REPRESENTATION

COLUMBIA THEMES IN PHILOSOPHY

COLUMBIA THEMES IN PHILOSOPHY

Series Editor: Akeel Bilgrami,
Johnsonian Professor of Philosophy,
Columbia University

Columbia Themes in Philosophy is a new series with a broad and accommodating thematic reach as well as an ecumenical approach to the outdated disjunction between analytical and European philosophy. It is committed to an examination of key themes in new and startling ways and to the exploration of new topics in philosophy.

Noam Chomsky, *What Kind of Creatures Are We?*

Thom Brooks and Martha C. Nussbaum, eds., *Rawls's Political Liberalism*

Alan Montefiore, *A Philosophical Retrospective: Facts, Values, and Jewish Identity*

Mario De Caro and David Macarthur, eds., *Naturalism and Normativity*

Jean Bricmont and Julie Franck, eds., *Chomsky Notebook*

Michael Dummett, *The Nature and Future of Philosophy*

Daniel Herwitz and Michael Kelly, eds., *Action, Art, History: Engagements with Arthur C. Danto*

John Searle, *Freedom and Neurobiology: Reflections on Free Will, Language, and Political Power*

Michael Dummett, *Truth and the Past*

Edward Said, *Humanism and Democratic Criticism*

Representation

THE BIRTH OF HISTORICAL REALITY
FROM THE DEATH OF THE PAST

Franklin Rudolf Ankersmit

Columbia University Press
New York

Columbia University Press
Publishers Since 1893
New York   Chichester, West Sussex
cup.columbia.edu

Copyright © 2024 Columbia University Press
All rights reserved

Library of Congress Cataloging-in-Publication Data
Names: Ankersmit, F. R. author.
Title: Representation : the death of the past and the birth of historical reality / Franklin Rudolf Ankersmit.
Other titles: Death of the past and the birth of historical reality
Description: New York : Columbia University Press, [2024] |
Series: Columbia themes in philosophy |
Includes bibliographical references and index.
Identifiers: LCCN 2023050328 | ISBN 9780231215909 (hardback) |
ISBN 9780231215916 (trade paperback) | ISBN 9780231561037 (ebook)
Subjects: LCSH: Leibniz, Gottfried Wilhelm, Freiherr von, 1646–1716. | Historicism.
Classification: LCC D16.9 .A645 2024 | DDC 901—dc23/eng/20240131
LC record available at https://lccn.loc.gov/2023050328

Cover design: Julia Kushnirsky
Cover image: Maria Sibylla Graff Merian, © British Library Board / Bridgeman Images

To the memory of my revered teacher
Ernst Heinrich Kossmann (1922–2003)

Ich habe mich hier keinem I. Müller und keinem Alten, sondern der Erscheinung selbst anzunähern gesucht, als welche eben so hervortritt, äusserlich nur Besonderheit, innerlich—und so verstehe ich Leibniz—ein Allgemeines, Bedeutung, Geist.[1]

—LEOPOLD VON RANKE

In ihr [Leibniz's thought] steckte ein epochemachender und entwicklungsfähiger, über alles naturrechtlichen Denken hinausführender Keim, der später im Historismus aufgehen sollte: die Idee der eigenartigen, spontan nach eigenem Gesetze wirkenden und sich enwickelnde Individualität die doch dabei die Abwandlung einer universalen Gesetzlichkeit ist.[2]

—FRIEDRICH MEINECKE

The eighteenth century had to find a new way and a new leader. It had to unearth the methodological treasure which lay hidden in Leibniz's doctrine; for this doctrine in its principle of the monad had given the clearest expression of the problem of individuality, and had assigned to individuality a firm position in a comprehensive philosophical system.[3]

—ERNST CASSIRER

1. Leopold von Ranke, "Erwiderung auf Heinrich Leo's Angriff," in *Leopold von Ranke's Sämmtliche Werke. Herausgegeben von Alfred Dove*, vol. 53.54 (Leipzig: Duncker und Humblot, 1890), 664, 665. Ranke's habit of speaking about historical individuals such as states or nations as "Gedanken Gottes" ("thoughts of God") is also definitely Leibnizian.
2. Friedrich Meinecke, *Die Entstehung des Historismus. Herausgegeben und eingeleitet von Carl Hinrichs* (1936: repr. Munich: R. Oldenbourg, 1965), 30.
3. Ernst Cassirer, *The Philosophy of the Enlightenment* (Princeton, NJ: Princeton University Press, 1951), 227, 228.

CONTENTS

PREFACE xi

Introduction
A New Vindication of Historicism 1

Chapter one
Premises and Axioms 15

Chapter Two
Leibniz and Historical Representation: The Basics 24
1. Against Narrativism 24
2. Leibniz and Representation 26
3. The Problem of the Phaenomena Bene Fundata 35
4. Application of Leibniz's System to Historical Representation 43
5. Three Final Comments 54

Chapter Three
Metaphysics, Individuals, Models, and the PBF 62
1. Historicism and Individuals 62
2. Strong and Weak Individuals 64
3. Leibniz on Individuals 75
4. Historical Representation: Metaphysics 82
5. Mobilization of the PBF 93
6. The Structural Similarity of the Scientific and the Historical Revolution 100

CONTENTS

Chapter Four
Signs, Semantics, Meaning, and Relational Statements   109
   1. Theories of Representation   109
   2. Representation and Signs   113
   3. Representational Meaning   126
   4. Monads and Relational Statements: The Internalist Approach   138
   5. Relational Statements About HRs: The Externalist Approach   150
   6. Relational Statements: From HRs to PBF   155

Chapter Five
Historical Knowledge, Facts, Arguments, Maxima and Minima   176
   1. Historical Rationality   176
   2. Facts About Past States of Affairs   179
   3. The Growth of Historical Knowledge   184
   4. Historical Texts as Signs: Maxima and Minima   201
   5. The Rationality of Historical Writing   213

Conclusion
Nontrivial Circularity   215

Epilogue
Intensionalism Versus Extensionalism: The Historical Period (Leibniz) and Its Enemies (Davidson)   225
   1. Why an Epilogue to This Book?   225
   2. Extensionalist and Intensionalist Truth   228
   3. What Are Intensionalist Phenomena?   233
   4. The Ontology of Intensionalist Phenomena   236
   5. Properties, Aspects, and Things   237
   6. The Limitations of Extensionalism   243
   7. Davidson on Conceptual Schemes   252
   8. Davidson's Radical Interpretation and the Historical Period   261
   9. Conclusion   274

GLOSSARY   277

BIBLIOGRAPHY   289

INDEX   297

PREFACE

A fragment written by the Greek poet Archilochus states that "the fox knows many things, but the hedgehog knows one big thing." Isaiah Berlin used Archilochus's metaphor of the fox and the hedgehog in the title of his essay on Tolstoy. It is not immediately clear exactly what Archilochus had in mind when he wrote this aphorism, so Berlin fortuitously came to our aid with an interpretation of his own: The hedgehogs are those who relate everything to a single central vision or organizing system by which they understand themselves and the world. The foxes, on the other hand, are those who pursue many ends, often unrelated and even contradictory, connected, if at all, only in some de facto way. To clarify his interpretation, Berlin offers some examples: Dante, Plato, Pascal, Hegel, Nietzsche, and Proust are the hedgehogs, whereas Herodotus, Aristotle, Montaigne, Goethe, Balzac, and Joyce should be seen as the foxes.

I suppose most scholars will have asked themselves at some stage in their careers whether they are a fox or a hedgehog in the sense used by Berlin. So it was with me. The question was easy enough to answer: I am the prototypical hedgehog. If I were asked to give the briefest possible summary of my intellectual preoccupations, just one word would suffice: *representation*. I addressed the issue of representation in three different contexts in the course of my scholarly career: in that of historical representation, political representation, and aesthetic representation. However, when dealing with these three contexts, I often exported what I had learned in one context to the two others, and vice versa, as a hedgehog is expected to do.

Some fifty years ago, historical representation was my point of departure when addressing the issue of historical writing. My idea was that historical texts are essentially representations of the past. Needless to say, this immediately raised the question of what representation actually is. The contemporary philosophy of language offered little help here. At that time, there were ongoing debates between the "representationalists" and the "antirepresentationalists." In those debates, representation was a mere spinoff from debates on truth. The notion of representation had nothing of any substance to add to the notion of truth. Moreover, one moved there from discussions about truth to the question of whether representationalism was a good idea or not. Conversely, I want to argue from representation to truth: that is, to begin with representation and to see whether there is such a thing as representational truth (there is, for that matter).

Nor did philosophy from the past prove to be more helpful. Few philosophers since the days of Plato and Aristotle have addressed the idea of representation as such. Aesthetic representation has received its share of attention since the eighteenth century, but representation never moved from there to the center of the philosophical scene. There is, however, one exception to this rule. And one might well call it a truly *huge* exception because it concerns a thinker who belongs to the select group of the five to ten greatest philosophers in two and a half millennia of Western thought. He is none other than Gottfried Wilhelm Leibniz (Leipzig, July 1, 1646–Hannover, November 14, 1716)—Freiherr von Leibniz since 1673. The notion of representation was central in his thoughts. One need only think here of what he wrote in a letter dated February 9, 1709, to Isaac Jacquelot about the essence of his thinking: "*le point de la représentation de l'univers dans chaque monade estant establi, le reste n'est que consequences.*" It was the discovery of my life. I recognized that anyone having decided to reflect on representation will have to state his position vis-à-vis his august predecessor: Leibniz. No theorist of representation can afford to ignore Leibniz. So I turned to Leibniz to penetrate the secrets of historical representation—and those of political and aesthetic representation as well. Leibniz has not disappointed me. On the contrary, this book is the result of forty years of sustained reflection on a Leibnizian account of (historical) representation.

For their unfaltering help and support, I would like to thank most warmly several of my colleagues whom I regard not only as colleagues but also as friends. Without our discussions and their invaluable comments on previous versions of this book, or parts of it, the book would have been a mere shadow of what it eventually has become. I am deeply indebted to Jaap den Hollander. Jaap has been my sparring partner during the writing of the book, and he is present on almost every page. Next I'd like to thank Jouni-Matti Kuukkanen, Herman Paul, Chiel van den Akker, Jonathan Menezes, Timme Kragh, Martin Jay, Jack Zammito, Toon de Baets, Klaas van Berkel, Reinbert Krol, Rik Peters, Allan Megill, Jeff Malpas, Jürgen Pieters, Daniel Woolf, Arthur van Essen, Stephen Bann, Jan Drentje, Jo Tollebeek, Zoltan Simon, Marek Tamm, Lydia Goehr, Ewa Domanska, David Carr, Brian Fay, Ethan Kleinberg, Robert Doran, Luis Vergara Anderson, Aurelia Valero, Mark Blum, Chris Lorenz, Jörn Rüsen, Hans Kellner, Piet Blaas, Mark Bevir, and Jianzhang Zhou for having accompanied me in such an exceptionally fruitful way on the journey of my scholarly career. No man is an island, as they say, and so it is with me.

I wish to end this preface with a special word of thanks to Luke O'Sullivan of the National University of Singapore. He expressed his willingness to copyedit the text of this book and to transform my wooden prose into efficient and elegant English. He did so with the greatest care and diligence. Moreover, he did not hesitate to pitilessly point out weaknesses in my argument. Last but not least, his suggestions for how to improve the book's argument often found their way into its final version. I am also most grateful to the two readers of the book for Columbia University Press: Daniel Woolf and Allan Megill. Their suggestions for how to improve the text have been most helpful. Moreover Allan was so kind to look with a critical eye at the text, and he prevented me from making many sins against the English language. Years ago he told me that "the English language is the easiest to learn, but the most difficult to master"—and so it is. For similar reasons, I am deeply indebted to Allan's student Tyler Ruvolo.

Sections 2 and 3 of chapter 2 are a revised and enlarged version of sections 2 and 3 of F. R. Ankersmit, "History as the Science of the Individual," *Journal of the Philosophy of History* 7 no. 3 (2013): 396–426.

I would like to thank Brill for permitting me to use this article in this book.

REPRESENTATION

INTRODUCTION

A New Vindication of Historicism

There is near unanimous agreement that historical writing underwent its "scientific revolution" in the second half of the eighteenth century. As was the case with the revolution of the sciences in the previous century, this revolution has been characterized in many different ways, and many factors contributed to its emergence. Nevertheless, no scholar of historical writing ever doubted that this scientific revolution in historical writing must be identified with the birth of "historicism," which is commonly associated with philosophers and historians such as Herder, Ranke, Humboldt, and Friedrich Meinecke (who in 1936 published a highly esteemed study of historicism's intellectual roots).[1]

Although the writing of history has gone through many changes over the past two and a half centuries, the basic pattern has persisted into the present day, just as a direct line still connects even the most exotic domains of modern science to Newton and his colleagues on both sides of the Channel. We must agree, therefore, with Beiser's claim about historicism in his masterful work, *The German Historicist Tradition*: "indeed, since it continues to exercise such enormous influence, it never really died at all. It continues to live in all of us, and it is fair to say that, as heirs of Meinecke's

---

1. Friedrich Meinecke, *Die Entstehung des Historismus. Herausgegeben und eingeleitet von Carl Hinrichs* (1936; repr. Munich: R. Oldenburg, 1965).

revolution, we are all historicists today."[2] This is also the message of this book: my aim is to demonstrate that historical writing as it came into being at the end of the eighteenth century and remains in the present day is basically historicist.

It is true that most historians will not regard themselves as historicists. The culprit here is the so-called crisis of historicism in the first decades of the previous century. The argument was (1) that historicism results in a bottomless relativism and (2) that this relativism compels us to abandon belief in the existence of eternally valid moral values. Neo-Kantianism (almost universally accepted in the academic world of that time) had inherited from Kant the conviction that values must be eternally valid in order to count as values we can allow to guide us in our moral dilemmas. This is obviously at odds with what history has to offer. This caused a profound and almost existential despair in the minds of neo-Kantian philosophers and of theologians, such as Ernst Troeltsch, also hoping for absolute and time-transcendent moral and theological truths. Historicism was accused of having been the source of the neo-Kantian's discomforts. Hence this "crisis of historicism."

Three comments are appropriate. In the first place, each historian, whether historicist or not, will recognize that no (moral) values have been valid for all times and places. So if the neo-Kantian and the theologian decide to remain stubbornly blind to this (for them) so unpleasant fact, and if they wish to avoid any future exposure to it, they will have to abolish *all* of historical writing—and not just historicism. Second, if there is such a conflict between plain historical fact and the neo-Kantian's dreams of eternal moral truths, had we not better awaken from these dreams? What's the use of hoping for something that will never be given to you? Third, and most important, it is not part of the meaning of the concept of norms and values that they should be universally valid. Only moral philosophers with a background in natural law philosophy or adhering to a more orthodox formulation of the Kantian categorical imperative will believe otherwise. Paraphrasing H. L. A. Hart's argument on the concept of law, we might argue that moral rules are "rules for action" and that these rules will depend on the kind of social order they should regulate. Each epoch has its own

---

2. Frederick C. Beiser, *The German Historicist Tradition* (Oxford: Oxford University Press, 2011), 26.

INTRODUCTION

set of such rules and is in need of time-specific rules; if one were to apply, for example, those of the Middle Ages to our own time, chaos would be the result. As moral beings, we are historically conditioned, and we can only rejoice in this. For only this enables us to cope in a more or less successful way with the social order in which we are living. It is self-evident that the historicity of norms and values does not exclude that their appropriateness can at all times be rationally discussed. On the contrary, reason may unite and guide us in our debates on what moral order we prefer and on how to achieve it. From this perspective, the crisis of historicism has been much ado about nothing, and one can only be amazed that historicists surrendered to their neo-Kantian opponents so easily and effortlessly.[3] Nevertheless, historicism never recovered from "the crisis of historicism," Reinhart Koselleck himself being the most striking illustration. His notion of the "Sattelzeit" is, if anything, an homage to the triumph of historicism if ever there was one; and yet he refuses to regard himself as a historicist. Even more bewildering is that his encyclopaedia of the *Geschichtliche Grundbegriffe* does not even have an entry on historicism!

In order to make his readers see the true nature of the historicist revolution and to recognize its persistence down to the present in all historical writing, Beiser asks us to consider the writings by Hans Martin Chladenius (1710–1759), whom he does not hesitate to praise as "the German Vico."[4] According to Beiser, Chladenius's revolutionary contribution to both our understanding of the nature of historical knowledge and the emergence of historicism is to be found in Chladenius's so-called perspectivalism. That is, the text the historian writes about the past must be regarded as a proposal to see part of the past from a certain "point of view." In *Allgemeine Geschichtswissenschaft* of 1752, Chladenius defined perspectivalism as follows:

> The point of view is the internal and external situation of a spectator in so far as there follows from it a certain and quite specific way of seeing, regarding, or interpreting the things we see. . . . It is a notion that goes together with

---

3. See Franklin Ankersmit, *Meaning, Truth and Reference in Historical Representation* (Ithaca, NY: Cornell University Press, 2012), 5, 6.
4. Beiser, *The German Historicist Tradition*, 27. Of no less interest is his observation that Ernst Bernheim (author of the widely read *Lehrbuch der historischen Methode* of 1889) saw Chladenius's *Allgemeine Geschichtswissenschaft* of 1752 as the first work to develop a systematic epistemology of history. An assessment that is still as true now as it was in 1889.

what is most important in all of philosophy, though it is still not sufficiently appreciated as such in philosophy, even though "der Herr von Leibniz" has drawn our attention to its role in metaphysics and in psychology.[5]

Beiser adds: Chladenius "complains that it [i.e., perspectivalism] is insufficiently recognized in current philosophy, which is a terrible omission because 'almost everything in historical knowledge depends on it. . . . We do not see historical things as in a mirror, as if narrative simply replicated the content of sensation; rather we see them according to the image or concept (*Bild*) that we form of them.'"[6] Next Beiser raises the question of whether perspectivalism opens the door to unbridled relativism. After all, perspectivalism, as defined by Chladenius, may seem to be the very codification of "subjectivism." However, Beiser points out that, according to Chladenius, any such fears are unfounded for two reasons: history is not distorted as long as the historian faithfully reports what the past looks like if seen from his point of view, and all possible points of view are points of view on one and the same historical reality.[7] So all these points of view have a solid *fundamentum in re*.

Beiser wrote an intellectual history of the historicist tradition. An exposition of what revolutionary implications Chladenius's perspectivalism had for the actual *practice of historical writing* itself is obviously quite a different enterprise. It fell, therefore, outside the scope of his book.

Nevertheless, the issue of how Chladenius's perspectivalism affected historical writing itself must be recognized as no less urgent than the issue Beiser addressed in his book. So we must also ask ourselves how Chladenius's perspectivalism succeeded in revolutionizing historical writing and did this so effectively that all historical writing up to the present day must be seen as heir to that revolution.

---

5. Johann Martin Chladenius, *Allgemeine Geschichtswissenschaft. Mit einer Einleitung von Christoph Friedrich und einem Vorwort von Reinhart Koselleck* (1752; repr. Vienna: Hermann Böhlaus Nachf, 1985), 100–1: "Der Sehepunkt ist der innerliche und äusserliche Zustand eines Zuschauers, in so ferne daraus eine gewisse und besondere Art, die vorkommende Dinge anzuschauen und zu betrachten, flüsset. Ein Begriff, der mit den allerwichtigsten in der gantzen Philosophie im Paare gehet, den man aber noch zur Zeit zu Nutzen noch nicht gewohnt ist, ausser dass der Herr von Leibniz hie und da denselben selbst in der Metaphysik und Psychologie gebracht hat." My translation.
6. Beiser, *The German Historicist Tradition*, 49.
7. Beiser, *The German Historicist Tradition*, 50, 51.

INTRODUCTION

Some thirty years before Beiser's book, the historian Reinhart Koselleck addressed this issue in a famous essay:

> Chladenius argued that it was ordinarily believed that a history and its representation should coincide. However, in order to represent part of the past and to assess it, a methodological separation was necessary: the past itself is one thing, but its representation is separate from it and can take different forms. A history as such can, in its uniqueness, only be thought as being free from contradiction, but each representation of it is broken perspectivally. . . . With this claim that a perspectivist account of history and a biased account of it are not one and the same thing, Chladenius created a theoretical matrix that is up till now still unsurpassed. . . . Chladenius's theory of knowledge has been an act of liberation. By expanding *autopsy*—traditionally narrowing and limiting the historian's room of manoeuvre [to] the perspective of the historian himself—historical writing acquired a hitherto completely unknown freedom of movement.[8]

Let us unpack this rich passage. To begin with, it contrasts a concept of history antedating Chladenius's momentous intervention with the concept of history resulting from it. Koselleck uses the word *autopsy* (i.e., having seen something for oneself) for the former. Indeed, this autopsy or "eyewitness" paradigm determined most of historical writing from antiquity until far into the eighteenth century (G. E. Lessing [1729-1781] still defended it). The paradigm demanded that the historian should present to readers the past as it must have been for the people who lived then, preferably by intimating that the historian had been an eyewitness to the events of the past recounted in the text. Put differently, the historian should present himself as if he is (or was) contemporaneous with the past he discusses. As soon as the historian fails in this, the spell is broken, and it becomes clear that the past as recounted by the historian is not the past itself but the past *as it is perceived* from a certain spatiotemporal point of view. The historian then sins against the requirements of the autopsy paradigm, and the story must

---

8. Reinhart Koselleck, "Standortbindung und Zeitlichkeit. Ein Beitrag zur historiografischen Erschliessung der geschichtlichen Welt," in *Vergangene Zukunft. Zur Semantik Geschichtlicher Zeiten* (Frankfurt am Main: Suhrkamp, 1979), 176–211, especially 185, 187. My translation.

therefore be distrusted: it cannot go beyond what we believe to be true on the basis of mere hearsay.

Chladenius's revolutionary move was to completely turn the traditional autopsy paradigm upside down. According to him, the participants in a particular event rarely see all of it and can be expected to be biased, so it is *their* account we should distrust. It is, on the contrary, precisely the historian living decades or even centuries later who can gather all the relevant evidence and critically analyze, compare, and dissect it to decide finally *sine ira et studio* from what "point of view" we had best look at certain aspects of the past. Next, there can only be a *best* point of view of looking at the past on the conditions that (1) multiple points of view are available (indeed, the more the better) and (2) a rational discussion is possible for deciding which of them is the *best*. Hence, instead of being a concession to "subjectivity," the introduction of the point of view opens up "the logical space of reasons" (Wilfrid Sellars). Paradoxically, subjectivity guarantees "objectivity."

Let us focus now on the first sentence of the quote. Koselleck claims here that, in the traditional autopsy paradigm, history and its representation were believed to coincide. Obviously, rejecting that belief implies that the two must be radically pulled apart. This means four things. First, the link between the past and historical knowledge is now completely broken. The past is one thing, and our knowledge of it is quite another. Second, that historical knowledge must essentially be *later* than what it is knowledge of. Historical knowledge is now the wisdom of hindsight, and historical writing is the science of the ex post facto. Third, as Koselleck strongly emphasizes, Chladenius's revolution was experienced by historians as nothing less than an *act of liberation*: they had now acquired the "hitherto completely unknown freedom of movement," allowing them to freely compare points of view with each other to establish which of them did best justice to the past. Fourth, this freedom of movement does not permit the historian to say just anything about the past that pleases him. In his *Monadology*, Leibniz (from whom Chladenius took the idea of the point of view) had insisted that monad A perceives more of the monadological universe than monad B if what B perceives is part of what A perceives. It is easy to understand what this must mean for historical texts if we see Leibniz's monads and their points of view as their models.

I stated a moment ago that the writing of history is the science of the ex post facto. Two closely related conclusions can be drawn from this. First,

INTRODUCTION

we can only know the "truth" about past events from a point of view that is *later* than the past events themselves. Second, the past can never know the truth about itself. Consider, for example, the unintended consequences of intentional human action. As Adam Ferguson most cogently pointed, out as early as 1767, that "nations stumble upon establishments, which are indeed the result of human *action*, but not the execution of any human *design*."[9] You intend to do something, but the result is often something wholly different. It was Napoleon's intention to subject all of Europe to his will, but the unintended consequence of his actions was that he ended up in Saint Helena. Doing so was the result of his *actions*, but it had surely not been his *design*. Similarly, we relied on science and technology to make our world as pleasant and as comfortable to humanity as possible—with climate change and our so very bleak future in the Anthropocene as unintended consequences. Three comments can be made about these unintended consequences. First, it is undoubtedly part of the historian's task to account for them. Second, they cannot be explained in terms of a historical agent's intentions: they are *un*intentional after all. And third, these unintended consequences must be located in some indefinite limbo between the past and the historian's present.

In sum, the truth about time T_1 necessarily includes the mention of many things that could not possibly be known at T_1. Arthur Danto once brilliantly expressed this idea as follows:

> And something of the same sort is true for the historical period considered as an entity. It is a period solely from the perspective of the historian, who sees it from without; for those who lived in the period it would be just the way life was lived. And asked, afterwards, what it was like to have lived then, they may answer from the outside, from the historian's perspective. From the inside there is no answer to be given; it was simply the way things were. So when the members of a period can give an answer in terms satisfactory to the historian, the period will have exposed its outward surface and in a sense be over, as a period.[10]

---

9. Adam Ferguson, *An Essay on the History of Civil Society*, ed. Fania Oz-Salzberger (Cambridge: Cambridge University Press, 1995), 119.

10. Arthur C. Danto, *The Transfiguration of the Commonplace* (Cambridge, MA: Harvard University Press, 1983), 207.

INTRODUCTION

This quote is one of the best things ever said about history by a philosopher of history. As is clear from the quote, we cannot associate the notion of historical reality with the past for two reasons. First, the past is (or was) a reality only for the people who lived in it. Let's call this "the past$_1$." But it is no longer a reality for the historian. He lives later when the past no longer exists. The phrase *past reality* is an oxymoron.[11]

So what could then justifiably be called "historical reality"? Surely, there must be such a thing as historical reality against which the truthfulness of historical representations can be checked. Historical writing is no less an empirical science than any of the other sciences. But, if so, where should we situate this historical reality? Equating it with the evidence the past has left us would be a grave mistake because then we would import past reality into present reality and delete the difference between the two.

Second, as we saw just now, much of what happened between the past and the historian's present will also have to be included in the historian's account of the past. Clearly, we are now speaking of a past that cannot be identified with the past$_1$. So let's call this "the past$_2$." It is a past that also contains things that happened *between* the past$_1$ and the historian's present. So what about the idea of seeing the past$_2$ as historical reality? There are a number of problems with it, but this is not the right place to enter into that. We can restrict ourselves to the observation that the very notion of the past$_2$ is inconsistent because it combines the fixity we associate with the notion of the past (one cannot change the past) with the infinite mutability of the point of view (it is part of the meaning of the notion of points of view that they can be multiplied ad infinitum). Nevertheless, if we wish to tie the notion of reality to that of the past$_2$, we have two possibilities. We can tie it to the past, but we will then have to abandon the mutability of the point of view, with the result of a relapse into the autopsy paradigm. But we can also tie it to the notion of point of view. Doing so allows us to hold onto the multiplicity of points of view. But this option is consistent only on the condition that historical reality is defined as the totality of all

---

11. Unless the conjunction of the words "past" and "reality" is meant to stand for what people living in the past regarded as their reality. But, for them, that reality was not "past" but "present"; and *for us* it was/is not *our* reality, i.e. the historian's reality. Needless to add, this book is written from the historian's perspective and not from that of the historical agent.

possible (historical) points of view (and not some subset of them). Now, if we express our agreement with Chladenius's revolutionary rejection of the autopsy paradigm, it follows that we have no choice but to adopt the latter option.

Hence, this book's main claim that *historical reality only comes into being when the past no longer exists*. As long as the past existed, it was reality. When historians start to write about what is from their point(s) of view the past, the past no longer exists. There is no such thing as "past reality."[12] But if we define reality as what is the inescapable touchstone of all of our knowledge of reality, then the manifold representations of past, present, and future that we have and the never-ending debate about them will satisfy this definition of (historical) reality.

This is what Peter Munz had in mind when he made his acute observation that most people tend to see the historical text as a mask behind which we must locate the past itself. The assumption is

> that behind the mask there is a face and that we might check the adequacy or truth of the mask by peeping at the face that is hidden behind it. But the ineluctable truth is that there is no face behind the mask and that the belief that there is is an unsupportable allegation. For any record we could have of the face would be, precisely, another mask. We cannot have proof that it is the genuine "record" of the face and every possible glimpse of the face would be, by its nature, yet another mask.[13]

---

12. Clearly this conception of the difference between past and present is predicated on that of existence: the past no longer exists in the present whereas historical reality does. It differs, therefore, from how Schiffman proposes to distinguish between past and present: "the distinction between past and present that constitutes 'the founding principle of history' rests on something other than a mere priority in time, it reflects an abiding awareness that different historical entities exist in different historical contexts. ... The flipside of this awareness is a sense of anachronism, triggered when we encounter things out of context. (Imagine Shakespeare dressed in jeans and a tee shirt.) For the sake of convenience, I will refer to the awareness of the difference between past and present as an *idea of anachronism*, for this idea enables us to distinguish between historical contexts." Zachary Sayre Schiffman, *The Birth of the Past* (Baltimore, MD: The Johns Hopkins University Press, 2011), 3. I have no quarrel with Schiffman's proposal for how to distinguish between past and present. Although my "ontological" proposal for how to distinguish the two may explain his proposal, whereas the opposite route cannot be taken.

13. Peter Munz, *The Shapes of Time. A New Look at the Philosophy of History* (Middletown, CT: Wesleyan University Press, 1977), 17.

INTRODUCTION

Clearly, Munz also wants us to identify historical reality with the totality of all possible historical representations.

If we are prepared to follow Munz here, we will find ourselves in agreement with Leibniz. Metaphysical reality is, for Leibniz, the totality of the substances or monads constituting the monadological universe, while each of them perceives that universe from its own point of view. For Leibniz there is nothing beyond or preceding them to which they owe their metaphysical status. Just as for Munz, there is no face under the masks that historians allegedly project onto it. Leibniz acknowledges no reality deeper than that of the monadological universe that we must regard as its "real" or "ultimate" foundation, or whatever term one would prefer here. For Leibniz, reality consists of an infinity of substances or monads seeing that reality from their own point of view, but there is nothing beyond these substances or monads and the point of view defining them. Consequently, the point of view a monad has is a point of view on *other* monads, and not on anything deeper beyond or prior to these monads. This is the essence of Leibniz's logic and metaphysics.

And so it is with Chladenius, who took his idea of the point of view from Leibniz, as we saw earlier. For Chladenius, no less than for Leibniz, the points of view proposed in historical representations are points of view on other such historical representations. Historical debate is a battle between historical representations. Although the weapons with which this battle is fought are true statements about past states of affairs, the scene of the battle is historical representation and not the past as described in these true statements—as we so much like to believe. It is as in Plato's allegory of the cave: we believe we see a battle about the past, but in fact, that battle is the mere shadow of the battle between historical representations.

Some readers may, indeed, see this as a (neo-)idealist or as a (re-)constructivist philosophy of history. But they would be wrong. The philosophy of history defended here fully and unreservedly recognizes the historian's ability to formulate statements that are true of states of affairs in the past. Statements are timelessly true or false—unless they contain components making their truth or falsity dependent on the temporal relationship between the historical states of affairs mentioned in them and the moment at which these statements are uttered. This is where statements about the past essentially differ from historical representations: in the latter the touchstone of truth lies not in states of affairs in the past but in other representations. I do not know of any idealist philosophy of history proposing this double standard for historical truth.

The account of the historical text presented here also requires the mention of facts situated between the past the text is dealing with and the time in which the text is written, so it could not possibly be regarded as offering a reconstruction of the past it is dealing with. Nor is it "constructivist" as understood by Leon Goldstein.[14] According to Goldstein, a reconstruction of the past is impossible because the past no longer exists; no account of the past could be compared to the past to establish whether it is a true reconstruction of the past or not. The only option left to the historian is, therefore, a maximally plausible construction of the past on the basis of the evidence presently available. First, replacing reconstruction by construction does not alter the fact that Goldstein leaves as little room as the reconstructivist does for the mention of facts situated between the past in question and the historian's own time. Second, the philosophy of history proposed in this book rejects the view that there should be any interesting epistemological differences between statements on the past, on the one hand, and on present states of affairs, on the other. It assumes that any acceptable epistemology for statements about existing states of affairs will also hold—*mutatis mutandis*—for statements about past states of affairs.[15]

Having rejected the adjectives idealist and (re-)constructivist, the account of historical writing given in this book is best characterized as "Leibnizian." Leibniz's substances or monads and the points of view defined by them emerge here in the guise of historical representations. And just as the rationalist Leibniz had an unfaltering belief in the rationality of science, this book demonstrates why historical writing is no less rational than the sciences. It is no less of a science than the empirical sciences.

Even more so, it shows that there is a structural similarity between the scientific revolution effected by Newton and the revolution in the writing of history of a century later, as discussed previously. Next, some striking similarities are argued to exist between the use of signs in mathematics

---

14. Leon Goldstein, *Historical Knowing* (Austin: University of Texas Press, 1976); and Leon Goldstein, *The What and the Why of History: Philosophical Essays* (Boston: Brill, 1996).

15. Danto's well-known notion of the so-called narrative sentences (i.e., sentences about an event that can only be formulated later than the event in question) does not necessitate a revision of an epistemology developed for statements about existing states of affairs.

and in the sciences, on the one hand, and historical representation, on the other. Moreover, the calculus, as discovered by Leibniz and Newton, is shown to play a decisive role in the debate about competing historical representations. Similarly, the notion of the model as used in mathematics and the sciences has its counterpart in historical writing. In order to see this, it must be pointed out, first, that physical and natural reality, with its mountains, trees, cities, and human beings, and so on, is described by Leibniz as the domain of the *phaenomena bene fundata*. That domain can be seen as a *concrete* model of the domain of Leibniz's *abstract* monadological reality. Similarly, in mathematics and the sciences, physical reality is a model of an abstract calculus or scientific theory—and *not* the other way around, as is the case with the model of a ship or of a national economy. Last but not least, so it is with historical writing. Leibniz's phaenomena bene fundata have their origin in historical representations. And I argue that these historical phaenomena bene fundata must be regarded as the concrete models of the intensionalist abstractions that historical representations will be shown to be.

One of the main conclusions in this book is that historical representation if seen from a Leibnizian point of view, on the one hand, and mathematics and the sciences, on the other, share more than is often believed to be the case and that there is a kernel of truth in the logical-positivist theory of "the unity of science." And finally, these elective affinities between the two are to be found in places where one did not look for them before.[16] In sum, this book has the ambition[17] to be the most comprehensive, cogent, consistent and uncompromising vindication of historical rationality, of (Rankean) historical writing and of history as an empirical science that has ever been proposed in the history of historical thought. Put in a

---

16. One of the best books on Leibniz is still Dietrich Mahnke, *Leibnizens Synthese von Universalmathematik und Individualmetaphysik* (1925; repr. Stuttgart: Friedrich Frommann, 1964). The book's interest is suggested already by its title. "*Universalmathematik*" refers to the world of mathematics and the sciences and "*Individualmetaphysik*" to that of the humanities. The word *Synthese* expresses Mahnke's conviction that Leibniz's monadology can be regarded as a "synthesis" of the two. The word is somewhat unfortunate. For what Mahnke had in mind with it is that Leibniz's system *precedes* the two (in the sense that both can be derived from it) rather than that the system should be logically later—so to speak—than them. In fact, the present book can be regarded as an attempt to prove that Mahnke's conviction (if understood as indicated here) was correct.

17. Of course, everyone is free to have his ambitions; it is up to others to decide whether a person succeeded in realizing his ambitions.

somewhat less provocative way, the book argues that the trajectory that mathematics and the sciences, on the one hand, and the writing of history, on the other, travel together is far longer than was hitherto believed to be possible. Next, seeing as much will deepen substantially our understanding of the practice of historical writing, of its rationality and of the nature of historical debate. Moreover, the book will unmask the extensionalist bias of almost all of contemporary philosophy and thus open our eyes for its its (unperceived) limitations.

Of no less interest is the following. Inconsistencies in Leibniz's thought—inconsistencies for which neither Leibniz himself nor any of his commentators ever found an acceptable solution—melt like snow in summer when Leibniz's system is read as a philosophy of history. I have in mind here the inconsistencies in Leibniz's account of the relationship between the domain of the substances or monads and that of his so-called phaenomena bene fundata. It is a problem with which he wrestled all his life, and he never succeeded in building a sufficiently strong and reliable bridge between these two domains. Hence, the amazing paradox is that the Leibnizian system serves the aims of the philosophy of history better than those he himself had hoped to realize with it. In this way, this book may also be of interest for Leibniz experts: in discussions about the best interpretation of Leibniz's thought, it may be helpful to see how it compares with the practice of some respectable science—in this case the writing of history. Einstein once said that philosophy is like chewing while you have nothing in your mouth. To the extent that there is some truth in Einstein's metaphor, the possibility to test interpretations of Leibniz against the realities of modern historical writing can only be welcomed because it will give philosophers something "real" to chew on.

Bertrand Russell had correctly pointed out in his book on Leibniz that his entire system can, in fact, be inferred from a fairly restricted number of first principles. And so it is in this book. In the first chapter, four premises are defined, and each individual claim about the nature of historical representation made in the remainder of this book is inferred from these premises. The book is structured in this way for two reasons. First, adopting this strategy guarantees that the book's argument will satisfy the highest standards of clarity and transparency. Second, much of contemporary philosophy of history begins with some tacit or implicit notion of historical writing, historical explanation, historical narrative, and so on that is believed to be so indisputable that it does not need to be explicitly articulated. Next, a number of conclusions are inferred from these tacit assumptions. The result is that the reader does not know what these conclusions are true of. This stands in the way of a meaningful discussion. To avoid this kind of impasse, a definition of historical representation is given in chapter 1 that is free from ambiguity and hidden meanings. This enables the reader to check at all times that what is inferred from this definition in the course of the book's argument is true, or not, of historical representation as defined in chapter 1.

Finally, this book also has a message for the philosophy of language in general. It is argued, first, that the text—whether historical or not—has a more complicated logical and semantic structure than is ordinarily recognized in the existing philosophy of language, although this complexity was anticipated in Tarski's semantic theory of truth. Next, the existing philosophy of language has a strongly extensionalist bias. There is nothing necessarily wrong with that, but it would be welcomed if philosophers of language were somewhat more aware than they presently are of the limitations of extensionalism and of the contexts in which intensionalism holds all the cards. Representation and (historical) texts are an example of these contexts. This issue is addressed in the epilogue to this book.

One remark on the text of this book. The meanings of the words used in it are the same as what these words mean in our daily use of them. Nevertheless, some technical concepts are introduced in the text. Each time this is the case, these technical concepts are carefully and intelligibly explained. At the end of the book, the reader will find a glossary of the main technical concepts.

Chapter One

PREMISES AND AXIOMS

Any meaningful discussion of historical writing, historical text, or historical representation is possible only after a strict definition has been formulated for the following phrases: historical writing, the historical text, historical narrative, historical explanation, and historical representation. Without these definitions, we simply don't know what we are talking about and what claims are supposed to be true. "Historical writing" is not something "out there" to which we can point as we can point to a river or a mountain and say "this is the Rhine" or "this is the Mont Blanc." This would be enough to ensure that a meaningful discussion about the geographical, physical, and geological properties of the Rhine or the Mont Blanc can take place without misunderstandings. However, when I speak the magical words *historical writing*, I may well have associations with that phrase that are quite different from yours.

For example, do myths belong to the genre of historical writing? Are Homer's *Iliad* or *La Chanson de Roland* examples of historical writing? What about chronicles and annals? And what about a historical novel such as Robert Graves's *I Claudius* or an article in today's newspaper on the war in Ukraine? Are the memoirs of a statesperson a historical text or only the material for a historical text *proprement dit*? And so on, and so on. Humanity has devised many ways of relating to its past during the course of its existence. As long as there is no agreement about what a work of history is and what it is not, the philosophy of history is doomed to being an endless *dialogue de sourds*. So before discussing historical writing, we need to define it. Only after having done so can we establish the truth of any claim made about it.

In this book, historical writing, works of history, and historical texts are defined as *representations of the past*. In line with my previous remarks, I will be the first to admit that this is an unprovable postulate. If others prefer some other conception of the nature of historical writing, I have no decisive argument against them, just as they will have no decisive argument against me. I chose this definition because I believe it to be the best starting point for understanding what goes on in historical writing. But this is, after all, mere belief. Nevertheless, in this book, a great number of conclusions are drawn from this definition, and these conclusions could be read as the reasons I have for my belief. The plausibility of my definition *can* be assessed, but only at the end of this book. At this stage, I must be content with emphasizing the necessity of choosing in favor of a decision—whichever it may be—and formulating that decision with a maximum of precision. Similarly, the geometer can only establish geometric truths about the circle after having defined it as the set of all points having the same distance to a point P.

The main weakness of almost all contemporary philosophies of history is that one simply starts talking about historical writing and then simply stops talking about it—having decided that enough has been said by now. The result is, at best, trivial circularity in the sense that the argument's conclusions express what was already present in it—in the form of implicit and noncontradictory assumptions at best, or in vague and patchy intuitions at worst. If one nevertheless comes to valuable and sustainable results, these are chance hits rather than the well-deserved rewards of a well-chosen strategy. I return to the issue of circularity in this book's conclusion.

This is only the first step. The next question is, "What then is a representation of the past?" My second premise is that the answer to *that* question is best given on the basis of Leibniz's notion of the substance or the monad. Once again, this is an unprovable premise or axiom. If one disagrees, so be it.

No binding conclusions can be expected from a debate about this and similar axioms. I prefer to avoid it and will explain, instead, what the axiom or premise means. For Leibniz, a thing *is* all that can truthfully be attributed to it—nothing more and nothing less—and so it is with historical representations (HRs) of the past. Historical texts (or representations) consist for the greater part of true statements about past states of affairs. Such as the statement that "the term 'representative democracy' was used for the first time in English by Alexander Hamilton in a letter he wrote in May 1777 to the Governor of Vermont." Or the statement that "the rule of law reigned supreme in the later Middle Ages, as was expressed in the dictum 'nihil in mundo quod non est in textu legis.'"

Think now of some HR that is comprised of the true statements about the past: s_1, s_2, s_3, and so on. Then this HR is, exactly as Leibniz states, nothing but the sum of all these sentences: s_1, s_2, s_3, and so on. For Leibniz, a thing is all that can truthfully be attributed to it. Put differently, a thing has the properties that can truly be attributed to it, no less and no more. Similarly, we can say of this HR that it has the properties of containing s_1, s_2, s_3, and so on—again, no less and no more. On this basis, we may formulate a brief, simple, and consistent definition of a historical representation as follows:

> A historical representation, HR, is (1) the total set of all the statements constituting that HR while (2) all these statements are assumed to be true of past states of affairs and can (3) be numbered from 1 to *n* such that each statement x follows statement x − 1 and precedes statement x + 1 (excluding an HR's first and last statement).[1]

---

1. It might be objected that this part of the definition of an HR is insufficiently precise because there is an infinity of possible HRs containing *that* set of statements. Undoubtedly so. So the definition should also state that this HR—say HR_1—contains *this* set of statements and *only* these. But the addition would be redundant because the definite article in "the total set" expresses this clause: "the total set of all the statements" is "*this* total set of statements" and not any *other* set, either longer or shorter. Finally, with regard to the numbering, it must be pointed out that statements are not identified by their content but by their number. The same statement may occur twice or even more often in an HR and will then be regarded as different because they have different numbers.

This is the sole axiom underlying all of my arguments in the chapters of this book.[2] The entire argument is derived from this one axiom, supplemented by two further Leibnizian principles: (1) the doctrine prohibiting contradiction (D_{et}) also known as the law of the excluded third, and (2) the doctrine of the identity of indiscernibles (D_{ii}).

Because of its prominent role in this book a few comments are in place about the latter. The doctrine states that if two things (A and B) share all of their properties they must be one and the same thing; or as Leibniz expresses it: "eadem sunt, quorum unum in alterius loco substitui potest, salva veritate." Elsewhere he defines D_{ii} as follows: "there are no two things that differ *solo numero only.*" Hence, substantial identity is equivalent to numerical identity—and vice versa. A more modern and compact way to formulate D_{ii} is: "$x = y$ if x and y are indiscernible."

Leibniz derived D_{ii} from his doctrine of sufficient reason (D_{sr}), stating that nothing is as it is without there being a reason or cause for why it is as it is. Leibniz's argument for D_{ii} is that no sufficient reason or cause can be given for God's creating two different things that are completely alike. Hence, just one of them will be "sufficient," to use the right word here.

It is undoubtedly an elegant argument, but it has the disadvantage of assuming that God does nothing without sufficient reason. To remove God from the scene, Russell proposed an argument in favor of D_{ii} not relying on God's supposed moral preferences:

> Suppose A and B to be two indiscernible substances. Then A would differ from B exactly as B would differ from A. They would, as Leibniz once remarks regarding atoms, be different though without a difference. Or we may put the argument thus: A differs from B, in the sense that they are different substances; but to be thus different is to have a relation to B. This relation must have a corresponding predicate of A. But since B does not

---

2. I shall mainly rely on Leibniz when developing my argument, but there is also a *structural similarity* between Leibniz's system and my own account of historical representation. Russell observes that all of Leibniz's system can logically be derived from five axioms or premises. See Bertrand Russell, *A Critical Exposition of the Philosophy of Leibniz* (London: Allen and Unwin, 1967): 4–8. So in both cases the procedure is to infer as many conclusions as possible from a minimum of assumptions.

differ from itself, B cannot have the same predicate. Hence A and B will differ as to predicates, contrary to the hypothesis.[3]

But "being different from" is a relational predicate and cannot be part of a substance's complete concept. In chapter 4, section 5, you will see that the Leibnizian system leaves no room for relational statements, which disqualifies Russell's otherwise ingenious argument from being a satisfactory alternative to Leibniz's appeal to God.

D_{ii} should be distinguished from proposals to answer the question of what is conditional for two things being identical; namely, "A and B are identical if they share all of their properties (I)." (I) is often mistakenly confused with D_{ii}. First, whereas D_{ii} is a claim about identity, (I) is a definition of it—or a proposal for such a definition. One might try to derive D_{ii} from (I), but no such attempt can be successful because (I) does not exclude the possibility that two (or more) things are identical, which is in conflict with D_{ii}. So other arguments will have to be found for proving D_{ii}; a deduction of D_{ii} from some variant of D_{sr} not relying on God's moral preferences being the most promising candidate.[4]

Each individual claim about the nature of HRs in this book is inferred from one or more previous ones on the basis of valid argument; in this way it can be ultimately retraced to the axiom and the two Leibnizian principles mentioned here. To achieve this, two conditions must be met. First, the structure of the argument must be as transparent as possible so the stage of the argument will at all times clear to the reader. Second, the words used must be of only two types: (1) words having a dictionary meaning and (2) technical terms. The latter should leave no room for ambiguity,

---

3. See Russell, *A Critical Exposition*, 58. Nevertheless, Russell's argument may help us see how to counter the Max Black hypothesis of two completely identical spheres being identical yet different. A first objection is that the spheres cannot be identical because they must necessarily be located in different places. However, for Leibniz individuals are individuated only by their internal predicates and not by external predicates such as location in space, so the objection is ineffective if used to improve on Leibniz. If space doesn't help, time does: these two identical spheres did not come into being *ex nihilo*. So they must have (different) histories, and a thing's history is surely defined by internal predicates. So Black's two spheres are neither identical nor the same—as he wanted us to believe.

4. See G. Rodriguez Pereyra, "Leibniz's Argument for the Identity of Indiscernibles in Primary Truths," in *Individuals, Minds and Bodies: Themes from Leibniz*, ed. M. Carrara, S. M. Nunziante, G. Tomasi (Munich: Franz Steiner, 2004), 49–61.

be without hidden semantic double bottoms, and be defined with quasi-mathematical precision.[5]

One can formulate so-called meta-sentences about HRs, such as "this HR is s_1," "this HR is s_2," "this HR is s_3," and so on.[6] These are called meta-sentences because they are *about* an HR and *about* the sentences contained by that HR, such as s_1, s_2, s_3, and so on. Put differently, they have HR and sentences such as s_1, s_2, s_3, and so on as their *object*. It must be emphasized that *these* meta-sentences are far from being a dispensable luxury! They do what this HR and s_1, s_2, s_3, and so on could never do on their own; namely, they tie them inextricably together.[7] Without them, an HR is an undefined and undefinable entity that nobody could possibly make any sense of floating freely through the world of words and written texts. However, these meta-sentences allow us to say that *this* HR is defined by possessing the properties of containing the sentences s_1, s_2, s_3, and so on—and only these. That is to say, an HR is *individuated* by the meta-sentences about it, such as "this HR is s_1," "this HR is s_2," "this HR is s_3," and so on. Because HR is explicitly mentioned in each of these meta-sentences, we can say that this HR is defined *recursively* by these meta-sentences.[8]

Four further remarks must be made about this recursive definition of HRs. First, there is the issue of the relation between individuation and reference. Suppose all possible HRs have been realized. In that case, reference to any of them will require the enumeration of *all* of their properties.

---

5. See the glossary in the backmatter.

6. These meta-sentences can be said to represent 'the operator of association'—a logical faculty of human understanding (effectively cancelling the distinction between knowledge and belief) deserving more attention than has hitherto been given to it. All the more so since most of what we act upon is neither knowledge nor belief but association. Association develops without logic or purpose, like a sprawling city, and a pattern in its development can only be projected on it with the wisdom of hindsight. It knows neither rules nor epistemology and yet produces the building blocks of the mental house in which we live. It precedes both knowledge and psychology. It is the stuff of which consciousness is made.

7. Their function is reminiscent of what the Scholastics called the *vinculum substantiale*—i.e., what binds the components of a substance (or a Leibnizian monad) together. Leibniz also used this notion, not for individual monads but for tying together individual monads within a so-called aggregate of monads. The human body is an example of such an aggregate of monads. See Leibniz's correspondence with Des Bosses in "Monadology." See G. W. F. Leibniz, *Philosophical Papers and Letters*, 2nd ed., trans. Leroy E. Loemker (Boston: Reidel/Springer, 1976), 610–11.

8. Conceiving of the HR as being the result of the kind of recursive definition allows us to do so without positing—with Russell—that there is some independent (preexisting) entity to which all of an HR's properties should be ascribed. Just as we may use a vase to keep a number of individual flowers together where the vase precedes the flowers. See Russell, *A Critical Exposition*, 59.

Individuation and reference will then be identical from a logical point of view. However, if not all possible HRs are realized, reference to any of them is possible by enumerating only those properties it does not share with all of the others, or some subset of them. In that case individuation and reference will differ.

But what about reference by means of proper names, such as HR_1, or uniquely identifying descriptions, such as "the HR that is mentioned on page x of book y written by historian z"? HRs are not the kind of things that exist prior to and independently of their being mentioned in language, as is the case with things such as King Charles III, Mount Everest, or the Andromeda Galaxy. We would need to have a list of all HRs to overcome this inconvenience. This list would have to mention on its left side the proper names of all HRs, such as HR_1, HR_2, HR_3, and so on, and on the right side an enumeration of all of their properties. Obviously, individuation is needed for dressing up the list.

Again, what about proper names and uniquely identifying descriptions if we have the list? We must also distinguish between the situation in which all possible HRs are realized and the one in which this is not the case. In the first case, proper names will work—but there will be no room for uniquely identifying descriptions (unless we are willing to regard the list of all of an HR's properties as such). In the second case, we can have uniquely identifying descriptions too. They consist of the list of an HR's properties that it does not share with any of the others.[9]

Second, we should not confuse the individuation of HRs with their identification. Individuation makes an individual into the individual that it is; identification picks out one individual from a set of individuals. Individuation sees "the inside" of an individual (HR) only; identification sees it "from the outside." Individuation is internalist; identification is externalist. Spatiotemporal denominations are irrelevant for the individuation of HRs, although they often occur in the statements predicated to an individual HR by the meta-statements referred to previously. Spatiotemporal denominations, however, are what identification prototypically relies upon. HRs themselves are, from a logical point of view, eternal.

---

9. Clearly this puts representational logic close to Frege. In both cases, the logical method is nominalist, but the status of the logical objects seems to require a realism akin to Frege's "Dritte Reich," although in this case we must think of an intensionalist realism.

That is, they are outside space and time, as numbers are. This is so even though the statements individuating an HR are typically about states of affairs in space and time. Identification could take place by relating an HR to the physical kind of thing we call a book—in this case a book written by a certain historian and having a certain title. Any copy of the book would permit identification.[10]

Third, HRs can only be defined "internally" (i.e., by meta-statements saying what is true of them) and not "externally" (i.e., by meta-statements saying what is *not* true of them). If you know what something is *not*, this information does not tell you what it *is* (contrary to the advocates of negative theology).[11] Moreover, as the meta-statement "HR_1 is *not* s_1" is either false about HR_1 (if HR_1 is s_1) or true of *any* possible HR not being s_1, it follows that it defines the *set* of all HRs not being s_1 and, hence, no *individual* HR.

Fourth, the logic governing the individuation of individuals is strictly nominalist. Properties are always attributed to an individual by individual meta-sentences, and never by law-like sets of them because the individuation procedure would then yield sets of individuals and thereby fail to individuate individuals. As St. Thomas put it, "*quod ibi omne individuum sit species infima*," although one feels tempted to comment that St. Thomas's *infima species* is not a *species* anymore.[12] The point is that there is no room whatsoever for a realist approach to—or account of—HRs.

In sum, there are *two* levels in a historical text: (1) that of the meta-sentences (whose presence in the text *only logic* compels us to recognize because that level does not manifest itself in historical texts themselves), and (2) that of the object-sentences (where the former have the latter—and HRs—as their object). Such sets of meta-sentences are also generated by other historical texts written by other historians. All of them together constitute the meta-language in which one can speak about all the sentences

---

10. Identification here has the character of *where* something can be found although not of *what* will be found there. It is indexical, although not in the sense of actually giving access to what is pointed to. See also pp. 88, 89

11. L. B. McCullough, *Leibniz on Individuals and Individuation: The Persistence of Premodern Ideas in Modern Philosophy* (Dordrecht: Kluwer, 1996); 34. McCullough is fairly successful in retracing most of Leibniz's later views to his *Disputatio*, i.e., his dissertation of 1663.

12. Or, as McCullough puts it, in the Scholastic tradition "singular being is 'greater' or more primary than the being of *species* or *genera*." McCullough, *Leibniz on Individuals and Individuation*, 39.

contained by all historical texts—i.e., their object-sentences. It is this metalanguage that constitutes HRs. Being blind to the presence of this metalanguage in all historical writing and historical representation reduces historical texts to nothing but massive and incoherent heaps of individual statements about past states of affairs. That is, the reader of a work of history must always read each individual statement as the component of a much larger set—namely, of that work of history *as a whole*. A whole comprises all of the historical text's statements from the first one to the last one and requires the construction of an equally large set of meta-sentences, which are needed to tie them together. This is a process that no working historian or the audience is aware of but that nevertheless takes place all the time—just as monsieur Jourdain did not know he was speaking prose.

But what is gained by these logical subtleties? As you will see, this metalanguage makes it possible to investigate from a logical point of view the problems that have traditionally been studied by philosophers of history. And then they will be seen in a new and different light. These problems include the relationship between historical writing and other scientific disciplines; the truth of historical texts; how historical texts relate to the historical past they are about; how historians explain the past; why we may have good reasons to prefer one historical text on some part of the past to some other; what these reasons are; and so on.[13] And for all of this, *nothing more is required than the axiom previously mentioned.* Answers to these questions can all be derived from it. Contemporary philosophy of history—especially if it addresses the issue of historical representation (or historical narrative, in the current so sadly misleading jargon)—has remained fruitless since its practitioners failed to observe the laws and customs of the philosophical country they had unwittingly entered. As the proverb says, "When in Rome, do as the Romans do." This book is an exemplification of what it is that one does in "Rome."

---

13. Alfred Tarski argued that speaking *about* the truth of sentence S necessitates a metalanguage having that sentence S as its object-language. So the sentence in the object-language must be given a name in the meta-language. This is achieved by quoting the sentence from the object-language in the meta-language, and placing it between quotation marks to distinguish it from the original sentence in the object-language itself. Hence, "'S' is true if S is true." Much the same procedure is followed here when moving from s_1, s_2, s_3, and so on to statements on HRs having the form of "HR_1 is s_1," "HR_1 is s_2," "HR_1 is s_3," and so on—where s_1, s_2, s_3 are part of subject-language and "HR_1 is s_1," "HR_1 is s_2," and "HR_1 is s_3" are part of the meta-language.

Chapter Two

LEIBNIZ AND HISTORICAL REPRESENTATION

The Basics

What an *abyss of uncertainty* whenever the mind feels that some part of it has strayed beyond its own border; when it, the seeker, is at once the dark region through which it must go on seeking, where all its equipment will avail it nothing. Seek? More than that: create. It is face to face with something which does not, so far, exist, to which it alone can give reality and substance, which it alone can bring into the light of day.[1]

1. AGAINST NARRATIVISM

Long ago I wrote a book titled *Narrative Logic*. The adjective *narrative* was meant to suggest that the book was a contribution to the then still pristine narrativist tradition in the philosophy of history demanding that the historical text should be seen as a *narrative* or a story. But I soon came to regret the title because both the novel and the historical text can be characterized as having a narrative form. Some philosophers of history have inferred from this fact that literary theories developed for the analysis of novels can also offer a better understanding of historical writing. I fully agree that a purely stylistic analysis of the text can be carried out just as well for a history book as for a novel. In practice, however, this is of little interest in the case of historical works because historians rarely have literary pretensions. And when they had, this diminished rather than contributed to the value of their writings—think of Carlyle in England, Michelet in France, or Bilderdijk in the Netherlands (although there are exceptions such as Theodor Mommsen who even won the Nobel Price for literature in 1902).

---

1. Peter Munz, *Philosophical Darwinism: On the Origin of Knowledge by Means of Natural Selection* (New York: Routledge 1993), 21. In a note Munz adds that these sentences are an adaptation of a passage taken from Marcel Proust's *Swann's Way, Part I*. The quote captures quite well the quasi 'miraculous' metamorphosis of the past into historical reality by historical representation. This book's cover is, so to speak, a visual metaphor of that quasi miraculous metamorphosis.

Moreover, history books and novels are quite different things.[2] Every well-educated person confronted with samples of both can faultlessly distinguish between them. So when it began to dawn on me that the word *narrative* was a standing invitation to philosophers of history to disregard the obvious differences between the novel and historical writing, I exchanged it for the word *representation*. I don't think I have used the term *narrative* since the late 1980s, except in contexts in which there was no doubt that historical texts were at stake.

Hence, I should have called the book mentioned just now *Representationalist Logic*.[3] Another good reason for wishing I had done so is that the logical backbone of the book was formed by Leibniz's theory of representation. Leibniz scholars such as Dillmann, Köhler, and Mahnke had already insisted that the notion of representation was of central importance for Leibniz.[4] The following chapters summarize my present view of the nature of historical writing and take Leibniz's theory of representation as their guide.

But the precedent was set by the first book ever written on what today we call "analytical (or critical) philosophy of history": namely, Johann Martin Chladenius's *Allgemeine Geschichtswissenschaft* of 1752.[5] So the philosophy of history presented here and in the next three chapters is, in fact, a return to both the birth of an analytical philosophy of history and that of the tradition of (German) historicism. There is nothing new under the sun. What is new in this book is not the conception of historical writing I defend but the way I do so. Put differently, underneath the myriad fashions that have been proudly and triumphantly advocated in both historical writing and in reflections upon it, a deeper substructure can be discerned that has not changed at all in almost three centuries. This book captures the

---

2. See Franklin R. Ankersmit, *Narrative Logic. A Semantic Analysis of the Historian's Language* (Boston: Martinus Nijhoff, 1983), 19–27.

3. Franklin R. Ankersmit, "Representationalist Logic," in *Other Logics. Alternatives to Formal Logic in the History of Thought and Contemporary Philosophy*, ed. Admir Skodo (Leiden: Brill, 2014), 103–23.

4. Eduard Dillmann, *Eine neue Darstellung der Leibnizischen Monadenlehre auf Grund der Quellen* (Leipzig: Hanse 1891); Paul Köhler, *Der Begriff der Repräsentation bei Leibniz. Ein Beitrag zur Entstehungsgeschichte seines Systems* (Bern: Francke, 1913); and Dietrich Mahnke, *Leibnizens Synthese von Universalmathematik und Individualmetaphysik* (1925; repr. Stuttgart: Friedrich Frommann, 1964).

5. Johann Martin Chladenius, *Allgemeine Geschichtswissenchaft. Mit einer Einleitung von Christoph Friederich und einem Vorwort von Reinhart Koselleck* (1752; repr. Vienna: Hermann Böhlaus Nachf, 1985).

metaphysical and logical characteristics of that substructure. I agree with Beiser's observation about historicism quoted in the introduction: "indeed, since it continues to exercise such enormous influence, it never really died at all. It continues to live in all of us, and it is fair to say that, as heirs of Meinecke's revolution, we are all historicists today."[6]

2. LEIBNIZ AND REPRESENTATION

Most people know little more about Leibniz's system than that it respects common sense less than that of almost any other great philosopher in the history of Western thought. Just think of how Leibniz summarized his system in the *Monadology* at the end of his life:

> So one can say that monads can only begin or end all at once, that is, they cannot begin except by creation or end except by annihilation. . . . There is likewise no way of explaining how a monad can be altered or changed internally by any creature, since nothing can be transposed in it, and we cannot conceive in it, as we can in composite things among whose parts there may be changes, that any internal motion can be excited, directed, increased, or diminished from without. Monads have no windows through which anything could enter or depart. Accidents cannot be detached from substances and march about outside of substances, as the sensible species of the Scholastics once did. So neither substance nor attribute can enter a monad from without.[7]

Thus, monads (or substances, as Leibniz called them until around 1695) remain what they are from the day of creation until the end of the world;

---

6. Frederick C. Beiser, *The German Historicist Tradition* (Oxford: Oxford University Press, 2011), 26.

7. Gottfried W. Leibniz, "Monadology," in *Philosophical Papers and Letters*, 2nd ed., trans. Leroy E. Loemker (Boston: Reidel/Springer, 1976), 643–53, see theorems 6 and 7 on 643. Leibniz's *Monadology* was published in 1714, two years before his death in 1716, and was meant to be a brief summary of several decades of intensive meditation on his monadological system. Nevertheless, the system's main elements were already present in his *Discourse on Metaphysics* (1686), as the following passage from the *Discourse* shows: "every substance is like an entire world, and like a mirror of God or of the whole universe, which it expresses, each in its own manner, about as the same city is represented differently depending on the different position from which it is regarded." Gottfried W. Leibniz, *Philosophical Papers and Letters*, 2nd ed., trans. Leroy E. Loemker (Boston: Reidel/Springer, 1976), 308.

no explanation can be given of their internal changes by an appeal to anything outside the monad itself; moreover, nothing penetrates into the monad from the outside—they are "windowless," as Leibniz put it in this quote. Many will reject this account of our world as just crazy—and one can only sympathize.[8] A few introductory remarks about Leibniz may therefore be helpful.

Since the notions of *representation* and of the *individual* are central both in my own account and in Leibniz's system, I focus primarily on these two concepts in this chapter. As previously noted, Leibniz himself was quite explicit that representation was the cornerstone of his thought.[9] In a letter to the Berlin court chaplain Isaac Jacquelot dated February 2, 1704, Leibniz wrote:

> the miracle or rather the admirable is this, that each substance is a representation of the universe in agreement with its perspective. This is the greatest richness, or the greatest perfection one can attribute to the activities of the Creator and to his creations, resulting in a multiplication of worlds in these numberless substantial mirrors, varying the universe to infinity. These simple substances are, so to say, all minor deities being all related to each other. So as soon as some point of representation of the universe is fixed, all of the rest automatically follows from it.[10]

---

8. When clarifying the notion of the phaenomena bene fundata (PBF) in the glossary, I explained why Leibniz opted for this seemingly weird construction. For a succinct and accessible introduction to Leibniz's thought, see Hans Poser, *Gottfried Wilhelm Leibniz. Zur Einführung* (Hamburg: Junius, 2005); especially the chapters titled "Die grossen Prinzipien" and "Die Monade als Substanz." As far as I know, this book has no equivalent in English in comprehensiveness and accessibility. The emphasis is on Leibniz as a philosopher of the exact sciences.

9. The authors mentioned in note 4 all agree about the centrality of the notion of representation in Leibniz's thought.

10. Leibniz to Isaac Jacquelot, February 9, 1709:

> Le miracle ou plutôt le merveilleux consiste en ce que chaque substance est une représentation de l'univers suivant son point de vue. C'est la plus grande richesse ou perfection que l'on puisse attribuer aux créatures et à l'opération du Créateur, et comme un redoublement des mondes dans ces miroirs innombrables de substance, par lesquels l'univers est varié à l'infini. Ces substances simples sont toutes comme des petites divinités respectives, depuis leur commencement, car pour de la fin, elles n'en ont point. Or le point de la représentation de l'univers dans chaque Monade étant établi, le reste n'est que conséquences, et vos questions, Monsieur, se résolvent, ce semble, d'elles mêmes.

The English translation is mine. See Carl Immanuel Gerhardt, *Die Philosophische Schriften von Gottfried Wilhelm Leibniz. Herausgegeben von C.I. Gerhardt*, vol. 3 (New York: Georg Olms, 1978), 464, 465.

So for Leibniz the (monadological) universe is built up of an infinity of individual monads, all mirroring or representing each other from a point of view specific to them. Consequently, anyone wishing to discover the secrets of representation—secrets going deeper than they might seem at first sight—had best turn to Leibniz.[11]

But two problems with the Leibnizian system present themselves straight-away. First, if each monad is windowless (as stated in the *Monadology*) and thus enclosed within its own "private world," how could there then be *one* universe that all substances or monads have *in common*? How could they be aware of one another, let alone represent each other? And, finally, if Leibniz defends this doctrine of the windowlessness of all monads (D_{wm}) and if monads cannot perceive each other, does it not follow that the perceptions of each individual monad might well be completely incompatible with those of all the others?[12] If so, each monad seems to live in its own universe, and so there must be as many universes as there are monads. But if not, and that claim can *ex hypothesi* neither be proven nor disproven by what is outside a monad, what purpose is served by claiming that their perceptions are all compatible with each other? So D_{wm} seems to be both absurd and useless.

To deal with these problems, Leibniz introduced his doctrine of the "*harmonie pré-établie*" or preestablished harmony (D_{ph}): when God created the world (i.e., the monadological universe), he took care that the perceptions or representations of all the monads should be in complete agreement—or

---

11. Evolutionary biology offers a historical representation of the evolution of life on this planet, so on those grounds alone it is valuable to have some understanding of historical representation. Representation is the basis of life itself. Recall that life began with DNA and RNA molecules that had developed spontaneously in the primal soup some four billion years ago—the latter probably before the former because of their being less complex. DNA is a double-stranded biological polymer made up of building blocks called nucleotides. These consist of a deoxyribose sugar molecule attached to a phosphate-group and a nitrogen-containing base. The bases in question are adenine, cytosine, guanine and thymine (A, C, G and T). The genetic code spelled out in the letters A, C, G and T remained the same down to this day for all of these four billion years. DNA and RNA molecules acquired the capacity to replicate themselves -hence, to produce "representations of themselves". Life is the transmission of information as encoded in matter—in this case in DNA and RNA molecules. Occasional changes in them explain evolution—and cancer. Life is definitely "Leibnizian." At the other end of the spectrum, this argument also applies to aesthetic and political representation.

12. Leibniz took over the idea from Francesco Suarez, the most important representative of the so-called second Scholasticism of the sixteenth century, although Suarez used the term *incommunicability*. See J. A. Cover and J. O'Leary-Hawthorne, *Substance and Individuation in Leibniz* (Cambridge: Cambridge University Press, 1999), 26. In both cases, the aim is to express the complete "self-sufficiency" of the monad: the monad could exist exactly as it is, even if it were the *only* monad.

"in harmony" with those of all the others. In contemporary terms we could say that Leibniz's cosmology contains the following three items: (1) God; (2) a (probably) finite set of variables, such that each value of a given variable corresponds to a certain state of that aspect of a possible world described by the variable in question; and (3) a computer of almost infinite computational power (the quantum-computer humanity might have in 2220, assuming humanity still exists). I separate God from these variables because Leibniz's theory of how the world in which we live came into being asserts that even God has to accept them as an unchangeable given. Leibniz mentions only one explicitly: the law of noncontradiction, to which God is no less subject than we are. What these other variables are, I could not say.[13]

Anyway, after having established the variables he had to work with—for better or for worse—God entered them into His quantum computer, and then typed in the words "what does the perfect world based on these variables look like?" Then He waited and waited. But no answer came. It gradually dawned on God that He had asked an impossible question, in the sense that even if He waited infinitely long His computer would not reply, either with an answer to His question or a "not found." Even God can ask questions to which no answer is possible. So he lowered his ambitions and typed instead, "What does the best possible world based on these variables look like?" And this time the computer did produce an answer.[14] God looked at the results, thought them over, and finally decided that "this is the world I will create."

The point of this modern creation story is that the existence of our world cannot be explained purely by an appeal to scientific laws because these also depend on the matrix of variables necessary to realize "le meilleur des mondes possibles." Leibniz's computer needs logic and mathematics only. Using the vocabulary at the end of chapter 5, one might say that Leibniz's best possible world is an HR with our world as its model (which I identified with Leibniz's domain of the *phaenomena bene fundata* in the glossary).

Next, thanks to God's intervention, monad M_1 will not perceive A_1 at place P and time T where monad M_2 perceives A_2 at that same place P and time T where A_1 and A_2 are distinct (there are admittedly problems

---

13. But it is possible that a close reading of Leibniz's *Théodicée* offers some interesting suggestions.

14. See chapter 5, section 4, for a mathematical explanation of why the latter question, unlike the former one, could be answered.)

occasioned by this notion of "the *same* place P and *same* time T" that I leave aside here).[15] The world that the monads all share can, thanks to D_{ph}, be described as the "point of view-less" substrate of all of the monad's representations. Of course, God's most praiseworthy effort to arrange the universe in agreement with D_{ph} is a *Deus ex machina* if ever there was one.[16]

Now, fortunately, this problem does not exist in the case of historical writing, or historical representation. Leibniz's D_{ph} is a given that is simply thrown in our lap and not in need of any theological foundation. With regard to Leibniz's monads or historical representations (HRs), we must strictly distinguish between (1) statements *about* monads or HRs and (2) statements that are *contained* by monads or HRs. Indeed, a statement S_1 about monads or HRs of the form "M_1 is p" or "HR_1 is p" is *ex hypothesi* analytically true; but so too would be a statement S_2 with the form "M_2 is non-p" or "HR_2 is non-p." Clearly, S_1 and S_2 can both be true—they are "compossible" as Leibniz put it. But since Leibniz advocates the doctrine of the excluded third *or* of noncontradiction (D_{et}), p and non-p are not compossible. That is the difference between statements about monads or HRs and those statements contained by them. Nevertheless, this gets Leibniz into difficulties: for what guarantees that that one statement "p" in one monad or HR does not have its counterpart "not-p" in some other monad or HR? This is why Leibniz appeals to God's computational faculties

---

15. Russell, for example, insisted that there is a serious problem here: "Thus Leibniz had two theories of space, the first subjective and Kantian, the second giving an objective counterpart, i.e. the various points of view of the monads. The difficulty is, that the objective counterpart cannot consist *merely* in the difference of points of view, unless the subjective space is *purely* subjective; but if it *be* purely subjective, the ground for different points of view has disappeared, since there is no reason to believe that phenomena are *bene fundata*." See Bertrand Russell, *A Critical Exposition of the Philosophy of Leibniz* (London: Allen and Unwin, 1967), 122.

So either there is *one* monad only—and Russell's problem will not present itself—or there is a *plurality* of monads, and there is no way to avoid it. Exactly the same problem is occasioned, of course, by time. Obviously, the difference between Leibniz and Spinoza is that the former had an infinity of monads or substances, whereas Spinoza had just one of them. One may therefore sympathize with Russell's complaint that Leibniz would have avoided many unnecessary problems if he had postulated just one monad instead of an infinity of them. However, had Leibniz followed Russell's advice, it would have prevented him from achieving what was undoubtedly his main aim; namely, to create a maximum of unity in a maximum of diversity. It is not unlikely that Leibniz's mathematical preoccupations—to be discussed in the last section of chapter 5—motivated him to attach so much importance to the issue of the reconciliation of the greatest unity with the greatest diversity.

to prevent contradictions between the statements contained by his monads (or their "perceptions," as he would call them).

Fortunately, the philosopher of history need not fear this problem in the case of historical representation. First, *whatever* the past may have been like, *whatever* may have happened in it, and *whatever* true statements can be made about what has happened in the past, we can be confident that it—i.e., the past—is consistent with itself. The past is what it was like, but not both what it was like and what it was *not* like—assuming that we will not come across Schrödinger cats in the past as investigated by historians. Second, let us assume that the historicist distinction between historical research (Geschichtsforschung) and historical writing (Geschichtsschreibung) is tenable, that historians have responsibly dealt with the evidence that the past has left us and, hence, that the statements constituting their HRs are all true.[17] Let's agree, furthermore, on the validity of the following two principles: (1) true statements are never incompatible with each other, and (2) we may agree with Leibniz's D_{et} so that all statements about the world are either true or untrue; *tertium non datur* (contrary to the dialecticians and n-valued logic).[18] It follows that what Leibniz needed D_{ph} for has effortlessly been realized in the case of HRs. It is as if past reality has been so kind as to do for the historian all the computations that Leibniz had so cheerfully outsourced to his omniscient God. Since the past is what it has been, and could not have been different from what it was, and since the contents of all HRs respect this trivial fact, the *harmonie pré-établie* of all statements mentioned in all possible HRs is assured. So Leibniz's D_{ph} is valid for HRs as well.[19]

---

16. "God could give to each substance its own phenomena independent of those of others, but in this way he would have made as many worlds without connection, so to speak, as there are substances, almost as to say that when we dream, we are in a world apart and that we enter into the common world when we wake up." Leibniz, *Philosophical Papers*, 493.

17. For this distinction, see section 4 of this chapter.

18. I'm undaunted by the protest that true statements are always formulated in a certain language and that what true statement S_1 states in language L_1 about some fact F may therefore conflict with what true statement S_2 states in language L_2 about that same fact F. In that case, I shall say that F can stand for both F_1 (what S_1 is true of) and F_2 (that S_2 is true of) and that the truth of S_1 does not exclude the truth of S_2. Compatibility of S_1 and S_2 has then been restored. If incompatibility stubbornly persists, we do well to distrust both L_1 and L_2 and look for an alternative language, L_3, capable of explaining and removing the incompatibility of S_1 and S_2.

19. It will be clear from the foregoing that Leibniz was a determinist and that his repeated attempts to reconcile his determinism with freedom failed to convince most of his commentators.

There is a second problem with the Leibnizian system that must be dispelled before entering more deeply into it in the next chapter. Leibniz requires us to conceive of the monadological universe as an infinity of monads, each of which mirrors all of the others, without there being anything outside or beyond this basic metaphysical fact. This invites the complaint that the Leibnizian universe has the nonsensical status of a house of mirrors in which everything mirrors everything else—but without there being *anything* to begin this endless mirroring process. If we accept Leibniz's metaphysics, we must postulate, in addition to his metaphysics, that something exists *outside* and *independent* of this endless mirroring process. That is, that something is actually mirrored by the mirrors, just as in a house of mirrors nothing is reflected as long as nobody enters it. However, this is at odds with Leibniz's claim that there is no reality outside the monads and their representations. For Leibniz, there is nothing behind, outside, or beyond representation and their representeds. As Cassirer forcefully put it:

> The universe, as represented by the monads, is the sum and the totality of all spatialtemporal phenomena: but precisely these phenomena themselves present to the mind in their order and with their intimate law-like connections a content and a fundament more certain and solid than could possibly be demanded. Here thought finds its final halt and objective destination. . . . So it is mere self-deception if some metaphysics would pretend to be able to go beyond this phenomena. Hence, Leibnizian philosophy has no answer to offer to the question of why there is this ever-changing manifold of representations.[20]

---

20. "Das Universum, das die Monaden vorstellen, ist die Allheit und der Inbegriff der räumlich-zeitlichen Erscheinungen: aber eben diese Erscheinungen selbst bieten in ihrer Ordnung in ihr durchgängiger gesetzlichen Verknüpfung dem Denken einen Inhalt and Grundbestand dar, wie er ein gediegener und sicherer nicht gefordert werden kann. Hier findet der Gedanke seinen Halt und sein objective Bestimmtheit. . . . Es ist lediglich eine Selbsttäuschung, wenn irgend eine Metaphysik glaubt noch hinter dieses Phänomen zurück gehen zu können. Auf die Frage warum überhaupt eine Vielheit und ein Wandel von Vorstellungsinhalten statttfindet, hat daher die Leibnizsche Philosophie allerdings kein Antwort mehr." Ernst Cassirer, "Einleitung," in *Hauptschriften zur Grundlegung der Philosophie*, Vol. 2, ed. G. W. Leibniz (Hamburg: Felix Mainer, 1966), 97. The translation is my own. Dillmann had previously expressed the same insight: "die Welt ist also nicht bloss, wie wir sagten, das Objekt der Substanzen, der Inhalt und der Gegenstand ihrer Tätigkeit, sondern diese *selbst* sind wesentlich auf dieselbe bezogen. Sie sind—es lassen sich eben keine bessere Bezeichnungen finden als diejenige welche Leibniz selbst gewählt hat—selbst Ausdrücke, Repräsentationen, Bilder, Spiegel, Nachahmungen des Universums, konzentrierte Welten, Welten im kleinen, und es gibt daher eine Unendlichkeit von Welten, wie es auch auch unendlich viele

This is absolutely crucial. To forget this is to miss the whole point of Leibniz's metaphysics. For if there *were* something behind Leibniz's monadological metaphysics, that something would immediately rob his metaphysics of its metaphysical status. That something could then triumphantly claim a metaphysical status for itself.[21] It would mean the premature end of the entire Leibnizian system. Seeing as much is *truly a condition* for all understanding of the Leibnizian system. If Leibniz's critics nevertheless continue to protest that there simply *must* be something that is mirrored, the discussion will follow the same path as that between realists and idealists. The realist always snaps at the idealist: "don't you see that chair and table over there? How could you possibly deny there is a reality outside ourselves?" To which the idealist will reply: "of course I see that chair and that table. But you have still not grasped my point when I said 'esse est percipi.'" So it is with Leibniz, although he would probably prefer to say that Being is both perceiving and being perceived (or representing and being represented). Put differently, in Leibniz's thought the representation and the represented are identical. You shall see why this claim, so weird at first sight, makes sense when the notion of the *sign* is discussed in chapter 4.

Third, there is Leibniz's notion of the individual. Let's start by stating where his thought still respects commonsense intuitions. We can all agree that the world presents itself to us as being built up of individual things. Wherever we look, from the universe itself, its galaxies, their stars and planets, down to molecules and atoms, and everything in between these two extremes, we find identifiable, individual things. However, the road Leibniz and the friend of common sense can safely travel together is regrettably short. His notion of the individual goes far beyond what we are ordinarily willing to grant to it. Leibniz conceives of the individual by thinking away everything that goes on, or should be located, between individual things, such as their interactions, their external relationships, generalizations over individuals, and so on.

Leibniz's world consists of individuals only. Recall D_{wm}. Leibniz took over that claim from the Scholastics, especially from Francesco Suarez (1548–1617). He first defended it in the doctoral thesis he wrote as a

---

Substanzen gibt." Quoted by Köhler, *Der Begriff der Repräsentation*, 145. All that is said here about substance is also true of HRs. See also the geographical metaphor discussed on p. 000.

21. As is explained in the glossary in the entry on "'Logic and metaphysics" one cannot uphold the existence of two metaphysics without contradiction.

seventeen-year-old lad at Leipzig, and he adhered to it for his entire life.[22] He continued to work it out systematically until his death in 1716. The result is a world in which all that one might situate between individuals is, so to speak, "packed up within" these individuals themselves. Universals and external relations are eliminated in the Leibnizian system. Consider, for example, the universal "being intelligent."[23] Suppose you have the following two statements: "John is intelligent" and "Peter is intelligent." Leibniz will insist that John's intelligence must be distinguished from Peter's intelligence.[24] Both intelligences are not the same because their exact nature will depend on to whom they are attributed. Universals are thus filtered out of Leibnizian monadological metaphysics. The only things left then are individuals, i.e., Leibniz's substances or monads. One can only agree, therefore, with Heimsoeth's observation that Leibniz has been the most extreme individualist in all of the history of philosophy.[25]

---

22. As Leibniz formulates it there, "omne individuum tota sua entitate individuatur." Quoted in Mahnke, *Leibnizens Synthese*, 78.

23. Relational statements are dealt with in the last three sections of chapter 4.

24. Here Leibniz comes close to the contemporary idea of tropes. If we leave out potential Scholastic predecessors, it can be said that the notion of the trope was introduced in modern philosophical parlance in Donald C. Williams, "On the Elements of Being: II." *Review of Metaphysics* 7, no. 2 (1953): 171–92. Tropes can be defined as follows: "Trope theory is the view that reality is (wholly or partly) made up from tropes. Tropes are things like the particular shape, weight, and texture of an individual object. Because tropes are particular, for two objects to 'share' a property (for them both to exemplify, say, a particular shade of green) is for each to contain (instantiate, exemplify) a greenness-trope, where those greenness-tropes, although numerically distinct, nevertheless exactly resemble each other. Apart from this very thin core assumption—that there are tropes—different trope theories need not have very much in common. Most trope theorists (but not all) believe that—fundamentally—there is nothing but tropes. Most trope theorists (but, again, not all) hold that resemblance between concrete particulars is to be explained in terms of resemblance between their respective tropes. And most (but not all) hold that resemblance between tropes is determined by their primitive intrinsic nature." See Anna Sophia Maurin, "Tropes." *Stanford Encyclopedia of Philosophy* (2018); https://plato.stanford.edu/entries/tropes/. See also chapter 3, note **25**, and section 5 of the epilogue.

25. "Leibniz ist insofern nach Heimsoeth der extremste Individualist den die Geschichte der Philosophie kennt. Zum vollständigen Begriff jeder Individualität gehört dabei auch die Unterschiedenheit von andern möglichen Wesen. Denn wenn etwa zwei individuelle Substanzen nicht durch eine 'différence interne,' sondern 'bloss durch die Zahl,' verschieden wären, so liesse sich kein Grund angeben, warum es zwei Dinge sind, während doch nach dem ontologischen principium rationis alles ein Grund haben muss." Quoted in Mahnke, *Leibnizens Synthese*, 125.

3. THE PROBLEM OF THE PHAENOMENA BENE FUNDATA

Hence, even if D_{ph} guaranteed that the perceptions the monads have are all in agreement with each other (as we saw a moment ago), this will surely not prevent us from regarding Leibniz's construction of the monadological universe as completely at odds with how we normally think of ourselves and of how we relate to the world outside us. Even if Leibniz reassures us by telling us that the perceptions of all monads perfectly agree with each other, the fact remains that Leibniz's notion of the windowlessness of the monads (and hence of ourselves) inevitably compels us to regard all of our perceptions as mere illusions.

This time, however, Leibniz is quick to meet our natural worries. For the world as we know it from daily life reappears in its familiar shape in Leibniz's system as the phaenomena bene fundata (PBF). These PBF constitute "the world as it appears to us"—but they are *not* reality itself (!), for that privileged status is granted exclusively to the totality of all the monads. Nevertheless, the PBF do have an absolutely reliable *foundation* in the monadological universe, which is why they are "bene fundata." So when we move from the world of the monads to that of the PBF, the monads react like the buds of flowers, as it were. They open up their petals and reveal their inner core to each other. For example, we human beings then see each other as we do now and can have a meaningful conversation while reacting directly to what our discussion partner will say. Similarly, an autumn storm will blow the leaves from the trees and metals will expand if heated—and we will see all these things with our own eyes. External relations, universals, the laws of nature, all of which were still slumbering in the monads, are now called into life and can become the potential objects of scientific research as we know it.[26] Consequently, science gives us knowledge of the PBF and not of substances of monads.[27]

A comparison with Kant may be helpful. Both Kant and Leibniz distinguish a phenomenal reality, a reality as it *appears* to us, from a deeper reality in which the former originates. Kant claims that nothing can be

---

26. In this way, universals *can* be said to be at least "potentially" present already in the monadological universe—thus qualifying the claim that it should leave no room for universals.

27. It should be added that this categorical statement is truer of the later than of the younger but still materialist Leibniz. The years between 1680 and 1685 roughly mark the transition from the younger to the later Leibniz.

known about this deeper "noumenal reality," and that only phenomenal reality is knowable. But for Leibniz it is the other way around. For him the real is to be found in the monadological universe, whereas the PBF that *are* accessible to us are, for him, a mere reflection of the deeper and more fundamental monadological universe.[28]

According to Kant, nothing can be said about noumenal reality apart from the observation that we must postulate it as "the cause of phenomenal reality." Much to Kant's irritation, Friedrich Heinrich Jacobi criticized this position right after publication of the first *Critique* as an impermissible transcendental use of the category of causality that was thus at odds with the Kantian system itself. So the Kantian system literally begged to be released from noumenal reality (*Ding an sich*), and idealists such as Fichte and Schelling happily complied. An unbounded idealism was the result.

For Leibniz no such solution was possible. The monadological universe could not be eliminated because it is the metaphysical basis of the phenomena bene fundata, and the latter could not be eliminated because they are how *we* perceive the world—or put differently, the phenomena are our world as a reflection of the monadological universe. The PBF are as deeply entrenched in the Leibnizian system as the monadological universe is. Leibniz was a brilliant physicist and arguably the greatest mathematician of his time and therefore not in the least inclined to take the phaenomena bene fundata *à la légère*. After all, they are the objects of all scientific research. Leibniz was thus obliged to present an acceptable explanation of how the two are related to each other.

It is no exaggeration to say that Leibniz wrestled with this problem all his life, and he never found a theory that gave both the monads and the PBF their due in a way that completely satisfied him. I cannot retrace his

---

28. Leibniz opposed the metaphysical domain of the monads and the "phaenomenological" domain of the PBF to one another. But Leibniz seems to have thought of this opposition in two somewhat different ways. His first view was that there is a level in which we situate the monads and another level where the PBF are located. His second view was that all things have two *aspects*, one monadological, the other phenomenological, a position that has a "hylomorphist" dimension. Rutherford remarked that "on the one hand, there is evidence linking Leibniz to a doctrine of phenomenalism, according to which bodies are nothing over and above the coordinated perceptions of unextended monads. On the other hand, there are grounds for taking him to be committed to the thesis that material things are in some sense aggregates of monads." See Donald Rutherford, "Phenomenalism and the Reality of Body in Leibniz's Later Philosophy," *Studia Leibniziana* 22, no. 1 (1990): 11. Leibniz wavered between these two options, favoring the second until the middle of the 1680s but inclining more toward the first later in his life.

long and arduous journey in detail here, but perhaps three remarks will suffice. First, at the beginning of Leibniz's philosophical career he was more inclined to a materialist emphasis on the PBF, whereas monadology gradually took over, especially in the *Discourse on Metaphysics* (1686), and culminated finally in his *Monadology* (1714). The main line of the argument he ordinarily preferred was as follows. To begin with, monads can only perceive, or represent, other monads. But these perceptions or representations must not be modeled on the commonsensical view of perception: monads are windowless. Another possibility would be to say that what monads actually see, perceive, or represent are phenomena belonging to the domain of the PBF. But that would result in a kind of short circuit between the monadological universe and the domain of the PBF, which is at odds with Leibniz's unswerving decision to keep the two apart from each other. The problem is that the monads are separate from each other, on the one hand, but must *seem* or *appear* not to be wholly different worlds, on the other. This seeming or appearing is then projected on the phenomenalism of our daily reality, i.e., the domain of the PBF. But this fails to explain anything, as Leibniz saw. Hence his appeal to the example of the rainbow to clarify his intentions. The droplets of water in the air cause the light of the sun to be broken in such a way that a rainbow appears to us even though we don't see these droplets. These droplets cause or "found" the rainbow, but the rainbow is all we see. So it is with the monads, or "constitutive unities" as Leibniz sometimes calls them, and "the matter or extended mass" constituting the PBF: "accurately speaking, however, matter is not composed of these constitutive unities but results from them, since matter or extended mass is nothing but a phenomenon grounded in things, like the rainbow or a mock-sun, and all reality belongs only to unities. . . . Substantial unities are not parts but foundations of phenomena."[29]

---

29 See Leibniz, *Philosophical Papers*, 536. So, in the end, monads do see, perceive, and represent other monads, although only in the guise of the PBF. This account will be contested by commentators questioning the accepted wisdom that Leibniz should be regarded as a phenomenalist. Their argument is (1) that Leibniz often uses the phrase "well regulated phaenomena" when discussing the PBF; (2) that, apparently, the two notions are interchangeable for him; (3) that the phrase "well regulated phaenomena" refers to fixed patterns in how (common sense) reality manifests itself (unlike dreams); and that (4) Leibniz endows that reality with a metaphysical status of its own. See, for example, Anthony Savile, "The Rainbow as a Guide to Leibniz's Understanding of Material Things," in *Individuals, Minds and Bodies: Themes from Leibniz*, ed. M. Carrara, A. M. Nunziante, and G. Tomasi (Munich: Franz Steiner, 2004), 193–203. But this

Second, Leibniz's problem was not epistemological. The epistemological relation between a knowing subject and an object of knowledge is not equivalent to that between the monads and the phaenomena bene fundata. There is no room whatsoever for epistemology in the Leibnizian system. One could say, at most, that the trajectory traditionally covered by epistemology has its equivalent in the relationship between monadological reality and the domain of the PBF. This is, again, where the Kantian and the Leibnizian differ from each other.

Third, and most important, the philosopher of history can, unlike the epistemologist and the philosopher of science, afford to remain indifferent to this problem in the Leibnizian system. The explanation is a certain peculiarity in the relationship between the historian and the past investigated by him. It is a peculiarity that is discussed at several points in this book, but here I restrict myself to an argument that may, as I hope, convince you intuitively. First, each book or article about the past proposes a certain point of view from which, according to the author of the book or article, the part of the past in question should be seen. Second, such points of view on the past are possible only from a perspective that is later than that part of the past. If you are still in the past itself, so to speak, you cannot position yourself outside it—but this is required for the very possibility of a point of view on what is investigated. It follows that both history and historical writing can only come into being when the past itself no longer exists. Put differently—recall my claim that "historical reality (i.e., the world of the HRs) only comes into being when the past no longer exists."

The claim sounds paradoxical: How could there possibly be a historical reality when the past no longer exists? The explanation is that we can

---

antiphenomenalistic reading is clearly at odds with the whole gist of Leibnizian monadological metaphysics. Assuming, then, that we must choose between a phenomenalist and an antiphenomenalist reading of Leibniz, I should say that the former seems to me to be the correct one. I follow Shohei Edamura's careful distinction between no less than six positions that could be ascribed to Leibniz on the issue. See Shohei Edamura, "Well-Founded Phenomenon and the Reality of Bodies in the Later Philosophy of Leibniz," https://www.seiryo-u.ac.jp/u/research/gakkai/ronbunlib/j_ronsyu_pdf/no43/08_edamura.pdf, and Shohei Edamura, "How to Connect Physics with Metaphysics: Leibniz on the Conservation Law, Force, and Substance," *Revista Portuguese de Filosofia* 74, no. 2-3 (2018): 787-810. To put it metaphorically, the monads perceive each other as "broken" through the medium of the PBF—and, again, what they perceive, they perceive in their own selves because monads are windowless.

certainly have *factual knowledge of the past* even though the past no longer exists. The evidence the past has left us and that can be investigated in the here and now is the basis for true or false statements about the past. It is true, too, that historians use these facts about the past in the books and articles they write about the past. But it is not these facts about the past that are at stake in historical debate; what is at stake in historical debate is the *historical* reality in which we must situate these points of view on the historical reality that historians propose. This, then, may explain how there can be a historical reality, not *in spite of the fact* but *thanks to the fact* that the past no longer exists (recall also what was said about this issue in the introduction). Historians use facts about the past not for a debate about *the past* but for a debate about *historical reality*. No one will doubt for a moment the importance about the past, i.e. about what statements about past states of affairs, or true or are not. This is where it all begins. But from there historical debate moves on to a debate about *historical reality*. And in these debates true statements about past states of affairs are arguments but never conclusions. Put differently, historical debate is soft where it seems hard and hard where it seems soft. I am well aware that one needs to turn a switch on in one's mind to grasp this absolutely pivotal fact—but it is as it is.[30]

Hence, the crucial question is: What *point* in that "space" (i.e., historical reality) offers us the best and most comprehensive point of view on historical reality? The statements about the past that constitute the historian's HR *define* that point (of view). So these statements about the past do two entirely different things: (1) they give us *information* about states of affairs in the past, and they also (2) *define such a point of view*. Historians appeal to facts about the (no longer existing) past to argue in favor or against (a) certain point(s) of view on historical reality (all of them part of historical reality as constituted by the totality of all possible HRs). At the same time, it is these facts about the past that nevertheless firmly attach the representations of the past offered by historians in their books and articles to the past and prevent them from floating in a timeless and indefinite historical limbo.

---

30. It is exactly the same kind of switch Cassirer urges us to turn if we wish to grasp Leibniz's thought. See note **20**.

Now, in theorem 57 of his *Monadology*, Leibniz wrote this: "Just as the same city viewed from different sides appears to be different and to be, as it were, multiplied in perspectives, so the infinite multitude of simple substances, which seem to be so many universes, are nevertheless only the perspectives of a single universe according to the different points of view of each monad."[31] Bearing in mind what was said about these points of view in historical writing, the parallels between them, on the one hand, and what Leibniz said here about his monads, on the other, will be obvious. But what about the city? It could not possibly be located in the monadological universe because that consists only of the perspectives from which the monads perceive each other. So the city must be located elsewhere.

The Leibnizian system being what it is, there seems to be only one alternative: the domain of the PBF. At first sight this seems to be in agreement with Leibniz's metaphor of the city seen from different perspectives. However, the Leibnizian system itself leaves no room for it. Had Leibniz held that the perceptions of the city from different perspectives were PBF nobody would object, but this would reduce the system to a banal platitude. The system owes its entire interest to the fact that the monads and *not* the PBF are "foundational." Precisely this requires Leibniz to offer a plausible explanation for how the domain of the PBF can be born from the perspectival perceptions that the monads have of each other. Although he searched his whole life for such an explanation, he never found one that satisfied him (or would have satisfied us).

In the account of historical writing given here, Leibniz's problem does not present itself. There is a decisive asymmetry between the Leibnizian system, on the one hand, and its application to historical writing, on the other, that may explain why Leibniz's problem disappears in the case of historical representation. The Leibnizian system leaves room only for the domain of the PBF apart from the monadological universe, whereas in the case of historical representation we have, apart from the HRs, *both* the PBF *and* the past. In the case of historical representation, this unfolding of Leibniz's PBF into two categories has its origin in the fact that "historical reality only comes into being when the past no longer exists."

This *absolutely crucial fact* makes it possible to do the following four things at the same time. It becomes possible (1) to deny to the past a

---

31. Leibniz, *Philosophical Papers*, 648.

metaphysical status and to reserve that status to historical reality only, i.e., the reality consisting of all possible HRs; (2) to leave room for the introduction of historical facts in the domain of the HRs; (3) to radically cut through all other possible ties between the past and historical reality; and (4) to explain why historical reality goes beyond the past in the sense of making room (in that reality) for saying things (either in terms of HRs or otherwise) that could never have been said in the past from which the facts expressed in HRs originate.

Observe that two and three mark the differences between the Leibnizian system and the account of historical representation given here. Because Leibniz's system had no counterpart of the category of the past, it leaves no room for two. Similarly, any radical cut like the one expressed by three would render the relationship between the monads and the PBF in Leibniz's system wholly inexplicable. Finally, there is a difference in the logical development, or the movement, so to speak, of the two systems. Leibniz's system demands that one can move from the monads to the PBF, and vice versa. In contrast, the movement proposed here for historical representation is from the facts of the past to HRs, and from there to the PBF (and in that order only). And this is, moreover, a one-way street. In sum, unlike Leibniz, the philosopher of historical representation is not compelled to argue that the first and third should be identical. Put differently, the philosopher of history retains considerable freedom to define the relationship between the HR and its PBF. To put it colloquially, whereas the PBF are for Leibniz a permanent pain in the ass, they are for the philosopher of history a most welcome windfall.

Our conclusion must be that the philosopher of historical representation must hold onto Leibniz's PBF but must redefine the meaning and content of the PBF in a manner consistent with the overall account of historical representation. Transplanting Leibniz's PBF to the domain of historical writing enables us to solve a problem that would otherwise be a very tough nut to crack. Recall the proposal to regard the representationalist universe of the HRs as historical reality. The proposal makes sense only on the condition that it is consistent with itself and does not occasion or allow any contradictions. Only statements about reality can contradict each other, but reality cannot contradict itself—as is stated in Leibniz D_{et} for monadological reality as well. For two reasons, the representationalist universe of the HRs satisfies this requirement of noncontradiction.

First, all the statements contained by HRs were postulated to be true. This postulate can be defended with the argument that these statements are true of the past—when it still was reality—and thus leaves no room for any incompatibility between them. The self-consistency of *historical reality* mirrors or repeats the self-consistency of *the past* when it still was reality.

Second, each HR—e.g., HR_1—is individuated by statements like HR_1 is s_1, HR_1 is s_2, HR_1 is s_3, and so on. Something similar can be said about the HRs: HR_2, HR_3, HR_4, and so on. So all these statements are true of either HR_1, HR_2, HR_3, HR_4, and so on, and *not* of any other(s). All statements defining an HR have a subject-term different from those individuating some other—so contradictions of these statements are impossible. Put differently, because all these statements are about one and the same subject—HR_1, HR_2, HR_3, HR_4, and so on—they are all inward-looking and thus avoid by force of logic any collision with other HRs. Clearly, we have here—for historical representation—the logical counterpart of the metaphysical claim expressed by Leibniz's D_{wm}. And it was D_{et} that enabled us to formulate it for HRs.

From the point of view of guaranteeing the self-consistency of historical reality, this is, of course, most welcome. But it has unpleasant consequences. The extreme tolerance that HRs show toward each other is a standing invitation to admit to historical reality the weirdest guests. For example, we could conceive of the possibility of an HR consisting of a haphazardly selected set of true statements about the past that makes no sense at all to its reader. The legislation for HRs knows no laws prohibiting such HRs. Self-evidently, we would like to get rid of such unwelcome guests. But on the level of the HRs themselves, no help is to be expected: they receive each conceivable HR in their midst with the greatest hospitality.

At this junction, the historical counterpart of Leibniz's PBF can be shown to be truly indispensable. In chapter 3 I show that these historical PBFs agree on all counts with those of Leibniz: (1) they are mere phenomena in the sense of lacking the metaphysical status of HRs, but (2) they are *bene fundata* because they have their roots in HRs and also because they have their support in historical fact *and* came into being via the rational procedures adopted in the writing of history and in historical debate.[32] I argue at the end of chapter 3 that the PBF, corresponding to the HRs to which

---

32. For these "rational procedures," see the last three sections of chapter 5.

they belong, are less tolerant with regard to their rivals than the HRs in question. And this is shown to be decisive. Put differently, addressing the issue of the PBF explains why, and how, the more vital and vigorous HRs can be separated from their less promising brothers and sisters on the basis of historical fact and historical argument. Here again we have a complete *harmonie pré-établie* with the architecture of the Leibnizian system. For Leibniz also acknowledges the fact that some monads see more of the monadological universe than some others, without seeing in this an argument to doubt the raison d'être of these less perceptive ones. Everything that exists has *eo ipso* an unalienable *right* to exist.

In sum, these historical PBF can be regarded as those derivations from their respective HRs that allow us to summon these HRs before a tribunal fit to judge their relative strengths and weaknesses. But that tribunal will not have at its disposal the a priori guaranteed self-consistency that governs the historical reality constituted by HRs. So an opposition as stark as that between compatibility and incompatibility will not help here. After all, these historical PBFs are mere phenomena. They lack a clear ontological status, and their contours are ordinarily vague, contentious, and disputable. Nevertheless, the contours of the PBF are drawn sufficiently clearly to permit a rational discussion about the pros and cons of the HRs to which they belong.[33] So via their PBF we have, after all, a solid grasp of the HRs themselves. Whereas Leibniz is at a loss as to how to link together his monads and his PBF in some credible manner, we have the historical PBF that enable us to summon HRs before the tribunal of historical rationality.

4. APPLICATION OF LEIBNIZ'S SYSTEM TO HISTORICAL REPRESENTATION

Leibniz's conceptions of the substance or monad and of the monadological universe will be used in this book for the development of a theoretical model for the discipline of historical writing. Let us begin with Leibniz's most fundamental, logical claim about his monads. According to Leibniz, the identity of each monad and the perspective from which it sees the monadological universe is both constituted and defined by the totality of the

---

33. See chapter 5, section 4.

perceptions it has of the monadological universe. Leibniz formulated this claim in terms of his so-called *praedicatum inest subjecto* principle. This principle states that a monad is nothing more and nothing less than the sum of all its properties, or of all that can be truly predicated of it. Briefly, a thing is the total set of *all of its properties*, nothing more and nothing less. When one property is left out or added, you will have another thing.[34]

The principle is often called Leibniz's doctrine of the complete concept (D_{cc}) because the concept of a thing contains a complete enumeration of all properties that can truly be predicated of it.[35] The inverse principle is that all the properties of a monad are logically derivable from the notion of the subject-term in sentences about that monad.[36] The notion of a monad M already entails that M has the properties $p_1, p_2, p_3 \ldots p_n$, so all sentences to the effect that M is p_1, M is p_2, M is $P_3 \ldots$ M is P_n are analytical truths. That is, the predicate is already *in* the subject.[37]

---

34. Leibniz took this doctrine from Francesco Suarez, but Cover and O'Leary-Hawthorne insist that Leibniz had his own reasons for believing the doctrine was fundamental. For Leibniz, it was the answer to the question with which everything begins, namely: "What is this? What is it to determine something?' Cover and O'Leary-Hawthorne quote Leibniz's *Nouveaux Essais*: "it seems impossible for us to know individuals or to define any way of precisely determining the individuality of any thing except by keeping hold of the thing itself." They comment that "Leibniz is clearly concerned to stress that no descriptive profile less than a super-rich one can serve in singling out a thing, and thus that no abstraction will succeed in providing unique singular reference. But Leibniz's point here is not that we *do* in fact secure reference by possessing the super-rich complete concept. Indeed he stresses here that 'only someone who is capable of grasping the infinite could know the principle of individuation of a given thing,' implying that we cannot know any such principle and so cannot ourselves grasp the complete concept (God is another matter). His point is rather that we cannot secure reference recognizing a profile—only an infinite description being sufficient on that score—and that we must know individuals by somehow 'keeping hold of them' in the way suggested by the *Confessio* passage." Cover and O'Leary-Hawthorne, *Substance and Individuation*, 178–79.

35. "In every true affirmative proposition, whether necessary or contingent, universal or particular, the notion of the predicate is in some way included in that of the subject. *Praedicatum inest subjecto*; otherwise I do not know what truth is." Leibniz, *Philosophical Papers*, 337.

36. Leibniz recognized that it was impossible to make relational statements about monads because such statements lack a subject-term in the proper sense of that word—but reacted in a strangely lackadaisical manner to it. See chapter 4, sections 3, 4, and 5 for a discussion of the problem of relational statements in both Leibniz and historical representation.

37. The Leibnizian system leaves no room for contingent truth. This has the unpleasant implication of eliminating human freedom—assuming that the domain of human freedom can be defined in terms of what is only contingently and not necessarily true of us. But for Leibniz even the most insignificant truths about us—for example, what we decide to have for dinner tonight—are essentially true of us no less than our decision whether we are ready to die for our country or not. D_{ii} left Leibniz no other choice: the person deciding to eat fish for dinner differs from the person having meat for dinner no less than the person who made the free choice to courageously die for his country differs from someone refusing to do so. D_{ii} denies Leibniz the possibility of recognizing that the same two substances that are "essentially" the same are "contingently" different.

This situation has its exact counterpart in historical representation. Suppose you have a historical representation (HR) consisting of the sentences $s_1, s_2, s_3, \ldots s_n$ about the past (where n is a finite number—no HRs are infinitely long), then this HR is recursively constituted and defined as the set of sentences HR is s_1, HR is s_2, HR is s_3 ... HR is s_n and by nothing more nor less than *this* set, and *only this* set of sentences.[38] Likewise, as with Leibniz's *praedicatum inest subjecto* principle, sentences of the form HR is s_1, HR is s_2, HR is s_3 ... HR is s_n are all analytically true.

Finally, note the asymmetry between Leibniz's monad and HRs, on the one hand, and the "moderate-sized specimens of dry goods" of daily reality, on the other.[39] It would be absurd to say of the latter that they are nothing more and nothing less than the sum of all their properties, or all that can be truly predicated of them. For they can boast of *also* existing apart from all that is or can truly be said about them. And no such thing is possible in the case of Leibniz's monads and HRs. But we can say such a thing without any absurdity if the things we are talking about are *linguistic* things. That might present a problem for Leibniz,[40] but HRs are *linguistic things* so the philosopher of history can accept this implication.

All properties that a thing has are *essentially* its properties. The inevitable conflict between Leibniz's D_{cc}, D_{sr}, D_{ii} and the belief in human freedom were central to Leibniz's correspondence with Antoine 'Le grand' Arnauld (1612–94). To Arnauld's objection that he found it hard to believe that his making, or not making, a journey to Paris should be part of his substance (or essence), Leibniz replied—assuming that Arnauld (or he himself) should decide to make the journey—"yet since it is certain that I shall make it, there must be some connection between me, who am the subject, and the execution of the journey, which is the predicate, *for in a true proposition the notion of the predicate is in the notion of the subject*. If I did not make the journey, there would therefore be a falsehood which would destroy my individual or complete concept, or of what God conceives of me or did conceive of me before he resolved to create me. For considered as possible, this concept includes existences or truths of fact or decrees of God upon which facts depend" (italics in original). Leibniz, *Philosophical Papers*, 334.

Leibniz had *le courage de ses opinions* and unflinchingly followed the logic of his scholastic argument to the very end. As we saw previously, this gives us Leibniz's so-called complete concept doctrine (D_{cc}) or praedicatum inest subjecto principle stating that "the whole entity, the individual substance itself, individuates" a claim that could be rephrased in Aristotelian terminology by saying that the individual substance must be an "infima species." Leibniz goes on to argue for D_{cc} by saying that anything less than the complete concept would entail that we can think of some subset of a substance's properties that is both necessary but not sufficient, and sufficient but not necessary, for individuating the substance in question—which is absurd.

38. For this claim see chapter 1.

39. J. L. Austin, *Sense and Sensibilia. Reconstructed from the Manuscript Notes by G. J. Warnock* (London: Oxford University Press, 1964), 8.

40. Leibniz never commented on the idea of "linguistic things," but his system presents no obvious obstacles to it.

Next, what is it that HRs represent? Much depends on this issue. The obvious candidate is of course "past reality." But for two reasons this answer is mistaken. First, the phrase *past reality* is an oxymoron: the past no longer exists, therefore it is no longer a reality. Second, it is not clear what this past reality could possibly be. The phrase suggests some misty and never precisely defined entity against which all possible HRs can be tested to discover their truth or reliability.[41] However, there is no evidence that there is any such thing. There is no super HR given to us apart from all the HRs that have and will be written by historians. Suppose such a super HR did exist; then why go on writing new HRs? For we would already have the final "truth" about the past, as expressed in this super HR. It would suffice to present the relevant parts of this super HR.

To account for the nature of historical knowledge we need only two things: (1) true statements about past states of affairs and (2) HRs. That is all we have and all we need; the dictum less is more never made more sense than here. The historian does not have *two* sources of information about the past to consider: (1) the facts about the past *and* (2) so-called past reality. The latter is either identified with the former, or it is an epistemological *fata morgana*. The notion of so-called past reality plays no role in the acquisition of historical knowledge; it is a wholly redundant irrelevance. Indeed, it is worse than redundant because it is an inexhaustible source of innumerable philosophical fallacies. In Wittgenstein's phraseology, past reality is "a wheel that can be turned though nothing else moves with it, is not part of the mechanism."[42]

---

41. This brings us to one of the most powerful—because it is subconsciously held—myths about the writing of history. People speaking about "past reality" (in the singular) ordinarily have in mind some spooky and elusive entity apparently believed to be spread out over the facts of the past, much in the way an infinitesimally thin and elastic sheet of plastic (household film coming closest to what I have in mind here) could be spread over a solid but rough and uneven floor. Above all, the sheet is thought to be removable without loss of form so that it can be carried from the past to the present to be investigated by the historian in the here and now. It is believed to be the intermediary between past facts, on the one hand, and historical narrative, on the other. In fact, this imaginary sheet of plastic could be said to be an intuitive inkling of the historian's PBF, as defined here. The idea of the imaginary sheet of plastic is, on the one hand, a cognitive illusion, but on the other, it hides in itself a profound insight in the nature of historical writing. It is the onerous but most rewarding task of the philosopher of history to separate truth from myth in the intuition.

42. Ludwig Wittgenstein, *Philosophical Investigations* (Oxford: Oxford University Press: 1974), section 271, 95e.

If HRs do not represent past reality, what do they represent? For an answer to that question, we must turn to Leibniz again. Leibniz's monads represent the monadological universe; but that universe consists of other monads, and of monads only. The answer that monads represent something that is outside all of them is, admittedly, tempting and seems commonsensical. But that answer is precluded by the very logic of the Leibnizian system because it would imply a reality apart from, outside, or beyond that of the monads. Such a suggestion is at odds with the very heart of the Leibnizian system.[43] Consequently, monads represent *each other*, and there is *nothing* outside, beyond, or behind the totality of the monads. As Leibniz wrote to Arnauld:

> The proposition which has occasioned this discussion is, I may add, very important and deserves to be established, for it follows from it that every individual substance [i.e., monad] expresses the entire universe in its own way and in a certain relationship, or from that point of view, so to speak, from which it regards it. It follows also that its subsequent state is the result, though free and contingent, of its preceding state, as if there were only God and itself in the world.[44]

And so it is with HRs. They represent the universe consisting of HRs and of HRs only and, hence, each other. This insight was expressed in what was, arguably, the most original book on the philosophy of history written in the previous century, namely, Peter Munz's *The Shapes of Time* of 1977.[45] Munz starts with the observation that most people tend to see the historical text as a mask behind which we must locate the past itself. The assumption is

> that behind the mask there is a face and that we might check the adequacy or truth of the mask by peeping at the face that is hidden behind it. But the ineluctable truth is that there is no face behind the mask an that the belief that there is is an unsupportable allegation. For any record we could have

---

43. See section 2 in this chapter.
44. Leibniz, *Philosophical Papers*, 337.
45. Franklin Ankersmit, "Peter Munz and Historical Thought," *Journal of the Philosophy of History* 15, no. 3 (2021): 378–95.

of the face would be, precisely, another mask. We cannot have proof that it is the genuine "record" of the face and every possible glimpse of the face would be, by its nature, yet another mask.[46]

Needless to say, Munz made exactly the same claim about HRs that Cassirer had made about Leibniz in section 2. According to Cassirer, the beginning of all wisdom about the Leibnizian system is that we unwaveringly resist each temptation to postulate a reality behind or beyond Leibniz's substances or monads. Here Munz states that it is no different with historical writing.

This parallelism of the Leibnizian system and historical representation can be elucidated in terms of the intimately related metaphors of the point of view and of scope.[47] Recall theorem 50 of the *Monadology*: "one created being [i.e., monad] is more perfect than another if one finds in it which will supply a reason a priori for what happens in the other. And it is because of this that it is said to act upon the other."[48] Leibniz's phrase to "supply a reason a priori for what happens in the other" indicates that the representational content of the latter can be derived from that of the former. In terms of the visual metaphor pervading Leibniz's writings, the scope of the latter is part of the scope of the former. Here, scope stands for how much, or little, a monad perceives of all other monads from the perspective specific to it and that defines it.[49] Crucial is the idea that the superiority of one monad to another is defined here exclusively in terms of one monad's scope comprising that of some other without involving anything outside or beyond the domain of the monads. For the only things that monads can "see" are other monads.

As an illustration, view a map of England and assume that the sea always blocks what you can see of the country. If you place yourself in Cardiff, the

---

46. Peter Munz, *The Shapes of Time: A New Look at the Philosophy of History* (Middletown, CT: Wesleyan University Press, 1977), 17. And—as will be done in this book—he infers from this the conclusion that "if we have a historical narrative, there is nothing over and above the narrative to compare it with.... We have only a narrative and nothing else. The most one can do is to check one story against another story. One can compare the two and any notion of 'truth' one can form must be related to such a comparison." Munz, *Shapes of Time*; 205, 206.

47. Both metaphors are admittedly not without their problems—as is the case so often with metaphors used in philosophical argument—and in some ways they are even at odds with Leibniz's own system. Fortunately, in chapter 5 I show that we can do without them, thus coming closer to his "true" intentions. However, in this chapter, the use of them is, I hope, forgivable.

48. Leibniz, *Monadology*, section 50.

49. For replacement of the metaphorical notion of *scope* by a nonfigural and, therefore, more acceptable one, see chapter 5, section 3.

whole of the South and Southeast of England will be outside your scope. If you place yourself in Liverpool, all that is to the left of the line from Liverpool to Cheltenham is outside your scope. But from London you can see almost all of England—although, again, Cheltenham limits what you can see. However, if you place yourself somewhere between Coventry and Northampton, the whole of England falls within your scope. Now replace all the cities, towns, and villages of England by Leibniz's monads—all of them seeing all of the others from a perspective that is specific to each of them (and that, in fact, even *defines* them)—and you will have a fairly good idea of Leibniz's intentions. The geographic "universe" of England is defined by all of its cities, towns, and villages (i.e., monads); that is, by all the perspectives they have on each other (that define their place on the map) where these perspectives—to uphold the metaphor—are logically prior to their actual geographical position (and *not* the other way around!). Nothing is then needed outside, beyond, or behind these cities as defined by the perspectives they have on each other to guarantee or support the consistency of this mental image.[50] You only have the perspectives the cities (i.e., monads) have on others—and nothing more than these—and yet it makes sense to say that one of them is more (or less) superior to some others. And if it is either of these two possibilities, this is determined by whether the perspective of one monad subsumes in itself that of some other. One might even consider the possibility of making a map of England on the basis of information about these perspectives *only*. That map would then play the role of a phaenomenon bene fundatum in this spatial metaphor.

It is no different with historical representation. Given a set of HRs, the most satisfactory monad is the one that is more comprehensive and

---

50. This metaphor may clarify what Leibniz had in mind when responding to Pierre Bayle's criticisms of his system: "Dies alles findet sich hier wie in einem perspektivischen Zentrum vereinigt, aus dem die Objektivität, die von jeder andern Stelle ausflieht, ihre Regelmässigkeit und die Übereinstimmung ihrer Teile erkennen lässt." Mahnke adds the following comment: "es ist also ein *objektiver* Perspektivismus, den Leibniz an die Stelle des subjektiven Relativismus setzt, nämlich eine universelle Systematik aller individuellen Erkenntnisstandpunkte" (italics added). Mahnke, *Leibnizens Synthese*, 13. This "objektiver Perspektivismus" reflects, next, that under certain circumstances the notions of representation and expression are interchangeable for Leibniz. As Köhler observes, "und da jetzt der Leser sich bereits ein Urteil gebildet und einzige Beobachtungen angestellt haben wird, will ich hier darauf aufmerksan machen, dass représenter und exprimer sich in der mathematische Bedeutung immer am besten mit 'Ausdrücken,' in der psychologischen Bedeutung mit 'Vorstellen' übersetzen lässt, während Leibniz beide Wörter promiscue gebraucht, allerdings für das objective Darstellen exprimer, für das subjektive Vorstellen représenter bevorzugt." Köhler, *Der Begriff der Repräsentation*, 115.

has a wider scope than the others. It is able—because of being the most comprehensive HR—to subsume the others in itself, and to "explain" the others from *its* point of view. Scope maximization is therefore the unfailing guide and measure of historiographical success.[51] It should be added, though, that an HR dealing with a big topic does not necessarily have a wider scope than one dealing with a much smaller one. An HR with an innovative analysis of the struggle between the Girondins and the Jacobins may well have a wider scope in this sense than one on the French Revolution as a whole that adds nothing new to what we know already about this *sublime* historical phenomenon.[52] A comparative judgment is always required: HRs on the French Revolution must be compared with other HRs on the Revolution. HRs on the conflict between the Girondins and the Jacobins must be compared with other HRs on that same topic. And, again, if one HR from among a comparable set of HRs best satisfies this demand of scope maximization, this is not because of anything that can be attributed to it from *outside* the representational universe (for example, because of an alleged correspondence to so-called past reality), but only because it can be said to be more perfect than these others because of its wider scope. The light of historical truth shines from *within*.

Two important conclusions follow from this for the nature of historical representation. First, HRs are essentially *competitive*. HRs are always striving to subsume as much of the scope of other HRs into themselves as possible. HRs always strive for two things: (1) to swallow up in themselves as many other HRs and as much of the scope of their rivals and (2) to widen their own scope as much as possible beyond those of their rivals.[53] An HR whose scope has been absorbed by some other has thereby lost its raison d'être and will cease to exist in practice (although not in theory because HRs are purely logical entities, no spatial and temporal denominations can be attached to them; in this way they can be said to be "eternal," just as numbers are: the number 356920897 has always existed, exists now, and will continue to exist forever in the future, even though no one ever mentioned it).

---

51. These claims are at this early stage of my argument necessarily no more than mere intuitions. A justification of them will be given in chapters 3 and 4.

52. I use the word *sublime* here in the Kantian sense, i.e., to denote a phenomenon transcending the categories of understanding on which we normally rely for making sense of the world in which we live.

53. Clearly, all this is mere idle metaphorical talk and, therefore, in need of argumentative proof. Such proof will be given in chapters 4 and 5.

Note that these observations about HRs concerning their competition and scope never move beyond the metaphysical limits of historical reality, which consists only of HRs. Again, HRs represent *each other* and not anything *outside* the domain of HRs.

Second, assuming that the practice of historical writing supports the claim of the competitiveness of HRs, we may conclude (1) that the representationalist universe must contain *minimally* two HRs and (2) preferably as many and various HRs as possible—which is in agreement with Leibniz's claim that his monadology "is the means of obtaining the greatest variety possible, but with the greatest order; that is to say, this is the means of attaining as much perfection as possible."[54] Here the spirit of Leibniz's monadology comes strangely close to that of a liberal market economy, as was argued by Joseph Vogl.[55] The representationalist universe of HRs is the historiographical pendant of the following characteristic Leibniz attributed to the monads and their interaction: "Now this mutual connection or accommodation of all created things [i.e., monads] to each other and of each to all the rest, causes each simple substance to have relations which express all the others and consequently be a living mirror of the universe."[56] This mirror image that an HR has of the universe also necessarily includes an image of itself—with the qualification that it can only be *an* image, and not *the* image of itself, because that image, too, will be codetermined by the image that other monads, or HRs, have of the monadological or representationalist universe.[57] Leibniz's thought has an amazing counterpart in the phenomenon of the so-called entanglement of photons

---

54. Leibniz, *Monadology*, section 58.
55. See Joseph Vogl, *Der Souveränitätseffekt* (Berlin: Diaphanes, 2015), especially chapter 6.
56. Leibniz, *Monadology*, section 56. In a letter to his good friend and sovereign lord and master, the Duke of Sachsen-Weimar, Goethe wrote that he had journeyed through Italy between the years 1787 and 1789 "um mich an den fremden Gegenständen kennen zu lernen." It worked; after his return he found that he had overcome the mental and psychological crisis that had paralyzed him since the early 1780s. Goethe's "experience" of Italy is prototypical of what the visit to Italy meant to generations of German poets, historians, philosophers, and novelists from Goethe to Hofmannsthal, Rilke, Burckhardt, Nietzsche, and Mann. The history of the German experience of Italy has impressively and masterfully been summarized in Henk de Jong, "*Kennst du das Land? Italië-reizigers, Rome-ervaringen en Duits historisch besef in de Negentiende Eeuw*" (PhD diss., Amsterdam University, 2020).
57. This claim could be reformulated as a rejection of the Kantian transcendental ego, an entity that is, according to Kant, the condition of the possibility of all knowledge, while not itself being part of the knowledge it makes possible.

and other subatomic particles that, according to contemporary quantum mechanics, go on to "remember" each other after a quantum event, even though one of them is in one part of the universe and the other in a wholly other part of it.

Now, if all HRs represent the same—i.e., historical reality as constituted by all possible HRs—it might seem to follow that all HRs must be the same too. But for three reasons this inference is wrong. First, Leibniz insisted that monads are more aware of what is relatively "close" to them than of what is more "remote." This necessarily changes from one monad, or HR, to the other, depending on the point of view from which they see the monadological universe. This can be reformulated to apply to what interests historians or what they choose as their subject matter. Second, each monad perceives the monadological universe with a mixture of clarity and obscurity that distinguishes it from all the others.[58] According to Leibniz, all monads perceive the whole universe, but not all of their perceptions make their way into the monad's consciousness. Some perceptions remain subconscious. Leibniz rather naively calls these subconscious perceptions "petites perceptions." Even though each monad perceives all the other monads in the monadological universe in principle, they will be conscious of them only in a tiny subset of the totality.[59]

This has its obvious analogue in the fact that only a very small subset of all possible HRs have been materialized, or "actualized," to put it

---

58. Monadological perceptions are conceptual. Clarity and obscurity must, therefore, be conceived in exclusively cognitive terms. In his important essay "Meditations on Knowledge, Truth and Ideas" (1684), Leibniz makes the following distinctions: "Knowledge is either obscure or clear, clear knowledge is either confused or distinct, distinct knowledge is either inadequate or adequate, and also either symbolic or intuitive." See Leibniz, *Philosophical Papers*, 291. Leibniz differentiates between these different kinds of knowledge as follows. Knowledge of a thing is obscure if we can discern it once we see it but cannot recognize it as the same thing when seeing it again. Knowledge of a thing is confused if we cannot enumerate all the necessary and sufficient conditions of the acquisition of knowledge. Knowledge is distinct if we dispose of all these conditions. Knowledge is inadequate if we don't know all of a thing's properties and is adequate if we have that knowledge. Symbolic knowledge is the kind of knowledge we have of a chiliogon (see chapter 4); and intuitive knowledge consists of what we know in terms of "ideas," such as mathematical propositions whose truth we perceive intuitively. This hierarchy of certainty is fully applicable to historical writing and gives us criteria with which to assess the strengths and weaknesses of historical knowledge. I interpret it as a program for enhancing the rationality of historical debate.

59. Herbertz suggests that Leibniz's notion of the "petites perceptions" implies a theory of consciousness. See Richard Herbertz, *Die Lehre vom Unbewussten im System des Leibniz* (New York: Georg Olms, 1980).

more accurately. However active historians may be in the future, not much improvement is to be expected here. However many HRs will be produced in the future (even by the now still unimaginable means of AI), the hope that an increase in their number is a sign of substantial progress in historical writing is like believing that the infinite has finally come within our reach after we have succeeded in counting from 100 to 100,000. Just as there will never be complete clarity in the representational universe at large, the number of true statements found in HRs will only ever be a tiny fraction of all the true statements that could be made about the past in principle. Since the number of all possible HRs is infinite, only a tiny fraction of them will be realized. One might, perhaps, sugar the pill by claiming that those HRs that have, are being, and will be actualized will, in all likelihood, be more important than those that will be allowed to slumber forever in corners of the representational realm no one will ever care to visit. For example, what sane historian would discuss the behavior of ants in South Africa when writing a book on the Russian Revolution?[60] An HR that did so would still be an HR, of course, but would universally be rejected as useless, even if entirely true.

Third, the representational universe consisting of HRs representing each other is exactly what we need not just to explain the possibility of historical writing but to guarantee progress in it. For the representational universe is where all HRs make their entry, where they all meet, and where each of them can show its relative strengths and weaknesses—thus providing the historian with the instrument indispensable for all meaningful historical debate.[61] Specifically, some points of view can then be found to be more perfect or superior to others in agreement with Leibniz's thesis stating that "one created being is more perfect to another one finds in it that which will supply a reason a priori for what happens in another."[62]

---

60. On the other hand, one might prefer a more optimistic view of this. Is there not something positive in the idea that we can discover an infinite number of historical truths? It is not depressing, but exciting, to think that there is always more to be known about the past (just as, presumably, there is always more to be known about nature). It can, of course, be frustrating to think that some things can never be known for lack of evidence; but the past has the potential to disclose new sides to itself.

61. See chapter 5 for further discussion.

62. Leibniz, *Philosophical Papers*, 648.

Given a set of HRs, the most perfect one is the monad that is more comprehensive than the others, in the sense that it can be said to be able to subsume the others in itself, and to *explain* the others from *its* point of view. So it is in historical representation. The most perfect available HR has this quality not because of anything attributable to it from *outside* the representational universe (for example, on the basis of so-called past reality), but because it does a better job of meeting the criteria for historical rationality internal to the domain of HRs themselves. Again, the light of historical truth shines from *within*.

5. THREE FINAL COMMENTS

I end this section with three comments extending the arguments made so far. First, Leibniz claims that no monad can have anything in common with any other in the monadological universe. If we translate this claim to the representationalist universe, we will get exactly the same picture. Recall that the identity of HRs is defined by nothing more and nothing less than the set of all of their sentences. Take now, for example, HR_1 and the true statements $S_a \ldots S_n$ it contains (unlike Leibniz's monads, the list is finite, as noted previously). Then HR_1 is defined by the meta-sentences HR_1 is S_a, HR_1 is $S_b \ldots HR_1$ is S_n, and so on, all of them having HR_1 as their subject-term. However, no *other* HR in the representationalist universe contains a statement having HR_1 as *its* subject-term. This is why they could not possibly have anything in common. This also explains why HRs are indivisible and cannot be added together, as Louis O. Mink has rightly argued.[63] As soon as one would try to do so, the subject-term will have to be exchanged for a new and different one. Monads and HRs have no constitutive parts, unlike a car or a computer; nor are they themselves the constitutive parts of larger monads. On the other hand, both monads and HRs can cluster together in what Leibniz called "aggregates" of monads (in the case of historical writing one might think of all the HRs on the French Revolution, or of other HRs on more or less closely related issues).

The fact that monads and HRs have nothing in common (i.e., are windowless) does not imply, however, that they are untranslatable into each

---

63. Louis O. Mink, *Historical Understanding*, ed. Brian Fay, Eugene O. Golob, and Richard T. Vann (Ithaca, NY: Cornell University Press, 1987), 11, 12, 26, 28, 79, 83, 87.

other. One could think of a dictionary containing entries stating how for two HRs (HR$_x$ and HR$_y$) the statements of the former can be exchanged for those of the latter. The length of the dictionary is infinite, because it contains all possible true statements about the past—but it is thinkable. Since seventeenth-century mathematicians such as de l'Hôpital, Bernoulli, and Leibniz himself demythologized the notion of the infinite, we need not feel any reluctance to work with it. And since Georg Cantor (1845—1918) mathematicians can deal with the infinite as easily as with any finite number. Following the procedure would result, in the end, in an exact copy of HR$_x$ or HR$_y$. Combining Leibniz's D$_{cc}$ with his doctrine of the identity of indiscernibles (D$_{ii}$), which states that two things are one and the same if all that can truly be predicated of the one can also be truly predicated of the other—or *"eadem sunt quorum unum in alterius loco substitui potest, salva veritate"* in Leibniz's formulation of the doctrine—the copy would then cease to be a mere copy, but actually *be* HR$_x$ or HR$_y$.

The dictionary would thus guarantee the possibility of translation of HRs into each other in terms of the statements defining them. Consequently, even though HRs are not translatable in terms of the statements *defining* them—statements of the form HR$_1$ is S$_a$—they *are* translatable in terms of the statements they *contain*. The difference is between the set of meta-sentences HR is s$_1$, HR is s$_2$, HR is s$_3$ . . . HR is s$_n$, on the one hand, and the set of object-sentences s$_1$, s$_2$, s$_3$ . . . s$_n$, on the other. The possibility of translation of HRs into each other is important because it ensures that historical writing is a scientific discipline and not an art—assuming that a defining characteristic of works of art is that they are, in principle, *not* translatable into each other. One cannot, therefore, discern in the artwork any fixed and well-defined elements or components that could function as the counterparts of the true sentences constituting an HR.

Perhaps one might now object that novels also consist of statements, and that therefore the novel wipes out this clear distinction between a scientific discipline of history, on the one hand, and literature, on the other. But the objection fails. All the statements of all possible HRs are compatible with each other. So one can start replacing the statements of an HR, say, HR$_1$ by those of another HR, say, HR$_2$. When all the statements of HR$_1$ have thus been replaced by those of HR$_2$, we will end up with HR$_2$. Translation has then been achieved. On the long road from HR$_1$ to HR$_2$, we may encounter some pretty weird HRs. But from a logical point of view, this is irrelevant:

they are all logically unexceptionable. In a novel, however, many, if not most, of the novel's statements are either false or without a truth-value (if one prefers that option). The translation procedure sketched just now for HRs will thus fail as soon as you come across statements that are incompatible with each other. This will occur very quickly in the case of the novel. The exchange of one for the other is then blocked. So the translation procedure will not work if one tries either to translate novels into each other, or novels into HRs, or vice versa. Novels, like all works of art, are untranslatable. If only because of this it is mistaken to believe that literary theory might deepen our understanding of historical writing. Though the reverse is true: after historical writing had come into being, one could conceive of the possibility of abandoning the historian's postulate of factual truth. Literature being the result. Literature, the novel, has its origins in historical writing. And it is not the other way around, since historical writing has its origins in myth and not in literature or the novel. Not surprisingly literature is of a much later date—it is often said that Cervantes's *Don Quixote* was the first novel—than historical writing. Literary theory can learn a lot of history and the reflections on history; whereas the latter two can learn nothing from the former.

Second, we can offer a further a comment on the notion of the point of view that Chladenius took over from Leibniz and that has been crucial for the account of historical representation in this chapter. Obviously, the notion must be understood metaphorically: space and time in the normal senses of these words belong exclusively to the phenomenal world and not to monadological reality. Nevertheless, the idea that the historical text always presents its readers with a point of view on the past has an immediate appeal to practicing historians. The majority of them will regard it as a simple truism that they write their historical texts to present their readers with what they hope is the best possible point of view on the part of the past they are discussing. "No bias, no book," as Michael Howard once succinctly put it.[64]

Philosophers of history, however, have always turned up their noses at the notion of the point of view; it was never properly explored in contemporary philosophy of history as far as I know. Why not? The problem is that if someone is silent on a certain topic you can't even tell why the person is

---

64. Michael Howard, "Lords of Destruction," *Times Literary Supplement*, November 13, 1981, 1323.

silent. Nevertheless, one can have suspicions. In all likelihood, three closely related convictions played a role here: (1) the idea that the notion of the point of view makes no sense in science and that, therefore, it is bad PR for historical writing to discuss the role it might play there; (2) that only an epistemological approach can further our understanding of historical writing;[65] and (3) that whoever uses the notion of the point of view opens the door for moral and political norms and values in historical writing. One can only agree with point one: the scientist is expected to tell us the truth and not what the truth is like if seen from a certain point of view. But in the introduction we found already when discussing Chladenius that the notion of point of view as used by historians by no means casts a doubt on the rationality of the practice of history. Point two is more interesting. Many philosophers believe that we must appeal to epistemology to explain science. Whether they are right or wrong is of no relevance here. Crucial is that the past no longer exists and that the very idea of an epistemological analysis of our knowledge of an object that no longer exists makes no sense at all. Hence, epistemology is not of any use in the philosophy of history—apart from in the context of the reflection on historical research (Geschichtsforschung). But point three needs closer scrutiny, if only because the role of moral and political norms in historical writing has always been a hotly debated topic in the philosophy of history.

Let us begin by distinguishing between (1) the notion of the point of view as it has been discussed in this book so far and (2) statements like "historian H sees the past from a Marxist point of view." Now, how do these two points relate to each other? The answer is that the two are indeed closely related: however, this is not necessarily an occasion for any fears or worries about the role of moral and political norms and values in the practice of historical writing.

Look at it this way. Suppose historian H has written his history of part of the past from a Marxist point of view. His history goes into the "machinery of historical writing and debate" as it was and will be expounded in the remainder of this book. At that stage, the fact that it was written from a

---

65. In opposition to the philosopher's confidence in epistemology, one could argue that epistemology had best be abandoned for an alternative theory explaining how human experience and knowledge is possible that is modeled on the account of historical representation given here. I hope to argue this bold claim some time in the future.

Marxist point of view has become wholly irrelevant. The only thing that matters is how the point of view defended by historian H compares to those proposed by other historians. How such a comparison proceeds is explained in chapters 4 and 5. But in that process the Marxist origins of historian H's book will play no role anymore. Any untoward prejudices will automatically be weeded out in historical debate—although, admittedly, not always straightaway. In sum, as long as the machinery of historical writing and debate functions as it should, we need not fear any nefarious effects from the role of norms and values in historical writing. Historical rationality prevails over norms and values. It follows that people worrying a lot about the role of norms and values in historical writing can be expected to have a low opinion of historical rationality.

In fact, it is rather the reverse: norms and values have excellent reasons to fear that the machinery of historical writing and debate might prove them wrong. Suppose that works of history written from a nationalist or Marxist point of view systematically underperform in historical debate. The conclusion must inevitably be that we'd better not subscribe to nationalist or Marxist norms and values. So historical writing can be seen as a most welcome experimental garden for moral and political norms and values. We need not try them out in sociopolitical reality to discover as much. Needless to say, all this holds only on the condition of an open and unprejudiced debate in the practice of historical writing. This puts the crown on the present argument. We cannot fail to be struck by the fact that this condition seamlessly agrees with the typically *liberal* demand of the freedom of expression. So *this* political norm is foundational for scientific historical writing—as it is for all the other sciences.

A third and last comment is that nineteenth-century historical thought distinguished strictly between historical research (Geschichtsforschung) and the writing of history (Geschichtsschreibung). The former establishes the facts about the past on the basis of the evidence that the past has left us; the latter integrates these facts into a historical representation. The distinction has always been brushed aside with the argument that only naive (logical)-positivists, never having heard of the "thesis of the theory-ladenness of empirical fact," could (still) believe in it. But three reasons can be given for why that thesis does not apply to historical writing.

First, there is the commonsensical argument that one and the same true proposition can appear in exactly the same phrasing and with exactly the same meaning in many different HRs. No HR on the French Revolution will fail to contain the proposition that "the Bastille fell on July 14, 1789," and its meaning in one HR will not differ in any interesting way from the one it has in any of the others.[66] Admittedly, complications might occur in the case of intensional contexts. But in an HR, in so-called intensional contexts, if occurring in representational texts, always take the form of a quotation, either of another HR or of a part of some other HR.[67]

Second, an HR contains sentences having the subject/predicate form, which may be true or false about the states of affairs in the past discussed in that HR. However, HRs themselves are *sets* of statements *lacking* the subject/predicate form. Sets of sentences, being mere sets, have neither subject nor predicate terms. That distinction arises only if one plucks one sentence out of the set and then takes it apart. The subject/predicate distinction makes sense only at the level of the sentence and cannot be imported from there into HRs.[68] To put it differently, tradition knows (1) statements having the subject/predicate form and (2) universal statements stating that it is true of every x that if x is f, it is also true that x is g. But no logic ever really cared about *sets of statements* interacting with each in a way that is typical of HRs. This is why historical representation's unhappy fate has always been to fall between two stools—and why this book enters hitherto a still unexplored and if only because of that territory being so fascinating.

But let's suppose the seemingly impossible to be possible. The result would be an absurdity. If HRs are defined by the statements they contain (as argued previously) and if, moreover, HRs partially determine their sentences (as is required by the thesis of the theory-ladenness of facts), the result would be a vicious circle from which no rescue is possible. Historians

---

66. It was first stated in the evening of July 14, 1789. Louis XVI had been hunting and on returning to Versailles was informed about what had happened in Paris. "Mais, c'est une révolte," he finally managed to say. One of his closest friends, the Duke de la Rochefoucauld-Liancourt, replied: "Non, Sire, c'est une révolution!" Clearly, when distinguishing so forcefully between a *révolte* and a *révolution*, the Duke had in mind the meaning we still associate with it.

67. Danto's "narrative sentences" are an example. This prevents the doctrine of the theory-ladenness of empirical fact from spilling over into the domain of historical representation because of the D_{wm}. See the epilogue for a further discussion of intentional contexts and their role in historical representation.

68. There is a third possibility, namely, statements with, so to speak, *two* subject-terms. This is the case with relational statements such as A is longer than B, A is older than B, or A is more informative than B. This category of statements will play a crucial role in my account of historical representation. See chapter 4, sections 4, 5, and 6.

may decide to rephrase sentences in their HRs with an eye to the argument of their HRs, but in that case the result is a *new* HR of which it is true, again, that it is defined by its statements, without defining (the meaning of) these statements itself. If meaning enters the scene—as we shall see it does later on—it does so in the interaction between HRs, and not in any alleged interaction between HRs and the statements they contain (although there may be, e.g., cross-references or intensional relations between an HR's statements at a strictly local level). So any attempt to apply the "thesis of the theory-ladenness of empirical fact" to the relationship between HRs and the statements they contain must be rejected as a nonstarter.

All of this has its counterpart in the domain of metaphysics as you shall see in chapter 3. We must at all times distinguish between (1) the metaphysics M_1 we all believe in when thinking of the reality in which we live, which consists of the sort of things surrounding us in daily reality; and (2) the completely different kind of metaphysics M_2 belonging to both Leibniz's monadology and to the domain of the HRs. What we say about the past in terms of true statements about the past belongs to M_1; but what is expressed in historical texts in terms of HRs belongs to M_2. There is not only a logical but also a *metaphysical* gap between the true statements that a historical text contains and the HR that is expressed by it. So anyone saying that there should be a sliding scale between a historical text's true statements and the HR expressed by it is confused and has not reflected carefully on the practice of historical writing. Worse still, he forgets that we can, indeed, *think* of two metaphysics, but that this fact does not diminish in any way that they mutually exclude each other. In sum, refusing or forgetting about the distinction between historical research and historical writing amounts to abandoning the distinction between the past, on the one hand, and historical reality, on the other; and this would obliterate the very basis of the account of historical writing given in this book.

It follows that the distinction between historical research and the writing of history, between historical representations and the statements they contain, is really *razor sharp*. Both pose their own problems: the problem of how to establish historical facts cannot be solved by an appeal to the instruments of historical representation, and historical representations will not tell us how to decide the truth or falsity of individual statements about the facts of the past. There are two entirely distinct levels of truth in historical writing: (1) the level of the statement (which may be true or false about some past state of affairs) and (2) that of HRs (which may be considered true or false only on the basis of historical debate about the relative merits of rival HRs).[69] This does not mean that the two levels should be entirely unrelated: an HR containing numerous factual errors on important issues will not be taken seriously by historians. But this is too obvious to be stated and not in need of further analysis.[70] In sum, everything is lost if one carelessly mixes up the two levels, or, worse still, treats the distinction as vague and indeterminate as, for example, the distinction between Western and Eastern Europe.

69. Chladenius had already seen this. Discussing what is "the subject" of historical writing, he argued as follows: "die Begebenheiten, und mithin auch die Geschichte sind Veränderungen. Veränderungen setzen ein Subject, ein dauerhaftes Wesen oder Substanz voraus. Folglich müssen 1. die Begebenheiten und Geschichte ein Subject haben, dahin dieselben gehören. Und so müssen 2. auch die historischen Sätze, Erzehlungen und Nachrichten, jedesmal ihr Subject haben, dessen Veränderungen darinnen vorgetragen werden. Nur, dass einmahl das Subject einer Substanz ähnlicher siehet und uns vorkommt, als das andere Mahl. Die Geschichte Cäsars haben ihr ungezweifeltes und zwar einiges Subject: insgleichen die Historie der Römischen Freyheit, die Historie der Enthusiasterey hat ein Subject, welches nicht von jedem sogleich als etwas substantielles dürffte angesehen werden." Chladenius, *Allgemeine Geschichtswissenschaft*, 11. Hence, Chladenius requires us to strictly distinguish between our speaking about the past and our speaking about historical texts about the past. On many occasions, I emphasized the utmost importance of this distinction. Both in historical writing itself and in the philosophy of history, the distinction is often lost with regrettable consequences. Note, furthermore, the pronounced Leibnizian ring of Chladenius's words.

70. Throughout this book it is assumed that historical representations (HRs) consist of statements that are true of past states of affairs. The implication is (1) that historical texts failing to satisfy this requirement are not HRs in the proper sense of the word, and (2) on a more practical note, other things being equal, that historical texts containing few factual errors are to be preferred to those having more of them, on the ground that the former come closer to being actual HRs. But this leaves undecided cases in which a historical text would be regarded as equal or perhaps even superior to the very best existing HRs on some topic, if only it did not contain a few irrelevant factual mistakes. How to cope with such problems is outside the philosopher of history's expertise and must, therefore, be entrusted to the practicing historian having the last word on what serves best the progress of the growth of historical knowledge. Decisive here is the relative importance of the fact(s) that a historian got wrong. The word *relative* implies that no general rules can be provided here.

Chapter Three

METAPHYSICS, INDIVIDUALS, MODELS, AND THE PBF

1. HISTORICISM AND INDIVIDUALITY

"Historicism is the exchange of a generalizing by an individualizing approach to human affairs and the social world." This is how Friedrich Meinecke proudly defined historicism in the preface to his magnum opus *Die Entstehung des Historismus* (1936).[1] He was expressing his agreement with the typically historicist claim that history is the science of the individual, whereas the sciences prefer to deal with the universal.

This historicist conviction that the writing of history requires a focus on the individual has often been criticized. It is repeatedly pointed out that the notion of the individual necessarily presupposes an acceptance of the universal. For example, how could we speak about *this* individual human being, such as Caesar or Napoleon I, without presupposing the universal "human being"? How can we speak about an individual nation, war, or economic depression without their also being instantiations of the universals

---

1. "Der Kern des Historismus besteht in der Ersetzung einer generalisierenden Betrachtung menschlicher Kräfte durch eine individualisierende Betrachtung." Friedrich Meinecke, *Die Entstehung des Historismus. Herausgegeben und eingeleitet von Carl Hinrichs* (1936; repr. Munich: R. Oldenbourg, 1965), 2. No less illustrative for Meinecke's conception of historicism is the epigraph he gave to his painstaking search for the intellectual origins historicism: "Habe ich Dir das Wort Individuum est ineffabile woraus ich eine Welt ableite schon geschrieben?" (Goethe to Lavater, September 20, 1780).

"nation," "war," or "economic depression"? Obviously, this can be split into a metaphysical and a logical claim. The metaphysical claim is that our universe consists of individual things possessing certain general or even universal properties; the logical claim is that the language used for speaking about these individuals takes the form of statements having the form of "I is φ," where "I" refers to an individual, I, and "φ" stands for a universal (property), such as "being black" or "being square," which is attributed to that individual. On the one hand, we have the numerical list of all the individual things contained by our universe, and on the other hand, completely independent of that list is another list with all the properties that these individual things may, or may not, have. All true and false statements connect an item on the former list with one on the latter.

Now, it is easy to see that this will not work for the individual things contained by Leibniz's monadological universe. That universe has no general properties. Suppose we have a monad M_1 with the perceptions p_1, p_2, p_3 ... and so on. Recall now the doctrine of the complete concept (D_{cc}). According to that doctrine, M_1 cannot be defined by p_1, p_2, p_3 ... and so on, but only by meta-sentences tying p_1, p_2, p_3 ... and so on to M_1: hence the sentences M_1 is p_1, M_1 is p_2, M_1 is p_3, and so on. M_1 has to be mentioned each time as the subject-term of these statements, so the monad M_1 is *recursively* defined by the statements: M_1 is p_1, M_1 is p_2, M_1 is p_3, and so on. Consequently, M_1's properties are not p_1, p_2, p_3 ... and so on, but M_1 is p_1, M_1 is p_2, M_1 is p_3, and so on. Self-evidently, all these properties having M_1 as their subject-term can be attributed to only *one* monad, namely, M_1 itself, and not to any *other* monad. They are not general or universal properties similar to being black or being square, which can be attributed to anything happening to be black or square.

Because Leibniz's notion of monads having perceptions is somewhat ambiguous in the sense of being unclear about whether the nature of these perceptions is defined by what they are perceptions *of,* or by what *has* these perceptions, the foregoing argument is even easier to defend for HRs. HRs are defined by the statements about past historical affairs that they contained. Moreover, whereas the number of perceptions that monads have is infinite, the length of HRs is finite. In the case of historical representations, we need not worry about any problems posed by individuals whose number of properties is infinite. Hence, we can assert without any ambiguity that the nature of HRs is recursively defined by all the properties they have and only by *them*. Likewise, if an HR, say HR_1, contains the statements about the past $s_1, s_2, s_3 \ldots s_n$ (n being a finite number), these properties are not $s_1, s_2, s_3 \ldots s_n$ but are M_1 is s_1, M_1 is s_2, M_1 is s_3 ... M_1 is s_n. Just like Leibniz's monadological universe, the representational universe only contains individuals and no universals—as is the case with the universe we are used to with its two lists: first of individual things, and second the general or universal properties that can be attributed to these individual things.

Hence, the metaphysics of the world in which we live, with its individuals that can be picked out by means of the universally ascribable properties they have, differs both from that of Leibniz's monadological universe and that of HRs, where no such thing is possible. Whereas the former universe has both individuals and universally attributable properties, the two latter have individuals only—although these are nothing but the sum of their uniquely attributable properties.

In chapter 2 I argued that in no philosophical system in the history of Western thought was metaphysics so logical and logic so metaphysical as in the Leibnizian system. Consequently, in all discussions of the Leibnizian system (and of historical representation), it is difficult to pull logic and metaphysics apart from each other. Nevertheless, to make my argument as clear as possible, I shall try to separate them as much as I can. This chapter thus focuses mainly on the metaphysics of the Leibnizian system and of historical representation, whereas chapter 4 is devoted to logical and semantic matters.

2. STRONG AND WEAK INDIVIDUALS

Sir Peter Frederick Strawson's *Individuals: An Essay in Descriptive Metaphysics* (1959) remains a classic statement of the contemporary notion of individuals, or "particular things" in Strawson's vocabulary.[2] Strawson

---

2. Even now, some fifty years after publication, Strawson's book is still one of the very few studies devoted to the issue of individuals and of individuation. See Peter F. Strawson, *Individuals: An Essay in Descriptive Metaphysics* (1959; repr. London: Methuen, 1964). McCullough argues that the issue is almost always avoided in favor of that of identification—but then individuals are given to us already. McCullough uses the example of an article by D. Wiggins stating that a theory about identity should address three questions: (1) the concept of identity or "sameness," (2) identity through change, and (3) what compels us to recognize substances as remaining the same. Here the question "what is an individual?" is not even asked. Although Strawson (and Goodman) discuss the issue of individuals, they are strangely uninterested in the question what kind of "entities" must be regarded as "individuals." See L. B. McCullough, *Leibniz on Individuals and Individuation: The Persistence of Premodern Ideas in Modern Philosophy* (Dordrecht: Kluwer. 1996), 11–12.

makes three claims about individuals, or particulars. First, "in mine, and as in most familiar philosophical uses, historical occurrences, material objects, people and their shadows are all particulars, whereas qualities and properties, numbers and species are not."[3]

Second, speaking about an individual requires that both speaker and hearer should know one or more individuating facts about it that are true of that individual and not of any other. For example, if both speaker and hearer know the fact that only one person was King of England from 1689 to 1702 and that this person was the Stadholder-King William III, this fact about him will ensure that we are speaking about one and the same individual when using the proper name William III. Or, to put it differently, that they are referring to one and the same person when using that proper name.

Third, as is suggested by the subtitle (*An Essay in Descriptive Metaphysics*), Strawson is well aware that a certain *metaphysics* is implied by this account of particulars or individuals. This metaphysics is the commonsense view of reality and our relation to it. It goes as follows: reality contains classes of individual things denoted by the general concepts in our language such as "human being," "tree," "cat," and so on, whereas individual members of these classes can be referred to by expressions such as "the human being, the tree, or the cat which is φ," where "φ" stands for some uniquely individuating fact expressed in universals about the human being, tree, or cat in question.

In sum, this division of reality into classes of individual things having certain properties denoted by general concepts is something assumed to be objectively given to us for no other reason than that this is how our language works. It is, therefore, the "descriptive metaphysics" we unwittingly subscribe to because our language so strongly suggests that this is what the world is like. If, for example, our language happened to consist of different *words* for "the redness of a" and "the redness of b," or for "a's being red" and "a's being black," we would spontaneously have accepted a

---

3. "Metaphysics had often been revisionary, and less often descriptive. Descriptive metaphysics is content to describe the actual structure of our thought about the world, revisionary metaphysics is concerned to produce a better structure. The products of revisionary metaphysics remain permanently interesting, and not only as key episodes in the history of thought. Because of their articulation, and the intensity of their partial vision, the best of them have been both intrinsically admirable and of enduring philosophical utility." Strawson, *Individuals*, 9.

wholly different descriptive metaphysics. We would have experienced the world in agreement with that metaphysics and have been just as blind to that metaphysics because we take it for granted that our world consists of things having certain properties.

The three claims just summarized in support of this view are not peculiar to Strawson; they do not sum up one haphazard opinion of one haphazard philosopher on one haphazard topic. On the contrary, Strawson's theory of particulars and individuals constitutes the very DNA of the philosophy of language as we presently know it.[4] This is clear from the writings of two of the founding fathers of the philosophy of language: Gottlob Frege and Bertrand Russell.[5] Frege's essay I have in mind is his most influential and best known work, "On *Sinn* and *Bedeutung*" published in 1892. Twentieth-century philosophy of language has moved far beyond Frege and Russell, but it has followed a path they had indicated. It is to them, therefore, that we should return to grasp why the twentieth-century philosophy of language is so consistently blind to the problems surrounding the notion of the individual in general,[6] how these problems manifested themselves in the writing of history, and of how historians succeed in accounting for a complex social reality by means of a complex text.

Kenny characterizes Frege's point of departure as follows: "Is identity a relation? If it is a relation, is it a relation between *objects*, or between *signs for objects*? The second answer suggests itself. Because—to take the example he [Frege] used in his 'Function and Concept'—'the morning star = the morning star' (namely, the planet Venus) is a statement very different in cognitive value from 'the morning star = the evening star.'" The former is analytically true, whereas the latter records a minor astronomical discovery.[7] It follows that equations such as a = b express relations between

---

4. Jorge J. E. Gracia, *Individuality: An Essay on the Foundation of Metaphysics* (Albany: State University of New York Press, 1988), xi, remarks that "it seems as if almost every major philosopher [in the analytic tradition] has had to say something about universals, and studies about the subject abound. On the other hand, in contrast with all this philosophical interest in and activity related to universals, discussions of the correlative notion of individuality are not abundant, and by comparison with the number and the depth of treatments on universals, may even be considered scarce."

5. See Gottlob Frege, "Über Sinn und Bedeutung," *Zeitschrift für Philosophie und philosophische Kritik* 100 (1892): 25–50; and Bertrand Russell, "On Denoting," *Mind* 14 (1905): 479–93.

6. This is where the contemporary philosophy of language differs so conspicuously from the Scholasticist tradition in which the problem of the individual was central.

7. Anthony Kenny, *Frege: An Introduction to the Founder of Modern Analytic Philosophy* (Oxford, Oxford University Press, 1995), 126, 127.

signs designating the same thing. Frege then goes on to argue that such equations can only provide information about the extra-linguistic world if the difference between signs such as a and b corresponds to a difference in the mode of presentation of what they both designate.[8] Only because "the morning star" and "the evening star" can thus be said to be different modes of presenting one and the same thing (i.e., the planet Venus) can the equation "the morning star is the evening star" succeed in expressing knowledge about the extra-linguistic world.

Self-evidently, Frege's argument only makes sense on the assumption that if we come across statements such as a = a or a = b, such statements must express *either* a relation between objects *or* between signs. The presupposition is that there is a clear-cut distinction between signs and objects, and that everything is either on the sign/language side or on the object/reality side of that distinction. This is the philosophical version of the common-sense view; and it is the view still advanced in Strawson's descriptive metaphysics. Strawson claims, just like Frege, that, on the one hand, we have individuals, or particulars, such as the planet Venus or Sir Walter Scott, and on the other, we can designate these *same* individuals with *different* phrases such as the evening star, the morning star, or the author of *Waverley* or the author of *Quentin Durward*. But this is, again, a statement about a property about the language that we happen to use rather than the claim about some incontrovertible truth about the relation between language and the world that it pretends to be.

---

8. Frege insists in a reply to Benno Kerry's criticisms that his model of meaning and reference will also be valid for contexts in which we speak about language. In such contexts, concepts can take the place that objects such as Aristotle or Kepler typically have when we refer to them by means of a proper name. Discussing Kerry, Frege writes: "he (Kerry) gives the following example: "the concept 'horse' is a concept easily attained," and thinks that the concept 'horse' is an object, in fact one of the objects that fall under the concept 'concept easily attained.' Quite so; the three words 'the concept "horse"' do designate an object, *but on that very account they do not designate a concept*—as I am using the word. This is in full accord with the criterion I gave—that the singular definite article always indicates an object, whereas the indefinite article accompanies a concept word" (italics added). Hence, in Kerry's example "the concept 'horse'" remains, indeed, a concept; but because it functions in the sentence mentioned by Kerry as an object, its being a concept is put within quotation marks, thus temporarily annulling its original logical character as a concept. See Gottlob Frege, "On Concept and Object," in *The Frege Reader*, ed. M. Beany (Oxford: Oxford University Press, 1997), 183–84. See also Gottlob Frege, "Letter to Husserl 24.5.1891: Extract," in *The Frege Reader*, ed. M. Beany (Oxford: Oxford University Press, 1997), 149–50, especially the scheme at 149.

Frege's argument loses, indeed, much of its a priori plausibility if applied to the writing of history. Suppose we have to answer this question: Is the Renaissance a sign or an object?[9] The main problem is that Frege's trick (if we may call it that) of juxtaposing two different designations of one and the same object does not work here. Suppose there is an object designated by the alleged sign "the Renaissance," what other sign can designate that object? Any attempt to give a sensible answer to that question, such as "the period between the Middle Ages and the Baroque," is not an alternative designation of that object (if it is one), but a more or less crude substitute for the alleged sign "the Renaissance" *itself*. So we've been moving in a circle here.

Next, *is* there an object designated by the Renaissance at all? From our point of view, this is already *une question mal posée* because it presupposes that we could conceive of that object without an appeal to the alleged sign. Whereas we have little difficulty in conceiving of objects such as planets or galaxies without there being signs for designating them, no such thing is possible here. In sum, the questions whether the Renaissance is a sign, *and* of what that sign stands for, make no sense in historical writing. It is *both*. (I return to this more elaborately in section 2 of chapter 4.)

One more aspect of Frege's argument demands our attention. When discussing proper names and their *Bedeutung*, Frege observes:

> the sense of a proper name is grasped by everybody who is sufficiently familiar with the language or totality of designations to which it [i.e., the proper name] belongs; but this serves to illuminate only a single aspect of *Bedeutung* [i.e., reference], supposing it to have one. Comprehensive knowledge of the *Bedeutung* would require us to be able to say immediately whether any given sense attaches to it [i.e., to the *Bedeutung*].[10]

Frege does not develop this comment, but it is worth doing so. The "comprehensive knowledge" Frege has in mind here would constitute the knowledge of the total set of *all* the senses that could be "comprehended" by

---

9. I do not place Renaissance between quotation marks here because that would suggest that the word already stands for a term, sign, or symbol. Whether or not this is so is precisely what is at stake in the argument. Of course, we remain free to speak—at this early stage of our argument—of the "alleged sign 'the Renaissance'" without committing ourselves to any claim about "the Renaissance" being a sign or not.

10. Gottlob Frege, "On *Sinn* and *Bedeutung*," in *The Frege Reader*, ed. M. Beany (Oxford: Oxford University Press, 1997), 53.

some specific *Bedeutung*. And, indeed, *if* we had such knowledge, we could immediately establish whether *some* sense is part of that set, or not.

But we don't have that knowledge. If we have only a subset S of that totality, we cannot be sure that the members of S (or even S itself) are not related to other *Bedeutungen* as well—i.e., *Bedeutungen* that *could* only be ruled out effectively by means of the *total set*, and by nothing *less* than that. But this total set is something that we shall never know, according to Frege. It follows that the members of S, and S itself, will function as a universal or as a general term, denoting a set of objects, all having in common the property or set of properties designated by members of S, or S itself. They denote all possible things in the world having the properties corresponding to the sense(s) defined by members of S, or S itself.

General terms or universals are the *faute de mieux* we appeal to in order to overcome the limitations caused by our lack of the comprehensive knowledge mentioned by Frege. If we *had* that comprehensive knowledge, universals would be useless, and their use would even entail a loss of knowledge. It would be as if every object in the world or any state of affairs in it had a proper name with a *full*, or comprehensive, meaning of its own. It would then suffice to utter that name to get access to its *Bedeutung*, and only *it*, instead of our being compelled to rely on some basically untrustworthy (set of) universals whose "intersection" happens to achieve the same goal—at least as far as our always imperfect knowledge permits us to believe.

For it is, in principle, always possible that more than just one *Bedeutung* or individual can be found at that point of intersection. The point of intersection is a universal itself, in much the same way that a point P on a plane is universally "true" of all lines and curves having point P in common in the sense of being part of them all. So in our less than perfect world, a world in which we do not have a comprehensive knowledge of all possible links between senses and *Bedeutung*, or a world in which the very idea of such comprehensive knowledge is even inconsistent with itself, *Bedeutungen*, or individuals, can only be thought of in terms of universals. And since the senses generated by the use of these universals will always fall short of this comprehensive knowledge of all the senses to be attached to a *Bedeutung* or individual, they will both remain incomplete and never be completely reliable if understood against the background of Frege's comprehensive knowledge.

Finally, it is, in fact, less absurd than Frege believed that in certain circumstances we should have access to this comprehensive knowledge. Think, again, of history. A moment ago we found, in the case of the Renaissance, that no satisfactory answer can be given to Frege's question of whether we have to do here with a sign or with what (i.e., an object) the sign stands for. The explanation is that in such cases we do actually *have* this comprehensive knowledge because historical texts on, for example, the Renaissance, are exemplars of what such comprehensive knowledge looks like with respect to the metaphysics of historical representation. The result is a fusion of sense and *Bedeutung*, of meaning and reference, whereas for Frege such a fusion is unthinkable. In that case no room is left for general terms or universals—which agrees, of course, with the account of the historicist's diagnosis of how matters stand with history and historical writing as briefly summarized in the introduction and as elaborated in chapter 2, and, of course, with Goethe's *individuum est ineffabile*. Put briefly, the sign/object distinction loses its point and purpose if faced with Frege's comprehensive knowledge—as is the case with notions like "the Renaissance."

I now turn to my second foundational text in the philosophy of language, namely, Russell's essay "On Denoting" of (1905).[11] Russell began with a discussion of things that do not exist, such as the round square or the present King of France. Even though this was the main issue of his essay, and even though this made him comment on Frege's essay "On Sense and Meaning," I shall not discuss it here and focus instead on what concerns us in the present context, namely, the analysis of singular true statements Russell derived from this discussion. Russell asks us to consider the statement "the father of Charles II was beheaded." He begins by stating that this proposition is asserting that "there was an x who was the father of Charles II and who was beheaded." Call this assertion (1). Next, Russell insists that the proposition also involves uniqueness: for it is not only true that there was an x who was the father of Charles II and who was beheaded but it's also the case that there was one, and only *one*, x of whom this is true. Charles II did not have two, or even more, fathers. Russell proposes to do justice to this element of uniqueness by stating that "if *anyone* is the father of Charles II, then this *anyone* must be identical with this x." Call this assertion (2).

---

11. Russell, "On Denoting."

METAPHYSICS, INDIVIDUALS, MODELS, AND THE PBF

Russell completes his analysis of this statement about the fate of Charles II's father by subsuming assertion (2) within assertion (1), thereby leaving the structure of assertion (1) intact. His basic strategy is to move from the phrase "the father of Charles II was beheaded" to "there was only *one* x having the property of being the father of Charles II and of being beheaded." Put differently, x is a variable running over all the items in this world requiring us to establish whether *all of* these items are fathers of Charles II and being beheaded, or whether only *some* of them are, or *none* at all, or just *one*—as happens to be the case here, of course. This is why this x is called the *variable of quantification*: it can stand for none, one, some, and all.[12]

Russell's strategy is thus to empty the subject-term of propositions of all content and to shift this content to the predicate part of the proposition while replacing the subject terms by these quantifiers: none, one, some, or all. In this way, Russell contributed to what became known after Quine as the "canonical notation" of the proposition. Strawson summarized it as follows:

> The relevant part of Quine's programme of paraphrase can most simply be summed up as follows. All terms other than the variables of quantification will be found, in canonical notation, to be general terms in predicative positions. The position of the singular term is reserved for the quantifiers and the variables of quantification; and since quantifiers themselves cannot count as terms, the only singular terms left are the variables of quantification.[13]

The result is that the subject-term in statements we usually see as the safe home, symbol, or expression of individuality has been wholly dissolved into universalist predicate terms. Only the variables of quantification still remind us of its once having been there. This is the complete triumph of the universal over the individual.

---

12. Mahnke observes that Leibniz's predicational logic and Russell's set theory mirror each other in their extremism. In the former, all predicates are swallowed up by the subject, whereas in Russell's set theory, universals select individuals. According to Mahnke, Scholasticism developed an embryonic variant of set theory that functioned as a "juste milieu" between these two extremes. Dietrich Mahnke, *Leibnizens Synthese von Universalmathematik und Individualmetaphysik* (1925; repr. Stuttgart: Friedrich Frommann, 1964), 35 ff.

13. Peter F. Strawson, "Singular Terms and Predicates," in *Philosophical Logic* (Oxford: Oxford University Press, 1973), 79.

The philosophy of language is often associated with the sciences and the sciences with the universal. It must then come as a bit of a surprise to us that in both these foundational texts of the philosophy of language the notion of the individual is still remarkably prominent. In fact, both texts seem to do little more than analyze and explain typically historical statements about individuals such as Aristotle, Kepler, Napoleon, Charles II, Walter Scott, and so on. It's almost as if Frege and Russell were doing the philosophy of history! But appearances are deceptive here because Frege's and Russell's argument is not a celebration of (historical) individuality but, instead, is an uncompromising attack on it. The individuals Frege, Russell, and Strawson have in mind are badly truncated individuals; individuals "with a huge hole in them," so to speak. They have had to suffer a far-reaching invasion of the universal. They are, therefore, what I shall call "weak individuals."

Frege's and Russell's argument produces these weak individuals by replacing the notion of the individual with that of the unique. Recall that Russell used the term *uniqueness* when insisting that any sound analysis of the statement "the father of Charles II was beheaded" should respect the fact that there is one and only one individual who was the father of Charles II. Hence, instead of the vocabulary of *individuals*, we now end up with that of *uniqueness*. But this tacit and unexplained shift is unwarranted.

Being an individual and being unique are different things and allow of different combinations. Think of the center of gravity of, say, a brick, to be defined as the point in that brick at which the resultant torque due to the force of gravity vanishes. Needless to say, the brick itself is an individual thing. But its center of gravity is not: we may *associate* it with certain silicon atoms in the brick. But this would be insufficient since precision requires us to proceed to the nucleus of one of the silicon atoms. However, having reached that level, quantum theory and quantum indeterminacy will take over, with the result that we now have to throw up our hands in despair.

But even if we were to push aside as unrealistic such impossible requirements with regard to the brick's center of gravity, even then we must reject any proposal to associate the point of gravity with any identifiable physical parts of the brick. For the truth of the matter is that the brick's point of gravity is not an *individual thing*; nor is it a mere *idea*, if only because of the quite real physical effects the brick's point of gravity will have for its behavior. Suppose we shoot the brick into interstellar space; it will then circulate there with an absolute precision around its spot of gravity. And physical objects do not rotate around ideas.

However, we can say about the brick's point of gravity that it is unique. No two bricks can be completely identical as is stated by Leibniz's law of the identity of indiscernibles (D_{ii}). Nor can any other point in or of the brick be regarded as a rival for the uniqueness of the brick's point of gravity: each object has only one point of gravity. It follows that this attribute of uniqueness must then be valid of the brick as D_{ii} stipulates.

So what about the relation between individuality and uniqueness? Do both terms have the same reference, as the foregoing seems to suggest? Having arrived at this stage we must distinguish between weak and strong individuals. It is easy to see that for weak individuals the notions of individual and uniqueness have a different meaning but the same extension. Take, once again, a brick (a weak individual). Each brick is individual and has minimally one property that makes it unique amongst all other bricks. For example, its point of gravity.

However, this does not work for strong individuals like HRs. For each property we propose as a candidate for a HR's uniqueness is a property that it shares with, in principle, an infinity of other HRs. The only way out seems to be to say that the totality of an HR's properties is *that* property of that HR that makes it unique among all other HRs. However that doesn't work either. For there also is an infinity of HRs having just *that* property, but a whole lot of others as well. A last desperate move would be to say that this HR is unique among all HRs having exactly the same set of properties as HR—and neither more nor less. But this comes down to saying that this HR is identical with itself—and it is impossible to see how an interesting notion of uniqueness could be derived from that trivial claim. It follows that anyone using both the term individual and that of uniqueness still speaks the (extensionalist) language of the weak individuals. Indeed, there both terms have a different meaning and a different extension. But if we speak the (intensional) language of strong individuals the term 'individual' has a well-definable meaning, whereas the term 'uniqueness' will have to be abandoned.

So, *if* the historicists were right that history is the science of the individual—as they were, in my view—philosophers of history must resist this shift from individuality to uniqueness. Trading individuality for uniqueness is tantamount to a betrayal of the heart of historicism—and is at odds with the notion of historical representation defended here. Uniqueness belongs to the vocabulary we use when speaking about weak individuals; we may say, for example, "Mozart's Don Giovanni is *unique* among all operas written in the eighteenth and nineteenth centuries" (1), whereas saying "this HR is unique" is like saying "no other HR than HR is identical with *this* HR" (2). The difference between (1) and (2) is the following. Statement (1) is, if true, a truth *de re*, whereas statement (2) is analytically true, hence, a truth *de dicto*. So, *if*, and I repeat *if*, the historicists were right when claiming that history is the science of the individual, philosophers of history should never go along with this shift from individuality to uniqueness.

Windelband made exactly this mistake when focusing on the *uniqueness* of historical periods, nations, styles of thinking, and so on. He called this their "idios," i.e., what was *unique* to them and what he opposed to the universal laws of the sciences. This view, as we saw at the outset of this chapter, has been criticized as the *ne plus ultra* of naivety because you will always need universal concepts for defining uniqueness. As far as it goes, this argument is, indeed, conclusive and irrefutable. Defending the historicist claim that the writing of history is "the science of the individual" requires never acquiescing in the replacement of the notion of the individual by that of the unique.

Russell's argument also reveals the mechanism behind this pumping dry of the subject-term and the individual it refers to that allowed this shift from individuality to uniqueness to take place. Russell's analysis empties the subject-term of all content in favor of universal terms or concepts. The subject-term referring to individuals or particulars thus dissolves into universal terms, and the domain of individuals is wholly overrun by the universal. The naked variables of quantification are all that remain to remind us of their existence before they were finally erased through the introduction of the canonical notation.

Almost all of contemporary philosophy, including German and French phenomenology and not only Anglophone philosophy of language and science, endorses some variant of what is known as "the thesis of the theory-ladenness of empirical fact" or as "the Myth of the Given" (Sellars).[14] The assumption is that we can only get access to reality—be this daily reality, the world studied by the scientist, or past reality as investigated by

---

14. See section 5 of chapter 2.

METAPHYSICS, INDIVIDUALS, MODELS, AND THE PBF

the historian—via the general, or universal, or the concepts embedded in human language. The implication is that the historicist's notion of history as the science of the individual is inconsistent if taken seriously. Obviously, in my view this is not the last word on the matter, but challenging the dominant view requires more explanation about the notion of the individual.

Finally, people losing themselves in idle and pointless distinctions are often accused of the vice of Scholasticism. But no philosophical tradition devoted more time and energy to the analysis of the notion of the individual than Scholasticism from the beginning of the Middle Ages down to Francesco Suarez in the sixteenth and Leibniz in the seventeenth centuries.[15] If one wishes to discuss individuals, Scholasticism is, in fact, a very good place to start. And it remains true, too, that Scholasticism discussed the individual and individuation in a manner fundamentally different from Frege, Russell, and Strawson and indeed from most if not all of the contemporary philosophy of language. It is in Scholasticism that we may find *strong* individuals, or "individuals without holes in them."[16] This is the topic of the next section.

3. LEIBNIZ ON INDIVIDUALS

Whereas modern theorists of individuals and individuation tend to be indifferent with regard to what *counts* as an individual (as opposed to the derivative issue of what we can say about individuals *once* they have been

---

15. For an excellent survey, see Jorge J. E. Gracia, *Introduction to the Problem of Individuation in the Early Middle Ages* (Washington, DC: The Catholic University of America Press, 1984).

16. HRs contain statements, and these statements express truths about weak individuals. So how can one have strong individuals (HRs) without presupposing the existence of weak individuals? If this observation were correct, it would follow that weak individuals are metaphysically more basic than strong individuals. This would obviously be at odds with Leibniz's claim that it is strong individuals that are prior. But this objection is easily answered. Leibniz's system only presupposes the truth of statements. It does not commit him to any view regarding what *makes* these statements true, nor about what categories of weak individuals would be required for doing so. Without inconsistency, Leibniz could even leave room for the possibility that these statements can be true without there being *any* weak individuals at all. Alternatively, or in addition, he could allow that there exists some *other* kind of truth-maker for these statements (as may be the case in pictorial representation). In sum, if confronted with Quine's problem of "what there is," Leibniz needs just two words in reply—strong individuals. "Unitas est entitas" as the Scholastics put it. Weak individuals are, for Leibniz, mere *phenomena bene fundata* and, as such, dependent on strong individuals (i.e., his substances or monads), not the other way around.

given to us), this was precisely the heart of the matter for the Scholastics.[17] They wanted to answer the question of what makes an individual into the individual that it is. From Boethius in the early Middle Ages, via Abelard, Thomas, Ockham, Duns Scotus, Henry of Ghent, Buridan, Suarez, and Leibniz, five principles were considered.[18] I focus exclusively on the most important one, namely, *indivisibility*. It is part of the meaning of being an individual to be indivisible. The etymology of the word *individual* already suggests as much. That is to say, you cannot remove from an individual one or more of its properties without it ceasing to be the individual that it is.[19]

17. McCullough, *Leibniz on Individuals and Individuation*, 3–12, observes that contemporary philosophical discussion about individuals normally assumes that "middle-sized dry objects" constitute the "ground floor" of individuals. One then moves on to what are regarded as the real problems occasioned by individuals, such as how identity persists through change, or the conditions for successful reference to individuals, and so on. However, the Scholastics (and Leibniz) started with the question: "What *are* individuals?"

18. The five principles were indivisibility, distinction, division, identity, and impredicability. See McCullough, *Leibniz on Individuals and Individuation*, 92; and J. A. Cover and J. O'Leary-Hawthorne, *Substance and Individuation in Leibniz* (Cambridge: Cambridge University Press, 1999), 11–16.

19. Gracia, *Individuality*, 30, also discusses these five principles of individuality, but his argumentation does not always convince. For example, he rejects the principle of individuality with the somewhat simplistic argument that if we think of individual things such as a man or a table, "these can be easily divided and broken up into parts, and yet they are no less individual for that reason." But this is not what the principle states: it states that an individual cannot be divided without *its* ceasing to be the individual that it is. This is lost in Gracia's argument. Observe, too, how Leibniz—who advocated the principle of indivisibility—defended it: "it is only *atoms of substance*, that is to say, real unities that are absolute destitute of parts, which are the sources of action, and the absolute first principles out of which things are compounded, and, as it were, the ultimate elements in the analysis of substance. One could call them *metaphysical points*. They have something vital, and a kind of perception, and *mathematical points* are the points of view from which they express the universe." Gottfried Wilhelm Leibniz, *Philosophical Papers and Letters*, 2nd ed., trans. Leroy E. Loemker (Boston: Reidel/Springer, 1976), 456.

Next, Gracia also rejects the principle of impredicability, which states that if we have a statement (1) "x is I" (where "I" stands for an individual to be predicated of x), statement (1) is true if x is I. Gracia objects that in this case the copula is not the copula of predication but of identity. I don't see why advocates of (1) would have a problem with this observation: they could quite justifiably even say that this is what (1) means and exclaim, next, that exactly this proves their point. As soon as you try to force the issue with a statement like (1), the copula changes color and turns from the "is" of predication into the "is'" of identity. What stronger proof of the claim that you cannot predicate substances, monads, or HRs of each other could one possibly wish for? Gracia, *Individuality*, 43–48, then goes on to say that individuality as impredicability only makes sense if one "identifies the world of things with the world of concepts and/or words." But why would this be so? Why could one not state in terms of concepts or words what is true of a thing if it is an individual?

Finally, after having rejected all five principles of individuality, Gracia proposes one of his own: namely, "individuality as non-instantiability." This principle states claims for individuals "the impossibility that they be instantiated. Socrates, for example, cannot become instantiated in the

It follows that the individual defines itself, or that its principle of individuation is *internal* and not *external* to it.[20] In this sense, we can even think of the universe as a whole as the prototypical individual. As Rutherford forcefully put it, for Leibniz "whatever is true of a substance must be true in virtue of its own nature, and not in the name of something else."[21] This claim clashes frontally with the thesis of the theory-ladenness of empirical fact or the Myth of the Given because, for these contemporary accounts, individuals are always *externally* defined in terms of a set of universal concepts that are uniquely true of them. We are faced with two different, and basically irreconcilable, paradigms for the concept of individuality. A great deal is, therefore, at stake here.

Now that we have an alternative meaning for the concept of the individual, the question arises regarding how individuals can be individuated using this concept. This brings us directly to Leibniz, whose doctoral dissertation, *Disputatio Metaphysica de Principio Individui* (1663), dealt with exactly that question. Since Benson Mates in *The Philosophy of Leibniz* (1986),[22] commentators have agreed that Leibniz never deviated much from what he said about individuals and individuation in the *Disputatio*.[23] In the *Disputatio*, Leibniz offers a survey of four principles of individuation: (1) negation, (2) existence, (3) Duns Scotus's *haecceitas*, and (4) individuation by the individual's complete concept. Leibniz deals only peremptorily with the first two (his rejection of the first two does not deepen our grasp of his concept of the individual, so I'll leave these two out of my exposition). Leibniz also deals only briefly with Scotus's *haecceitas*, but here his criticism is of more interest. He rejects Scotus's *haecceitas* because this notion of the so-called common nature still has a reminiscence of the general and

---

way 'human beings' can." But this is at best a rather odd way of stating individuality. It is, moreover, open to the fairly obvious objection that Socrates's individuality is in fact "instantiated" once, and only once; namely, in the case of Socrates himself.

20. McCullough, *Leibniz on Individuals and Individuation*, 30; Cover and O'Leary-Hawthorne, *Substance and Individuation in Leibniz*, 28, 29.

21. Donald Rutherford, "Metaphysics: The Late Period," in *The Cambridge Companion to Leibniz*, ed. Nicholas Jolley (Cambridge: Cambridge University Press, 1995), 126.

22. Benson Mates, *The Philosophy of Leibniz: Metaphysics and Language* (New York: Oxford University Press, 1986).

23. McCullough's *Leibniz on Individuals and Individuation* is a careful account of the dissertation and of its scholastic antecedents. Leibniz always remained close to the *Disputatio*, so McCullough could be quite brief about Leibniz's later views on individuals.

the universal in it. It strikes Leibniz as something that is abstracted from individuals, as a mere *ens rationis* (say, a fiction of the mind), and is therefore *outside* individuals themselves.[24] Leibniz's nominalism is obvious to anyone here. Even the properties individuals have should not tempt us into discerning in them the presence of the universal because they are always the properties of *this* individual and precisely this makes them unique.[25] Properties have no existence *outside* individuals, in contrast to the realist conception of universals. We have only the "instantiations" of properties *in* individuals, and properties therefore participate *also* in the individuality of the individuals in which they manifest themselves.[26] These instantiations are, in fact, synonymous with the notion of the "aspect" that I have

---

24. Peter King renders the gist of Scotus's argument as follows: "Duns Scotus holds that in each individual there is a principle that accounts for its being the very thing it is and a formally different principle that accounts for its being the kind of thing it is; the former is its individual differentia, the latter its common nature. . . . The individual differentia and the common nature thereby explain what Scotus takes to stand in need of explanation: the individuality of Socrates on the one hand, the commonalities between Socrates and Plato on the other hand." See Peter King, "The Problem of Individuation in the Middle Ages," *Theoria* 66 (2000): 176–78. King adds that for Scotus the individual differentia are logically prior to any common nature: "there is no whiteness that is not whiteness of some given intensity." This qualification brings Scotus close to Leibniz.

25. This must remind us, again, of what has been known since D. C. Williams as tropes denoting what one might call "the essence of an occurrence." Examples are "Bill Clinton's eloquence, Sydney's beauty, or Pierre's love of Héloïse. Bill Clinton's eloquence is understood here not as participation in the universal eloquence, nor as the particular quality of Clinton's eloquence, but simply as Clinton's bit of eloquence, an eloquence that he and he alone has." Trope theory can be defined as "the view that reality is (wholly or partly) made up from tropes." Tropes are things like the particular shape, weight, and texture of an individual object. Because tropes are particular, for two objects to "share" a property (for them both to exemplify, say, a particular shade of green) is for each to contain (instantiate, exemplify) a greenness trope, where those greenness tropes, although numerically distinct, nevertheless exactly resemble each other. Apart from this very thin core assumption—that there are tropes—different trope theories need not have very much in common. Most trope theorists (but not all) believe that—fundamentally—there is nothing but tropes (this is the conception of tropes defended in the epilogue to this book). Most trope theorists (but, again, not all) hold that resemblance between concrete particulars is to be explained in terms of resemblance between their respective tropes. And most (but not all) hold that resemblance between tropes is determined by their primitive intrinsic nature. See the introduction by Anna Sophia Maurin, "Tropes," *Stanford Encyclopedia of Philosophy* (2018), https:/plato.stanford.edu/entries/tropes/.

26. Leibniz follows a line of argument here that began with Abelard, was continued by Ockham, and is visible above all in Buridan's extreme nominalism. But in spite of his sympathy for nominalism, Leibniz pays little or no attention to their writings. Perhaps he believed they had little to add to Suarez's perfection of this way of thinking about individuation.

proposed elsewhere.[27] The result of Leibniz's theory is the radical claim that Laurence McCullough formulates as follows:

> *Individuals have nothing in common with each other. They are individual throughout and thus at most similar to each other, never the same.* The mind abstracts universals under which different individuals can be thought to be the same (italics added).[28]

Here we truly have strong individuals without any universalist holes in them robbing them of their individuality, individuals who are individual *through and through* and are sufficiently robust to repulse all attacks made on them in the name of the theory-ladenness of empirical facts *e tutti quanti*. Strong individuals neither contain nor produce universals; whereas the weak individuals of commonsense experience celebrated in the analytic tradition literally "drink and sweat out" universals.

This leaves us with the fourth principle of individuation, namely D_{cc}, or the doctrine of the complete concept. I have noted this doctrine previously, but we can now explore it further. Leibniz takes it over from Suarez. But he nowhere clearly says why, and even his most competent modern commentators have been confused about this absolutely crucial issue.[29] Nevertheless, the background to Leibniz's commitment to D_{cc} is clear enough. Recall Leibniz's belief that the principle of indivisibility gives us the primary meaning of individuality. According to that principle, you cannot remove from an individual even a single one of its properties, accidents, or aspects without its ceasing to be the individual it is. It follows that all of an individual's properties are essential to it in the sense of determining its identity. This, then, is exactly what D_{cc} asserts: namely, that all of an individual's properties are contained in the individual's complete concept and can therefore be analytically derived from it.

---

27. See Franklin Rudolf Ankersmit, *Meaning, Truth and Reference in Historical Representation* (London: Cornell University Press, 2013).
28. McCullough, *Leibniz on Individuals and Individuation*, 38.
29. Cover and O'Leary-Hawthorne, *Substance and Individuation in Leibniz*, 175–83, relate the issue to reference, but reference is a notion that plays no role at all in Leibniz's logic and metaphysics. Nor *could* it play any role because reference can only be achieved by the complete notion of what is referred to—which reduces all reference to *self*-reference.

In sum, there are two accounts of the notion of the individual. On the one hand, there is Frege's, Russell's, and Strawson's *weak* individual, including such apparently absolutely solid and unquestionable realities as the hammer with which we may accidentally, but very painfully, hit our fingers, or stolid and indifferent trees causing dents in our cars. Their status as individuals seems to have its foundation in our most elementary encounters with the world. But their being part of a seemingly objective reality wholly independent from ourselves cannot hide the fact that they are very *hybrid* and *misty* individuals from a logical point of view (I'm well aware that we need these hybrid and misty individuals to deal with the realities of our daily life, in spite of their doubtful metaphysical status). They are hybrid in the sense that the individual and the universal are always mixed up in them; misty in the sense that as individuals they consist for the greater part of holes and fissures allowing us to freely look through them. They end up being even completely transparent, as in the case of Russell's evaporation of the individual in favor of the general. On the other hand, we have Leibniz's *strong* individuals, his substances or monads. Admittedly, these may *seem* to be hybrid and misty too, at first sight, because we cannot see, touch, smell, or hear them. In fact, however, they are pure individuals, defining themselves internally, untainted by anything outside themselves, be it other individuals or universals. They are wholly windowless, as Leibniz would say. They are as logically solid as rock; even more so in truth because a rock is, after all, only a weak individual too. Finally, anticipating the issue to be discussed in the epilogue of this book, it could be said that weak individuals are extensionalist, whereas strong individuals are intensionalist.[30]

We are not compelled to choose between these two conceptions of the individual. This would mean falling victim to narrow-mindedness and

---

30. See the glossary for the meaning of extensionalism and 'intensionalism.

31. Daily life would become impossible if we abandoned weak individuals for strong ones exclusively. We would then be reduced to the state of newborn babies, unaware of the existence of houses, trees, cats, and so on. However, it seems reasonable to suppose that the infant first becomes aware of certain unities in its perceptions of the world and that what then goes on is captured best what has been about strong individuals in this chapter. At a later stage, certain recurring patterns may occur in these unities, so that these strong individuals gradually give way to weak individuals to which certain properties can be attributed. And then we enter daily reality as we all know it. We are newborn babies—with Leibniz—before becoming grown up adults—with Frege and

dogmatism. It would be ridiculous to deny that there are weak individuals. Nothing is further from my mind than doing so.[31] Recognizing their presence in our daily world is a condition of all our successful interactions with it. Rather, we should recognize that *both* conceptions of an individual have their proper domain of application. They are complementary rather than opposed to each other—as extensionalism and intensionalism are. The Scholastics and Leibniz were interested in the question of what makes an individual into the individual that it is; Strawson, Frege, and Russell took the existence of individuals more or less for granted and asked themselves the quite different semantic question of how we can refer to them by means of proper names or identifying descriptions.

On the other hand, this complementarity should not blind us to the fact that both approaches to the individual point in completely opposite directions. The modern approach presupposes the separation of language and the world, thus giving rise to the issue of how language can referentially or epistemologically be tied to the world. The Scholastics and Leibniz, however, are not concerned with this demarcation line between language and the world. Without actually denying that different kind of individuals can be found on either side of it, they concentrate on the strong individual (thus removing epistemological problems from the philosopher's agenda).[32] Individuals are then no longer subject to the conditions for connecting what lies on either side of this demarcation line between language and the world. In the next section, I argue that we need Leibniz's notion of the strong individual without holes in it, the individual that is an individual through and through, to make sense of historical representation.

Russell. In this sense, writing history is a reenactment of a primeval phase of human development (see Ankersmit, *Meaning, Truth and Reference*, chapter 7). But it is primeval in the sense of being decisive. Everything begins with it, and it is therefore a proper subject of research for philosophers of language trying to explain our use of language and how it relates to the world. If philosophers of language were to take seriously the project of accounting for all our uses of language and not just some of them, they would realize that historical writing presents them with problems they have never dealt with until now.

32. One could say that HRs are linguistic things and as such transcend the demarcation line between language and the world of things. It could be objected, however, that these "things" do not belong to the world of weak individuals. However, in discussing the notion of the sign, we shall find that the sign always requires something "physical," e.g., something that can be written on a piece of paper (in the case of mathematics or historical representation), painted on a canvas, or cut from a piece of marble (in the case of the visual arts).

4. HISTORICAL REPRESENTATION: METAPHYSICS

Most contemporary philosophers assume as a matter of course that we should distinguish between the world, or reality, and the things it contains, on the one hand, and the language we use for speaking about the world, on the other. To put it metaphorically, words and the world are like two parallel planes that never intersect with each other. But how can we speak about the world at all if these two planes never intersect? Obviously, the fact is there, but how do we account for it?[33] Self-evidently, if such an intersection existed, it would be the proper point of departure for an investigation of how language and the world are related. But, alas, the very idea of two parallel planes rules out the possibility of such an intersection *ex hypothesi*.

Worse still, it is not clear what such an intersection could look like. Admittedly, Christianity has an answer to this question: "and the Word became Flesh and dwelt among us, and we beheld His glory, the glory of the only begotten of the Father, full of grace and truth" (John 1:14). But the appeal to religious certainties has gone out of fashion in philosophy. Philosophers prefer to take the language/world dichotomy as an indisputable given. They find it self-evident that it is one of the philosopher's main tasks to investigate the epistemological relationship between language and reality and to forget about dogmatic claims—theological or otherwise—about any actual intersections of language and the world.

One could try to play down this problem about the relationship between these two planes of reality and language by arguing that words, in whatever form, are no less part of the world than mountains, roses, and dogs. Does the language user perhaps dwell in some quasi-heaven elevated far above the "world" of mountains, roses, etcetera, for no other reason than that some whim of evolution gave the person access to this supernatural position? Obviously not: the use of language does not involve anything as dramatic as a move outside or beyond the natural world. But this sobering truth is regrettably unhelpful because the problem of the relationship between language (even though it contains *things* like HRs) and the world

---

33. Clearly, if formulated this way, the question seems to ask a question that can only be answered by showing how the acquisition of language fits into the evolutionary development of homo sapiens. That approach is adopted in chapter 6 of my forthcoming book *Peter Munz's Evolutionist Philosophy of History and the Anthropocene*.

will then reappear within "the world" itself. One part of the world is now to be thought of as language, and another part of it as that of things, e.g., mountains, roses, or dogs. And then the whole problem of the relationship between language and the world will announce itself again, although this time within the "world." We'd best place this world within quotation marks now because it must be a world that is different from the world that we were speaking about a moment ago. At this stage, the person holding onto the view that the world/language distinction is exaggerated might try to argue that language is expressed via sounds—and are sounds not part of the world? But this runs into the same problems as the previous proposal. Surely, we want to be able to distinguish quite clearly between the sounds of an erupting volcano or the clap of thunder, on the one hand, and the tender words a lover whispers in the ears of his beloved, on the other. Volcanoes don't talk.

Another strategy is to say that this so-called world/language distinction is, in fact, a distinction that originates within language itself. This seems to remove the drama of the distinction: the proper functioning of language requires a going together of words and things or of language and the world. To implement this strategy, we can return to the two lists mentioned at the beginning of this chapter: the list enumerating all the things in the world around us, and the list of the universals that can be used for establishing their properties and for referring to them in terms of their identifying descriptions.

It could then be argued that language *itself* succeeds in *uniting* world and language; the list enumerating all things in the world takes care that things have access to language, whereas the other gives us universals. It has been argued since the Medieval realists that universals do exist. If so, language may perform the job of tying itself to the things of the world without positioning itself outside of the world. But precisely this claim makes this position dubious as well. What if one is a nominalist, stating that universals—an indispensable components of language, after all—are a mere *flatus vocis* and do not exist, but yet still somehow succeed in tying themselves from their habitat in a some nonnatural limbo to the tangible things of the world in which we live? Moreover, it may be true that subject-terms often refer to things in the world, but referring to your pet does not make it enter the domain of language itself. In sum, the world/language distinction is not so easily upset, to say the least.

The apparent impossibility of getting rid of the distinction originates in the Strawsonian, Fregean, and Russellian metaphysics that underlies much, if not most, contemporary philosophy (of language and science), as we saw in section 2. This (extensionalist) metaphysics argues that there is, on the one hand, a (physical) reality to which the status of metaphysical reality is granted, and on the other, there is the language we use for speaking about it.[34] The uncertain metaphysical status of language is the result. It is peculiar, then, that epistemologists always begin with language: if (physical) reality has a metaphysical status one hesitates to grant to language, why not begin from *there*? The obvious strategy would be to commence with a stage in which (physical reality) is assumed to be there and then to derive language from it somehow. All the more so because this is how things actually went: first there was the world, and language came only at a stage billions of years later. However, proceeding in this way is an impossible assignment—how could one even *start* such a strategy without using language (and by doing so tacitly or implicitly assuming it to exist)? Apparently, language is like the proverbial piece of sticking-plaster that you cannot get rid of no matter how you try. Nevertheless, at least recognizing the problem would be helpful.[35]

Leibniz's monadology offers an entirely different (intensionalist) metaphysics with which to approach the problem. It contains individuals only, and these individuals are nothing but the predicates they contain. They *are* (in the truly metaphysical sense) the total sum of the statements M is s_1, M is s_2, M is s_3, and so on—nothing more and nothing less than that. The question whether they are things or language is meaningless because the question presupposes that the distinction between things and language makes sense.[36] Leibniz's monads and HRs are, if anything, linguistic

---

34. This opposition runs parallel to the contrast between particulars (things in reality) and the general (the general concepts of language). Cover and O'Leary-Hawthorne, *Substance and Individuation in Leibniz*, 174, write that "the singular is more basic than the general, both in the mind of God and in the created world.... The priority of the singular is vital to Leibniz's metaphysical vision." But if this is correct, contemporary philosophy of language, having language and the general in its constitution, did not start where philosophy ought to start. The question then arises of what revisions could remedy the consequences of this false start.

35. The issue of the relationship between language and the world is further elaborated in chapter 4, section 6.

36. Because of the parallel between that distinction and the distinction between extension and intension, it follows that the value of the latter distinction is also doubtful in the case of Leibniz's monads or of HRs. However, one could say that HRs in the end have more affinity with intensionalism than with extensionalism (as exemplified, for example, by Russell's logic of sets).

things and, hence, both—or neither, if you prefer that option. The kind of metaphysics presupposed in contemporary philosophical debate also contains individuals, but these individuals owe their status as individuals to proper names or uniquely identifying descriptions—such as "the first man on the moon" (Neil Armstrong) or "the man who wrote the *Principia Mathematica*" (Newton). If asked the admittedly odd but nevertheless inevitable question of "what it means to have knowledge of a proper name," the answer is that this meaning is expressed by means of a uniquely identifying description that may take the place of the proper name in question *salva veritate*. Hence, a proper name stands for a uniquely identifying description—and is no more than that.

As the term itself suggests, a semantic hierarchy can be discerned in the notion of the uniquely identifying description: (1) the level of the identifying description formulated in terms of a set of universals, and (2) these universals are chosen by the speaker in such a way that they intersect only in one place. For example, the universals "King of France" and "being guillotined" intersect on that spot in language (and on that spot only) from where we may descend confidently—historical reality being what it is—to the past reality of Louis XVI, King of France from 1774 to 1792.

The genealogy of strong individuals knows of no such hierarchy. The two levels distinguished just now have coalesced here into only one level. These strong individuals come into being in a linguistic universe that they constitute *themselves*. It is as if they reenact a linguistic counterpart to God's creation of the world. In fact, this is much like how Leibniz conceived of the creation of the monadological universe, or as if language were forced in the model of Frege's "comprehensive knowledge" discussed in section 2. To use a popular term today, there is no *slippage* when moving from the monadological universe of Leibniz's monads or the representational universe to the language of these monads or HRs, and vice versa. Everything that is said on one level has its exact and exclusive counterpart on the other. Nothing ever gets lost in the process of moving from one to the other. That is one of the nice things about the domain of intensionality. Whereas there always is such slippage between the language about weak individuals and the world these weak individuals inhabit. We can never be sure that a language that is sui generis so badly handicapped by its dependence on universals will cover reality as effectively as we expected and hoped it would. There is always the possibility that more individual things in the world correspond to the intersection of the universals we had chosen to refer to one individual only. To put it metaphorically, because weak individuals are individuals with holes in them, a strong draught in them continuously blows unforeseen things in and out. Epistemology is then needed to keep the slippage within acceptable bounds.

Nevertheless, it does not follow that the Leibnizian system should leave no room at all for the world/language distinction, and it does so on two levels: at the level of the monads themselves and at the level of their properties. Let's start with their properties because the issue here is simple. Leibniz claims that his monads have perceptions, and nothing in his system precludes that some of these perceptions will be perceptions of mountains or animals, whereas others are of what people have said or written. The former belong to the domain of physical reality (or the world) and the latter to that of language. Nothing prevents us from distinguishing between mountains or animals, on the one hand, and language, on the other—just as in non-Leibnizian metaphysics. Leibnizian metaphysics is wholly indifferent with regard to our wish to retain that distinction on this level. If one wishes to do so, that's fine for anyone looking at the matter from the Leibnizian metaphysical viewpoint.

As for the world/language distinction at the level of the monads themselves, it should be said that Leibniz has a hierarchy of monads. The highest in the hierarchy are those that perceive the most of the monadological universe; or, as Leibniz puts it elsewhere, the place of monads in the hierarchy is determined by the degree to which they are "conscious" of the monadological universe. At the top of the hierarchy is God and those creatures in the domain of the PBF best informed of the world in which they live, and at the bottom are those monads having only the most elementary information about this world. In concrete terms, at the top of this "great chain of being" we will find human beings, after them the animals, then plants, and finally, physical objects. This list demonstrates that for Leibniz the difference between human beings and animals is only one of degree. One welcome implication is that he urges us to always treat animals with as much respect as we treat each other (whether human beings normally treat each other with respect is, of course, an entirely different matter).[37] It would be better to be Leibniz's dog than Descartes's. Leibniz even grants

---

37. Even this may not always be of much help for animals. There is much truth in the comparison of the death camps of the Nazis with bio-industry.

the status of individuals to physical objects such as mountains, rocks, or heaps of stones, although they have only the most minimal degree of consciousness. He does so on the (questionable) grounds that if we perceive them in the domain of the PBF, they must have their counterpart—either as "aggregates" of monads or as individual monads with a very low degree of consciousness—in the world of the monads. The Leibnizian system is committed to pan-psychism.

If Leibniz is willing to go this far, why not consider written texts as another category of monads, next to human beings, animals, plants, and mountains or rocks? A text, as an expression of human thoughts, must stand fairly high in the hierarchy of Leibniz's great chain of beings. It is human thought frozen in letters that have been written or imprinted on a piece of paper (or these days, encoded in digital form). Self-evidently, we are dealing here with the category of monads of which HRs will be a prominent part. As such, we can find a niche for HRs within the Leibnizian system *itself*.

HRs can even be said to be the *prototypical* monads because they fit into the structure of Leibniz's system more easily and naturally than Leibniz's own substance or monads. Had Leibniz asked himself what example he had best appeal to when conveying to his readership the gist of his thought, the writing of history would have been the answer. The structure of his thought can be projected with relative ease onto that of the writing of history, and vice versa. Most of the trouble occasioned by the Leibnizian system arises from the question of how to relate the domain of the monads to that of the PBF. In chapter 2 I suggested that we need not worry about that issue insofar as historical representation is concerned: in the latter the PBF are an asset rather than a liability. Next, what was said about the perceptions of monads also holds for the properties of HRs: if HR_1 has the property "HR_1 is s," then s can be about both the world and about language. It's even easier for the HRs themselves: they are *things*, individual things from a metaphysical point of view, but they consist of *language* only. So metaphysics (the world) and language coincide here again.[38]

---

38. If "the world" and language are thought to coincide here, this can also be said to raise the issue discussed previously of where language is born or how it arises out of "the world." An evolutionary account of the emergence of language, of its costs as well as its benefits, would be best suited to answer these questions. For such an account, see chapter 6 of my forthcoming book, *Peter Munz's Evolutionist Philosophy of History and the Anthropocene*.

This applies to all HRs, whether we are dealing with Hellenism, the Rise of the Bourgeoisie, the Dual Revolution (Hobsbawm), the Interbellum period, the Cold War, or any other HR. All that is said about weak individuals in the statements contained by HRs is a mere shadow when compared to strong individuals such as Hellenism or the Cold War. Even a genius such as Leonardo da Vinci is wholly swallowed up by a strong individual such as the Renaissance, and so it is with Kant and the strong individual of the Enlightenment. It is these strong individuals that constitute historical reality, whereas the weak individuals mobilized in their name are merely fodder for these linguistic Leviathans.

An adequate understanding of historical writing compels us to distinguish between two (incompatible[39]) kinds of metaphysics. On the one hand, there is the world consisting of the things we have knowledge of in terms of the universals that are true of them. This is the non-Leibnizian world consisting of weak individuals. Knowledge of them can be expressed by statements having a proper name or a uniquely identifying description as their subject-term to which a certain property is attributed by the statement's predicate-term. So it is in extensionalist metaphysics. On the other hand, there is the reality of the totality of all possible HRs we can know only "by knowing these individuals in their fullness"—if I may put it in this regrettably clumsy way. Here each property that is attributed to an HR is already part of the subject-term, as is claimed in D_{cc}. Because of this, the totality of all possible HRs constitutes an intensionalist metaphysics.[40]

There is no shortcut between our knowledge of weak and strong individuals. It might be objected now that it is easy enough to think of such a shortcut: suppose we give an individual HR a proper name of its own such as H_x or provide a uniquely identifying description of it such as "the HR written by historian H on topic T." We can then refer to this HR and formulate true statements about it that differ in no interesting way from the kind of statements we may make about weak individuals. So it may seem. However, such proper names or uniquely identifying descriptions don't give you knowledge of that HR. What they can do, at most, could be compared with referring to an envelope that you can never open to read the letter it contains. It is as if you made a promising start with your attempt

---

39. See for this the entry on "logic and metaphysics" in the glossary.
40. See the epilogue for the extensionalism/intensionalism dichotomy.

METAPHYSICS, INDIVIDUALS, MODELS, AND THE PBF

to refer to something and then suddenly found yourself completely in the dark. Reference here is rather a matter of "indicating" or of "pointing to the place where" you may find what you are looking for. But *what* you will find there remains a mystery. Again, you can have knowledge of an HR only if you know *all of its properties*.

Hence, the kind of comprehensive knowledge that is never given to us in the world of the weak individuals, according to Frege. For in that world we never have more than a mere *part* of that knowledge—however extensive the part in question may be. Nevertheless, the part we have can always most conveniently be divided into a part giving us secure access to an indefinite much larger part, and that larger part. The former is to be identified with uniquely identifying descriptions: such descriptions express the knowledge (1) that there is only one thing in the world satisfying it and (2) that this thing is what the description is true of. Think of the uniquely identifying description: "the man who was born in Schönhausen on April 1, 1815, who founded the second German 'Reich' and was the greatest hypochondriac of his time." From the Big Bang until the end of time there is nothing anywhere in the universe to which that description can refer but to Otto von Bismarck. Having singled out Bismarck from all other things in the universe thanks to this identifying description, we got access to an inexhaustive source of more knowledge about him. This is, in fact, a real miracle. It's almost like doing astronomy without telescopes, with only language for a lens on the universe.

Unfortunately, there is no room for this version of astronomy in the world of the strong individuals; the explanation is that the knowledge we have of them cannot be divided into a uniquely identifying description and what that description gives access to. Because the number of HRs (or monads) is infinite, any allegedly uniquely identifying description is true of the *set* of all HRs (or monads) containing that description. It might be objected, however, that in the practice of historical writing the number of HRs is finite. But even then there can and will be a considerable amount of overlap between individual HRs. Moreover, chapter 5 explains that a permanent proliferation of HRs is part of the logic of historical writing. So overlap will increase rather than decrease in the development of historical writing.

Nevertheless, we might argue that the idea of this overlap is precisely what enables us to make room in the world of strong individuals for an equivalent of the uniquely identifying description.[41] We might divide a set of HRs into what they all have in common and a part where there is no overlap. A well-considered selection of an HR's sentences not belonging to the overlap might then set this HR apart from the others. That selection could be regarded as a uniquely identifying description of this HR. The problem with this option, however, is that HRs are indivisible. Suppose you have the HRs HR_1 and HR_2 and you divide each of them where they overlap and where they do not. But after having done so, HR_1 will result in HR_3 and HR_4 and HR_2 in HR_5 and HR_6. And let's say HR_3 and HR_5 stand for where H_1 and H_2 overlap and HR_4 and HR_6 for where they do not. As we saw in section 4, HRs are (co-)determined by how they compare to other HRs. That comparison presupposes that we have complete HRs and not amputated parts of them, such as where they overlap in the sense of sharing a certain set of properties (i.e., true statements about past states of affairs). Hence, dividing an HR in a part that overlaps with (some) others and a part that does not will, at best, yield three different HRs; even four, if we hold that HR_3 and HR_5 will retain the "memory" of their origin in HR_1 and HR_2, respectively, and thus differ from each other in spite of reflecting their overlap between HR_1 and HR_2. So the attempt to find room in historical representation for an equivalent of uniquely identifying descriptions has been stranded on the indivisibility of HRs (and monads).

The metaphysics of the weak and the strong individual are incompatible with each other—as is the case with their corresponding conceptions of reference, truth, and meaning and of more technical instruments such as the uniquely identifying description. This incompatibility is, of course, inherent in the very conception of a metaphysics: you cannot subscribe to two different metaphysics at one and the same time. But likewise, there is no possible competition between the two: there can *sui generis* be no common ground between them. If there were, these two competing metaphysics would evaporate at once, leaving us with only their common ground. Next, the hope of perfecting one metaphysics by introducing into it elements of some other is equally absurd. Finally, the attempt to build a bridge

---

41. The proposal that the phrase "the HR written by historian H" could be regarded as a uniquely identifying description of that HR must be rejected for the same reason that the GPS location of a house is not a uniquely identifying description of the house that happens to be built on that location. If anything, it identifies a location but not what is built on that location.

between the two while leaving both of them intact—more or less[42] in the way Leibniz always tried to tie together in some plausible manner his monadological universe and the domain of the PBF—is tantamount to attempting to square the circle. And anyone pondering the metaphysics implied by the practice of a scientific discipline—such as the writing of history—will have to respect this categorical ban on a "double metaphysics."

The metaphysics of weak individuals nowhere patently conflicts with the realities of daily life and of the sciences, so it seems to follow that we ought to dismiss the metaphysics of the strong individual as an impractical oddity. The latter is, perhaps, an interesting construction and has, indeed, the merit of being devoid of inner contradictions, but it is a philosopher's pipe dream—and will never be more than that. But in fact it is *precisely* this double metaphysics (in the form just discussed) that is ideally suited for understanding historical writing—although we must avoid at all times and at all costs any short circuit between the two metaphysics. That is to say, we should not, at least in the present context, juxtapose these two metaphysics and then make up our mind about them. Instead, we must take our position on the precipice, as narrow as it is deep, separating both metaphysics and wonder what the world is like if seen from that precipice.

Recall once more my claim that "historical reality only comes into being when the past no longer exists"—i.e. "the birth of historical reality from the death of the past" that is this book's subtitle. This claim invokes the metaphysics of *both* strong and weak individuals—and the transition from the latter to the former—while insisting, at the same time, that each of the two "normally" goes its own way while carefully avoiding a conflict or even the *hint* of a contact between them. It's like this. There was a time when the past still existed, and whether one is a constructivist or not, no sensible person will deny that we can have cognitive access to it via the traces the past has left us. We can investigate archaeological remains, archives, inscriptions, works of art, and so on and establish on the basis of these data facts about the past that were unknown in the past the historian writes about. Even so, these kinds of facts, at least *in principle*, could have been established in the past itself. As long as historians focus on this type of issue, they are, in a sense, the contemporaries of the people who lived in the past—even if they

---

42. Admittedly, Leibniz never went as far as granting to the domain of the PBF a metaphysical status of its own.

make use of ultra-modern research instruments unavailable to the people in the past themselves. As long as historians do only this kind of research, their metaphysics is that of the weak individual.

But when historians return to their own time with all their research data in their luggage, they may ask what the past in question looks like from the perspective of their own time. Indeed, has any historian ever done anything else? Could any historian possibly see the past from another perspective than that of their own time? Even if they were to try to do so, that *other* perspective would be what *they*, from the perspective of their own time, believe that the perspective of some *other* time might be like. It is precisely this that condemns the effort to futility. There is no way to escape from one's own time; historians are tied as inextricably to the time in which they live as they are to their own shadows. But at this point, the gap between past and present opens up in which *historical reality*, all historical *knowledge* and historical *discussion*, originates. As long as the past still exists, it is a logical impossibility that its history can be written.[43] As soon as you start to write history, you have left the past behind you. If the words *past* and *present* have any meaning, part of their meaning is that nothing can be both past and present.

---

43. On the one hand, this enables us to draw the line between historical writing and journalism (needless to say, doing so is in no way detrimental to the status of journalism—on the contrary), on the other, it raised since the birth of historicism the problem of so-called contemporary history. The problem never really prevented historians from writing contemporary history. Even Ranke himself wrote some books that we would now label as contemporary history. The answer to the problem of contemporary history is that the borderline between past and present is always vague and permeable from both sides. For a well-considered analysis of the problem of contemporary history, see Jaap den Hollander, "Contemporary History and the Art of Self-Distancing," *History and Theory: Studies in the Philosophy of History* 50, no. 4 (December 2011): 51–68. Den Hollander has a clairvoyant solution to the problem occasioned by contemporary history: "I finish with an unsolved riddle, namely how can we identify a historical period like modernism without a contrasting period in the present? . . . Without narrative interpretations of the present we do not seem to have a counterpoint to our interpretation of the past. Perhaps we should pay more attention to the future. After all, the crucial distinction of time is not between past and present but between past and future." Hollander, "Contemporary History," 67. Den Hollander's suggestion of some ten years ago is now almost universally accepted. In our Age of the Anthropocene, the category of the future has become no less part of our experience of time than the past and the present. For this see Zoltán Boldiszár Simon and Marek Tamm, *History and Theory* 60, no. 1 (March 2021): 3–23, and the excellent Zoltán Boldiszár Simon, *History in Times of Unprecedented Change: A Theory for the 21st Century* (New York: Bloomsbury Academic, 2019). And with this the always so vexing problem of contemporary evaporated more or less spontaneously.

Historical writing, insofar as it really fills this gap between past and present, gives us these strong individuals of the HRs—and the type of metaphysics going with them. As long as we find ourselves in a world strictly enclosed within the demarcations of the present, the individuals surrounding us (including our own selves) will only be weak individuals. The strong individuals, being the irrefutable proof of the gap between past and present, are then still absent. But if anyone believes it should be possible to inhabit *both* the past and the present, the problem of reconciling past and present is not a *philosophical* one—for from that perspective *no* such reconciliation is possible—but an *existential* one that each of its advocates will have to tackle as well.[44] Or not, of course, in case he allows himself to go wherever the winds of existentialist speculation will blow them. We can only "live" what must necessarily remain a mystery for the philosopher. Philosophy can sui generis never demonstrate that, which is why it should be wrong to go beyond philosophy. Any attempt to do so will be philosophy all over again.

5. MOBILIZATION OF THE PBF

One more issue needs to be discussed in this chapter. What has just been said enables us to shed some new light on the word *representation* if it is used for historical representation. The word can be taken apart, separating the prefix, "re-," and the noun, "presentation." Our first intuition is that doing so captures what historical representation involves: there has been a past, and that past is then re-presented (again) by a historical representation. But having learned (1) to strictly distinguish between the past and historical reality and (2) that it is part of the notion of historical representation that the latter can never be reduced to the former, it must now be clear that HRs can never be seen as representations of the past in the sense suggested by separating the word in this way. This claim has its ultimate justification

---

44. One could in this context think of all the discussions about memory, commemoration, "lieux de mémoire," forgetting, trauma, and mourning and the historical experience of the 1990s and of the first decade of this century. These discussions have in common pulling the past within the precincts of the present. Even though the effort neutralizes the philosophy of history, it has the greatest dignity and deserves the greatest interest.

in the "incompatibility" of the metaphysics of weak individuals (we must associate with the past) with the metaphysics of the strong individual going together with historical representation. But that certainly does not imply that the past and an HR representing it are *wholly* unrelated: they are unrelated only insofar as the dimension of *representation* is involved. It is true that statements about historical facts individuate an HR; but it is the HR, and *not* the facts mentioned in it, that represent historical reality. At the same time, the *historical facts* mentioned in an HR firmly tie that HR to that part of *the past* to which these facts also belong.

This is not all. HRs promote historical knowledge—a task for which the truth about the facts of the past is indisputably a necessary condition. If there are no facts about the past, then there can be no HRs either. But whereas facts can be checked against the past, no such thing is possible with HRs. To begin with, we cannot compare an HR with the past itself to decide about its plausibility. Anyone making the attempt has in fact presupposed the truth of a certain HR that they believe to be so convincing that they have unwittingly identified it with the past itself. The decisive refutation of all such attempts is that we only ever find HRs in a work of history—and whatever we may wish to say about the past, a work of history it is not. Nor can individual HRs be checked against historical reality, if we understand this to mean that we have first an HR and second that part of historical reality that corresponds to it.[45] We may check the statement that Jean Bodin published in *Les Six Livres de la République* in 1576 against the relevant historical evidence (a copy of the published work), but there is no similar object against which to check the HR detailing the transformation of medieval monarchies into modern states. HRs are part of historical reality themselves, and there is no second or alternative reality outside historical reality with which to compare them.

However, the definition of reality is to be self-consistent. And *this* fact gives us the key to explaining how HRs are checked for their credibility. The answer is disarmingly simple: *HRs are checked against each other*. This can be done by taking into account the PBFs corresponding to them, as I argued in chapter 2. Once we have several HRs on more or less the same historical topic, in principle it is possible to find out which of them is the

---

45. See chapter 2, note 41.

best. And then the criterion of guaranteeing the consistency of historical reality supersedes all others. However, three important qualifications must be made: (1) HRs satisfy *this* criterion sui generis already because they are all strong (and windowless) individuals, so that they cannot possibly be inconsistent with each other; (2) HRs can *nevertheless* meaningfully be compared with each other; and (3) in spite of (1), HRs have a level where (in-)consistencies *may* and even *will* occur. That level, and the criteria of (in-)consistency obtaining there, is discussed in chapter 5. For the time being, I focus exclusively on the preliminary issue of why and how HRs can be compared. This brings us back to the domain of the historical PBF: the claim here is that HRs can be meaningfully compared, although not as HRs, but because their PBFs can be compared.[46]

Leibniz's monads constituted the reality of the monadological universal, but apart from that reality Leibniz also postulated the domain of the PBF corresponding to his monadological universe. The relationship between the two remained an unsolvable mystery. It can be shown, however, that in the case of historical representation, that relation is far from being an embarrassing mystery. It is actually the cornerstone of our account of historical representation.

In chapter 2 it was established that HRs represent *each other* and not anything *outside* them.[47] With the help of what I have just said about the historical PBF, that is only part of the story. We must also take into account that each of the HRs represents the representational universe in a way that is unique to it. HRs owe their uniqueness to the statements about the past (and not, as we have stressed, about historical reality) constituting them. But these true statements define only individual dots that are representationally meaningless when taken by themselves. They need to be connected by association[48] to form some coherent and recognizable whole that is meaningfully comparable to other such wholes (corresponding to other HRs). The dots together with these webs that can be woven around them constitute the domain of an HR's PBF. Moving from the dots to the whole and integrating them in one way or another

---

46. The results of such comparisons are expressed in terms of relational statements about HRs. The possibility of such relational statements is discussed in chapter 4, sections 4–6.
47. See chapter 2, section 2.
48. See for this note **6** of chapter 1.

has to respect, minimally, the laws of nature and those of both individual and collective human behavior. Association then does the rest. This permits, admittedly, of a certain margin of freedom and indeterminacy. But historical debate as discussed in the next two chapters will bind these margins of freedom within ever narrower limits.

Crucially, these webs are and will remain mere *phaenomena* together with the PBF of which they are part, even though they have their origin in the august metaphysical reality of the HRs. You cannot touch, see, hear, or smell them. Nevertheless, they are *bene fundata* thanks to the *origin* they have in their respective HRs. They are *bene fundata*, moreover, because they are supported by hard historical fact and because the networks of which they are the nodes are constructed on the basis of the best and the most solid knowledge we have of the phenomenal world today.[49]

But the dots can be connected by association with each other in infinite ways, and how this is done can also overlap with other HRs. However, far from being a regrettable lack of precision and certainty in the practice of historical writing, this indeterminacy is, in fact, a blessing in disguise because it creates (1) the possibility for an interaction between the PBF corresponding to different HRs; and (2) the commensurability and comparability of the PBF makes it possible to establish which HR out of a set of HRs on more or less the same subject can be considered the most plausible. If it is objected that all this is only a "just so story," and therefore some further argument will be needed to grant that story its credibility, I can only agree. To counter this objection I'd like to appeal—do not freak out!—to developments in mathematics dating back to the later nineteenth century.

It was believed for a long time, following Aristotle, that mathematical concepts, such as points, lines, or space, are abstractions from what is given

---

49. It is tempting to see this account of historical representation as an alternative to epistemological approaches to human experience and knowledge. The first step would be to accept the data of sensory experience as physiological *facts* that can only be investigated by neuro-scientific and other related biological approaches to which the philosopher has nothing to add. Next, these data of sensory experience are said to result in a *representation of the world* we live in. A philosophy of representation of this kind might explain such a "computation" as resulting in what we regard as "reality" or "the world." That reality would be the counterpart of Leibniz's domain of the PBF, which entails that we see that reality, instead, as a reflection, or a phenomenological manifestation, of the totality of *representations* in terms of which we become conscious of the data of our sensory experiences. As this sentence suggests, an account of human experience and knowledge would then both need and explain the notion of consciousness.

to us in experience. This seemed to suggest that the philosopher of mathematics should investigate the nature of points, lines, and spaces empirically. Thus John Stuart Mill still argued in the 1840s that three plus two must be five because it can be established *empirically* that regardless of whether you add *two* apples, stones, or cats to *three* apples, stones, or cats, the result will invariably be *five* apples, stones, or cats. Arithmetic, Mill believed, was therefore an empirical science.[50]

However, at the end of the nineteenth century, Frege and a number of mathematicians, most notably David Hilbert (1862–1943), replaced the Aristotelian view by requiring that all intuitive ideas about points, lines, and so on should be given up. All that can validly be said about these objects is stated in the axioms defining them. Next, in mathematics (for example, in geometry) only those claims are valid that can be inferred from these axioms by valid argument.[51] Mathematics was thus formalized in the sense that all material content was eliminated from it. There is a significant parallel here with the step from the statements *contained* by an HR to that HR itself, which is where the formalization takes place in the account of historical representation that follows.[52] But that does not imply that the truths of geometry are without use or consequence for our knowledge of reality! On the contrary, *precisely* because they were emptied of all empirical content, a mathematical theorem can be used for *any* empirical content, *whatever*

---

50. The surprising implication seemed to be that there must something shared by widely different things as pebbles, political parties, or Kepler's laws that manifested as soon as one started to add them up. See Ernst Cassirer, *Substanzbegriff und Funktionsbegriff. Untersuchungen über die Grundfragen der Erkenntniskritik* (Darmstadt: Wissenschaftliche Buchgesellschaft, 1994), 37–38.

51. Descartes had already taken an important first step in this direction. His so-called analytical geometry replaced the lines, circles, and ellipses of Euclidian geometry with purely algebraic terms. For example, the algebraic equation for the circle is $(x-m)^2 + (y-d)^2 = r^2$, where (m, d) fix the circle's center and r its radius. Leibniz took a further step by giving a mathematical definition of infinity that made it possible to calculate with the infinite. This mathematization of the infinite left no room for any semantic speculations about what the infinite essentially is. Put differently, the infinite is nothing more and nothing less than what the mathematician can *do* with that notion.

52. This has the interesting implication that *all* of contemporary philosophy of history still operates on a quasi-Aristotelian level. This is not meant to imply that contemporary philosophy of history is wrong in all that it says. Similarly, all the syllogistic figures of Aristotelian logic remain as valid as in the days of Aristotle himself. But no help can be expected from Aristotelian logic in understanding the problems occasioned by modern science and mathematics. So it is with contemporary philosophy of history: even if there is nothing wrong with it in its own terms, it cannot further our understanding of the nature of historical writing that came into being with the historicism of the early nineteenth century.

it is, if it is translated in the terms of that theorem. As is commonly said, mathematics is true of all possible worlds.

Each instance of empirical content satisfying these requirements is called a *model* of some abstract, empirically void, mathematical calculus. For example, one could say that adding two apples, stones, or cats to the three apples, stones, or cats (we already had) will add up to five apples, stones, or cats, are three different *models* of the abstract calculus stating that 3 + 2 = 5. In this respect I emphasize that models in mathematics and the sciences have a character exactly the reverse of what we ordinarily associate with that notion. One may build, for example, a model of an airplane to learn about its aerodynamic properties. In such cases (as indeed with the models used in economics), we are first given an empirical reality, such as an airplane or a national economy, and we then build a model of it imitating its properties and behavior under certain circumstances. But in mathematics and the sciences it is the other way around. There we begin with an abstract formal calculus, or mathematical theorem, that is devoid of any content and derived from a set of axioms. It is only subsequently that we investigate what aspects of reality can (1) be regarded as models of the abstract calculus and that can (2) be explained with the help of that abstract calculus. These explanations are far more exact and reliable than the inferences based on the uncertain and shaky things such as the models we may construct of the weather or of national economies. In the first case, we are doing science. Deriving conclusions from a model in the traditional sense of that word is the derivation of uncertainty from uncertainty, which is the case with model-building in economics as well.

In the case of the airplane or the national economy, the "theory" is a model of reality. But in mathematics, certain parts of reality are a model of the abstract mathematical calculus. Much the same holds, in principle, for scientific theories that are expressed in terms of mathematical equations. As Dupuy put it:

> A model is an abstract form, as it were, that is embodied or instantiated by phenomena. Very different domains of phenomenal reality—hydrodynamics and electricity, for instance, or light and sonic vibrations—can be represented by identical models, which establish an equivalence relation among them. A model is the corresponding equivalence class. It therefore enjoys a

transcendent position, not unlike that of a Platonic Idea of which reality is only a pale imitation.[53]

On the one hand, we have the abstract mathematical calculus, and on the other, we have an indefinite number of *models* of the calculus in the domain of reality that, by virtue of their origin, can all be regarded as applications of these models to some area of scientific research.

Historical representation is no different.[54] HRs are the historian's counterpart to the abstract calculus of mathematics. The different ways in which the dots designated by some HR can be connected in historical reality on the level of the PBF are the different *models* corresponding to the HR in question.[55] When a kindred HR comes along, relevantly similar HRs are awakened to life by the prospect of a fruitful discussion between their respective advocates.[56] Other HRs continue their slumber until prodded into action by the proximity of an HR intelligible as one of their kindred. The domain of the historical PBF—and, as we shall see, that of historical knowledge—is born from these encounters of HRs, in the form of the interactions between the models of the PBFs they entail. Each HR always has its boots on the ground, so to speak, in the guise of its PBF and models. They *cannot* interact on the level of the HRs themselves, but on *that* level they can and they do so.

---

53. Jean-Pierre Dupuy, *The Mechanization of the Mind: On the Origins of Cognitive Science* (Princeton, NJ: Princeton University Press, 2000), 29, 30. I owe this reference to Jaap den Hollander.

54. Had Leibniz known the notion of the model, he might have tried to solve his problem of the relationship between the monads and the PBF by claiming that the latter—i.e., phenomenal reality—is a model of the former. Leibniz's conception of the relationship between mathematics and reality is suggestive here: "ainsi quoique les méditations mathématiques sont idéales, cela diminue rien de leur utilité, parce que les choses actuelles ne sauraient s'écarter de ses règles; et on peut dire en effet, qu'est en cela que consiste la réalité des phénomènes, qui les distingue des songes." Quoted in E. Cassirer, *Leibniz's System in seinen Wissenschaftlichen Grundlagen. Text und Anmerkungen bearbeitet von Marcel Simon* (Hamburg: Felix Meiner, 1998), 113.

55. This is how I understand Ranke's observation about his reading of Leibniz quoted in the first of the two epigraphs to this book. The HR is a strong individual to which no universal can be applied, but historical models and the PBF can be described with the help of universals. Nevertheless, these models and the PBF will never wholly renounce their origins. They remain somewhere between the strong individual and the universal—perhaps where we would like to situate "the general."

56. This part of my argument replaces my earlier appeal to metaphor in previous accounts of the nature of historical writing. With this new formulation of this part of my theory of historical representation, the last remnant of figural language it contained has been replaced by literal language.

6. THE STRUCTURAL SIMILARITY OF THE SCIENTIFIC AND THE HISTORICAL REVOLUTION

In the introduction Frederick Beiser related the birth of historicism to Hans Martin Chladenius's perspectivalism. It meant the end of the autopsy model of historical writing that had dominated Western historical thought virtually unchallenged for two thousand years. Furthermore, according to Koselleck, Chladenius's perspectivalism revolutionized historical writing by "liberating" historical writing from the shackles of the autopsy model. But it is, arguably, the true sign of Chladenius's genius that he did not stop there but took a second even more daring step.

This second step is best explained by taking our departure in a well-chosen metaphor that Chladenius proposed in the sixth chapter of *Allgemeine Geschichtswissenschaft*, appropriately titled "the metamorphosis of history in narration." He invites readers to think of a battle and then argues with the cogency worthy of a Stendhal in his *Le Rouge et le Noir* or a Tolstoy in his *War and Peace* that for as long as the battle continues nobody knows exactly what is going on. All of the participants have what Chladenius calls "a mirror image" of the battle, depending on the point of view from which they see it. Admittedly, some of the participants—such as the strategists of the two armies—will have a better mirror image of it than some subaltern infantryman. But even the strategists will not have a point of view allowing them to see *all* of the battle; for example, they will not have access to the mirror images of these subaltern infantrymen. So most of the battle will remain in the dark for all of the participants. Here we seem to have come to the limits of what perspectivalism can give us.[57]

Only after the battle is over and when we know who won and who lost can these limits be overcome—although even then only partly. But how? Above all, without abandoning perspectivalism because that would mean a return to the autopsy model. The question therefore is: What enables the historian to retain the fruits of perspectivism while overcoming its limitations? Chladenius's clear and unambiguous answer is narration (Erzählung).

---

57. Johann Martin Chladenius, *Allgemeine Geschichtswissenschaft. Mit einer Einleitung von Christoph Friederich und einem Vorwort von Reinhart Koselleck* (1752; repr. Vienna: Hermann Böhlaus Nachf, 1985), 114.

What was said just now indicates what Chladenius expects from narration. It is true that the point of view possesses an autonomy of its own with regard to what it is a point of view upon. This is why, as we have seen, perspectivalism is superior to the autopsy model. Nevertheless, each point of view remains tied to what it is a point of view on; that tie is specific to that point of view and what is seen from it and, moreover, what distinguishes it from how *other* points of view correspond to what *they* are points of view on. In this way the autonomy of the point of view remains restricted. Similarly, however long the leash connecting you and your dog may be, your dog will never be completely free. The leash will always be there in the end. So more is needed to see *all* of the battle between these two armies that Chladenius had in mind.

This is where narrative comes in, according to Chladenius. You can only *narrate* some part of the past on the condition that you have taken up a position that is *later* and, therefore, *outside* that past itself—a position you can only claim for yourself after having cut through *all* these ties between Chladenius's mirror images and what they mirror.

Even after having cut through these ties, you can still meaningfully say that the past can be seen from different points of view. However, in that case, the phrase "point of view" will have acquired a different meaning: the point of view will then combine in itself (1) a point of view that is located in the *present* and not in the *past* (i.e., what it has in common with *all* other points of view defended by historians writing on the same part of the past) as well as (2) where it *differs* from all of them—because of a difference in historical subject matter or in the presentation of it. The *vertical* relationship between the points of view and what it is a point of view upon is essentially exchanged for the *horizontal* relationship between points of view.

In sum, when moving from the past to the present of the historian, the picture is as follows. The people who lived in the past saw their world from their own point of view (resulting in the mirror images they had of their world). When moving to the present, all these points of view are wiped out in favor of the points of view defended by historians and whose nature is defined by where they differ from other such points of view. Differences in points of view on the past have now been transfigured into the differences between historical points of view as expressed in historical narratives. The provocative implication is that *these* points of view have no identifiable counterpart in either the past itself nor in the way it was seen by the people in the past themselves: they live their lives in an entirely different, exclusively narrativist realm. Much is therefore to be said for Chladenius's characteristic of this transfiguration of points of view as "the metamorphosis of history into narration." Chladenius summarizes his argument (albeit somewhat obtusely) as follows:

> If we wish to recognize the true nature of history, or, rather, of historical narration, it will not be enough to know the different manners in which the events of the past were pictured—as if in a mirror—by the participants, as was explained in the previous chapter. We will need, in addition to this, one more "action of the soul" ('Handlung der Seele') which *precedes* all narration and which I will call "the metamorphosis of history," since the events of the past can never be narrated exactly as they have been experienced, but only in agreement with a certain image ('Bild') that is gained from experience and its representation by memory ('Gedächtnis'). For we don't narrate things from experience and true representation, but *after* these two: and we allow us to be led by the picture ('Bild') which is printed in our soul by experience (author's translation).[58]

Surely, this is a complicated argument, but the gist of it is as follows. Narration is a mental activity having no ground in the past itself; it is a category we must appeal to for imposing a *form* on the past that the past (and the experiences constituting it) does not have itself. Hence, Chladenius's notion of a "metamorphosis of the past into narration." It has a quasi-transcendental status, but with a strong emphasis on the "quasi" because it certainly is not Chladenius's intention to reduce the past to the sorry status of the Kantian noumenon.[59] It is guided, as Chladenius somewhat obscurely puts it at the end of the quote, "by the 'image' ('Bild') which is printed in our soul by experience."

The result of this metamorphosis is an image ('Bild'). But this could not possibly be an image in the way that these mirror images we discussed a moment before were images. The latter were images in the sense of

---

58. Chladenius, *Allgemeine Geschichtswissenschaft*, 115, 116.
59. A transcendentalist analysis of historical narrative was proposed long ago in Hans Michael Baumgartner, *Kontinuität und Geschichte: zur Kritik und Metakritik der historischen Vernunft* (Frankfurt am Main: Suhrkamp, 1972).

mirroring the past, if seen from a certain point of view to be situated in the past itself. At that stage "the dog leash" between the point of view and what it is a point of view of was still there. But with the metamorphosis effected by narration, "the dog leash" is finally cut through. So *this* image ('Bild')—let's call it *Bild*—must strictly be distinguished from the mirror images of a moment before.

Leibniz's metaphor of the rainbow may give an idea of how the two relate to each other.[60] The myriad individual droplets of water breaking the light of the sun are the counterpart of the mirror images, whereas the rainbow must be seen as the counterpart of the *Bild*. Just as the rainbow is an astounding metamorphosis of what happens in the individual drops of water, so it is with the metamorphosis of the many mirror images into the unity of the historian's *Bild*. As will be clear, the *Bild* is both more and less than the past. In the sections in chapter six, Chladenius discusses the many ways in which this difference between the mirror images, on the one hand, and the *Bild*, on the other, may manifest itself. Preservation of *content* there may and even will be—to a certain extent at least—but there will be a complete metamorphosis of *form*. Chladenius's word *metamorphosis* must, therefore, be taken literally rather than metaphorically. When we do so, it will give us a domain of forms possessing an autonomy of their own with regard to the past: these forms have no longer a *fundamentum in re*. This compels us to think of a domain consisting of these *Bilder* only—just as Leibniz's monads and HRs (and Munz's notion of a mask without a face behind it) exclude a reality existing outside of themselves.[61] Thanks to this autonomy, Chladenius's *Bilder* constitute historical reality itself—as is the case with Leibnizian and historical representation—and where historical debate is a debate about *that* reality.

If we replace Chladenius's term *Bild* by *representation* and read the foregoing gloss of the quote from Chladenius again, it comes quite close to what was said at the end of the previous section about models and historical PBF. In both cases, either the *Bilder* resulting from the metamorphosis of the mirror images or the representations presented by the historian acquire

---

60. See chapter 2, note 29.
61. In chapter 4, Leibnizian representation reverses the hierarchy of the represented and the representation: representation precedes the represented.

a stunning autonomy with regard to the past. Even more so, these images or representations claim for themselves the status of existence at the expense of the past (that no longer exists). Admittedly, what fails in Chladenius is the differentiation between the level of the image (or of historical representation) and that of the historical models or PBF. But there *must* be a level where the struggle between Chladenius's images or HRs takes place, and this level could not possibly be that of these images of HRs themselves. For reasons previously explained, the postulate of that second level follows as a matter of course from his account of the metamorphosis of the past into *Bilder* by narrativization. At that level we can say that it contains the models, or in Leibnizian language the PBF, generated by Chladenius's *Bilder* or by HRs.

To conclude, what has been argued so far about historical representation can be traced back to Chladenius's *Allgemeine Geschichtswissenschaft*, which can be said to have enacted the revolution in historical writing, although that revolution still had to be realized in the practice of historical writing. Nevertheless, Chladenius opened the way for historicism, which is the heart of the practice of historical writing to this day, and so it will remain for as long as history will be written.

The scientific revolution of the seventeenth century has undoubtedly been the most important single event in all of the history of mankind: no other event so dramatically and in so short a time changed the face of the world. Not surprisingly, the scientific revolution has been analyzed and discussed from numerous perspectives. For each theory about its emergence and nature, many others can be cited, and the choice for any of them is inevitably to a certain extent arbitrary. I hope I may be forgiven for taking Bernard Cohen's *The Newtonian Revolution* as my guide.[62]

Cohen considers Galileo's credentials for having been the initiator of the scientific revolution, but he decides, in the end, that the honor must be granted to Newton. This is not so surprising when we take into account his observation that "there is evidence aplenty that in the age of Newton and afterwards, his *Principia* was conceived to have ushered in a revolution in the physical sciences. And it is precisely this revolution whose

---

62. I. Bernhard Cohen, *The Newtonian Revolution. With Illustrations of Scientic Ideas* (Cambridge: Cambridge University Press, 1980), 12.

characteristic features I aim to elucidate."[63] To capture the nature of the Newtonian revolution in science, Cohen distinguishes between Newton's "scenario" and his "style."[64] The former stands for how Newton himself conceived of the method he had applied when writing *Principia*, whereas the latter is the term Cohen uses for how he *actually* proceeded. Indeed, Newton did not practice what he preached.

Newton formulated his scenario as follows:

> the main Business of natural Philosophy is to argue from Phaenomena without feigning Hypotheses, and to deduce Causes from Effects, till we come to the very first Cause, which certainly is not mechanical. ... This Analysis consists in making Experiments and Observations, and in drawing general Conclusions from them by Induction, and in admitting of no Objections against the Conclusions, but such as are taken from Experiments, or other certain Truths. For Hypothesis are not to be regarded in experimental Philosophy.[65]

And Cohen concludes:

> Newton would have us believe that he had himself followed this "scenario": first to reveal by "analysis" some general results that were generalized by induction, thus proceeding from effects to causes and from particular causes to general causes; then, on the basis of these causes considered as principles, to explain by "synthesis" the phenomena of observation and experiment that may be derived of deduced from them, "proving the Explanations."[66]

Cohen admits that in some of his works, such as in *Opticks* or on chemistry, the theory of matter or of gases, Newton employed this empiricist or positivist procedure. But in the work on which his fame of having revolutionized science rests—i.e., his *Philosophiae Naturalis Principia Mathematica*—he proceeded in a quite different, if not entirely opposite, manner.

To begin, he sinned against his distrust of hypotheses (*hypotheses non fingo*) by simply assuming there to be such a thing as gravitational force,

---

63. Cohen, *The Newtonian Revolution*; 9.
64. Cohen, *The Newtonian Revolution*; 12, 13.
65. Cohen, *The Newtonian Revolution*; 12.
66. Cohen, *The Newtonian Revolution*; 13.

while admitting he had no explanation for it (and this is still the case: there is no universally acknowledged theory of quantum gravity enabling an integration of quantum theory and Einstein's general relativity). Predictably, most of the contemporary criticism of the *Principia* focused precisely on this. But of more importance in this context is that Newton does not use mathematics in the *Principia* to infer conclusions from empirical fact or observation (as the empiricist or inductivist might be inclined to do) but as a language enabling him to speak about certain physical phenomena, such as the movement of bodies that by centripetal forces tend toward one another. He used mathematics metaphysically. As Newton puts it himself at the outset of his discussion of these forces and their effects on the movements of bodies:

> For this reason I now go on to explain the motion of bodies that mutually attract one another, considering centripetal forces as attractions, although perhaps—if we speak in the language of physics—they might more truly be called impulses. For we are here concerned with mathematics: and therefore, putting aside any debate concerning physics, we are using familiar language so as to be more easily understood by mathematical readers. . . . He then enjoins the reader "not to imagine that by those words I anywhere define the kind, or the manner of any action, the cause or the physical reason thereof, or that I attribute forces, in a true and physical sense, to certain centres (which are only mathematical points); when at any time I happen to speak of centres as attracting, or being endowed with attractive powers."[67]

To put it bluntly, if we wish to understand the phenomena of physics, we shall have to start by replacing the language used for speaking about physical phenomena with the language of mathematics (with which we are all supposed to be familiar). This is the physicist's analogue of the language of the HRs. Not reality, but mathematics itself generates its truths; similarly, a statement about a HR must be true—not because it expresses a truth about some state of affairs in the past—but because it can logically be derived from the notion of that HR (as is stipulated by D_{cc}). And as becomes clear from the second part of the quote, the use of mathematical language and

---

67. Cohen, *The Newtonian Revolution*; 73, 74.

METAPHYSICS, INDIVIDUALS, MODELS, AND THE PBF

its abstractions also allows him to refrain from all speculation about what gravitation actually *is*. That question belongs to the domain of physics and fortunately falls outside the scope of mathematics. Elsewhere he presses the point a little bit further:

> I use the word attraction here in a general sense for any endeavor whatever of bodies to approach one another, whether that endeavor occurs by the action of the bodies either tending towards one another or agitating one another by mean of spirits emitted, or wherever it arises from the action of aether or of air or of any medium whatsoever—whether corporeal; or incorporeal—in anyway impelling toward one another the bodies floating therein.[68]

This is what Cohen regards as the scientific revolution as effected by Newton: the scientist should treat problems in the exact sciences as if they were exercises in pure mathematics and link experiment and observation to mathematics in a notably fruitful manner. "The Newtonian revolution in the sciences was wrought by and revealed in the *Principia*. For more than two centuries, this book set the standard against which all other science was measured; it became the goal toward which scientists in such diverse fields as palaeontology, statistics, and biochemistry would strive in order to bring their own fields to a desired high estate."[69]

The structural similarity of (1) what was said in a previous section on the use of models in the sciences, (2) the *Bild* in Chladenius's revolutionary revision of the historian's task, and (3) the Newtonian revolution of science will be obvious to anyone. In each of the three cases, the focus on phenomena is temporarily interrupted by a move toward pure abstraction. In all of them, this movement is a *"reculer pour mieux sauter"*: the withdrawal into pure abstraction is made to secure the boldest and longest possible leap forward in the domain of (empirical) phenomena. In cases (1) and (3), this is a move from the observation of empirical fact and the (statistical) regularities that can be discerned in them toward an abstract calculus. Or, as Newton puts it, it is a shift from the (extensionalist) language of physics to the (intensionalist) language of mathematics. Finally, what is said in the latter will be compared with the data of experience and observation. We now

---

68. Cohen, *The Newtonian Revolution*; 74.
69. Cohen, *The Newtonian Revolution*; 16.

know, after Duhem, after the demise of logical-positivism, and after Quine, that this comparison with what is empirically given to us is, in both theory and practice, a comparison of one scientific theory with other competing theories. The same pattern can be upheld for (2). There is the extensionalist language expressing truths about historical states of affairs. Next comes the shift to Chladenius's *Bild*—or representation in the terminology used in this book possessing no *fundamentum in re* in what can be expressed in terms of extensionalist language. The intensionalism of that language must be identified with the meta-sentences recursively defining an image à la Chladenius or an HR. Finally, there is the stage of the comparison of these images or HRs in terms of the models or historical PBF implied by them. The structural similarities of the scientific revolution of the seventeenth century and the revolution in historical writing of a century later will need no further clarification. In both cases, the achievements of the scientific revolution remain part and parcel of scientific practice to this very day.

People with a nostalgic turn of mind could even see this as a belated compliment to the now wholly forgotten thesis of "the unity of science."

This book ends with an epilogue on extensionalism and intensionalism; it is, in a way, the book's apotheosis. It is shown there that we must distinguish between an extensionalist and an intensionalist use of language or, if one prefers to put it more dramatically, between extensionalist and intensionalist language. The former is used to speak about reality (extension); whereas the latter investigates what valid conclusions can be reached from processing certain linguistic signs by means of the relevant algorithms (the latter issue is elaborated in chapter 4). Four things can be said about these two languages: (1) they cannot be translated into each other without loss of meaning; (2) statements made in either of them will never conflict with statements made in the other [(1) and (2) measure the unbridgeable gap between the two]; (3) all sciences need both of them, even though in some of them extensionalism will marginalize intensionalism whereas in others it is the other way around, with the result that each science should at all times search for the *juste milieu* between them that suits it best; and (4) the *juste milieu* can often be located on different places within one and the same science.

Chapter Four

SIGNS, SEMANTICS, MEANING, AND RELATIONAL STATEMENTS

1. THEORIES OF REPRESENTATION

Until now I have been discussing historical representation without going beyond what was said in chapter 3 about the notion of "representation," but this topic is central to this chapter and chapter 5.[1] Our attention shifts from the metaphysical question of the nature of historical representation to the more logical and semantic questions of the linguistic instruments required for the expression of historical representation. Keep in mind, however, that it is impossible to separate metaphysics and logic from one another in the

---

1. In this chapter and in chapter 5, historical representation is often compared with mathematics. There is more common ground between them than ordinarily is believed. My argument comes close to Mahnke's *Leibnizens Synthese*. Mahnke read Leibniz as aiming at a synthesis between (universal) mathematics and the metaphysics of the individual often associated with historical writing. In Dietrich Mahnke, *Leibnizens Synthese von Universalmathematik und Individualmetaphysik* (1925: repr. Stuttgart: Friedrich Frommann, 1964), 15–16, Mahnke writes: "die diskrete Zahleinheit der Arithmetik, die kontinuierliche Funktionseinheit, das Differential and zugleich das Integral der höheren Analysis, das chemische Atom, die physikalische Kraft (genauer das Energiequantum) mit ihrem mathematischen Wirkungsgesetz, die organische Form und Entelechie der Biologie, die Bewusstseinseinheit der Psychologie, das inhaltslogische Subjekt, das alle seine Prädikate 'enthält,' die juristische Person und die Entwicklungseinheit der Geschichte, die 'kleine Welt' oder 'kleine Gottheit' der Mystik und zuhöchst die sittlich-religiöse Persönlichkeit des Christentums mit ihrer ewigen Bestimmung—dies alles fliesst in dem einen Begriff der Monade zu einem synthetischen Ganzen zusammen.... So verschmelzen bei ihm [i.e., Leibniz] Monismus und Pluralismus im

account of historical representation given below: whatever is said about the metaphysical nature of HRs has its consequences for the logic of historical representation, and vice versa. So it is with Leibniz and so it is here.

I identify three distinct theories of representation. The first is what one might call the "projection theory." Think of the problem of how to project a sphere (e.g., the earth) on a flat plane (e.g., a map) so the figure on the plane is the representation and the sphere is the represented. There are many ways to do this: by means of a cylindrical projection (made famous by Mercator), or by pseudocylindrical, pseudoazimuthal, conic, pseudoconical, or polyhedral projections. Each of these has many variants, but in all of them it is crucial that the projection is determined by a mathematically defined rule. This projection rule fixes what point of the represented corresponds to some point on the representation, and vice versa. This is why the problem of projection is part of the mathematical subdiscipline of topology.

The projection theory can also be compared to a scale drawing such as an architectural plan or engineering diagram that serves as a guide for building a house or constructing a machine. A feature of this version of the projection theory is that the relation between the representation and what is represented is debatable. For example, as long as the house is under construction, we would say that the working drawing is the represented and the house is the representation of the drawing in terms of bricks, cement, beams, and so. However, once the building of the house has been completed, the opposite view seems to be the most plausible one. But all in all, the projection theory is remarkably indifferent with regard to what counts as the representation and what should be seen as the representation and what as the represented. The explanation arguably is that what one might call "translation rules" define the relationship between the representation

---

Begriff der Harmonie (als Einheit in der Mannigfaltigkeit), substantielles Sein und Heraklitisches Werden und zufällige Tatsachenwahrheit im unendlichen Rationalisierungsprozess, Determination und Freiheit im individuellen Gesetz oder in oder in der verschiedenartigen Repräsentation des Allgemeinen durch das Einzelne und endlich—was gegenwartig vielleicht das aktuellste Interesse bietet—logisch-idealistische *Universalmathematik* und irrational-realistische *Individualmetaphysik* in der formalen Äquivalenz der qualitativ differenzierten und subjektiv verlebendigten Erlebniswelten." See also Mahnke, *Leibnizens Synthese*, 196. Mahnke hoped to argue for the synthesis of a universal mathematics with a metaphysics of the individual in a later book, but unfortunately that book was never written. Mahnke's fascination with Leibniz's thought has similarities with Ernst Cassirer, whose philosophy of symbolic forms also grew out of his encounter with Leibniz's philosophy of mathematics and of science. See Heinz Paetzold, *Ernst Cassirer. Zur Einführung* (Hamburg: Junius, 1993), 31ff.

and its represented, doing so with exactitude so that the direction in which one moves from one to the other is immaterial. Needless to say, these translation rules will affect an isomorphy between the representation and its represented, making the choice between which is which fairly arbitrary. Isomorphy is the only thing at stake, after all.

Another illustration from a wholly different field of our freedom of choice between what we wish to see as the representation and as the represented is the following. Think of reproduction in plants and animals. An individual plant's or animal's DNA guarantees that this individual is a fairly reliable copy of its progenitor(s). Is the represented the progenitor(s) or the DNA passed on by the progenitor(s) to the individual? Or should we see the individual as the represented and its progenitor(s) as the representation representing that represented? It may seem that we have hit here upon the limits of what meaningfully can be done with the concept of representation. It is as if you mishandled the screw cap on a bottle with the outcome that you can't get if off anymore.

Stephen Puryear speaks of "isomorphic correspondence" when discussing the projection theory, claiming that Leibniz should have adopted it.[2] Passages can be found in Leibniz's writings that seem to confirm this claim, but Leibniz often said things that are impossible to reconcile with what is universally recognized as the main thrust of his argument. So it is here. There is unanimous agreement among Leibniz experts that his monadology is essentially perspectivist because each monad seeing the monadological universe from its own point of view is the core of his notion of the monad. Scholars are also agreed that all variants of the projection theory share the aim of eliminating perspectivism and that all variants of the projection theory aim at avoiding perspectivalism. A perspectivalist map of a country or a city would come close to being useless. Similarly, the idea of a working map that presents a house or a machine from a certain perspective would be a disaster for the builder of that house or machine. Clearly, Puryear's theory fails to account for Leibniz's manifest intentions right from the start.[3]

---

2. Stephen M. Puryear, *Perception and Representation in Leibniz* (Pittsburgh, PA: University of Pittsburgh Press, 2006), 3.

3. Puryear frequently pays tributes to the inferentialism of his PhD supervisor Robert Brandom. But a fruitful cooperation between Brandom's inferentialism and Leibniz's concept of representation is not easy to imagine. See, e.g., Zachary Micah Gartenberg, "Brandom's Leibniz," *Pacific Philosophical Quarterly* 102, no. 1 (March 2021): 73–102.

The other two theories that dominate current debate about representation are the resemblance and substitution theories. According to the former, a representation *resembles* what it represents; think of the drawing of a tree and the tree itself. This is called the *resemblance theory* of representation.[4] But think now of a round red spot on a map of France representing Paris.[5] This spot does not resemble Paris at all. Nevertheless, in the practices of mapping and map reading, the red spot can be said to represent—or to *stand for*—the actual city of Paris. Some would say that it functions on the map as a *substitute* for the actual city of Paris—just as for the child, in Ernst Gombrich's well-known example, a hobbyhorse will function as a *substitute* for a real horse.[6] This is why this theory of representation is called the *substitution theory* of representation.

Observe, furthermore, that substitution seems to be part and parcel of all representation as defined by the resemblance theory. The drawing of a tree not only resembles the real tree but will in the eyes of the spectator also function as a substitute for it. Put differently, the resemblance theory is actually resemblance plus substitution. This is why theorists such

---

4. The resemblance theory has an a priori plausibility that is hard to deny—probably because of its vagueness. But as soon as it is put on the rack of critical assessment, it loses much of its appeal. Nelson Goodman wittily pointed out that a painting of Blenheim Castle resembled more a painting of, e.g., the Duke of Marlborough than Blenheim Castle. Two pieces of canvas with dots of paint on them resemble each other more than both resemble the huge building of this name constructed by Sir John Vanbrugh between 1705 and 1722. So you're absolutely nowhere without criteria for resemblance. This might seem to send us back to the projection theory because it supplies us with such criteria. But even if we grant that this takes away part of the weakness of the resemblance, the substance of Goodman's criticism of the resemblance theory remains intact. Clearly, a lot of additional work is needed to make the resemblance theory do what is expected from it. This does not mean that the curtain has fallen for the resemblance theory; however, the resemblance theory and its close relative the isomorphic correspondence theory are clearly in need of considerable further clarification and refinement.

5. There is still a reminiscence of the projection theory here, with the difference that the point of view has now entered the scene. If one says "this drawing is a good representation of x," this statement is essentially incomplete; the qualification "if seen from the point of view or the perspective of point P" must be added. If seen from another perspective, the drawing will be entirely wrong—unless x has the form of a sphere.

6. Ernst Gombrich, "Meditations on a Hobby Horse," in *Aesthetics Today*, ed. Morris Philips (New York: New American Library, 1980), 172–85. Gombrich's view of representation was anticipated by Edmund Burke: "poetry, taken in its most general sense, cannot with strict propriety be called an art of imitation. . . . But *descriptive* poetry operates chiefly by *substitution*; by the means of sounds, which by custom have the effect of realities." Edmund Burke, *A Philosophical Enquiry Into the Origins of Our Ideas of the Sublime and the Beautiful* (Oxford: Oxford University Press, 1992, italics added), 157.

as Gombrich, Goodman, and Danto—in keeping with the motto "less is more"—prefer the substitution theory to the resemblance theory. If one seeks the simplest theory of representation, a theory defining the absolute minimum condition for something to be called a representation, this preference for the substitution theory is understandable. But in cases like those of portrait paintings, plans for a house, designs for a machine, and anatomical atlases of animal or human organs, substitution is not enough. Resemblance here is a *conditio sine qua non*. Much depends on what is expected from a representation. The portrait painter depicting his sitter as a dog turd will soon have to look for another job, unless the painter had acquired the quasi-sacred status of a Mondrian or a Picasso.[7] The more expectations one has of a representation, the better these expectations are served by the resemblance theory; the fewer demands or expectations one has, the more the resemblance theory may develop from an irrelevance into a real nuisance. Think of a map representing the cities depicted on it by aerial views: interesting but obviating useful information about the city's direct surroundings. Moreover, this is not the kind of information for which we consult maps. In sum, the substitution theory is a necessary but not always sufficient condition of adequate representation.[8]

2. REPRESENTATION AND SIGNS

Both the substitution and resemblance theories separate what is represented (a tree, the city of Paris) from its representation (the drawing of a tree, a red spot on the map). Most people think this distinction cannot meaningfully be questioned. What could be the use of the representation of a represented if this representation would give us the represented all over again? Representation is then either useless, because it sends us back to the represented, or impossible, because Leibniz's D_{ii} rules out the possibility of two *different*

---

7. There is nothing new under the sun here. Think of the third person from the right with the red nose and his hat almost dropping from his head on Frans Hals's *The Regents of the Old Men's Alms House*, which is in the Frans Hals Museum in Haarlem. Clearly, we're looking at an old drunkard. It is likely that the person in question (and his family) acquiesced in being depicted in this way for no reason other than that it was Hals—already a celebrity during his lifetime—who painted this "regentenstuk."

8. The last two theories of representation mentioned here are modeled on Peirce's theory of the sign. The resemblance theory agrees with the sign as icon, and the substitution theory with the sign as symbol. It is difficult to think of a counterpart for the sign as index.

things (the represented and its representation) being exactly the same. Yet contrary to what is suggested by Leibniz's D_{ii}, I hope to show that the identity of the represented and the representation is part and parcel of the theory of representation presented by Leibniz himself.[9] That is to say, first, that the representation *is* the represented *as* represented by the representation; and second, that the represented *is* the representation representing that represented.[10] Compare it to what is involved in "thinking a thought." If you think a thought, there is not, on the one hand, the process of thinking which itself is wholly devoid of thought, and on the other, the thought existing completely apart from the process of thinking. The two always go together: if you think, a thought must be present, and if you have a thought, you must have been thinking. Admittedly, a difficult and even mind-boggling idea.

But, as you shall see, the identity of the represented and the representation is not only a feature of Leibniz's monadological metaphysics as defined by D_{wm}, D_{cc}, D_{ii}, and D_{ph}, but it can be shown to be true of historical writing as well.[11] Before arguing these two claims, however, I briefly discuss pictorial representation, for two reasons: first, that even there the claim of the identity of the represented and the representation is less absurd than it might seem; and second, this smooths the transition to the subsequent topics of historical representation and Leibniz's notion of the sign.

---

9. To avoid misunderstandings, I emphasize that this theory of representation should not be confused with the projection theory of representation. In the latter we may label the house as the representation and its working drawing as its represented, or the other way around, but that does not allow us to wipe out all differences between houses and working drawings. In the variant of representation under discussion here, however, there truly is an identity of the representation and the represented.

10. Herbertz hinted at this possibility, although without grasping its full significance: "wir könnten demnach die Bedeutung der drei im Frage gestellten Begriffe etwa durch folgende Bestimmung festlegen: jede geschaffene Monade ist eine Art Mikrokosmos und repräsentiert somit in ihren eigentümlichen und charakteristischen Weise, das gesamte Universum (representer).... Da die Monade nun aber ein Kraftwesen ist, dessen Kräfte Vorstellungen sind, so ist jeder Ausdruck ein Vorstellungsmässiger (perceptions). Kurz, die Monade repräsentiert das Universum dadurch, dass sie es in ihren Perzeptionen zum Ausdruck bringt." Put differently, the representation (monad) *is* its represented (the universe). See Richard Herbertz, *Die Lehre vom Unbewussten im System des Leibniz* (New York: Georg Olms, 1980), 43.

11. This is the main thesis of Louis Couturat, *La Logique de Leibniz d'après des Documents Inédits* (Hildesheim: Olms, 1961), 43. Couturat's claim finds support in Leibniz's formula "cum Deus calculat et cogitationem exercet fit mundus," quoted in Mahnke, *Leibnizens Synthese*. Cassirer also defends the view that Leibniz's philosophy presents us with a fusion of logic and metaphysics, although with the qualification that logic is the stronger partner of the two. See Ernst Cassirer, *Hauptschriften zur Grundlegung der Philosophie*, vol. 2, ed. G. W. Leibniz (Hamburg: Felix Mainer, 1966), 90.

Leibniz finds a metaphysical justification for the identification of the representation and the represented in the identity of being and of being perceived. The following comparison may be helpful for understanding this apparently counterintuitive claim. Think of a landscape and a painting of that landscape. It seems natural to say that the painting is the representation and the landscape the represented. But is it? Think of two painters painting the same landscape and producing two different paintings of the same landscape. Then there must *also* be two different representeds. For representeds always correspond to representations; and if representations differ, their representeds must do so as well.

This is, of course, at odds with our intuition that if two painters paint one and the same landscape there can be only *one* represented—i.e., the landscape itself. The explanation is that each of the two painters focused on that *aspect* of the landscape that found its way to his representation of it.[12] The aspect is both part of the landscape itself (just as what we see of the moon is *part* of the moon itself, and not some fiction coming into existence somewhere on the trajectory between the moon and ourselves), and at the same time, part of the representation's represented. The notion of the *aspect* is helpful because the notions of perception and being perceived ("percipere" and "percipi")—of representation and of being represented—are inextricably fused together in it. The *aspect* ties the perceived and perceived thing together: the aspect is both part of the thing perceived and determined by the *unique* spatial position of the perceiver with regard to the thing perceived.[13] Our commonsense thinking about representation—stating that the landscape *itself* is the represented and *not* the aspects these two painters somehow foisted on it—must be rejected because it fails to do justice to the refinement proposed here. This is where Leibniz's theory of representation is more precise and radical than the resemblance and substitution theories: (1) it dissolves "the" landscape into its "aspects"; (2) it identifies the latter with the representation's represented; and (3) it proposes

---

12. I remind the reader of what was said on the aspect in section 3 of Chapter 3. See, moreover, Franklin Rudolf Ankersmit, *Meaning, Truth and Reference in Historical Representation* (London: Cornell University Press, 2013), 68–71. When entering a dark torch-lit chamber, the aspects illuminated by the light are aspects of the furniture itself (and not of the torch light). The notion of the aspect will be discussed more elaborately in the epilogue.

13. The idea of the aspect discussed here resembles the notion of the model mentioned at the end of chapter 3.

a theory of the sign (discussed later) in which the representation and the represented are the *same*—although each is under a *different description*.

An obvious objection is what is then left of the landscape itself? It seems to have gotten lost somewhere on the way from the landscape, via its aspects, to its representation. But advocates of Leibniz's theory of representation will ask: What *more* is there to a landscape than the sum of all of its possible aspects (or representeds)? Every time someone produces something of which they triumphantly exclaim "this is the landscape *itself,* or part of it," the Leibnizian will imperturbably add it to an ever-lengthening list of the landscape's representeds and repeat that the belief that there is a "real" landscape apart from the totality of all of its possible representeds (or aspects) is an illusion. Pursuing this debate further can only result in adding one more chapter to the endless story of the struggle between Berkeleyan idealists and the realists.

Let us return to historical representation. Whereas discussion in the previous paragraph ended in the stalemate between the idealists and the realists, in this case the balance tips in Leibniz's favor. The key passage is from Arthur Danto:

> [T]he historical period considered as an entity . . . is a period solely from the perspective of the historian, who sees it from without; for those who lived in the period it would be just the way life was lived. And asked, afterwards, what it was like to have lived then, they may answer from the outside, from the historian's perspective. From the inside there is no answer to be given; it was simply the way things were. So when the members of a period can give an answer in terms satisfactory to the historian, the period will have exposed its outward surface and in a sense be over, as a period.[14]

The idea is that a certain time is a historical period only "from the outside"; if seen, or experienced, "from the inside," it is not experienced under that description. It is simply how things were at that time. Something is a historical period only from a perspective or point of view later than it. This may seem like a trivial insight, but it has an unexpected implication for how we must conceive of historical reality. To see this, we must

---

14. Arthur C. Danto, *The Transfiguration of the Commonplace* (Cambridge, MA: Harvard University Press, 1983), 207.

start with the recognition that events as such are neither past, present, nor future; it is only the speaker's temporal position with regard to them that makes them so. Hence, events are part of past reality only when we have *discovered*, *decided*, or *concluded*—and compelling existential considerations obtain here!—that we *now* live at an essentially later time. But right from *that* moment on, past reality exists no longer; it has died back like the withered branch of a tree from which life has withdrawn. As long as the past still existed, it is not yet *historical* but *actual* or *present* reality. Common sense demands that we situate historical reality in the past itself—this is the historical ontology almost universally accepted in the contemporary philosophy of history. But, following Danto, we must recognize this as an error: *historical reality only comes into being when the past no longer exists.*

Let us return now to the realist's indignant exclamation: "but what has happened to the landscape!?" In the case of Leibniz, it is sufficient to remind the reader of Cassirer's warning that we should at all times avoid looking for something behind or beyond the monadological universe (see chapter 2). Avoiding this mistake is the beginning of all wisdom regarding the Leibnizian system. So it is here: just as there is nothing behind, outside, or beyond the monads representing each other, so there is nothing behind, outside, or beyond representations and their representeds. There is nothing behind the masks historians press on the past, as I quoted Peter Munz in chapter 2. From a metaphysical point of view, they are identical and impossible to separate from each other.

If we nevertheless posit "something" that all these representeds are allegedly aspects *of*, this something is not an entity to which we can glue all these aspects because that something could never be more than the *sum* of all these aspects. So it is with historical representation: the represented, or historical reality, is not "the past" but what is represented by the historical representation, and these two are as impossible to separate from each other as the letter "a" is inseparable from what that letter stands for. This example is far from arbitrary. You shall see shortly that the historical text is, from a logical point of view, a *sign*. I do not recoil from the assertion that the philosophy of history is condemned to impotence as long as it ignores the issue of the sign-like or symbolic character of the historical text. The philosopher of history who ignores this issue is like an arithmetician trying to do arithmetic without numbers. Let me explain.

As long as the philosopher of history's theoretical vocabulary is comprised of HRs only, he can do no more than mention, identify, or refer to them using phrases such as "'the HR proposed by the historian H in his book entitled B" or the "HR presenting a so-called *micro-storia* of a certain Menocchio." But it will be impossible for him to theorize about or to operate with them. Only when he has at his disposal the notion of the *historical text as sign* is the way open for theory formation allowing him to operate with more than just one representation.

Now, in an absolutely crucial essay, Leibniz discusses a chiliogon, a polygon with a thousand equal sides. His argument is that we have the *word* chiliogon—what he refers to as its *notion*—but not its *idea*. He means that we cannot imagine a chiliogon. We cannot form a mental image of it, such as one may have of a triangle, a pentagon, or an octagon. But the geometrician may make use of these ideas to go beyond them and discover the properties of the chiliogon as a *thing* (i.e., as an *intensional object*). This is how the three concepts of notion, idea, and things are related in Leibniz's semantics. Hence, even though we have no idea (or grasp of the meaning) of the word *chiliogon*, we use that word when appealing to the ideas of "thousand," "equal," and "side" (as previously mentioned in accepted geometrical truths) in order to deepen our knowledge of the thing chiliogon. As Leibniz puts it:

> Yet for the most part, especially in a longer analysis, we do not intuit the entire nature of the subject matter at once but make use of signs instead of things, though we usually omit the explanation of these signs in any actually present thought for the sake of brevity, knowing or believing that we have the power to do it. Thus when I think of a chiliogon, or a polygon of a thousand equal sides, I not always consider the nature of a side and of equality and of a thousand (or the cube of ten), but I use these words, whose meaning appears obscurely and imperfectly to the mind, in place of the ideas which I have of them, because I remember that I know the meaning of such words but that their interpretation is not necessary for the present judgment. *Such thinking I usually call blind or symbolic*; we use it in algebra and in arithmetic, and indeed almost everywhere.[15]

---

15. Leibniz, *Philosophical Papers and Letters*, 2nd ed., trans. Leroy E. Loemker (Boston: Reidel/Springer, 1976), 292 (italics added).

If we use words like chiliogon for "blindly" or "symbolical" geometrical argument (*calculatio caeca*), they do not stand for something else (e.g., their meaning) but for themselves. You use them, and do so in an amazingly effective way as long as you refrain from asking yourself what (e.g. meaning) they stand for. They have then become empty *signs*. *I define the word* sign *here as the symbol that stands for itself.* As it is with numbers and letters—3, 7, m, or r—stand for themselves: it makes no sense to ask *what else* 3, 7, m, or r still stand apart from 3, 7, m, or r. for. It might be objected that these letters stand for certain sounds. But compare the different ways in which the letter "a" is pronounced in the English words *bad* and *all*, or in the French *beau*. The individual letter, simply as such, is no guide to its pronunciation. If we see the letter "a" on a piece of paper, it merely says *this is the letter "a."* This explains why Leibniz's *calculatio caeca*—as we find it in arithmetic and in mathematics—is possible with *signs* only. As soon as the sign stands for more than just itself, it ceases to be a sign, calculation with it has become impossible.

The absolutely crucial move Leibniz makes here is the following. He urges us to cut through all the ties between a term (such as "chiliogon"), on the one side, and how we imagine a chiliogon (if we are able to do so) at all, or the meaning we may give to the word or what it may refer to, on the other. His argument is that as soon as we forget this, the "calculatio caeca," conditional for all mathematics, has become impossible. Think, for example, of reference and try to imagine how reference would function in arithmetic. At first sight it may seem that we ought to know what we mean or what we refer to when multiplying numbers. However, suppose we wish to multiply: (1) "the natural number between the natural numbers 34 and 36," and (2) "the natural number between the natural numbers 6 and 8." Obviously, both phrases are referential: (1) refers to the natural number 35 and (2) to the number 7. Observe, now, that the arithmetician cannot calculate the product of (1) and (2); for the simple reason that you can multiply numbers, but not *references*. You can multiply what a reference refers to, but not references themselves. To put not too fine a point on it, the multiplication, addition, or division of references is just sheer nonsense. But the multiplication of the *signs* 35 and 7 is wholly unproblematic—the outcome being the *sign* 245. Arithmetic is about operations with *signs* having neither meaning nor reference. Signs are what they are, and that's the end of it.

So why is that so? The answer is that the signs 35 and 7 are *self-referential*: that is why they do not refer to, nor stand for anything outside themselves. And this it is precisely why the *calculatio caeca* of the multiplication of 35 and 7 is possible at all: for as soon as you start to ponder about what "the meaning" of 35 and 7 might be or where to locate their "reference," you have constructed around 35 and 7 an imaginary world robbing them of their capacity to function any longer in arithmetic as they should. They can only perform their job if being completely "naked," so to speak. Arithmetic is done *blindly*, you do it as if you were a machine (without any memory or associations), simply performing the operations that the signs 35, ×, 7 urge you to perform, and as any other person might perform them, or even a machine.

And now it comes: this has, as we have seen, its counterpart in HRs. In historical representation the representation is the represented; it is, therefore, also true of the text of a historical representation that it stands for itself—no less than that the letter *a* or the number 32 stand for themselves. You may associate a whole lot with a historical text, just as you may associate with the letter *a* the first letter of the name of your first love or with 32 the age you had when receiving your PhD. But as it is with this letter *a* and this number 32, so it is with the historical text: the meanings or references we may give to them never go beyond being mere associations. Historical texts are like the main buildings in the city in which you live. Each inhabitant of your city will have his own associations with them. And each may be happy with those he or she has. But this is wholly irrelevant to those buildings themselves. Nor does it affect their function in your city in any way. However, this does not preclude in the least that some of the associations some of your fellow-citizens will have with these buildings are far more informed and of far more interest than those of some others! And a strictly rational discussion can make clear to all of the city's inhabitants which associations will tell us more about the past and the present of our city than others.

When discussing the resemblance and substitution theories of representation, we found that symbols ordinarily represent or stand for something *other* than themselves. Hence, we could see signs as symbols in which the difference between the representation and the represented has been reduced to zero. Earlier, I used the example of a red spot on a map that stood for Paris, representing or symbolizing that city. The distance between

SIGNS, SEMANTICS, MEANING, AND RELATIONAL STATEMENTS

the representation and the represented remains huge here. But think next of a ship and a model of that ship: the difference is already much smaller. In the case of a painting and the most exact copy that modern science can produce of it, the representation and its represented are almost identical. Ultimately, in the *sign* the representation and its represented become identical. It might, paradoxically, be said that the sign is the *perfect* representation because it perfectly represents its represented. Perfect representation cannot be found in art, but only in mathematics and the natural and human sciences, including the science of history. For all of them, the use of signs is a condition of the possibility of their success.

But we should not conclude from this that the notions of the representation and the represented have become *identical* in the sign. Their *extension* now is the same, but this is not true of their *intension*. We need this *sameness* in extension and this *difference* in intension precisely in order to define the sign as the symbol in which the extension of representation and the represented coincides whereas their intension does not. Put differently, we need the distinction between extension and intension to establish that on the level of extension the representation and the represented coincide, whereas the intension of the notions of representation and of the represented do not. Furthermore, it remains necessary to use the two words—representation and the represented—to locate the notion of the sign within a broader account of representation. Here lies the link between the metaphysics (extension) of representation—discussed in the previous section—and Leibniz's semantics of representation (intension).

Signs alone are not sufficient, however. Signs are also part of a sign system, or an "alphabet," as it is sometimes called. A sign system can be as simple as the numbers 0 and 1 to 9, or the letters of the alphabet itself (as with the letter algebra introduced by François Viète in the sixteenth century). Moreover, the alphabet should allow for "blind reasoning" (Leibniz's *calculatio caeca*) with the help of some appropriate algorithm. For example, if one wishes to multiply two-hundred-sixty-two by thirty-seven in the decimal system having as an alphabet the signs 0 and 1 to 9, one begins by transforming these English words into the sign system in use (which is an art in itself that has to be acquired) by writing down the signs 2, 6, and 2 (in that order) and then 3 and 7 below it. Next one multiplies 2 by 7 giving 14, one writes down 4 and adds 1 to 6 multiplied by 7, resulting in 43. And writes 3 to the left of the 4 we had already. Next, one multiplies 7 and 2 and writes

18 before the 3 mentioned just now. And so on, as we were taught to do at elementary school. We thus reach the number 9,694 by "blind calculation." Indeed, one performs such a calculation blindly, in a machine-like way, almost as if one were not aware of what one is doing.

But the conditions for proceeding in this way are not always satisfied. Think, for example, of Roman numerals such as I, II, IV, IX, LIII, or CXIII. As a sign system it is unexceptional, albeit awkward and complicated. Although addition and subtraction are sometimes still possible, there is no algorithm for multiplication and division in this sign system. However, the introduction of *meaning* in mathematics is far worse than a maladaptation of sign and algorithm, as in the case of Roman numerals. Indeed, the secret of mathematics is the ability to do everything with the signs on the paper in front of you that an algorithm allows you to do, on the condition of *never* thinking about the *meaning* of what you are doing. As soon as meaning enters mathematics, everything is lost because *meaning* is incompatible with signs standing for nothing but themselves. Meaning returns us inexorably to the domain of words standing for something other than themselves, as for example the word *chair* stands for an object of a certain form and structure. Leibniz's *calculatio caeca* has then become impossible. Blind calculation is possible only with meaningless signs; never with letters, words, or generally speaking, with language having a meaning.

This theory of signs and algorithms was one of Leibniz's greatest discoveries. It earned him the honor of being called the father of mathematical and symbolic logic.[16] Sybille Krämer summarized it as follows:

> Operative writings fulfil a double task: they serve as a medium and, at the same time, as an instrument for mental operations. Put metaphorically, with them languages are employed as a technique. It is this double function, to represent and, at the same time, to calculate with what is being represented, in which the intellectual power of calculation has its roots. What makes them into a "symbolic machinery," into a mechanical "amplifier of the

---

16. As Mahnke perceptively observes, the claim follows "ohne weiteres aus der von Leibniz schon anderthalb Jahrhunderte vorausgeahnten Entwicklung der Mathematik im 19. Jahrhundert; die *Metageometrien* und überhaupt alle nur formal-axiomatisch definierten Systems können sich in keiner Anschauung über ihre Gegenstände ausweisen, sind aber doch nicht 'leer', wie man nach Kant annnehemen müsste." Leibniz anticipates "die Grundtendenz der ganzen modernen

intellect" is that the rules of the symbolic operation are not guided by what the symbols mean.[17]

By referring to signs as operative writing, Krämer is emphasizing that the sign is always something we can write down. It has a distinct physical form on paper that cannot be exchanged or confused with other signs.[18] Here the sign does indeed represent, as Krämer writes, but she forgets to add the decisive qualification that it represents *itself*. As we have seen, it is precisely this feature that makes it a sign. This is true of both the numerical signs we use in the decimal system and of algebraic letters. Leibniz's blind calculation always requires something *with which* we can calculate. In the absence of signs providing the algorithms of arithmetic with their input and their numerous counterparts in mathematics, we would have nothing to work with when wishing to perform a certain calculation. We would then be like a bricklayer without bricks.

Wissenschaft, jedes Erfahrungsgebiet in ein streng deduktives 'System' umzuwandeln, dass derart aus dem das System definierenden Axiomen rein logisch-analytisch folgt, dass jede Frage, die nur mit den Begriffen des Systems operiert, aus diesem Zusammenhänge beantwortbar ist." . . . "Leibniz's Ansicht deckt sich in der Tat völlig mit der jetzigen Auffassung Hilberts, der in seinen letzten Schriften. . . eine Neubegründung der ganzen bisherigen Mathematik unternimmt, die an der logischen Methode der Formalisierung und Axiomatisierung festhält, aber doch das anschauliche Operieren mit ausserlogischen, sinnlich gegebenen Zahl-und Formelzeichen zur Führung des Existenzbeweis mit heranzieht." Mahnke, *Leibnizens Synthese*, 201–203.

17. See Sybille Krämer, "Kalküle als Repräsentation. Zur Genese des operativen Symbolismus in der Neuzeit," in *Räume des Wissens: Repräsentation, Codierung, Spur*, ed. H. J. Rheinberger, M. Hagner, and B. Wahring-Schmidt (Hrsgb.) (Berlin: Akaddemie, 1997), 115–16: "Operative Schriften erfüllen eine doppelte Aufgabe: Sie dienen als ein Medium und zugleich als ein Werkzeug geistiger Arbeit. Metaphorisch gesprochen: Mit ihnen werden Sprachen als eine Technik eingesetzt. Es ist also diesen Doppelfunktion, zu repräsentieren un zugleich mit dem, was repräsentiert wird auch zu operieren, worin die intellektuelle Wirkungskracht der Kalküle wurzelt. Was sie zu eine 'symbolische Maschine,' zu einem mechanischen 'Intelligenzverstärker' macht, ist, dass die Regeln der symbolischen Operation keinen Bezug nehmen auf das, was die Symbole jeweils bedeuten." I'd like to thank Jaap den Hollander for alerting me to Krämer's work.

18. There is here a thought-provoking parallel between the notion of the sign and that of information as formalized by Claude Shannon in his seminal paper of 1948 entitled "A Mathematical Theory of Information" and about which Rudolf Landauer coined in 1961 the famous slogan "information is physical." Considering Landauer's slogan it need no longer surprise that information plays an important role in modern cosmology. One may think here of Stephen Hawking's so-called information paradox of black holes. See Thomas Hertog, *On the Origin of Time. Stephen Hawking's final theory* (London: Penguin Random House 2023); 219–21, 230–33. It makes one wonder whether the notion of the sign could be the *trait d'union* or "missing link" between the notion of knowledge and that of information in information theory.

Calculation would then be impossible. But as soon as we have signs and an appropriate algorithm, we can calculate with the signs regardless of what the signs *mean*—where a meaning is understood as something that necessarily differs from what it is the meaning of. To put it more strongly, signs are meaningless. Yet their meaninglessness is not a handicap; rather, it is what guarantees the possibility of achieving correct results of blind calculation. In all operations with signs—as in mathematical equations— meaning and reference are absent.

My claim is that Leibniz's argument enables us to establish both what the use of signs in the *Naturwissenschaften* and the *Geisteswissenschaften* (historical representation) still have in common, and how they move from there into different directions. According to Krämer, in mathematics and the sciences the sign is a unique physical mark on paper that represents itself and that enables algorithmic calculation. Signs are no less indispensable for the historian than they are for the mathematician and the scientist. But there are no algorithms facilitating a *calculatio caeca* with historical signs. This is where mathematics and historical signs differ dramatically and where each of them goes its own way. Nevertheless, signs are no less indispensable for the historians than they are for the mathematician. To make this clear, we must distinguish between two functions of texts expressing HRs: we must distinguish between the text *as such* and the text as the vehicle of historical knowledge.

We have to do this with the text *as text* when saying, for example, that it has a certain title, consists of ten chapters, that sentence number x in the text states s (and where s is no less a mere sign than the text itself *as text*), and so on. *As such* the text is a symbol, albeit an unusually complex one. Moreover, it is a symbol standing for itself, and hence a sign. Insofar as the text represents itself, it is both a representation and what is represented by that representation. The *second* function of the sign manifests itself when we say that, for example, this text does, or does not, contribute to our knowledge of the domain of the historical PBF for reasons a or b; or more specifically, that this HR is "better" than some other.[19]

---

19. The issue of why and when we can say these kinds of things about historical texts is discussed in chapter 5.

SIGNS, SEMANTICS, MEANING, AND RELATIONAL STATEMENTS

Let's begin with the analogies between mathematical and historical uses of signs. First, neither in mathematics nor in historical representation are any changes allowed once the form of the sign has been fixed by means of a self-referentially defined description. Arithmetic would be impossible if one were able to freely exchange the signs 4 or 7 for the signs 5, 8, e (the natural logarithm), or π. Nor is any freedom permitted with regard to the application of algorithms. Suppose an arithmetic calculation were to yield the number 123,456; this number cannot then be exchanged for the numbers 123,455 or 123,457 on the grounds that such a tiny change could not possibly make any real or, to put it more appropriately, any *meaningful* difference. Indeed, the latter may be true if you think of how many dollars you have in your bank account. But in arithmetic such a lackadaisical attitude would lead to contradictions and to an annihilation of the algorithms of arithmetic. The objection that the physical forms of signs can vary, so that (for example) the sign of the number zero can appear on a computer screen as a square rather than a circle, is beside the point. We know that the archetypical sign has the properties of a circle, and if we see a square instead of a circle, we are meant to see a circle.

The same is true with the historical text *as sign*; as soon as any change has been made to it, it is no longer the *same* sign (as D_{ii} makes clear). The objection that in history, as opposed to arithmetic and mathematics, omitting or adding two to three sentences to a historical text will make little or no difference because this leaves the text's *meaning* unaffected, fails straightaway because historical texts, *as signs*, have no meaning.[20] Signs have (physical) properties but no meanings. Observe, furthermore, that Leibniz's D_{cc} requires us to respect the integrity of the historical text *as sign*. The change of even one word in a historical text treated as a sign is tantamount to the exchange of one historical sign for another.

---

20. The objection was put forward in Jouni-Matti Kuukkanen, *Postnarrativist Philosophy of History* (Basingstoke: Palgrave MacMillan, 2015), 77, 79, 80–86. See also, Franklin Rudolf Ankersmit, "A Dialogue with Jouni-Matti Kuukaanen," *Journal of the Philosophy of History* 11, no. 1 (2017): 38–59; and Jouni-Matti Kuukkanen, "Moving Deeper Into Rational Pragmatism: A Reply to My Reviewers," *Journal of the Philosophy of History* 11 (2017): 59–83.

3. REPRESENTATIONAL MEANING

These considerations also compel us to be more precise than we often are about the phrase "the meaning of the text." To begin with, saying that the historical text or an HR has no meaning is not meant to deny that its statements have a meaning. As statements about past states of affairs, they undoubtedly have a meaning. But one cannot add all these meanings together to establish the meaning of the historical text. One cannot add these meanings together like one may add up the amounts on the credit and debit side of a balance sheet. A barrier immediately run up against are all the meta-sentences tying the text's statements together. If the text has n sentences, it has n–1 of these meta-sentences. There are two possibilities. Either one understands these meta-sentences as they must be understood in the context of the text of which they are part—but then we have the historical text all over again—or one decides that they have nothing to add to the meanings of all of the text's object-sentences—but then the text disintegrates into an incoherent chaos of many thousands of isolated individual statements. In sum, there is no plausible matrix for how to move from a historical text's individual statements to the text as a whole. Needless to say, the argument at the end of chapter 2 about the unbridgeable gap between the level of historical research (i.e., the statement) and that of historical writing (i.e., the text) has been repeated here, although from a different perspective.

Because the text *as* text is a sign and, hence, cannot be said to have a meaning, the phrase *the meaning of a text* can only stand for the meanings we *project* onto, or *associate* with, the historical text as sign—as we may tie a horse, a dog, a cart, or whatever to a hook in the wall of a farmhouse or a tavern that is wholly indifferent regarding whatever one decides to tie to that hook. I deliberately say meanings in the plural to highlight one more misleading aspect of the phrase *the meaning of the text*: apart from the mistaken belief that the text has a *meaning* (as distinct from saying it *has* the property of containing a certain statement), we should also reject the belief that there could be *one* meaning for each text (for example, the meaning the historian having written it wanted to attach to the text and that should be the text's readers exclusive object of interest). As it is with numbers, the sign 5 is a symbol standing for itself, hence a sign without a meaning of its own; on the other hand, the compositions of five houses, five trees, or five chairs—attaching the nouns houses, trees, or chairs to the English word corresponding to the 5—*do have* a meaning because they can be part of meaningful sentences or of larger parts of such sentences.

In fact, one could attribute to the text *any* meaning—think, for example, of someone who badly burned his hand when reading text T and who is always reminded of the pain when reading T later in life. Meaning is primarily associative, but that does not entail that meaning is wholly random. Contrary to the opinion of Quine, there is such a thing as analytical meaning: everyone will agree that X is an unmarried man if the statement "X is a bachelor" is true. And we could only say such a thing on the condition that the words *unmarried man* and *bachelor* have exactly *the same meaning*. So the *meaning* of these two words must be something quite specific: a semantic coin uniting word and meaning like a coin's heads and tails, so to speak. One might call this "analytical meaning" or "dictionary meaning" because the dictionary tells us by what other words a word can be replaced, *salva veritate*.

A moment ago I compared meaning to what is attached to a hook in the wall of a tavern. Analytical meaning is, in this metaphor, like a notice above the hook stating "only for horses and carts." Thus one is free to exchange a cart for a horse, or vice versa. But as soon as we move beyond the fixed ground meaning has in words and after it takes to the air, it will go wherever the winds blow it, although this does not mean that we could neither explain nor predict the direction into which it decides to move. Even more so, to a certain extent a speaker or writer may determine the climatological circumstances under which the meanings created will undergo their take-off. But sooner rather than later the moment will come when the person can only acquiesce in the direction it takes. Eighty years after its publication date, what is the meaning of Thomas Mann's masterwork *Doktor Faustus* (1947)?[21] It is beyond any doubt a most sensible and important question, but it is impossible to answer. Each answer to it will, in fact, merely be a new item to be added to the list of the meanings of that great book. Our semantic coins fail us here.

---

21. See note 24 in this chapter for a reference to the book.

Some general comments can be made about these problematic cases, which happen to be the only cases in which the discussion of meaning really makes sense. We do not discuss analytical or dictionary meaning. In literature and historical writing, it is often (correctly) argued that a text's meaning is ordinarily intertextual and codetermined by the meanings attributed to other historical texts in the way suggested by Saussure.[22] These meanings are vague and ill-defined sets of associations floating in the semantic sky. In these cases, we have no dictionaries to define or fix them. The crucial fact here is that meanings, as such, are not communicable; they only become so thanks to the *written signs* to which they are attached. They need the sign as a kind of semantic hatstand to serve the cause of historical representation. Paradoxically, *meaningful* discussion in history is possible only thanks to *meaningless* signs. But again, what is tied to these hooks in the wall is by no means entirely arbitrary.

To see this, recall that HRs always go together with a set of models to be situated in the domain of the historical PBF. HRs are meaningless signs and form together historical reality; outside that reality lies the domain of the PBF, i.e. that of the basically unstable set of meanings that can be associated with each PBF in historical reality.[23] Decoupling text (i.e. an HR) and meaning (i.e. the PBF)—resulting in the 'historical text as sign' and, next, the domain of the PBF in which the PBF of different HRs have a controlled freedom to interact with one another—is one of the main (very Leibnizian) moves in this book. Self-evidently, this move was inspired by Leibniz's radically pulling apart of the domain of the monads and that of the PBF. Two consequences follow.

First, in contrast to what was just said, one might acquiesce in the phrase "that HRs have (a) meaning(s)," but only on the all-important condition

---

22. See Ankersmit, *Meaning, Truth and Reference*, 141–52. There is already a hint of this intertextualism in Leibniz himself: "I agree that in order to judge the concept of an individual substance, it is well to consult the concept I have of myself, just as we must consult the specific concept of a sphere to judge its properties. But there is a great difference between the two, for the concept of myself in particular and every other individual substance is infinitely more inclusive and more difficult to grasp than is a specific concept such as that of a sphere, which is incomplete and does not include all the circumstances necessary practically to arrive at a particular sphere. To understand what this *I* is, it is not enough that I sense myself as a substance that thinks; I must also distinctly conceive that which distinguishes me from all other spirits." Leibniz, *Philosophical Papers*, 334. The statement is also of interest because it is clearly at odds with Leibniz's view that monads can only be defined internally and with his doctrine of the windowlessness of the monads.

23. See chapter 3, section 5.

that "having a meaning" is to be understood here *referentially*. That is, an HR *refers* to a meaning (or meanings) rather than *having* one; being signs, they are meaningless themselves. They will refer to as many meanings as were given to them in the course of time, and like a good parent they will love each meaning as much as any other. But because of their somewhat dispassionate relationship with their children moving from an HR to its children is an indicator in what direction you should move rather than an exposition of what you will find when walking in the direction indicated. For that depends on how the children of an indefinite variety of HRs will interact with each other. And just as in human life, such interactions are hard to predict. The referential function of HRs can, therefore, be never more than this hook tying *meanings* to the *meaningless* wall of the sign.

However, in cases where intertextuality does not interfere with the relation between sign and its meaning, that relation is better explained causally than referentially. Music is a good example here (although even there the referential relation will never be wholly absent). Think, for example, of the score of a Bach cantata (or of the digital information on a CD of that cantata). In both cases we undoubtedly have to deal with *signs*. The score—the music's sign—is just as little arbitrary as is the HR constructed by the historian. Bach invested all of his musical genius in writing it. He knew very well what he wished to achieve with it. Nevertheless, the cantata will mean different things to the director of the orchestra, to the musicians performing it, and to each individual listener in the audience. It is as if the long road from the score as sign to the emergence of meaning has to pass through a filter—which in the case of music is peculiar to each individual person and allowed to be so—to decide what that meaning will be.

A causal conception of the relation between sign and meaning is thus much more plausible than a referentialist one. To use a spatial metaphor: whereas the relation between sign and meaning is vertical in the case of historical representation, it is horizontal in the case of music. In historical representation, the movement is downward from the sign to its models, PBF, and meaning(s). All of these may be kicked in any direction by the mechanisms of intertexuality, but the link with "their" sign will never be lost. Music, on the other hand, is "composed" in the form of a sign. But from there it moves away horizontally in an unpredictable chaos of processes that entangles the music with human feelings of every kind that only permits of a causal analysis. For example, suppose someone is in good spirits and then decides to listen to the aria "Wacht auf, wacht auf, ihr Adern und ihr Glieder" (Bach, Cantata 110); what then is the music's meaning, and what has the listener added to it?

What the music "means," if performed, cannot be defined in terms of its score in the same way that the linguistic meaning of terms or expressions is often defined in terms of the truth-value of sentences in which they occur. There is just one score, whereas the number of meanings that can be attached to it equals the innumerable states and aspects of the human soul. The very endeavor to define linguistic meaning in such a way is based on the assumption that meaning can be determined in terms of something not belonging to the realm of meaning. But this does not work for musical scores. These are mere sheets of paper with little blots and lines of ink on them. To be sure, scores can *causally* generate musical meaning—and are carefully and diligently drawn up to do just this—but they have no meanings themselves.[24]

Finally, one might object that scores *do* have a meaning; we should see them as a complex sets of instructions for musicians for what they should do with their instruments. But this is beside the point. For the instruction for use by the musicians and their greater or lesser talent for following them, the technical properties of their instruments guaranteeing that they will produce a certain sound if touched in a certain way at a certain place, and so on, are mere phases on the long causal trajectory between the score and the meaning of the music. Musical meaning is found only and exclusively at the *end* of that trajectory.

---

24. Western music and composers from the sixteenth century onward have been successful in subjecting their musical will to this so erratic causal process from sign to meaning. Part of the explanation of its success is, perhaps, the system developed in the West for the *notation* of music. That notation allows us to write down every kind of music developed in the West from Hildegard von Bingen to Schönberg. This is only possible thanks to the meaninglessness of the notation itself: the notation is not prejudicial to any kind of music composed in the West. However, the innovations of the twentieth-century musical avant-garde left us with signs only. Avant-garde composers no longer tried to keep control of the trajectory from sign to meaning and regarded precisely this as their triumph in the history of Western music. The same can be said—with some exceptions—of the visual arts in the same period. The process was summarized by Thomas Mann, *Doktor Faustus. Das Leben des deutschen Tonsetzers Adrian Leverkühn, erzählt von einem Freunde* (1947; repr. Frankfurt am Main: Fischer Taschenbuch, 1990), 320. "Das Langweilige ist interessant geworden, weil das Interessante angefangen hat langweilig zu werden" ("the boring has become interesting, because the interesting has become boring"). Just replace "the boring" by "the meaningless" to grasp the point. Is there one sentence with which one could better capture Derrida's writings than this one?

The second consequence is that the meanings to which HRs refer are the models or PBF accompanying an HR. These models and PBF live in a wholly different world than the HRs to which they belong, just as horses and dogs live their lives in a world different from that of the wall and the hook in it—apart from an occasional encounter when they are tied to that hook in the wall. In the world of the HRs nothing ever changes—apart from the fact that the number of "actually realized HRs" continuously increases. To the extent that historical writing progresses, ever more *possible* HRs will be actualized, or awakened from their eternal sleep, by historians. But the world of the models and PBF to which they refer is a far more unruly one. Saussure's differentialist or intertextualist conception of meaning suggests a permanent battle between HRs, in which the HRs themselves remain far from the front, leaving the dirty work to the soldiers on the ground that they command, namely, their models and their historical PBF.[25] If the HRs win the war, it is thanks to the courage and self-sacrificing effort of their soldiers. But HRs themselves never die; they may have been defeated in the battles they fought, we may forget about them, but eternal life has been granted to them. Their models and historical PBF, however, can be wiped completely and forever from the historiographical record. Indeed, historical writing is war—and in chapter 5 I examine the weapons with which it is fought.

The semantic dichotomy between the historical text *as sign* and the *meaning* of the historical text finds support in the fact that some famous historical texts, such as those written by Burckhardt, Huizinga, or Braudel, have been given many different meanings. If signs were to have a unique meaning, if sign and meaning were firmly and inextricably tied together, they would cease to be signs and become words. But words stand for something other than themselves, namely, their meaning. It is true that there *are* signs with only a single meaning. Traffic signs are an obvious example. But their meaning is not the result of a fight between their PBF: they owe it instead to a binding legislative decision. The legislator has decreed that the meaning of a sign with a red and a black car in it means that overtaking is prohibited, and that meaning is not subject to debate as may, incidentally, still be the case with words. This puts the category of signs to which traffic signs belong miles apart from the issue of meaning and historical representation.

---

25. For a further elaboration of the application of Saussure's intertextualism to historical representation, see Ankersmit, *Meaning, Truth and Reference*, 141, 142.

Nevertheless, this might be moving too quickly. A moment ago I spoke of the permanent war between HRs and the weapons used in it. One of these weapons undoubtedly is the coherence of an HR's text. This issue is discussed more fully in chapter 5, but at this stage, a few comments are appropriate. Think of a (relatively) incoherent HR. Obviously, the models and PBF of this HR will find themselves in a relatively weak position with regard to HRs whose beginning is also already an anticipation of its end and whose end a reminder of the beginning—what Louis O. Mink once so aptly characterized as the criterion for what must be seen as the best historical narrative.[26] In contrast to the former, the latter forms a relatively strong unity, and this will emphasize its being an entity not to be overlooked so easily in the fastidious representationalist universe.

From a logical point of view, each individual HR is assured of being part of that universe—and in this way little is required of it. Yet ordinarily their individuality is difficult to recognize because their presence remains submerged in a host of other similarly inarticulate HRs. In English we say someone "can't see the forest for the trees," meaning they have lost sight of the overall picture and become lost in the details. But it is equally true that the trees can lose their individuality if seen from a distance. The notion of individuality is carried over from the individual trees to the wood as a whole. Or, to use Leibniz's own example, the sound of an individual wave breaking on the beach loses its individuality in the sound of the surf if heard from a certain distance. But the individual wave nonetheless makes a sound of its own. So it is with HRs: they only exist on the condition of having a unity that clearly separates them from other HRs. As Cusanus said: *coincidit itaque maximitati unitas, quae est entitas* (the more unity there is, the more being there will be). The Scholastics put it more succinctly: *unitas est entitas*.[27]

---

26. "Action and events, although presented as occurring in the order of time, can be surveyed as it were in a single glance as bound together in an order to significance, a representation of a *totum simul*.... The end is connected with the promise of the beginning as well as the beginning with the promise of the end, and the necessity of the backward reference cancels out, so to speak, the contingency of the forward references. To comprehend temporal succession means to think of it in both directions at once, and then time is no longer the river which bears us along but the river in aerial view, upstream and downstream in a single survey." Louis O. Mink, *Historical Understanding*, ed. Brian Fay, Eugene O. Golob, and Richard T. Vann (Ithaca, NY: Cornell University Press, 1987), 57.

27. Note the comparatives in Cusanus's claim. We return to the role of comparison in historical debate in chapter 5, section 4.

There is a lesson here applicable to the relationship between HRs and their models and PBF. Recall John Stuart Mill's argument as to why 3 + 2 = 5. Mill's theory suggested a relationship between models and our world according to which the model will always work, regardless of what we apply it to—apples, molecules, or airplanes. Of each type of x, it is true that if we have three of them, and if two of that same type are added, we will end up having five of them. Models of this type can hardly be improved upon. But ordinarily the domains to which a model can be applied are much more restricted. That the very structure of some scientific theory permits it to be applied at first sight to wholly unrelated natural phenomena is an expectation or hope that is by no means always, or even frequently, realized. By analogy, HRs whose models remain closer to the 3 + 2 = 5 type must possess in their PBF and their models a (relatively) powerful instrument for ensuring their hold on the domain of the PBF. This can be translated into a desideratum for the expression of HRs in historical texts: an HR keeping close control of its PBF and models is to be preferred to another HR whose PBF and models are quick to fall under the spell of HRs that are its rivals. Such HRs are like molluscs in the animal world that are easily ripped apart.

The historical text consists of words and statements. Words and statements have meanings. Most Anglo-Saxon philosophy addressed the problem of the meaning of words and statements. From the perspective of historical representation, these words and statements must be regarded as being a pure given that is not in need of closer investigation—at least not from the perspective of historical representation. However, the historian's concern is not the *meaning of words and statements* but their *selection*. The philosopher of historical representation only comes into action after issues of the meaning of statements have been settled and the question arises of which statements should be selected for an HR whose PBF and models have the solidity of a reinforced concrete block. Obviously, this is one more reason the doctrine of the "theory-ladenness of empirical fact" is useless if HRs are at stake. In HRs, semantic coloring is always work in progress, whereas in statements the results of semantic coloring can ordinarily be taken for granted. Nevertheless, one may discern a place where the metaphysics of the strong and the weak individual come infinitesimally close to each other. The historian wishing to give the HR the best cards in its struggle with others must ensure that the models and PBF of the HR are best equipped in their struggle with those of others. Obviously, this has consequences for the historian's text *as* text. It requires that the historical text be as closely knit and to have as few loose ends as possible. More concretely, assuming that the historian wishes to defend a historical thesis with the HR (and its PBF and models), the text should be organized in a way that gives readers the impression that all the statements of the HRs can be derived from, or be related to, this thesis as if this were a matter of simple deduction. To put it metaphorically, the historian must work from the bottom up when building this thesis, whereas the finished work of history will be read from the top down. Readers will treat the HR's individual statements as seeming to follow directly from the overall thesis.

Achieving this effect must be the historian's goal when selecting the words and statements for the text—and, again, in this selection procedure the *meaning* of these words and statements is a given. Their meanings are semantic coins, so to speak. The historian will therefore closely scrutinize at all times what effect the metaphysics of weak individuals has on the meaning of the words and statements in the text to bolster as much as possible the strong individual of the HR. Here we may discern the demarcation line between the metaphysics of the weak and that of the strong individual. But we must never forget, *if* the historian has selected a certain word or statement for inclusion in the HR because of its meaning, this leaves the meaning wholly unaltered. Again, the doctrine of the theory-ladenness of empirical fact can never be transposed to the domain of historical representation.

With regard to an HR *as text*, it is as if all of its words and statements are like the building material, the bricks, the cement, the beams, and so on needed for the construction of a building. The building presents itself as a united whole, and all of its parts make their own indispensable contribution. In keeping with Leibniz's demand for maximum unity in maximum diversity, the more *diverse* the materials used for achieving a unified whole, the better it is. So the best HR should resemble the staircase Balthasar Neumann designed for Schloss Augustusburg at the commission of Clemens August, Prince-Archbishop of Cologne, where the immense variety of forms between the staircase's overall structure and its tiniest details are in a subtle and supreme balance, rather than those bare and chilly houses consisting of straight lines and corners only that Le Corbusier so admired. Houses, that he ominously described as *"des machines à vivre,"* thus revealing the fascism of his architectural aims and ideals.[28] If these goals are achieved in the HR's text, the HR in question will be able to transmit its own *unity in diversity*, together with its suggestion that all of the text's words and statements derive from a central idea, namely, that of an HR's models and PBF. Then its author can confidently send this HR into combat with the rival HRs awaiting it on the battlefield of historical debate. In sum, the idea that HRs should aspire to *become* like traffic signs, in the sense of being as tightly connected to their meanings as traffic signs are, is not such a bad one after all.

We may assert that there is a continuing interaction between different HRs, even though this is an interaction in which the HRs themselves are not involved. They delegate that interaction to their models and PBF and can then only wait to discover what representational meanings will, in the end, be attached to them (as signs). Next, the outcomes of these interactions will decide the strength of the tie between the HR as sign and its models and PBF. In the case of a successful HR, that tie will remain strong. But in the case of an HR that has been more or less wiped out, it will wear desperately thin. Nevertheless, however tenuous the connection between an HR and its PBF or models may have become thanks to a defeat in battle, and however wildly an HR's meaning may change in the course of these battles, the tie between them will never be entirely cut. Even if all an HR's PBF and models have been completely overrun by those of other HRs, it will be possible to identify in the domain of the PBF and models the place that particular HR's PBF and models formerly occupied. Identifying that place is the task of the discipline of historiography, the history of historical writing. The fact that this discipline exists, and that its results are respected, proves that even in the case of wholly forgotten HRs, the tie with its PBF and models is never wholly severed. Historians know that everything has

---

28. Le Corbusier's fascism—as documented by Xavier de Jarcy and Francois Chaslin—need not surprise. For Augustusburg, see Wilfried Hansmann, *Schloss Augustusburg in Brühl* (Worms: Wernersche Verlagsanstalt, 2002). See also H. Hubert Krins, *Barock in Süddeutschland. Mit Fotografen von Joachim Feist* (Stuttgart: Konrad Theiss, 2001); above all see Schloss Ludwigsburg, Schloss Solitude near Stuttgart, Wallfahrtskirche Wies, Wallfahrtskirche Vierzehnheiligen, Schloss Pommersfelden, and the Kaisersaal of the Residenz in Würzburg. I have always found its surprising that you will find neither in France nor in England many castles or churches that can compete with these architectural masterpieces of the German baroque and rococo. However, something similar could be said about the music and the philosophy of that time. The shift from Neumann to Le Corbusier is a perfect illustration of Thomas Mann's "the boring has become interesting, because the interesting has become boring" quoted in note 24.

its history and that this must be true of their own discipline as well, as Gadamer powerfully argued.

We could, therefore, attribute to a historical text *as text* a fixed and unchanging meaning only in the strictly hypothetical limiting case that *all possible* HRs have been written. If the writing of history were ever to reach that ideal condition, a dramatic insubordination of the PBF with regard to their respective HRs would take place: the PBF would then take the revolutionary step of dropping the P off the PBF and declaring *themselves* to no longer be mere phenomena but to have become *past reality*. Historical debate would then have come to an end. The HRs existing in that final apocalyptic stage of the history of historical writing could pride themselves on presenting the final historical truth about *past reality*. Indeed, representational or historical reality and past reality would have coalesced—and the phrase *past reality* would no longer be the oxymoron it is now.

Historians would have completed for historical reality the task that Leibniz had assigned to God in his system. As long as this stage has not been achieved, however (and it never will be, if only because there never will be complete certainty about the future), historians will have to rely on historical rationality in their never ending efforts to approximate this perfect God-like grasp of historical reality as well as possible.[29] Each new HR has, therefore, a *double* value: it makes its own contribution to the growth of our knowledge of the past, and it also adds to the number of HRs we have of historical reality. It is, as such, one more step in the direction of achieving "a full historical universe"—in the sense that all possible HRs have been realized—and, hence, on the infinitely long and never ending road to the actual realization of a fusion of past and present. That fusion is achieved if the meanings associated with HRs are no less fixed than those of the words defined by our dictionaries. We then speak about the past as if it were the present and vice versa. If this is what historical writing aims at, it is undoubtedly true that the more historical HRs we have, the better it is. That is, the endless proliferation of HRs permanently reminds us of the metaphysical abyss between "the past" and "historical reality."

There is, therefore, one final welcome aspect to an infinite proliferation of HRs within historical reality. As long as there are fairly few HRs on a

---

29. And, hence, also about the HRs to be developed in the future.

given topic and they remain relatively remote from each other, they will live their life in a relative isolation. Their meanings (i.e., models) must remain vague and diffuse. No one can say with any degree of certainty or precision what the meaning of an HR is. Their meanings are no clearer than Leibniz's notion of a chiliogon. We may know all the facts about the past that could possibly be known—as is the case with Danto's "Ideal Chronicler"—but as long as there is no historical writing resulting in HRs, no knowledge of historical reality is possible.[30] This can only change for the better with the arrival of a wealth of HRs differing from each other as much as possible; the desiderata in historical writing of certainty and precision can then be approximated ever more closely. The paradox is that we have, on the one hand, a never ending and merciless battle of the HRs, and on the other hand, they need each other for their very existence. This also may explain why the phrase *historical writing* is so appropriate; the historian needs the writing of meaningless signs to find out about the meaning of history. As one cannot multiply two-hundred-sixty-two by thirty-seven without writing down signs on a piece of paper, so historical writing is conditional on the possibility of historical knowledge.

This brings us once again to the common ground shared by mathematics (and the sciences) and historical writing. In both cases, everything begins with the sign. Just as mathematical models relate mathematics to physical reality, historical models relate HRs to their PBF and models. But from there both move in different directions. The notion of meaning is our clue here: mathematics can only thrive as long as it excludes meaning. Signs and algorithms are all the mathematician needs; even the smallest dose of meaning added to this minimalist instrumentarium will poison it. But discussions of meaning are the historian's avenue to historical knowledge.

---

30. The same view was defended by Michael Oakeshott. Luke O'Sullivan summarizes the relevant part of his historical thought as follows: "this notion of historical understanding is reminiscent of the Hegelian owl of Minerva: it is precisely because historical theorizing is exclusively retrospective and non-participatory that it can assemble an understanding of a past event which transcends the standpoint of anyone who figured in it. Historical thought is not subject to the spatio-temporal limitations of the particular actor, but the price that we pay for the wisdom of this kind of hindsight is an appreciation of the past that is inherently inapplicable to our own practical ends." See Luke O'Sullivan, "Worlds of Experience: History," in *The Cambridge Companion to Oakeshott*, ed. Efraim Podoksik (Cambridge: Cambridge University Press, 2012): 42–64, see especially 51.

Nevertheless, there is a parallelism beyond this. Mathematics knows signs such as the number π; √, sin, cos, logarithms in general, and the natural (Euler) logarithm e in special; the infinite ∞ as the sign for the infinite (i.e., not its meaning [!]); the imaginary number √ − 1, and so on. The history of mathematics can be written in terms of the development of these signs. To mention the most obvious example, the introduction of the signs dy/dx and ∫(fx) marked the greatest leap forward in all of the history of mathematics; and without them the world in which we live would have been completely different from what it looks like today. The introduction of these signs (and the science and technology made possible by them) has, arguably, been the greatest revolution in all of the history of *homo sapiens*. Although the differences outweigh the similarities, the same could be said of the historian's signs. For the discovery of the historical sign—incidentally not much later than the discovery of the calculus, as we saw in the previous chapter—was conditional on the possibility of historical knowledge (to put it in Kantian phraseology). Only after that discovery was the continuous interaction between the models and PBF of HRs set into motion, and only then did the growth of historical knowledge became a possibility. Whether this revolution in the writing of history changed the course of recent human history less or more than the revolutionary discovery of calculus, I leave to the reader to decide. For the time being, suffice it to state that in both cases the revolution lay in the discovery of the *sign*. In brief, the birth of historicism was for the writing of history what the discovery of the calculus was for mathematics. And with the twin of these two revolutionary discoveries, the dark abyss opened up into which humankind will disappear in a foreseeable future.[31] We have become so advanced that advance provoked the end of mankind.

4. MONADS AND RELATIONAL STATEMENTS: THE INTERNALIST APPROACH

Leibniz's monadological universe consists of monads. These monads consist, in their turn, of statements attributing properties to them. The following two things can be said about these statements. First, each of them

---

31. This is the story to be told in my forthcoming book, Franklin Rudolf Ankersmit, *Peter Munz's Evolutionist Philosophy of History and the Anthropocene*.

expresses a property of the monads that is true of that monad, and only true of that monad, because each of them has that monad as its subject-term. Second, all of these statements together (regardless of whether there is only one or an infinity of them) individuate that monad in the sense of fixing its nature: the monad *is* that total set.[32]

There are also relational statements: i.e., statements expressing a certain relationship between two different things. Examples are "Peter is older than John," "this piece of rope is longer than that one," or "a Bentley is more expensive than a Toyota." As is clear from these examples, relational statements differ in form from the only type of statement we can find in the Leibnizian universe: statements having the form of a subject-term to which a certain property is attributed (as in "monad M contains [i.e., is] sentence s"). Relational statements have no subject-term—or two, if you prefer to see it that way. The problem is whether it is possible to move from Leibniz's type of statements to relational statements, and vice versa; and if so, how.

Even a child, on being told that "Peter is forty years old" and "John is twenty years old," is capable of inferring from this the relational statement that "Peter is older than John." We might be inclined to see no problem here, but, alas, the Leibnizian universe itself takes a far less relaxed view. It proves to be disappointingly inhospitable toward relational statements. It will complain that it has no idea of what these relational statements might mean and that they are in what it considers to be a foreign language. It demands that we translate these statements into its own language, which consists exclusively of sentences in subject/predicate form. However, satisfying this demand is far from easy. It may even be impossible.

---

32. We should distinguish between internal and external relations: the former are relations between the components of one and the same thing, the latter are relations between (the components of) two or more different things. The former do not occasion serious problems for Leibniz's system. Think, for example, of the following statement expressing an internal relationship: "'s_1 (temporally) precedes s_2' in the monad M" where s_1 and s_2 are two properties attributed to M in the year x. This statement can then be translated into "'M is s_1' for a perception of M in May" and "'M is s_2' for a perception of M in September." The relational statement has been replaced by two statements of the desired subject/predicate form, both having M as their subject-term. This section therefore deals exclusively with external relations that resist easy reduction to subject/predicate statements.

SIGNS, SEMANTICS, MEANING, AND RELATIONAL STATEMENTS

In fact, Leibniz had recognized the problem himself as his correspondence with Clarke indicates.[33] Leibniz invited Clarke to think of two lines (L and M), L being the longer and M the shorter one. The ratio or proportion between L and M can then be described by a statement informing us about the ratio of their respective lengths having either L or M as its subject-term. But there is a third possibility, namely, a statement merely expressing the ratio (i.e., the relation) of the lengths of L and M.[34] Leibniz goes on to say:

> But which of them will be the subject in the third way of considering them? It cannot be said that both of them, L and M together, are the subject of such an accident; for, if so, we should have an accident in two subjects, with one leg in one and the other in the other, which is contrary to the notion of accidents. Therefore we must say that this relation, in this third way of considering it, is indeed out of the subjects; but being neither a substance nor an accident, it must be a mere ideal thing, the consideration of which is never useful.[35]

Although Leibniz was aware of the problem, he was never much interested in it. It is not easy to explain why. Perhaps his extreme nominalism made him believe (with the Scholastics) that relational statements were merely constructions of the human mind, just like universals, and therefore devoid of interest (that is, they did not reflect any essential metaphysical or logical truths). This interpretation is suggested by another passage in Leibniz's writings in which he discussed the relation of "being the father of" or "of being the son." One cannot be a father without there being someone who

---

33. Samuel Clarke (1675–1729) defended Newton against Leibniz in the struggle over which of them had been first to formulate the calculus. Today the consensus is that both invented it independently between 1674 and 1684. It is often said that Leibniz's contribution to the calculus was much more influential than Newton's because of Leibniz's careful attention to his notation. Leibniz published his discovery of the calculus in an article titled "Nova Methodus pro Maximis et Minimis," *Acta Eruditorum* (October 1684): 467–73. The full title if translated into English is as follows: "A new method for maxima and minima, and for tangents, that is not hindered by fractional and irrational quantities, and a similar kind of calculus for the above mentioned." It is from this title that this branch of mathematics takes the name "calculus." In 1695 the marquis de l'Hôpital pulled Leibniz's and Newton's formulations together into the calculus as it is known today.

34. This possibility involves a loss of information by remaining silent about which of the two lines is longer. It is not immediately clear how this loss of information can be avoided without the use of statements having L or M as their subject-terms.

35. Leibniz, *Philosophical Papers*, 704. Russell recognized the importance of the passage. See Bertrand Russell, *A Critical Exposition of the Philosophy of Leibniz* (London: Allen and Unwin, 1967), 13.

is that person's son, and vice versa, so these two phrases express a relationship. When discussing this example in his correspondence with Des Bosses, Leibniz states there could not possibly be accidents that are in two subjects at one and the same time—which is typically the case with relational statements:

> I do not believe that you will admit an accident that is in two subjects at the same time. My judgment about relations is that paternity in David is one thing, son-ship in Solomon another, but that the relation common to both is a merely mental thing whose basis is the modification of the individual.[36]

In this case, one could possibly still go along with Leibniz. Why could one not attribute to David the property of paternity, or that of Kingship, without having to state that he was the father of Solomon or the King of Israel? The two accidents of being a father and of being a king remain safely contained in the complete notion of David, but without implying a corresponding accident in Solomon or Israel.[37] As you shall see, however, unlike the case of relations such as being longer or shorter than, and so on, the problems raised by these kinds of relational statements cannot be so easily circumvented.

Leibniz's disinterest was unlikely to have been feigned because he was always open to serious criticisms of his thought. Precisely this fact makes his lack of interest in the problem all the more surprising. Leibniz was one of the most brilliant physicists of his time. He knew better than almost anyone at the end of the seventeenth century that the physicist's knowledge of nature is not expressed in terms of statements about the properties of things but in terms of mathematical equations stating the *relationship* between the variables on either side of the "=" sign.[38] The physicist's theories are the

---

36. Leibniz, *Philosophical Papers*, 609.
37. For a discussion of this example, see L. B. McCullough, *Leibniz on Individuals and Individuation: The Persistence of Premodern Ideas in Modern Philosophy* (Dordrecht: Kluwer, 1996), 173ff.
38. See Ernst Cassirer, *Substanzbegriff und Funktionsbegriff. Untersuchungen über die Grundfragen der Erkenntniskritik* (Darmstadt: Wissenschaftliche Buchgesellschaft, 1994), 27: "Die Logik des Gattungsbegriff, die, wie wir sahen, unter dem Gesichtspunkt und des Substanzbegriffs steht, tritt jetzt die Logik des mathematischen Funktionsbegriff gegenüber. Das Anwendungsgebiet dieser Form der Logik aber kann nicht im Gebiet der Mathematik allein gesucht werden. Vielmehr greift hier das Problem sogleich auf auf das Gebiet der Naturerkenntnis über: denn der Funktionsbegriff erhält in sich zugleich das allgemeine Schema und das Vorbild, nach welchem der moderne Naturbegriff in seiner fortschreitenden geschichtlichen Entwicklung sich gestaltet hat."

paradigmatic example of our knowledge of the domain of the PBF, so one would have expected Leibniz to realize that the best way to overcome the main weakness of his system—i.e., his failure to account for how the monadological universe and the domain of the PBF hang together—would be to show how to translate statements about monads into relational statements.

To deal with the problem of relational statements, let us write *a* has a relation to *b* as (1) *aRb*, where R stands for relations such as longer than, older than, higher than, and so on. Then our question is whether *aRb* can be transformed into the two nonrelational statements (2) *a* is *x* and (3) *b* is *y*, where *x* and *y* are properties attributed to *a* and *b* individually. This question cannot be answered straightaway, however. To begin with, relations between a and b always concern a specific property—such as length, color, or weight—that is shared by a and b. A first problem is that the transformation of (1) into (2) and (3) requires further knowledge about a and b. Supposing that a and b are compared with regard to length, the transition from (1) to (2) and (3) is possible only on the condition that more is known about the actual length of a and b. At this stage we might be tempted to believe that it would be enough to know that a is longer than b—or vice versa. But we would then presuppose having knowledge already of the kind of knowledge we wish to explain—namely, what we mean by saying that *aRb* (where R stands for the relationship of being longer [or shorter] than). Suppose that we know the length of a and b: a is half a meter and b one meter and half. In this case, the transition from (1) to (2) and (3) seems warranted. Indeed: the statement (1) → [(2) & (3)] is then undoubtedly true.

However, *meaning* not *truth* is the problem here. For the meanings of (1) and [(2) & (3)] are different: (1) expresses a relationship between two lengths, whereas [(2) & (3)] merely states the length of a and b without pronouncing how these lengths relate to each other. Moreover, one can meaningfully say that a is longer then b without having any knowledge of a's and b's actual length (i.e., any knowledge going beyond the mere knowledge that a is longer than b). Apparently, translating relational statements into strictly nonrelational statements (or vice versa) really is a big problem. Again, more generally, one may wonder whether such translations are possible at all. The upshot is that relational statements may occasion unexpected problems making us stumble where, at first sight, the going seemed easy and without any serious hindrances.

Let us now return to Leibniz. Leibniz's problem with relational statements can be approached from an externalist or an internalist perspective. The externalist approach demands us to regard substances or monads as a whole. Within the internalist approach, the focus is on the components of a monad making it into the monad that it is. The Leibnizian system seems to leave little or no room for the externalist approach because it requires one to take a position outside the monadological universe. Within Leibniz's conception of the monadological universe, it is difficult to find a place for such an "outside." God's point of view, perhaps? The monadological universe is all there is. However, as we shall find in the next section, this need not be the last word on this issue. It will become clear that there is room for the externalist approach after all, and even more so, that we must adopt it when moving from Leibniz's substances or monads to question whether relational statements about HRs are possible.

Following the internalist approach for Leibniz's system, we will find that the problem of relational statements affects the Leibnizian system more deeply than we might have surmised—or than Leibniz had realized himself. We saw that his system, by its very nature—and in particular thanks to the doctrine of the windowlessness of the monads (D_{wm})—leaves no room for relational statements. There is no bridge between monads for relational statements to sit on, to put it metaphorically. Or no tube between two vessels making them into communicating vessels, in case you prefer that metaphor.

But perhaps I am moving too fast here. For Leibniz, recall that each individual monad *perceives* all of the others and that each of them consists *exclusively* of all the *perceptions* that it has of all the others. One might then ask: Does not perception create a *relationship* in the proper sense of that word between the perceiving monad and the one that is perceived? If so, the problem in question would take on truly alarming proportions because the Leibnizian system leaves no room at all for relational statements. However, if a positive answer must be given to the question asked just now, they are as numerous in it as the perceptions that monads have of each other. Obviously, this is a problem requiring closer scrutiny.

This dilemma is occasioned by Leibniz's claim that the monads *perceive* each other—a claim that is absolutely central to his system. To deal with it, I begin with a general comment on relational statements and apply it to the role of perception in the Leibnizian system. To begin, note that two levels can be discerned in all relational statements. At the first level, there is a reciprocity in *all* relational statements that seems to be the heart of them. Consider the relational statement (1) "A is older than B." In that case, there is reciprocity in the sense that if A is older than B then (2) "B is younger than A." But reciprocity *follows* from relationality, and the possibility that the claim of relationality goes beyond that of mere reciprocity exists (in fact, this actually is the case). Next, in this example, there is reciprocity with regard to *age*. And so it is with perception: if a perceives b, b is perceived by a. Clearly, reciprocity is what all relational statements have in common; they may do more than expressing mere reciprocity (and, again, they do), but the latter indisputably is an indelible part of the very meaning of relationality.

Focusing on reciprocity may help us decide whether perception threatens to upset the integrity of the Leibnizian system and, if so, to locate the exact place where it does so. Specifically, we should consider the possibility (1) that reciprocity is all that the Leibnizian system needs and (2) that reciprocity must be distinguished from what is expressed by relational statements, so (3) the dangers for the Leibnizian system embodied by relational statements can be staved off by demonstrating that the relational statements the system *seems* to invite are, in fact, innocuous statements about reciprocity. In that case, we would have the best of both worlds: the Leibnizian system as it is *and* relational statements in the innocuous attire of reciprocity.

To distinguish the relation of reciprocity from relation in the proper sense of that word, I propose to attach the sign r (the "r" of reciprocity) to R; hence, "Rr" stands for this relationship of reciprocity. Let us agree, furthermore, that reciprocity is always reciprocity with regard to some specific property that things may have, such as age, price, weight, perception, and so on. The sign Rr is therefore in need of a qualification with regard to what property a and b are related; for example, Rr_a concerns age, Rr_p price, Rr_w weight, and so on. So (1) and (2) can now both be rewritten as aRr_ab (3) and bRr_aa (4), where "$_a$" stands for reciprocity with regard to age. If we are content to state that a and b are related with regard to age, we can acquiesce in (3) and (4) having in common the argument Rr_a. But if we also wish to account for the fact that a is older than b and that b is younger than a (as is the case in the relational statement "a is older than b"), we should appeal to the two descriptivist (i.e. nonrelational) denominations accompanying the category of age: (a) "old," as in the description "person P is old," and (b) "young," as in the description "person P is young."

In agreement with this (3) and (4) can be rewritten as $aRr_{a(o)}b$ and $bRr_{a(y)}a$, where "$(_o)$" stands for "being old" and "$(_y)$" for "being young," and where "$_{(o)}$" and "$_{(y)}$" indicate how a and b must be located with regard to each other on the spectrum between being old and being young. A similar story could be told for the property of price moving between the nonrelational properties of "being expensive" and that of "being cheap," or with regard to the property of weight moving between the property of "being heavy" and that of "being light." This will give us, respectively, the relational statement of $aRr_{p(e)}b$ and $bRr_{p(c)}a$ where "$_p$" stands for price, "$_{(e)}$" for "being expensive" and "$_{(c)}$" for "being cheap," and the relational statement $aRr_{w(h)}b$ and $bRr_{(w(l))}a$. where "$_w$" stands for weight, "$_{(h)}$" for "being heavy," and "$_{(l)}$" for "being light."

Let us now apply all this to the perceptions that Leibniz's monads have of each other. Suppose monad M_1 perceives monad M_2. This gives us the following relational statement: $M_1Rr_pM_2$ (1) stating that M_1 and M_2 are related to each other with regard to the property of perception, expressed as "$_p$". Distinguishing between "perceiving" expressed as $(_{pe})$ and "being perceived" gives us $M_1Rr_{p(pe)}M_2$ (2) and $M_2Rr_{p(bp)}M_1$ (3), where R stands for the relation of reciprocity, Rr for the relation of reciprocity, "$_p$" for perception, "$_{pe}$" for perceiving, and "$_{bp}$" for being perceived. Okay.

But this is not yet all. Up till now we left out a crucial aspect of Leibniz's notion of perception and representation. In our pedestrian world, you may perceive me *while I do not perceive you*. But this is different with Leibniz's monads: if monad M_1 perceives monad M_2, monad M_2 perceives monad M_1 *as well*. Being perceived by M_1 is only half of it. We must read the Leibnizian *"esse est percipere et percipi"* in two directions, so to speak. Hence this *extra* dimension of the reciprocity of perception in Leibniz. Because of the relationship of reciprocity, each statement about a substance's or a monad's perceptions also entails a statement about the perceived substance or monad to the effect that it perceives the perceiving monad. But even this extra dimension can easily be accounted for in terms of Rr by simply adding to (2) and (3) the two relations $M_1Rr_{p(bp)}M_2$ (4) and $M_2Rr_{p(pe)}M_1$ (5).

The four relational statements, (2), (3), (4), and (5), if taken together, express how Leibniz understands representation. Reciprocity endows each substance or monad with the quality of essentially being a mirror of what happens in all of the others. Representation is, basically, perception. It is reciprocal in the sense of mirroring and of being mirrored: "*esse est percipere et percipi.*" I'd like to remind the reader of my argument in section 2 of this chapter about the (extensionalist) identity of the representation and the represented. All substances and monads are mirror images of each other to the extent that a monad's self-knowledge is also knowledge of other monads, and vice versa: "*esse est percipere et percipi.*" Self-evidently, what is true of the argument of perception also holds for arguments about seeing, hearing, smelling, liking, hating, loving, writing, describing, or whatever you have. All of these verbs denote mere qualifications of perception.

We must conclude that we did not come across any signs of there being anywhere a decisive asymmetry between R and Rr: all that can be said in terms of the former can be said in terms of the latter as well. Apparently, there are no insurmountable obstacles for the translation of statements about the reciprocity of the perceptions of monads into purely relational statements. If perception is at stake (the property that is so much all-pervasive in the Leibnizian system), there is no difference at all between aR_pb and bR_pb, on the one hand, and aRr_pa and bRr_pa, on the other. No threshold—suggestive of entering some new domain—will be overstepped in the transition of one to the other.

Because Rr is all that the Leibnizian system needs, I had hoped to stave off the problems for that system as occasioned by relational statements by demonstrating that Rr must be distinguished from R in the proper sense of the word. But, alas, that hope has proven to be idle. If R upsets the Leibnizian system, Rr does so as well.[39]

On the one hand, this is a most welcome outcome because it leaves the door of the monadological universe wide open for scientific knowledge, which is typically expressed by mathematical equations stating what relations obtain between different variables. But on the other hand, not only Leibniz himself but all of his commentators (as far as I know) unanimously denied that Leibniz's monadological universe should allow

---

39. Matters are even worse because this relational equivalence of perception with being perceived is already manifest at the level of the individual monads of HR *themselves*: "so it is well to make a distinction between perception, and *apperception*, which is consciousness or the reflective knowledge of this inner state itself and which is not given to all souls or to any soul all the time." Leibniz, *Philosophical Papers*, 637.

relational statements. Indeed, the Leibnizian doctrine of the windowlessness of the monads epitomizes it all. So Leibniz—and we—are in trouble. One may choose for relationality giving us science, but then the Leibnizian system must be completely reorganized—probably so completely that nothing will be left of it. Or one may succeed in somehow digging a deep abyss between R and Rr, but then science will have to go first. Even then, one may wonder what other havoc Rr may create in the Leibnizian system because of its all too obvious affinity with R. Worst of all, the problem does not announce itself in some isolated and hidden corner of the Leibnizian system, *it is literally all over the place*.[40]

A solution to this contradiction might be to allow monads and HRs to swallow all those other monads and HRs to which they are tied by means of relational statements lock, stock, and barrel. In that way, what the relational statements express could be subsumed within one monad while, at the same time, the content of all these other monads or HRs will have to be predicated on the subject-term of the HR that is swallowing all of the others. Once this process has begun, however, there can be no end to it short of the production of just one monad or HR for the whole universe.[41] However, this idea of a monad or HR swallowing up all the others presupposes that monads or HRs can be predicated on each other, but this is not possible, as the Scholastics emphasized. They pointed out most cogently that substances or individuals cannot be predicated on each other with one exception, namely, when a substance or an individual is predicated on itself. Think of the statement "x is S," where S is a substance in the predicate position; then x can be true if x = S. So even the radicalism of this proposal does not bring us closer to a solution of the problem.

But now it comes. Much to our relief we find that there is a way out of this profoundly worrying dilemma. In contrast to what was argued a moment ago, it can be shown that R and Rr are quite different beasts after all.

---

40. This response invites a perverse reading of Leibniz's system as, in fact, the descriptive metaphysics of a world only containing individuals that, in stark opposition to the author's intentions, have lost *all* content, so that no true statements about them are possible. All we have are the *name*s of individuals *and* relational statements stating how these individuals relate to each other. The names of individuals have no other function than that of providing the hooks for the relational statements.

41. Several of Leibniz's commentators—Russell among them—have argued that if Leibniz's postulate of an infinity of substances or monads were exchanged for only *one* substance or monad comprising the entire universe, the system would gain significantly in plausibility.

To begin with, it is undoubtedly true that relational statements are reciprocal: "if L_1 is longer than L_2," then "L_2 is shorter than L_1." But this is a reciprocity of a different kind than we encounter in Leibniz. For L_1 will be longer to an infinity of other things, say, $L_1 \ldots L_{\infty s\,(1)}$; similarly L_2 will be shorter than another infinite set of things, say, $L_2 \ldots L_{\infty 2}$. Put differently, not just L_1 but an infinity of things are longer than L_2, and there is also an infinity of things that are shorter than L_2. Hence, in the relations ". . . being longer than" or ". . . being shorter than . . .," an infinity of lengths can replace the dots, *salve veritate*. Now, this is essentially different with the kind of reciprocity Leibniz had in mind. Consider the four *seemingly* relational statements $M_1 Rr_{p(pe)} M_2$ (1), $M_2 Rr_{p(bp)} M_1$ (2), $M_2 Rr_{p(pe)} M_1$ (3), and $M_2 r_{p(bp)} M_1$ (4): these are true only and exclusively of M_1 and M_2. Leibniz's universe has, in agreement with D_{sr}, only one M_1 and only one M_2. Next, one can make an infinitely long list of all statements having in common with (4) the property of having M_1 as its subject-term and another one sharing with (5) the property of having M_2 as its subject-term. Each of these lists will recursively define, respectively, M_1 and M_2. Moreover, each statement on this list will have only one counterpart in the other—as is the case with (4) and (5). This, then, is where these two lists differ essentially from the two lists one may make of all the lengths satisfying the relation of ". . . being longer than . . ." and ". . . being shorter than . . .". It follows that statements (2), (3), (4), and (5) are, contrary to appearances, not relational statements *at all*, and that reciprocity is a necessary but not sufficient condition for a statement to be a relational statement. That is the difference between Rr and R.

Another argument leads to the same conclusion. Consider once again length as our example. In this case, we can think of an imaginary line on which all possible lengths can be compared with each other. This line supports transitive statements of this form: if b is longer than a and if c is longer than b it follows that c is longer than a. So it is with price, weight, and with relational statements in general. But transitivity would not work for monads perceiving each other. Admittedly, it is true that if monad M_2 perceives monad M_1 and if monad M_3 perceives monad M_2, monad M_3 will also perceive monad M_1. But monad M_3 does not perceive monad M_1 *because* monad M_2 perceives monad M_1. Perception is not transitive. M_3 perceives monad M_1 because in Leibniz's monadological universe each and all monad(s) perceive all of the others. It is true that monad M_1 can perceive monad M_2's perception of monad M_3, but these are different things, which we shall see when discussing the distinction between first- and second-order observation in the epilogue.

At most one could characterize statements about the perceptions monads have of each other as *quasi*-relational statements. They do express a *correspondence* between what Leibniz calls "the accidents" in the monads M_1 and M_2—which is, however, less than a *relation* between them in the proper sense of the word.[42] Rr does not express *relations* but *correspondences*. This is where and why Rr and R differ. If we have a list of statements for each individual member of set S_1 to which individual members of set S_2 correspond, this list cannot be said to express a relationship between the members of set S_1 and set S_2. This is the kind of correspondence that Leibniz had postulated for his monadological universe with his doctrine of preestablished harmony (D_{ph}), and it cannot be translated in terms of a relationship in the proper sense of that word. The statements (2), (3), (4), and (5) are not relational: their reciprocity—or rather correspondence—is accounted for by the logic and the metaphysics of the Leibnizian system. Reciprocity reflects how Leibniz constructed his monadological universe, but it possesses no agency of its own. Put differently, Leibniz has devised his system in such a way that it automatically dissolves all *seemingly* relational statements on monads into nonrelational statements about the correspondence of the accidents in individual monads.

In sum, with the fact that Rr holds for the relationship of reciprocity in the Leibnizian system, we discovered one type of relationality that is compatible with it. It is, basically, a metaphysically founded relationality of

---

42. This raises the question of how the notion of "correspondence" relates to the account of relational statements that was given here. Let's take the relational statement $aR_{(n)}b$ (1) where "$_n$" stands for the set of natural numbers, "g" for greater than, and "s" for smaller than, which gives us $aR_{(n[g])}b$ (2) and, thanks to the relation of reciprocity, $aR_{(n[s])}b$ (3). Now, (1) only becomes a definite statement if a is known. Suppose the value of a to be the natural number 7 and b to be the natural number 5. It then follows that the natural number 6 satisfies (2) and (3) together. Put differently, the natural number 6 corresponds to the two relational statements (2) and (3) if a is 7 and b is 5. In this way, a relation of correspondence between the numbers 5, 6, and 7 can be derived from (minimally) two relational statements. Whether one is prepared to regard this relation between 5, 6, and 7 as a "relation" is of course optional. One could justifiably say it is not because this "relation" of "correspondence" can be distinguished from "normal" relational statements. But one could also say that they constitute a deviant Leibnizian set of relational statements that are strictly discerned from the set of "normal" relational statements.

correspondence. But there is no room for all other types of relationality in the Leibnizian system.

Finally, the foregoing argument can also be regarded as a further clarification of (D_{wm}). The problem is *not* that monads could have no perceptions of each other, as D_{wm} seems to say. They *do* have such perceptions and, moreover, these perceptions individuate them. The issue is that in Leibniz's system these *perceptions* (or accidents) are completely severed from their corresponding accidents of *being* perceived in the other relevant monads. The fact of their reciprocity does not alter this. It is in this sense that the monads are windowless. This is so even when the two statements "M_1 perceived M_2" and "M_2 is perceived by M_1" seem to say exactly the same thing, apart from the former being in the active and the latter in the passive voice. What one might call the metaphysical fact in the Leibnizian universe of M_1 and M_2 being related with regard to the variable of perception and of their being united leaves intact the division between perception and being perceived. So, in the end, Leibniz's windowless monads are truly as closed as closed can be. This is why Leibniz needs an omniscient God to ensure that all the accidents of perception correspond exactly with all the accidents of being perceived in the relevant other monads.

5. RELATIONAL STATEMENTS ABOUT HRS: THE EXTERNALIST APPROACH

There is no room for relational statements in the Leibnizian system. Moreover, the system is unable to account for the kind of statements typical of the sciences. These include mathematical equations expressing relations between physical variables such as mass, temperature, velocity, acceleration, pressure, and so on. The philosopher of history might be tempted to acquiesce in this because such statements are irrelevant to historical writing. So it might seem that Leibniz's incapacity to offer a plausible account of relational statements is of no real concern for historiography. However, this conclusion would be too hasty. As so often is the case, if you decide to travel together with someone because of the benefits you expect from it, you must also be to prepared to share with him the less pleasant parts of your common journey. The crucial, but definitely unpleasant fact here is that historical representation involves relational statements, even inevitably so. Think of the statement "HR_1 is better (or more convincing, or more plausible) than HR$_2$." What would historical writing be like if such statements were excluded?

Most people would now react by saying "what's the big deal here? Don't we all know what we mean when saying that one HR is better than some other?" Undoubtedly so, but the sting is in "what we *mean* by saying that one HR is better than some other." That is, we must be capable of explaining what such relational statements mean *in terms of the Leibnizian system*. As long as we are incapable of providing a convincing answer to that question, we will be unable to clarify the nature of historical knowledge and of its growth. It must be shown, therefore, why the assertion that one HR is better, more convincing, or more plausible than some other is not just an irresponsible claim but one that can be argued to have its solid support in the nuts and bolts of Leibniz's philosophy of representation.

Before proceeding further, recall that in the previous section a distinction was made between an internalist and an externalist approach to the problem of the relational statement in Leibniz's thought. If the internalist approach was followed in the previous section, I now adopt the externalist approach. That is, the focus here is not on the problem of the relationship of statements on the *perceptions* that monads have of each other but on relations between monads (and HRs) as a whole.

When accounting for these relational statements about monads and HRs that are indispensable for mapping the growth of historical knowledge, I begin with the attempts that have been made to do so within the parameters of the Leibnizian system. The first such attempt was made by Bertrand Russell in 1900, when Russell embarked on the long journey that would result in *Principia Mathematica*.[43] That he believed it worthwhile to write a book on Leibniz at this stage of his career reflects Russell's great respect for Leibniz. Russell's rescue operation anticipated his analysis of statements like "the present king of France is bald" or "the father of Charles II was beheaded" set out in "On Denoting" (1905). In chapter 3 this analysis took the form of a statement expressing the relationship between a number of properties and a quantifier stating whether the statement is true of zero, one, several, or all things. This was also Russell's main move when trying to reconcile Leibniz's logic of the monads with the logical nature of relational

---

43. Bertrand Russell and Alfred North Whitehead, *Principia Mathematica* (Cambridge: Cambridge University Press, 1962).

statements. He translated all statements about monads into statements saying that there is one, and only one, x having the properties p_1 to p_n.

We are left with a set of universal properties, p_1 to p_n, and a variable of quantification stating p_1 to p_n to be true of no x, or of one and only one x, of some x, or of all x. Hence, whereas Leibniz banned relations from his universe, relations are omnipresent in Russell's world (in the sense of relating all the properties p_1 to p_n to each other). Leibniz's problem with relational statements simply evaporates. However, where strong individuals are omnipresent in Leibniz's universe, they are banned from Russell's, so we have gone from one extreme to the other. One can hardly expect Leibniz to agree with Russell's reduction of his strong individuals (i.e., the monads or HRs) to the status of mere variables of quantification.

Since Russell, many attempts have been made to bridge the gap between relational statements and the Leibnizian system. Cover and O'Leary-Hawthorne's book on Leibniz's notion of the individual is of particular interest. According to them, all of Leibniz's commentators, from Russell to Mates, have investigated whether we can move from relational statements to Leibniz's metaphysical definition of the monad or substance. Cover and O'Leary-Hawthorne are convinced that any attempt to tackle the problem in this way is doomed to failure. They invite us to approach it by asking instead whether Leibniz's metaphysics leaves room for relations. This is the right approach; we would be well-advised to follow their analysis. They begin by arguing for the futility of all attempts to reduce relational statements to statements exclusively containing assertions about the internal, nonrelational properties of Leibniz's monads.

One such attempt is as follows. Think of two completely identical objects, O_1 and O_2. One might be tempted to say that the relationship between them can be reduced to two sets of statements about where the components of O_1 and O_2 find themselves in three-dimensional space. But what is lost in translation is precisely the dimension of relation. Stating where O_1 and where O_2 are in space says *nothing* at all about their spatial *relationship*. As Cover and O'Leary-Hawthorne categorically put it: "there aren't relational ways things are, out there in the world, wherever one chooses to find them."[44] In agreement with the externalist approach, such

---

44. J. A. Cover and J. O'Leary-Hawthorne, *Substance and Individuation in Leibniz* (Cambridge: Cambridge University Press, 1999), 67.

relationships are projected on things from the outside, as it were, whereas these things themselves can afford to remain wholly indifferent about what is projected on them. O_1, at whatever spatial location it happens to be, is wholly "unconscious" of how its location relates to O_2 and can afford to be so; this is different from the internalist approach in which this relationship is not part of O_1's complete concept, which will contain only O_1's internal, *non*relational denominations.[45] The same holds for O_2. Leibniz couldn't have agreed more. More generally, nothing is to be expected from translating relational statements such as aRb (where R asserts a relation R between a and b) into statements about the corresponding accidents in both a and b. Again, the semantic ingredient of how a and b relate to each other would be lost.

A final proposal is that "a predicate F is relational if and only if it is not possible that both (i) there exists some substance x that is F and (ii) there exists no y that is distinct from x."[46] The advantage of this proposal is that the relational ingredient has now been wholly absorbed by x. This avoids predicates with a foot in both substances at once, to repeat Leibniz's terminology in the previous section. But this is no help either because the relationality of F is then preserved within the substance x. We are confronted again with the question of the reducibility of F to x's purely internal properties. Like all the other attempts at reducing relational to nonrelational denominations, we end up building a house around a problem. The problem may be invisible to all who just walk around the house, but anyone entering it will discover straightaway that the problem is still there.

Cover and O'Leary-Hawthorne then propose a new strategy for dealing with the problem of moving from nonrelational denominations to relational statements. Their argument is as follows. Think of the following two nonrelational statements: (1) Gaius is wise, and (2) Titus is wise. These describe the "monads" called Gaius and Titus quite separately, with no relation between them. But from here we may move to (3) "Gaius is similar to Titus," which obviously *is* relational. Similarity expresses a symmetric relationship between two things (here Gaius and Titus) that are said to be

---

45. Another problem with this attempt to rescue Leibniz is that it confuses the epistemological issue of the spatial location of O_1 and O_2 with the question of whether, within Leibnizian metaphysics, spatial denominations can be seen as internal properties.

46. Cover and O'Leary-Hawthorne, *Substance and Individuation in Leibniz*, 68.

similar. In this case, we have two strictly monadic statements, (1) and (2), and a relational statement corresponding to them. More generally, suppose there is a thing T_1 of which the set of sentences S is true, and another thing T_2 of which the same set S is true as well. In that, case relational statements like (3)—in this case T_1 is similar to T_2—are possible. The set S justifies the relationship of similarity. The claim that relationships are always projected on things "from the outside" has been neutralized because the relationship has its ground in what is internal to T_1 and T_2.[47]

The impasse that relational statements and purely monadic ones are irreducible to each other has thus been overcome: we now have a model for how to move from monadic statements to relational ones. It has been shown how the two can be reconciled within the parameters of the Leibnizian system. It might still be objected that it is not yet clear how asymmetric relations, such as being larger or smaller than, or being the father or being the son of, fit into this model. And next, that the meaning of (1) and (2) is different from (3) because (1) and (2) are silent about similarity, which is mentioned in (3). Cover and O'Leary invest considerable time and energy in defusing these objections, but I leave this aside because a more important issue demands our attention.[48]

Cover and O'Leary-Hawthorne call their theory the "supervenience model," which seems appropriate within the externalist approach discussed here. It explains how, in Leibniz's system, relational statements and purely monadic statements can be reconciled with each other. The idea is that the former are "supervenient" upon the latter. That is to say, there is a clear demarcation line between statements (1) and (2), on the one hand, and statement (3), on the other, and there can be no question of the former invading the world of the latter. Nevertheless—and this is decisive—on

---

47. This argument invites the question whether one (or more) of the statements of S about T_1 and T_2 can be replaced by statements that are (1) true if S is true and (2) formulated relationally. For example, suppose that the length of T_1 is two meters, that of T_2 one meter, and that a statement S about T_1 says "T_1 is two meters." S can then be replaced by the statement S: "T_1 is twice as long as all things that are one meter long." In that case, the relational statement "T_1 is twice as long as T_2" can be analytically derived from the notion of T_1 and the fact that T_2 is one meter long. Analyticity then guarantees relationality. However, the conclusion only follows if the premise is added that T_2 exists. But this premise cannot be part of the notion of T_1 for two reasons. First, monads (or HRs) cannot be predicated of other monads (or HRs). Second, it is excluded by the windowlessness of monads and HRs. See Cover and O'Leary-Hawthorne, *Substance and Individuation in Leibniz*, 67.

48. For the full argument and these objections, see Cover and O'Leary-Hawthorne, *Substance and Individuation in Leibniz*, 77–83.

the basis of monadic truths, relational statements *can* be formulated. That was the point of Cover and O'Leary-Hawthorne's argument. Hence, the Leibnizian system leaves room for relational statements, while avoiding a clash between the acceptance of relational statements, on the one hand, and Leibniz's D_{cc} stating that any truth about a monad permits of (re-)formulation in terms of statements having the subject/predicate form, on the other.

Cover and O'Leary-Hawthorne sum up by saying that "monadic facts simply determine relational ones; reduced relational facts obtain because the monadic, reducing ones obtain. And conversely? No."[49] The argument seems unexceptional, but this emphatic *no* is somewhat discouraging. Admittedly, unlike their predecessors, the authors convincingly show that the borderline between relational and monadic statements is permeable after all, albeit in one direction only, alas. But we can state two reservations. First, consider a relational statement like "Gaius is similar to Titus." Should it not be noticed that this similarity concerns the property of ". . . being wise"? Remember that we replaced the R in aRb by aRrb to express that a and b are related from the perspective of r (i.e., reciprocity). Adopting this kind of notation might be a good idea here as well.

Second, we still need a reason to explain why one can move forward from (1) and (2) to (3), but not backward from (3) to (1) and (2). Apparently, something was lost when moving from (1) and (2) to (3) that is impossible to retrieve for the journey backward from (3) to (1) and (2). What that could be is unclear. This does not enhance trust in Cover and O'Leary-Hawthorne's supervenience model. Worse still, we are interested precisely in the backward movement: we wish to know whether one can move from relational statements (such as HR_1 is better, or more convincing, than HR_2) to HRs, and if so, how. But Cover and O'Leary-Hawthorne's categorical no suggests there is no hope of doing so. We seem to have ended up back at square one.

6. RELATIONAL STATEMENTS: FROM HRS TO PBF

After this disappointing conclusion, I had best directly address the problem of relational statements about HRs in the hope of discovering whether the problem of the reducibility of relational statements about HRs to HRs has a solution or not. In fact it does; but to get to it, a detour

---

49. Cover and O'Leary-Hawthorne, *Substance and Individuation in Leibniz*, 82.

is necessary. This detour begins with the apparently entirely different issues of the self-consistency of reality and of our speech about reality. Scientists are not obliged to dabble in metaphysics, but if compelled to do so, they will probably assert the self-consistency of the physical reality they investigate.[50] The metaphysical assumption in question is that physical reality—understood as a *metaphysical* entity—is not *both* what it *is*, and what it *is not*. It is what it is.

Although physicists before 1900 would have agreed with this assertion, quantum mechanics has demonstrated the existence of natural phenomena that are at odds with this assumption: light can be both photons and waves. But this objection is easy to defuse. Light cannot be both photons and waves, and *not* be both photons and waves. Put differently, quantum mechanics cannot be both true and not true. There is a catch here, of course. In talking about truth, we are dealing with statements about language, i.e., the language of quantum mechanics, and not about *metaphysical* reality. This suggests how difficult it is to express in language the metaphysical claim I have in mind here. Using language to talk about the metaphysical nature of reality is making use of an instrument that almost inevitably invites the phenomenon you wish to catch to slither from your hands like an eel. Consider this notion of "self-consistency," with which we began: there is nothing in all of *metaphysical reality* even remotely resembling the word *self-consistency* because metaphysical reality contains no language.

This is why all speech about metaphysical reality is doomed to roughly the same impasse we came across when discussing the two paintings of the same landscape in section 2. In this comparison, the two paintings were on the same level as language, whereas the landscape itself must be situated in metaphysical reality. Generally speaking, trying to speak about the metaphysical nature of reality is, at least in this case (for in others this might be easier), like trying to jump over the world/language demarcation—while using language. The result is that inevitably you will find yourself in the domain of language *again* after having made the jump. There is, indeed, much wisdom in the view that one should avoid metaphysics like the plague.

---

50. Note that we are speaking here of the self-consistency of metaphysical reality and not the self-consistency or compatibility of true statements about reality.

Two qualifications must be made, however. First, the debate on metaphysics takes on an entirely different complexion when the metaphysical reality we are talking about is *language itself*. Self-evidently, this qualification is of specific significance in our discussion of historical representation—for language has been elevated there to the sublime status of being a metaphysical reality itself (recall the argument that HRs constitute historical reality). Languages are, after all, no less part of metaphysical reality than landscapes are—admittedly, a part allowing us to speak about metaphysical reality and having the peculiar faculty of presenting us with a linguistic mirror of the latter. But do mirrors themselves not belong to reality as well? Hence, only thanks to a rude and arbitrary decision could we claim that there should be, on the one hand, a metaphysical reality, and on the other, a *je ne sais quoi* called language.

The second qualification is that this assessment does not entail that metaphysical problems must always be meaningless. In this context, it is worthwhile to distinguish between two kinds of metaphysics. On the one hand, when Aristotle coined the term, he had in mind the study of a more fundamental "reality" underlying the phenomenal reality studied by physicists and other scientists. Many proposals have been made throughout the centuries for how to conceive of that metaphysical reality. Strawson called this variant of metaphysics "revisionary metaphysics." On the other hand, modern metaphysics investigates the conception(s) of reality implied by our use of language. Strawson spoke of "descriptive metaphysics" in chapter 3 when contrasting the notions of weak and strong individuals. The former enterprise is the more doubtful one. It is of no use in science, although it may be appropriate for discussing, for example, the "condition humaine."

However, if we return to metaphysical reality in the Aristotelian sense and try to capture it in terms of language, the most one can do is to conclude any effort to that end with a few rhetorically well-considered and suggestive words and end with lamely saying, "I hope you get an idea of what I have in mind." In a metaphysical discussion of the "condition humaine," an appeal to some well-chosen novels may prove helpful as well. But in the case of the metaphysical reality one might wish to associate with scientific research even such help is absent.

However, one notable exception to the rule of the idleness of metaphysical speculation in scientific research is historical representation, where

Aristotelian and Strawsonian descriptive metaphysics coincide. Again, metaphysical speculation about the nature of historical reality is guided by a logical inquiry into the historian's language.

This is why the issue of metaphysics is different for the sciences, on the one hand, and the writing of history, on the other. Recall the equivalence of logic and metaphysics in the Leibnizan system, which will hold as well for historical writing if analyzed in agreement with that system as I have done in this book. Specifically, Leibniz's doctrine of noncontradiction has its metaphysical counterpart in the notion of the self-consistency of historical reality. It is what it is and not anything else. Although the physicist will in all likelihood agree with the metaphysical claim of the self-consistency of physical reality, it is difficult to see what the cash-value of that willingness is for physicists. Next, speculations about the self-consistency of metaphysical reality immediately become entangled in the old wasp's nest of determinism versus indeterminism. The determinist will support self-consistency, and the indeterminist will express his doubts about it (it is, perhaps, not impossible to be an indeterminist *and* to believe in the self-consistency of metaphysical reality).[51]

All these problems will disappear like snow melting in the sun as soon as we drop the adjective "metaphysical" and understand "reality" as no more or less than physical reality *as it is studied* by physicists and other scientists. The notion of a self-consistent reality then becomes a completely natural and unproblematic one. It says no more than that all our beliefs about physical reality should be minimally consistent with each other. Needless to say, in the practice of science this desideratum will not always be satisfied. Scientists often disagree with each other, but this is not a problem. As soon as inconsistency manifests itself, a scientific debate begins to decide who is right and who is wrong. In this way self-consistency is ultimately restored; at the same time, it becomes clear that inconsistency is not a liability but an

---

51. For example, by subsuming indeterminism in a conception of metaphysical reality, making the statement analytically true. One might argue that indeterminism is part of the metaphysical reality in which human beings live, after having included indeterminism in the notion of metaphysical reality. But I assume that most people will regard this as a piece of sophistry. And right they are. However, the greatest things are sometimes born from what seems to be mere sophistry. Think, e.g., of a = a. See also note 1 of the epilogue for the role the principle played in Leibniz's thought.

asset because it contributes to the growth of scientific knowledge.[52] Better still, inconsistency is a necessary condition of such growth.

In historical representation, the picture is much the same, apart from a difference on the level of metaphysics. In historical representation, logic and metaphysics are (as in Leibniz) two sides of the same coin, with the qualification that the self-consistency of historical representation pulls along the self-consistency of historical reality in its wake. This fact gives us the tools for solving the problem with which we began: the problem of relational statements about HRs. The self-consistency of metaphysical reality can readily be proven here. All HRs—constituting the representational universe—have the form of statements of an HR having that HR as its subject-term. So no HR could possibly be inconsistent with any other—even if an HR were to have as one of its properties the property of containing a statement incompatible with a statement contained by another HR, or even one that is incompatible with another one in *one and the same HR* (although both possibilities are strictly ruled out, in fact, by our definition of HRs stating that all the statements they contain should be true of the states of affairs described by them). Self-evidently, this is a welcome starting point: the guaranteed impossibility of contradictions is to be warmly welcomed. But it has its disadvantages as well because the self-consistency of all HRs in metaphysical historical reality entails that it will be just as hospitable to the most absurd and ridiculous HRs as to the very best HRs that have ever been written. Self-consistency may satisfy the logician, but this only proves that the logician does not have the right kind of judgment when it comes to the practice of historical writing. Here one has to sort out the sensible from the hopeless HRs.

---

52. Leibniz makes a somewhat similar argument, see Gottfried Wilhelm Leibniz, "The Principles of Nature and of Grace Based on Reason," in *Philosophical Papers and Letters*, 2nd ed., trans. Leroy E. Loemker (Boston: Reidel/Springer, 1976), 639. "Now we must rise to metaphysics and make use of the great, but not commonly used, principle, that nothing takes place without a sufficient reason: in other words, that nothing occurs from which it would be impossible for someone who has enough knowledge of things to give a reason adequate to determine why the thing is as it is and not otherwise. . . . Further, assuming that things must exist, it must be possible to give a reason why they should exists as they do and not otherwise. . . . This final reason for things is called God." Leibniz here formulates his doctrine of sufficient reason stating that for everything a cause or reason can be found that explains why things are as they are and not otherwise. However, his argument is restricted to the domain of metaphysics. He does not say whether, or how, the doctrine of sufficient reason applies to the domain of the PBF. He may have thought it so obvious that it was unnecessary to say so.

In considering how to do this, remember that at the end of chapter 3 we encountered for the first time the notion of the model and of the historical PBF. These notions can be of help in our problem of relational statements about HRs. The crucial fact here is that we are not allowed to transpose the self-consistency of historical reality, which we have established applies in the domain of the HRs, to the domain of the PBF or models as a matter of course—for they do *not* belong to historical reality. But our apparent helplessness on descending from the self-consistency of historical reality to the insecure domain of the PBF and models is, in fact, a blessing in disguise. It is crucial that we can *postulate* the self-consistency of the domain of the PBF on the ground even though it lacks a *metaphysical* foundation; it is a *logical or scientific desideratum*. It is such a desideratum because of Leibniz's D_{et}: the doctrine of noncontradiction forbids contradictions on the level of the PBF and models. Of course, that does not in the least preclude contradictions from actually presenting themselves. This is where the domain of the PBF differs from historical reality; D_{nc} only tells us that we are not allowed to *acquiesce* in contradictions outside the domain of historical reality. Put differently, it defines a condition for meaningful historical debate. In the same way, it was the willingness to abandon the support of any metaphysical guarantees that opened the road for the growth of scientific knowledge. In sum, at the level of the models and PBF to be associated with HRs, the historian is in much the same position as the scientist: in both cases self-consistency is a postulate not having support or justification in metaphysics.

If self-consistency in historical representation could boast of possessing metaphysical support, the paradox is that historical writing would be robbed of the condition ensuring the possibility of progress in our historical knowledge. So it is a blessing for historical writing that the domain of the PBF and models are *not* part of historical reality—and that they are, to a certain extent, mere provisional fictions deprived of a metaphysical status that we must abandon as soon as better and more promising fictions become available. Put differently, D_{et} compels us to postulate the self-consistency of the domain of the models and PBF, and that postulate, in turn, guarantees both the possibility and the meaningfulness of debate between historians. I call this postulate "the presumption of consistency." Put differently, the input from the HRs in terms of their models and PBF and "the presumption of consistency" stake out together the terrain where the joust between HRs is situated. The latter guarantees that the models and PBF of individual HRs cannot possibly escape from each other and are thus, whether they like it or not, compelled to contribute to the growth of historical knowledge. The growth of historical knowledge is possible only thanks to that presumption of consistency. Without it the very notion of the growth of historical knowledge is a mere *flatus vocis*. How could we establish that growth without the measuring tape that the presumption of consistency puts at our disposal and without the urge to achieve agreement that is driven by the presumption of consistency, which thus promotes the growth of historical knowledge? The postulate of "the presumption of consistency" has an analogue in Leibniz's argument as to why we are justified in believing in the veracity of the PBF in spite of their merely phenomenal character. He could not deny this veracity without condemning his own scientific work to irrelevance.

When discussing Leibniz's solution, Daniel Garber begins with Leibniz's (well-attested) phenomenalism and then asks how Leibniz moved from there to the belief in the existence of an external world containing material bodies in space and time. The answer is coherence.[53] Thus Leibniz writes in an essay with the telling title *De Modo Distinguendo Phaenomena Realia ab Apparentiis* (1683/1686):

> Yet the most powerful criterion of the reality of phenomena, sufficient even by itself, is success in predicting future phenomena from past and present ones, whether that prediction is based upon reason, upon a hypothesis that was previously successful, or upon the customary consistency of things as observed previously. Indeed, even if this whole life were to be only a dream, and the visible world only a phantasm, I should call this dream of this phantasm real enough if we were never deceived by it when we make good use of reason.[54]

Consistency is, as Leibniz put it himself, "the sign of truth." One can interpret this either in a phenomenalist or an antiphenomenalist way. The phenomenalist will say that, according to Leibniz, coherence will make PBF look *as if* they were real, whereas they are, of course, nothing

---

53. Daniel Garber, *Leibniz, Body, Substance, Monad* (Oxford: Oxford University Press, 2009), 282.
54. Quoted in Garber, *Leibniz, Body, Substance, Monad*, 288.

but *mere* phenomena. The antiphenomenalist will say, however, that coherence proves that they are *real*. Garber defends the antiphenomenalist position. He writes that in the 1680s and 1690s "Leibniz's view of body and the physical world is grounded in a world of corporeal substances, substances understood on analogy with organisms, not mind." A few sentences later he even writes that there "seems to be no toehold for a monadological metaphysics in this period of Leibniz's thought"[55] But this goes much too far. In the *Discourse on Metaphysics* written around the same time (1686), the most important ingredients of Leibniz's monadological metaphysics were already present. It makes little sense to believe that Leibniz defended two separate metaphysics at one and the same time, one for the monadological universe and another one for the domain of the PBF (containing "us" and the physical phenomena of this world).[56]

It is of the greatest importance to add this notion of "the growth of historical knowledge" to our conceptual arsenal. It is presupposed by our justified belief in the possibility of meaningful historical debate. But it also makes us aware of an aspect of historical writing that is too often neglected in the philosophy of history today. The notion of the growth of historical knowledge is suggestive of historical writing as, above all, a collective enterprise. Of course, progress can only be made in the writing of history thanks to the efforts of individual historians. But philosophers of history tend to focus exclusively on the level of what a particular historical narrative H_1 contributed to historical knowledge, what we owe to historian H_2, and so on, while remaining blind to what happens at the "collective level" where the growth of historical knowledge can be established.

What philosophers of history often forget is that *with* and *between* all these individual contributions, a domain of generally gradually accepted historical knowledge grew up. This domain is admittedly difficult to retrace

---

55. Garber, *Leibniz, Body, Substance, Monad*, 267.
56. What is the case, however, is that Leibniz wrestled for much of his life with the incompatibility of the materialist antiphenomenalism of his youth and his later monadological metaphysics—an incompatibility that was built into the very architecture of his system—and that he tended to oscillate for many years between the two positions. But there can be no doubt that a monadological metaphysics was triumphant in his later years. In any case, the passage quoted here clearly agrees with our phenomenalist reading of Leibniz.

to the contributions to historical knowledge by individual historians. It requires serious work in historiography and perhaps social and intellectual history to do so. But it forms the background generally shared by all academic historians that enables them to understand each other and to identify without too much difficulty what each of them has to say about historical reality. The form in which the growth of historical knowledge manifests itself most clearly is in the more or less spontaneous intuitions historians have when reviewing history written by their colleagues. A number of ingredients go into producing this historical sense. Historians ask themselves whether their colleagues have done their homework properly: did they consult all the sources relevant for this research topic; did they interpret them correctly; did they read all the available secondary literature; and does what they did with it in their own work of history make sense? Finally—and this is where historians' intuitive gut feeling about their colleagues' work of history will be decisive—does their book or article meaningfully contribute to the existing state of the art on some historical topic? The essential question is: Can what they have written be seen as contributing to the growth of historical knowledge?

When grappling with that question, historians mobilize all the PBF and models amassed in their mind over many years of historical scholarship. The domain of these PBF and models is often much wider than the domain primarily associated with the topic in question. It may happen, for example, that a historian of eighteenth-century England has a very low opinion of a recent book on the conflict between King Philippe IV le Bel of France (also known as "le Roi Hibou" because of his owlish way of looking at people) and Pope Boniface VIII, even if that historian knows little more of that part of the Middle Ages than what is remembered from undergraduate days. Reviews may nevertheless prove their gut feeling to have been right. The explanation is that there is a greatest common denominator among all the PBF and models belonging to the HRs that can be regarded as having been written in the same era. This greatest common denominator reflects the overall state of the art of historical knowledge for a given epoch in the history of historical writing, and it is not something that can be traced back to a small well-defined set of exemplary works of history. Having appropriated a substantial part of that common denominator is the mark of a professional historian.

Next, this greatest common denominator is the standard for deciding whether a work of history is a valuable contribution to historical knowledge. Specifically, if one HR is better than another one, this is a promising start. But how it compares to this greatest common denominator is truly decisive. One could say that this greatest denominator is the *language* that all professional historians have learned to speak. A few words spoken in that language are ordinarily sufficient to make clear whether their speaker will be recognized as "one of us" by other historians.[57] Even an amateur historian who has amassed an impressive knowledge of some specific historical topic will fail this test straightaway in a brief exchange with a professional historian because he does not speak "the historian's language." Admittedly, the historian's language comes deceptively close to ordinary language. It is often argued that there is, in fact, no difference at all between ordinary and historical discourse, and that it is, moreover, an advantage of historical writing that the historian can address the layperson in their own language, unlike the scientist.

It is true that the difference between the historian's language and ordinary language is subtle. But the subtleties are real and comprise a node in a web of other important and revealing truths about the interaction between historians. The difference between the historian's language and ordinary language is a one-way street. Whereas the historian notices at

---

57. Most philosophers of history would not be recognized as "one of us" by historians. That is a bad thing insofar as philosophers of history more often than not have insufficient insight into what really goes on in the practice of historical writing. As a result, they easily ask the wrong questions about the practice of historical writing, thus becoming easy prey for the GIGO principle. Before philosophers of history reflect on the nature of historical writing, they could begin by talking to historians, asking them what they think the writing of history is about. Bruno Latour spent a year in scientists' laboratories before writing *Science in Action. How to Follow Scientists and Engineers Through Society* (Milton Keynes, UK: Open University, 1987). That would be a valuable experience if not a *conditio sine qua non* for good philosophy of history. The problem is aggravated by the fact that, in their reflections on historical writing, many philosophers use philosophical instruments unsuitable for addressing its real problems. They not only lack understanding of what their topic of investigation actually is but also appeal more often than not to kinds of philosophical theories that are inapplicable to the practice of the writing of history.

The result is that one answers questions that nobody, for excellent reasons, ever bothered to ask. One is reminded of the joke of the drunkard returning home in the dead of night who is found by a policeman on his knees under a lantern. "What are you doing there?" asks the policeman. Answers the drunkard: "I am looking for the key of my house." The policeman then asks: "why are you looking for it under that lantern and not near the front door of your house?" Replies the drunkard: "because there is light here."

once whether he is talking to a colleague or not, the layperson all too readily endows the historian's language with the same aura of truth and credibility that he correctly attributes to statements belonging to ordinary language. This is why, in fact, historical language is, at least potentially, such a dangerous instrument.

The layperson is only too ready to swallow what historians say, believing that all that is said in historical discourse is no less true than statements such as those of the next-door neighbor's son who went to university last year or the man living across the road who walks his dog four times a day. Political criminals such as Hitler, Trump, and Putin have routinely exploited this lack of awareness by ordinary people of this difference between history and ordinary language. This is all the more reason to invest time and energy in teaching history at school with the aim of giving people an inkling of it, and so immunize them against such political Pied Pipers. That may help all of us to avoid political disasters. In sum, there is an asymmetry between how the historian and the man in the street experiences the historian's language. But precisely this asymmetry proves that historical language is an artificial language, no less than that of the physicist. Both differ from ordinary language, but the historian is aware of the difference, whereas the layperson is not.

Finally, if there were no such common denominator securing both the possibility of the growth of historical knowledge and the standards for establishing it, historical writing would remain in the position of the arts. Everyone can see that the art of one period differs from that of a previous or later one, but whether there is progress is impossible to say. Taking myself as an example, I see the history of painting after 1700, and above all after 1900, as a history of continuous decay; but I am well aware that very few people would agree with me on this. No one can tell with certainty who is right about this. No one can actually *prove* that my reactionary ideas about art are wrong, whereas those who happily go along with all the extravagancies of modern art are right. And, indeed, before the rise of historicism, the writing of history was an art rather than a science, albeit "the science of the individual" that it is today, as we saw in chapter 3.

If the writing of history ceased to be an art, this was not simply the result of the achievements of the individual great historians of the last two centuries, such as Ranke, Droysen, Fustel de Coulange, Burckhardt, Marx, Theodor Mommsen, Huizinga, Braudel, Pocock, and so on. There have *always* been great historians: think of Herodotus, Thucydides, Tacitus, Beda Venerabilis, Otto von Freising, Francesco Guicciardini, P. C. Hooft, Lord Clarendon, Voltaire, David Hume, or Edward Gibbon.[58] But this never succeeded in transforming the writing of history in the science it became two and half centuries ago. Nineteenth-century historicism introduced a form of "scientific historical writing," giving overwhelming credibility to the conviction that there truly existed such a thing as the growth of historical knowledge. That has been the independent variable, so to speak. This idea was the real paradigm shift in the history of historiography. But explaining what made this momentous transition possible requires reference to the idea underlying the concept of the growth of historical knowledge, namely, the presumption of consistency and its adoption by all professional historians.

After this long detour, let us return to the problem of the possibility of relational statements on HRs. Recall that the issue is crucial because there can be no meaningful historical debate and no growth of historical knowledge if statements like "HR_1 is better, more convincing, and so on, than HR_2," cannot be given a meaning. We have not found a way yet to move

---

58. The suggestion is that the works written by these "great historians" from the past and the present are neither a necessary nor a sufficient condition for the growth of historical knowledge. See Jaume Aurell on the question, "What is a Classic in History?" Jaume Aurell, "What Is a Classic in History?," *Journal of the Philosophy of History* 16, no. 1 (2022): 54–92, at 84, presents a list of such "classics" that many would consider perfectly reasonable, although it includes historians such as Michelet and Spengler. But there will also be general agreement that Michelet, Spengler, and Toynbee—whatever lasting interest their writings may have—did not really contribute to the growth of historical knowledge. They were not the Newtons, the Einsteins, or the Lavoisiers of historical knowledge. They belong to a category of their own, which rarely intersects with the practice of historiography. If a historical classic has such a side effect, it was ordinarily unintended. Aurell quotes from Lionel Gossman's *Between History and Literature*: "because [Michelet] was such a 'bad' historian by certain standards, he helped to transform historiography and continues to inspire the most innovative historians, from Lucien Febvre to Braudel." Aurell goes on to say: "there must be a certain 'un-orthodoxy' and 'non-conventionality' among the historians able to create a classic work of history." This gets to the heart of the matter: a classic is a *wholly random event* from the perspective of the history of historical writing. This explains why it is atypical for a historical classic to contribute to the growth of historical knowledge (although this in no way diminishes the interest that such classics may have). No historian can know in advance that they are writing a historical classic, even if they like the idea of writing one and have the intention to do so, because this status depends on a critical reception that they do not control. If their book does become a classic, they can only conclude that they unintentionally spoke "with two tongues": one used to address their colleagues and the other for the edification of a much wider audience. A historical classic is a wonderful thing, but the growth of historical knowledge is better still.

from relational statements of the form HR_1 R HR_2 (in which R expresses relationships such as is better than, is shorter than, is of a more recent date than, and so on) to nonrelational statements about HRs such as HR_1 and HR_2. This is the bad news; the good news is that thanks to the PBF and models and, above all the presumption of consistency, we can work *around* the problem. With the presumption of consistency, we can claim—or at least reasonably postulate—that all models and PBF are comparable and commensurable with each other. This allows us to compare the models and PBF that can be derived from different HRs. Finally, we can attribute different sets of models and PBF to each of the HRs—and we can do so in such a way as to explain what it *means* to say, e.g., that HR_1 is better than HR_2 without relying on relational statements. Let me illustrate this argument with a concrete example.

Leibniz can be read as recommending that historians should focus on trend breaks or tipping points.[59] An example of such a break was the meeting on New Year's Eve 1564 of the Council of State of the Netherlands (then still comprising both the Northern and the Southern Netherlands) attended by the governess Margaret of Parma and with the Frisian lawyer Viglius van Aytta as its president. The debate seemed destined to a stalemate. Then Prince William of Orange and Count of Nassau—later Prince William I—stood up and gave a flaming, complex, and principled speech (as he would do on some other occasions). He ended by saying, "as far as he was concerned he was prepared to hold on to Catholicism, but that he could not permit that Kings should rule over the minds of their subjects, thus robbing them of their freedom to believe and of religion."[60] This was little less than revolutionary,[61] certainly in an august institution of state

---

59. See the end of chapter 5.
60. René van Stipriaan, *De Zwijger. Het leven van Willem van Oranje* (Amsterdam: Querrido, 2021), 213
61. "Revolutionary" is used in the context of the birth of the modern absolutist state as personified by King Philip II. But what Prince William stood for in his speech had, in fact, its roots in the Middle Ages. The Dutch revolt was a conservative revolution. What we refer to as our fundamental civil rights as codified in the French *Declaration de l'Homme et du Citoyen* of August 1789 and the American *Bill of Rights* of September 1789 reflect the typically medieval aversion of all kinds of tyranny. A medieval prince hoping to establish a tyrannical regime met immediately with staunch opposition from the magnates in his realm and, at a later phase, of the Third Estate. *No historical myth is both so stubborn and so utterly wrong as that of "medieval tyranny."* The opposite is true: fundamental civil rights and the rule of law will always be in danger in countries not having their roots in the European Middle Ages, such as Russia and China.

such as the Council of State that was expected to always obey the will of its sovereign lord and master, King Philip II of Spain. Most, if not all, of its members were profoundly shocked by these terrible things being said aloud and openly, even if they agreed with them privately; Viglius van Aytta even suffered a heart attack after a sleepless night after the meeting. The meeting of the Council of State was a trend break because it suggested that the nobility (and even some of the highest nobility) tended to choose for the Protestant cause and was on the verge of making common cause with the people. It was now only a matter of time until the civil war—known as the Eighty Years War in which the Dutch fought for their independence from Spain—broke out in 1568.

We need to agree on the following assumptions to operationalize the notion of the PBF and models for historical debate. First, we must assume that HRs can be said to exist forever and so to have existed already before they were "actualized" at the moment of their individuation, whereas an HR's PBF and models only come into being when the HRs to which they belong have been actualized. Second, we must assume there is a plane of PBF and models that is defined by the existing PBF and models. Outside that plane of PBF and models there is *nothing*. And emphatically not "the past." Third, we must assume that the relative success or importance of an HR's PBF and models is expressed in terms of the amount of surface of the plane of PBF and models that they covered. The greater the surface covered by an HR's PBF and models, the more successful its corresponding HR can be said to be. Fourth, we must assume that "individuated" HRs coagulate in clusters (e.g., on the emergence of the modern state; on the French Revolution; on the absence of socialism in the USA after 1945, or on the significance of the proceedings of the Council of State of the Netherlands in 1564). In such clusters, HRs will tend to overlap with each other. The degree to which the surface covered by an HR's PBF and models exceeds that of an already existing cluster is the measure of its success, all other things being equal.

Let's now return to this meeting of the Council of State on December 31, 1564. Assume that we have ten HRs on this momentous event in Dutch history and that the PBF and models that can be derived from these HRs cover the surface of the PBF from PBF_1 to PBF_{100}, and that none of them cover more than 25 PBF. Let's assume that all PBF's are of more or less equal historical significance. This is not a realistic assumption, but let us defer further discussion of this for now.[62] Suppose that recently two new HRs (HR$_1$ and HR$_2$) have been written about what happened in Brussels on New Year's Eve 1564, the lead-up to the event and its aftermath, and that an expert on this part of Dutch history was invited to review the two HRs. Suppose also that his conclusion took the form of the following indisputably relational statement: HR$_1$ is better than HR$_2$.

How do we translate the relational statement HR$_1$ is better than HR$_2$ into nonrelational statements about HR$_1$ and HR$_2$—or what is the *meaning* of that relational statement in terms of pure Leibnizian language? As is ordinarily the case with someone reviewing two new books, let us imagine that this reviewer also concludes that both books have their merits because both add substantially to what had been known. In fact, the reviewer shows that the two books together increase the number of known PBF from PBF$_{100}$ to PBF$_{125}$. As is also common, he argues that one of the two is stronger where the other is weaker, and vice versa. Nevertheless, in the last resort, he still prefers H$_1$ to H$_2$. He summarizes his final conclusion by saying that H$_1$ covers the PBF from PBF$_{75}$ to PBF$_{125}$, whereas H$_2$ covers the PBF from PBF$_{80}$ to PBF$_{110}$. We are assuming that all PBF are of fairly equal importance, so the reviewer's conclusion is perfectly reasonable.

This example suggests how to translate relational statements about (windowless) HRs into *non*relational statements about an HR's PBF and models. In this example, the translation would take the following form: the relational statement "HR$_1$ is better than HR$_2$" means that (1) it is true of HR$_1$ that it covers the PBF from PBF$_{75}$ to PBF$_{125}$ and also (2) it is true of HR$_2$ that it covers the PBF from PBF$_{80}$ to PBF$_{110}$. It must be emphasized, finally, that these two statements are *about* HR$_1$ and HR$_2$ and not *part of* HR$_1$ and HR$_2$ (i.e., the problem addressed in the previous section). Were they actually part—or would become part—of the HRs in question, they would have to be added to the list of statements recursively individuating both HRs, hence, to the lists HR$_1$ is s$_1$, HR$_1$ is s$_2$, HR$_1$ is s$_3$ ... HR$_1$ is s$_n$ and HR$_2$ is t$_1$, HR$_2$ is t$_2$, HR2 is t$_3$ ... HR$_2$ is s$_n$. HR$_1$ and HR$_2$ would then automatically become new HRs, say HR$_x$ and HR$_y$, closely resembling HR$_1$ and HR$_2$, apart from the fact that HR$_x$ contains the statement HR$_1$ is s$_2$ and HR$_y$ the statement HR$_y$ is s$_3$, which are *not* on the list of statements recursively individuating HR$_1$ and HR$_2$. To make such statements possible at all, we

---

62. The issue is discussed in greater detail in chapter 5.

must postulate a meta-language allowing us to speak about HRs situated on the object-level of that new language.

This meta-language is, indeed, absent from the Leibnizian universe, which originally made us distrust the possibility of the externalist approach to the problem of relational statements in that universe. But generation of the domain of the models and PBF justifies—by courtesy of the demands of symmetry—the generation of this meta-language. A fact suggesting, once again, the surprising observation that the Leibnizian system is more successful in accounting for historical writing than for realizing the goals Leibniz himself had hoped to achieve by means of it. If one wishes to explain and justify the Leibnizian system, the best thing to do is to take historical writing as one's example. This will also be our reliable guide for deciding what is right and what is wrong in the Leibnizian system.

In general, the relational statement (1) HR_1 is better than HR_2 can be replaced by (2) HR_1 corresponds to the PBF and models covering the surface S_1 and (3) M_2 corresponds to the PBF and models covering the surface S_2, where (2) and (3) are nonrelational and nowhere conflict with Leibniz's logic and semantics. Just like statement (1), statements (2) and (3) must be situated on the meta-level; that is, they have statements about HR_1 and HR_2 as their object-level. Statements (2) and (3), plus the specification of the meanings of S_1 and S_2, express the nonrelational meaning of (1). In this way relational statements can be translated into nonrelational statements without coming into conflict with Leibniz's logic and semantics.[63]

One final remark. We may now recognize the complexity of the historian's language: (1) on the lowest level we have the PBF; (2) then come the models; next (3) the statements expressing individuating truths about HRs having their origin in true statements about past states of affairs; (4) then the level of the HRs themselves; (5) the meta-sentences tying an HR's sentences together; and finally (6) the level of the meta-language of relational statements and nonrelational statements about HRs. The postulate of such a meta-language for speaking about relational statements and nonrelational statements about HRs may remind us of Cover and

---

63. Leibniz's use of the metaphor of the rainbow to explain the relationship between the monads and their PBF has been discussed. The main idea is that the "phenomenon" of the rainbow is the phenomenalist counterpart to the quasi-monadological domain of myriad individual droplets of water refracting and reflecting the light of the sun. We do see these monads, but only in their phenomenal guise of the rainbow.

O'Leary-Hawthorne's supervenience model because it is clear that relational statements such as "Gaius is similar to Titus" should also be situated on the meta-level.

The philosophy of history has made little progress in the last fifty years because its practitioners have been insufficiently aware of the need to separate these different layers of the historical text. As a consequence, they have unwittingly mixed them, thus preventing solid and lasting results from emerging in their discussions. The most nefarious example of this mixing up of levels is the failure to isolate truths *de re* from truths *de dicto*. As was suggested on several occasions, in contemporary philosophical terminology one distinguishes between *extensionalist* and *intensionalist* truth; the former is a truth about objects of reference and the latter a truth about linguistic meaning.[64] If we think of two statements—(1) "Emperor William II was a warmonger," uttered by someone just having read Fritz Fischer's *Griff nach der Weltmacht* of 1961, and (2) "Fischer's Emperor William II was a warmonger"—it will be clear that (1) is ambiguous in a way that (2) is not. Statement (1) may refer either to Emperor William II, who lived from 1859 to 1941 and was German Emperor from 1888 to 1918 *or* to the representation of William II's intervention in European politics that was proposed by Fischer. If understood in the first way, statement (1) is an extensional truth or a statement *de re*, and it may well be false; if understood in the other way, statement (1) is an intensional truth, or a truth *de dicto*, and is undeniably true.

In the practice of both historical writing and in the philosophy of history, this distinction is often forgotten. The result, not only in historiography but in human life as well, is that truths *de dicto* tend to crowd out truths *de re*. This process reaches the ultimate low point in the widespread belief that if Hitler, Trump, Putin, or Xi Jinping say that something is true, it must be true just because *they* say so. Language betrays its very raison d'être here. Needless to say, these autocrats are surely responsible for this degeneration of language—but those who are too lazy, too uninterested, or just too stupid to be aware of this degeneration of language are even more culpable. Autocrats can only play their nefarious role in world history thanks to the laziness, lack of interest, and the sheer stupidity of their followers for whom the word *freedom* has no meaning.

---

64. This distinction is central to the epilogue in this book.

Freedom, free debate, the free exchange of opinions from which Truth is born presuppose each other. One cannot have one of them without the other three.

The real revolution of the eighteenth century was not the American or the French Revolution but the revolutionary recognition that political truth can only be born from free public debate and from the desire of truth. Even the monarchs of that century discovered that not they, but "l'opinion publique est la reine du monde." They knew they had to choose now between being a tyrant or an enlightened despot serving the cause of freedom and political Truth for the benefit of people they ruled. Since then politics was firmly tied to Truth—religion being the first and most prominent victim of this revolutionary re-arrangement.

Then, in our own time, the completely unthinkable happened. To begin with, just think of this. About half of the officials of the present government of the United States believe, if asked, this government to be illegitimate, since the 2020 elections "were stolen" by Biden, whereas the other half quietly, and without demur, acquiesces in this absurd situation. The only explanation of it must be that *both* halves consider political Truth to be a matter of only minor concern. Could a government taking itself seriously possibly demonstrate less self-respect? Can it hope to function properly if half of its officials, if not more, doubt and/or reject its legitimacy? It cannot, if we conceive of the well-ordered State (regardless of its form of government) as a unified and consistent whole, acting as if it had one mind and one heart. Civil society is disunited, but it is the State's supreme task to create unity out of disunity—as the motto of runs: 'e pluribus unum'. The sovereign State is *eo ipso* 'un et indivisible', as the French revolutionaries put it. A State with many minds and hearts *is* no State, as Jean Bodin argued so cogently some five hundred years ago. If we agree with Bodin that a shared conception of political Truth is conditional for a social organization to be a State, then the present American State reveals itself as a body politic in state of decomposition.

Next, each lawsuit begins with establishing what are the *indubitable facts or truths* that are of relevance for it. Without them a judge cannot responsibly make a judgment. Doing this is sometimes difficult, at other occasions relatively easy. Now, anyone having a TV knows or could know that it is an *indubitable fact* that the former president of the United States incited to a rebellion and attempted a coup on January 6, 2020. Television viewers saw him do so before their own eyes. Similarly, we have all heard Trump's phone call with Brad Raffensperger on January 4, 2021. Who would need further proof—if he is not a political pervert? However, the peculiarities of the American judicial system compelled it to inflate the problem of establishing this simple and *indubitable fact* to the sublime size of having to establish, for example, whether our universe will implode or expand until it reaches a state of complete equilibrium. Or whether psychoanalysis is helpful or useless.

Hard, *indubitable truth* was thus debased into doubtful legal speculation. The Brazilian Supreme Court and the Superior Electoral Tribunal succeeded on June 8, 2023 in banning Bolsonaro from office till 2030—so in a mere half year after a mob attempted on January 8, 2023 an imitation of the storming of the Capitol. In stark opposition to this, the American State and its judicial system are stretched beyond the limits of their power in their effort to deal with the former president's coup of almost four years ago. The American judicial system is remarkably successful at keeping incarcerated a staggering 1 percent of the country's population. But making Trump pay for his countless crimes with the instruments available to it is like trying to catch an elephant with a butterfly net. In this way they confirm Putin's and Xi Yinping's contention that democracies are a thing of the past: even *at home* they can no longer answer the challenges of autocracy! So within soon they will join the club of autocracies. First of all the United States; the European democracies will follow a bit later.

More important, it is not hard to see that this transformation of simple fact into an inextricable juridical labyrinth must have the unintended result of robbing these lawsuits of the former president of all credibility in the eyes of the American public. If he is found guilty his followers will see this as proof of the "weaponization" of the DoJ against the former president. If he is acquitted the Democrats will interpret it as one more proof of their party's well-attested mix of timidity and cowardice (Merrick Garland being a fine example of that mix). The Democrats have no fighting spirit when having to stand up against the Republicans. However—and this is the bottom line—in *both* cases the *indubitable truth* that the former president attempted a coup in order to stay in power will disappear completely behind the horizon and be replaced by wholly different concerns.

In this way the American judicial system, being what it is, unintentionally undermined the belief that there exists such a thing as Truth in political debate—as well as the belief that Truth, and not a juridical clash of arms is, or ought to be, decisive. The present American political and judicial system never possessed the means to offer sufficient protection to the State and its Constitution. As so unexpectedly became clear after 2019. Even the Civil War never came so close to political suicide. The best way to countervail the adverse effects of the dysfunctioning of the American judicial system would be to pull the establishment of fact, on the one hand, and the issue of what verdict can be argued to be the best on the basis of these facts, on the other, as far apart from each other as Geschichstsforschung and Geschichtsschreibung are in the writing of history.

But an even more important historical lesson is to be learned from the Trump episode: it has exposed the major weaknesses of the American Constitution and is, therefore, an implicit call to a thorough revision of it in order to prevent such episodes from happening again. The issue should have been top priority right from day one of the Biden administration. The main difference between American democracy and its European counterparts is that the latter were regularly updated after their many revolutions with the aim of how to rewrite their constitutions so that nobody would think again that a new revolution might be a good idea. When James Madison, Alexander Hamilton, John Jay and others drafted the American Constitution the French Revolution still had to break out. So much of the historical and political wisdom incorporated in European constitutions is absent from its so venerable older American brother. Its main weakness being that it does not locate political decision-making in the debate between the government and the people's representatives. Had it done so, a Trump government would have fallen within a few months after its inauguration. Furthermore, having next to each other two representative chambers with the same powers is not a very good idea either. Either they agree (and then one of them is superfluous) or they disagree (and then you're in an impasse). But for Americans the Constitution is a secular Bible preferably read in a fundamentalist way. So one could not possibly expect them to change their Constitution. "Nemo obligatur ultra vires," as it says in the *Justinian Digest*. But, alas, this will not save the United States (and the Western world in general) from the dire consequences of this fatal incompetence.

Needless to say, this gradual decomposition of the American body politic started long before the misdemeanors of the former president and the American political system's present wrestling with how to deal with them. But with the wisdom of hindsight one might say that the present degradation of political Truth into mere partisan opinion was, in fact, what this gradual degeneration of American politics aimed at the whole time. Indeed, the electorate of what can boast to be the oldest democracy in the world—famously hailed by Tocqueville as Europe's political guide!—no longer cares about Truth. Even though it has free and unhindered access to it. And though neither King, nor Pope, not even an autocrat's propaganda hid it from them. Tocqueville's freedom-loving Americans morphed into Hilary Clinton's pitiable "deplorables." The Big Lie is the Truth for the major part of the American electorate. Deeper than this an electorate cannot sink. It no longer has the right to be free. Tyranny and corrupt government will be its well-deserved reward. [65]

In order to protect other still existing democracies from a similar fate a new *historicist* Enlightenment—in all of these democracies—would not be such a bad idea.

---

65. The present American electorate has sunk even deeper than that of Russia. Since the beginning of Mongol rule in 1240 down to the present, tyrannical rule—at some times harsher, at others somewhat less so (as under Nicholas II)—was Russia's fate. With regard to Russia one is reminded of the Marquis de Custine's book *De La Russie* of 1839, which could be summarized with the assessment that in Russia one person is born to rule with the rod of iron while the rest are born to passively undergo that rule. How could the ideas of freedom, free debate and truth ever take root in a country in which tyranny is almost a law of nature? So one can hardly blame the Russian electorate for believing that Ukraine has no right to exist and is ruled by Nazis, if this is what Putin and his propaganda inculcated in it. Or whatever nonsense Putin decides to inject into the Russian mind. Alas, *mores mori tardius*.

Chapter Five

HISTORICAL KNOWLEDGE, FACTS, ARGUMENTS, MAXIMA AND MINIMA

1. HISTORICAL RATIONALITY

This chapter addresses the issue of how to conceive of the growth of historical knowledge and of what I call "the rationality of history" that supports and guarantees it. In the natural sciences, no one doubts that progress has been made in our knowledge of a vast array of domains of scientific research, although there have been exceptions such as Kuhn's claim of the incommensurability of scientific paradigms. But that was a long time ago, and even Kuhn later retracted most of the claims that had made the first edition of *The Structure of Scientific Revolutions* a bestseller. The problem of the growth of historical knowledge is a harder nut to crack.

For example, Fritz Fischer's *Griff nach der Weltmacht. Die Kriegszielpolitik des Kaiserlichen Deutschland* (1961) argued that the outbreak of World War I was part of Germany's well-considered strategy to become the hegemonic European nation-state. Gerhard Ritter replied that Wilhelm II and the German Chancellor Bethmann-Hollweg had no such plans, and that Austria, Russia, and France were no less guilty of the outbreak of the war than Germany. This debate has continued into the present. For example, John Röhl and Sir Richard Evans follow Fischer, whereas Niall Ferguson and Christopher Clark in his brilliant *The Sleepwalkers* remain closer to Ritter. Others, such as Wolfgang Mommsen, occupy an intermediate position.

After sixty years of intensive debate, there is still no agreement. It is difficult to think of stalemates in the sciences that have persisted as long about such an absolutely crucial issue.

No historian will deny that substantial progress has been made in the interim, insofar as no historian today can afford to defend either Fischer's or Ritter's position in their original form. This is what the growth of historical knowledge typically looks like; it should be situated *between* HRs, so to speak, rather than be identified with the success of individual HRs. We can conclude that progress has been made in both the sciences *and* in historical writing, although in different ways. The philosopher of science and the philosopher of history must, therefore, present different explanations of how progress is possible and the form that it takes.

In chapter 4 I argued that thanks to the presumption of consistency the models and PBF of HRs may all be regarded as commensurable with each other. Because they can be meaningfully compared with each other, we may speak of HRs that are better, more convincing, and so on than some others. But we must now discuss the aspects of the historical text that are typically at stake in such assessments. In particular, we should distinguish between three aspects: (1) the facts about the past mentioned in HRs, (2) the explanatory success of HRs, and (3) the HR *as* text.

The best book presently available on how to decide between rival HRs is Kuukkanen's *Postnarrativist Philosophy of Historiography*.[1] Kuukkanen also discerns three issues to be taken into consideration, but his splitting up of the problem is somewhat different. Under the rubric of "three dimensions of evaluation," Kuukkanen mentions: (1) the epistemic dimension, (2) the rhetorical dimension, and (3) the discursive dimension. To identify the similarities and differences between my approach and Kuukkanen's, a few remarks are in order.

The epistemic dimension is, according to Kuukkanen, "a close relative of 'cognitive'":

"Cognitive" here signifies any appropriate and *reasonable* criteria that make a historiographical thesis or expression concerning the past—that is, as a knowledge claim—*compelling* to accept. "Epistemic" is here a sub-concept of

---

1. Jouni-Matti Kuukkanen, *Postnarrativist Philosophy of Historiography* (Basingstoke, UK: Palgrave MacMillan 2015).

cognitive and a more restricted notion referring not to truth-conducivity as it typically does but to the *relation* in which a historical presentation stands *with its objects of research* (the past) and *with evidence* directly (italics in original).

Second, the rhetorical dimension:

I have chosen the term "rhetorical" because the point is that every work of history attempts to persuade its readers to accept a central historiographical thesis. It is important to notice that we are not talking about just any kind of persuasion, but of a specific form of argumentative persuasion that relies on informal argumentative strategies and reasoning.

Third, the discursive dimension:

A discursive dimension amounts to something "external" because it refers beyond the text itself to the historiographical argumentative context. It is evident that no historical work appears as a self-contained piece from an intellectual vacuum but emerges, instead, inevitably as molded by existing historical knowledge and historiographical arguments.[2]

Moreover, Kuukkanen does not keep these three elements strictly apart from each other. He prefers to regard them as a continuum, although the dimension of argument is most prominent.

There is nothing wrong with Kuukkanen's treatment of these three criteria as a continuum, but note that he does not differentiate between "the past" and "historical reality" in the way I have been doing throughout this account of historical writing. Second, and more important, Kuukkanen does not explicitly distinguish between establishing historical fact and issues pertaining to historical representation. His view is presumably that *argument* is decisive in both cases and that, therefore, the dimension of argument (present in both the rhetorical and the discursive dimension) covers *both*. If so, I must disagree because arguments about factual truth have another character than arguments about representational plausibility.

2. Kuukkanen, *Postnarrativist Philosophy of Historiography*, 156–58.

Arguments about factual truth deal with *the past*; arguments about representational plausibility deal with *historical reality*.³ Furthermore, arguments about factual truth deal with *weak* individuals, whereas arguments about representational plausibility deal with *strong* individuals. These two types of arguments occasion quite different types of questions in the practice of historical writing. The method for dealing with either is useless if applied to the other. It would be like trying to write a letter with a shovel or to dig a patch of grass with a pen.

Kuukkanen's distinctions also suggest that he would reject the idea that an HR *as such* can be regarded as an argument. In consequence, he effectively treats the issue of argumentative cogency as if it is restricted to the domain of establishing historical fact. However, I also situate the debate about HRs within "the logical space of argument" (to paraphrase Wilfrid Sellars), while acknowledging that HRs are arguments of a peculiar type: they are arguments in which the argument and its conclusion coincide. Put differently, if a historian was asked what their arguments were for defending a certain thesis and, replied "just read the book again," this would be an entirely appropriate and adequate response to the question.⁴

Two more differences are worth nothing. The first—although it is perhaps a matter of emphasis—is that what Kuukkanen refers to as the "discursive dimension" is integral from our point of view to the kind of argument we are ascribing to HRs *as such*. The second is that the dimension of the HR *as text* is altogether missing from his list. However, there is an overlap, and much will become clear when the criteria for the relative epistemic or cognitive success of HRs is expounded.

2. FACTS ABOUT PAST STATES OF AFFAIRS

Let us begin with establishing facts about the past. We routinely distinguish between states of affairs in the past and factual descriptions of these states of affairs. If, in talking about the past, we say "it is true that . . ." or "it is a fact that . . .", a description of a past state of affairs typically follows after

---

3. Recall, again, the historicist distinction between historical research (Geschichtsforschung) and historical writing (Geschichtsschreibung).

4. Schubert was once asked during one of his "Schubertiades" what he meant by one of the first of his impromptus. His answer was to sit back down at his piano and play the impromptu again.

the dots. States of affairs are part of the past; facts are true descriptions of them. But for two reasons these true descriptions are a less reliable basis for historiographical certainty than might be hoped.

First, (logical-)positivists believed that descriptions could capture the absolute truth about states of affairs—the paradigmatic example being the "picture theory of the true statement" Wittgenstein defended in the *Tractatus*.[5] But that optimistic view was abandoned long ago. It is now universally recognized that the truth of descriptions of states of affairs (partly) depends on the language in which these descriptions are made. Here, the word *language* is often replaced by *theory*. For example, the statement "the earth is flat" will be true for an advocate of the flat-earth theory but mistaken for the person rejecting that theory. The resulting doctrine of the so-called theory-ladenness of fact states that theories are always involved in the formulation of statements about states of affairs. Consequently, we will never get access to states of affairs without the interference of theory. As long as facts are at stake, I have no problem with that doctrine.

Second, Danto famously pointed out that true descriptions of some state of affairs in the past also depend on the temporal relation between the past state of affairs in question and the moment when the description was made. For example, only after 1648 could it truthfully be said that "the Thirty Years War broke out in 1618." Even someone knowing *all* that could possibly be known in 1618 (called the Ideal Chronicler by Danto) could *never* have made that statement because of their ignorance of the future. To do so, one would have had to have known that the war would end in 1648 and would therefore be called—albeit only after 1648—the Thirty Years War.[6]

These two considerations entail a systematic indeterminacy between statements about states of affairs (or events) in the past and these states of affairs themselves. Some authors, such as Paul Roth, even go so far as to eliminate the event itself behind the veil of its descriptions: "what the unit-event is, depends on the telling of it. Given the instructions to record 'everything that happens, as it happens' the problem is not that there is

---

5. Ludwig Wittgenstein, *Tractatus Logico-Philosophicus*, trans. C. K. Ogden (New York: Dover, 1999), 4.021: "The proposition is a picture of reality, for I know the state of affairs presented by it, if I understand the proposition."

6. Arthur C. Danto, *Narration and Knowledge: With a New Introduction by Lydia Goehr and a New Conclusion by Frank Ankersmit* (New York: Columbia University Press, 2007), chapter, 8.

too much for an Ideal Chronicler to record: the irony is that there are no things in the abstract to be recorded. The Ideal Chronicler never gets started because there are no ideal events to chronicle."[7] Roth doesn't even shy away from the ultimate step when speaking with manifest satisfaction of the historian's capacity "to change the past."[8] But this is going too far. The historian cannot make Hitler stay just a little longer in the *Bürgerbräukeller* in Munich on November 8, 1939—with the result that he would have been blown to smithereens by Johann Elser's bomb. We may describe and interpret these events in whatever way we like; we may categorize the objects in the past in any way we prefer; but no amount of redescribing or rewriting the past will ever wipe this kind of event from the historical record, or erase it as a historical state of affairs. Unlike facts, historical states of affairs don't care at all about how they are or will be described—they stubbornly remain what they have always been—so if we are talking about states of affairs in the past, our talking about them cannot change them in the slightest.

Even more important is the following consideration. Previously I mentioned the doctrine of the theory-ladenness of empirical fact: the claim that the description of facts is codetermined by the language or theory in terms of which the description is formulated. The conclusion is that the establishment of fact and theory are inseparable. The conclusion is correct. But there is a temptation to believe that the same must be true of the establishment of facts, and the HRs mentioning these facts. Consequently, fact and historical representation are as inseparable as fact and theory. Put differently, the fact that the statements about the past resulting from historical research are (often) integrated in an HR suggests a continuity between historical research and historical writing. This is often seen as proof that no clear-cut distinction can be made between the two. But this is wrong.

To see why, let us look at Chiel van den Akker's argument:

Although a chronicle and a narrative [Van den Akker's term for a historical representation] may mention the same event, even its description may be graphically or sonically identical, containing the same marks in ink or pixels or producing the same noises in the same order; the truth-conditions, hence

---

7. Paul Roth, *The Philosophical Structure of Historical Explanation* (Evanston, IL: Northwestern University Press, 2020), 29.
8. Roth, *Philosophical Structure of Historical Explanation*, 42.

the meaning of these statements will differ, for as part of the truth-conditions of statements in a narrative there belongs a reference to the historical theses of that narrative, and such reference obviously is lacking in a chronicle consisting of events descriptions.[9]

Van den Akker's claim is not difficult to explain. Let the results of some piece of historical research be expressed by the statements $s_1, s_2, s_3 \ldots s_n$. Now, as previously established, the corresponding HR_a doesn't have the form $s_1, s_2, s_3 \ldots s_n$; a mere conjunction of statements is no historical representation. These sentences must be made to belong to each other somehow. This is why I argued that a historical representation HR_a only comes into being if $s_1, s_2, s_3 \ldots s_n$ are recursively read as a definition of HR_a; that is, as a set of meta-statements having the form $\{(HR_a \text{ is } s_1), (HR_a \text{ is } s_2), (HR_a \text{ is } s_3) \ldots (HR_a \text{ is } s_n)\}$. Now, the meaning of the statements $p_1, p_2, p_3 \ldots p_n$ clearly differs from that of the statements $(HR_a \text{ is } s_1), (HR_a \text{ is } s_2), (HR_a \text{ is } s_3) \ldots (HR_a \text{ is } s_n)$. The former are about the past, whereas the latter are about an HR. Van den Akker is, therefore, correct that there is an unbridgeable gap between a true statement about a historical state of affairs *as* based on historical research and that *same* statement *as part* of the HR mentioning it. In the latter case, that statement must be read not *only* as a statement about the past but *also* as a statement about the HR containing it.

Philosophers of history have typically seen only the *first* function of that statement and systematically ignored its *other* function. No philosopher of history (as far as I know) ever recognized that the sentences of an HR also recursively define that HR: they never appreciated that HR_a requires us to read the statements $s_1, s_2, s_3 \ldots s_n$ in an expanded form, as follows: $\{(HR_a \text{ is } s_1), (HR_a \text{ is } s_2), (HR_a \text{ is } s_3) \ldots (HR_a \text{ is } s_n)\}$. They have never realized, in other words, that logic requires the phrase "HR_a is ..." to be persistently there, but it is at the same time always omitted because, taken in context, the phrase can clearly be treated as redundant. Obviously, no reader of HR_a will ever feel tempted to see its sentences as the properties of some *other* HR than HR_a and therefore feel the need to endlessly repeat the phrase "HR_a is ...". Nevertheless, the phrase is always logically implied.

---

9. Chiel van den Akker, *The Exemplifying Past. A Philosophy of History* (Amsterdam: Amsterdam University Press, 2018), 67.

All this demonstrates that it is imperative to grant to linguistic entities such as HR_a a logical status of their own, on the same level as proper names, subject- and predicate-terms, sentences, theories, and so on. Failure to do so ensures that all reflection on narrative or representation inevitably remains groping in the dark. It will then be like trying to count without numbers. What my argument shows beyond doubt is that the logical difference between historical research and historical writing can only be clarified thanks to the kind of logical entity indicated by the sign HR_a.

To sum up the results of this section, historians may employ (socio-)scientific theories (whether from economics or some other social science) to make sense of their archival research. In that case, the doctrine of the theory-ladenness of empirical fact correctly claims that the historian's facts will be formulated in terms of these theories. Note, however, that normally such theories have been formed in the present or in a recent past, and they may be applied to a past centuries ago. Hence, these theories are *eo ipso* assumed to be resistant to temporal change and, in that sense, *a*historical. Put differently, their being used to describe historical facts refers us to a level in the practice of the writing of history on which the intrinsic asymmetry between past and present claimed by modern historicist historical writing does not yet manifest itself. Their use is, therefore, restricted to the level of historical research (Geschichtsforschung), i.e., the level of the establishment of historical facts (including their proper description). This level, as I have argued on several occasions, is logically and semantically distinct from the level of historical writing (Geschichtsschreibung).

The shift from the former to the latter is made as soon as facts about the past are integrated in an HR, but this integration will not alter their meaning. What *may* change—sometimes dramatically—is the representational meaning to which they contribute. As Van den Akker's argument made admirably clear, one and the same fact, under one and the same description, may occur in quite different HRs. In that case, that same fact will contribute to different historiographical meanings just as one may use one and the same set of pebbles to form different patterns, but these pebbles will remain exactly the same in each pattern. Similarly, some fact may contribute to different historical meanings—and thus *seem* to change its semantic color accordingly—while remaining the same fact all along. We cannot change the facts of the past whatever these facts are made to do in different HRs. Hence, we must insist that historical representation does not determine the *description* of historical states of affairs (whether in terms of ordinary or of theoretical language). Nor does it decide the question of meaning, as the doctrine of the theory-ladenness of empirical facts tries to claim—it decides *exclusively* about the *selection* of those facts.

3. THE GROWTH OF HISTORICAL KNOWLEDGE

I briefly touched on the notion of "the growth of historical knowledge" in chapter 4, and what was said there allows me to elaborate on it further. The distinction between historical research and historical writing entails that the growth of historical knowledge occurs in both domains. We now know far more about the past than we did a hundred or even fifty years ago, and we have also refined our HRs during the same period. HRs have therefore been indispensable conditions of the growth of historical knowledge. It may sound odd to treat the growth of historical knowledge in this way because we tend to think of HRs as "serving their own purpose" exclusively and to be indifferent to what seems to be nothing of their business—as, for example, such a thing as the growth of historical knowledge.

At first sight there seems to be no determinable link between the concept of the historical representation, on the one hand, and that of the growth of historical knowledge, on the other. And, indeed, it needs a more comprehensive scope to see that there *must* be such a link. Specifically, at this stage recall that historical reality only comes into being thanks to HRs: no HRs, then no historical reality either and, hence, no entity to give the notion of the growth of historical knowledge any meaningful content. In this way, an HR's raison d'être extends beyond—or transcends—its *own* role in historical debate. Put differently, the growth of historical knowledge has its proper locus *between* HRs rather than *in* them. In sum, we must associate the triumphs of modern historical writing not with *individual* HRs but with the unintended result of their interaction. One is reminded of Leibniz's metaphor of the sound of the surf (equivalent to the growth of historical knowledge) we hear when approaching the sea and that cannot be retraced to the sound of individual waves (equivalent to individual HRs).

To put it provocatively, if all possible HRs had been realized, that would mean the end of the growth of historical knowledge—not because no more HRs could be written now but because there is no longer any space between them within which historical knowledge could grow. It follows that historical knowledge grows fastest when only a few HRs are around; if the number of HRs increases, the growth of historical knowledge will undoubtedly continue but its pace will gradually decrease. The stronger historical knowledge becomes, the weaker the position of HRs with regard to it will become; the latter will lose more and more of their grip on the sentences constituting them. And the meta-sentences keeping them together will ever more easily make common cause with those of other HRs that come infinitesimally close to them. In the end, HRs will dissolve into the individual sentences constituting them and be no more than mere static overpowered by the overwhelming presence of historical knowledge. Historical writing (if we may still call it so) will then consist of historical knowledge, on the one hand, and a chaos of information about individual states of affairs in the past, on the other. HRs will still exist—they never die—but they will have lost their power to organize the chaos of factual knowledge about past states of affairs.

Needless to say, this situation will never materialize. From that perspective, these considerations are without any practical value. Nevertheless, it sometimes pays to think through an idea to its ultimate logical consequences. And, indeed, there is a lesson in what was said just now: it makes us aware of the surprising fact that historical representation and historical knowledge do not have the same agenda—as we would naively have surmised—and that, to some extent at least, they even exclude each other. For the original sin of HRs is their innate desire to dominate all other HRs; this desire has the unintended consequence of always contributing—however small!—to the death of the domain of the HRs. A proper understanding of the writing of history requires, therefore, the recognition of this dialectical opposition between historical representation and historical knowledge—with the qualification that the latter necessarily presupposes the presence of the former.[10] Without HRs there is no historical knowledge.

---

10. All this may remind us of the second law of thermodynamics as established by Rudolph Clausius (1822–1888), which states that nature strives to maximalize entropy (Clausius coined that term) and to achieve a state of equilibrium. Or of a maximum of disorder, or chaos and a minimum of order. Life is, as Erwin Schrödinger showed, the perennial struggle against the second law. A struggle it will always, sooner or later, lose. The second law is, arguably, the most important law of physics; it dicates even the fate of the universe, as Clausius himself saw already.

Pursuing this comparison, historical representation is on a par with sucking order out of a system. For this is exactly what historical representation does: by means of its perspectivism it sucks order out of the chaos of myriad individual states of affairs in the past. After the historian has

At the same time, conceiving of the growth of historical knowledge as the *unintended* result of the interaction of HRs seems to discourage—to say the least—any effort to answer the question of how individual HR's may hope to contribute to it. Unintended results are necessarily outside the reach of what can be intentionally achieved. Consequently, the very idea of historical rationality must be an illusion. Needless to say, the conclusion is absurd. The undeniable fact that there exists such a thing as rational action is perfectly compatible with the observation that rational action may have its unintended (and ordinarily irrational) results—either on the level of the individual or of that of the collectivity. Similarly, the fact that the growth of historical knowledge is the unintended result of HRs does not diminish in the least the urgency of a reflection on the issue of historical rationality—and, indeed, a great deal was said about that issue in chapter 4. So let's return to it again.

As so often, Leibniz's monadology is illuminating; it helps us to see how the use of the phrase "the growth of historical knowledge" can be justified in logical terms. The following metaphor repeatedly recurs in Leibniz's writings:

> Just as the same city viewed from different sides appears to be different and to be, as it were, multiplied in perspectives, so the infinite multitude of simple substances, which seem to be so many universes, are nevertheless only the perspectives of a single universe according to the different points of view of each monad.[11]

---

done their job, order has accumulated in the HR. But precisely by doing so, the historian increases chaos or entropy in the system as a whole, and the result is that later historians will need an even stronger "will to power" to create order in the chaos—and so it will go, on and on. In the end, all order will have been removed to the level of representation, reaching a state of equilibrium—a maximum of entropy—on that of historical fact. Representation stands for order; entropy, equilibrium, and chaos stand for historical knowledge. Both in nature and in historical writing, entropy is the final state.

11. Gottfried Wilhelm Leibniz, "Monadology," in *Philosophical Papers and Letters*, 2nd ed., trans. Leroy E. Loemker (Boston: Reidel/Springer, 1976), section 57. See also his correspondence with Arnauld, in Gottfried Wilhelm Leibniz, *Philosophical Papers and Letters*, 2nd ed., trans. Leroy E. Loemker (Boston: Reidel/Springer, 1976), 337: "the proposition which has occasioned this discussion is, I may add, very important and deserves to be firmly established, for it follows from it that every individual substance expresses the universe in its own way and in a certain relationship, or from that point of view, so to speak, from which it regards it. It follows also that its subsequent state is the result, though free and contingent, of its preceding state, as if there were only God and itself in the world. Thus each individual substance or complete being is a world apart, independent of every other thing but God."

Leibniz uses this metaphor when he wishes to clarify his view of the relationship between the monadological universe and the domain of the PBF. The idea is as follows. You have, to begin with, all the perspectives from which you can see the city. If one has seen the city from only a few perspectives, one's idea of it will be imperfect. But if one walks around the city with paper and pencil while sketching it from every conceivable perspective, and then finally combines all the sketches one has made, one may draw a map of the city as it *really* is. Needless to say, in Leibniz's metaphor the perspectives correspond with the monadological universe—where there is also nothing but perspectives, and where the city itself (allegedly) is a PBF and, as such, part of the phenomenal reality in which we live.

We all know the proverb *omnis comparatio claudicat*. But Leibniz's metaphor is a particularly unhappy one. To begin with, the city precedes in the perspectives one may have on it. In this way, Leibniz's metaphor turns the essence of his own system upside down: the domain of the PBF is now suggested to be prior to that of the monadological universe. Second, the perspectives that the monads have are perspectives on *each other* and emphatically *not* on a PBF. The latter reading would entirely wipe out the clear-cut distinction between the *reality* of the monadological universe, on the one hand, and the merely phenomenal domain of the PBF, on the other. This distinction is no less crucial in Leibniz's system. So the metaphor is likely to spread confusion rather than to bring clarity to readers of the *Monadology*.[12]

Nevertheless, the metaphor can still be helpful. Historians feel a genuine affinity for Leibniz's ideas of the perspective and of seeing the world from a certain point of view.[13] They are in the habit of saying things like "from what point of view has this historian studied a certain part of the past?" or "this historian offers a new and interesting perspective on a much-discussed part of the past," and so on. We may infer that these visual metaphors of the point of view and the perspective express some fundamental truth about the nature of historical representation.

It is not difficult to discern what that truth is. Suppose you are looking for the best point of view from which to see Leibniz's city—the point of

---

12. The metaphor of the map of England previously proposed is therefore to be preferred to Leibniz's metaphor. See pp. 48, 49.
13. See chapter 2, section 5.

view giving you the most informative perspective on it. Self-evidently, the closer you come to the city, the more information about it would become available. If you were standing right in front of the city, your whole field of vision would be filled with a wealth of details about houses, streets, and trees. You would be overwhelmed with information and would have every reason to be content—if this were what you were looking for. But precisely this should make you hesitate: is it not better to exchange the position giving you access to these heaps of exact but chaotic information for a point of view allowing you to survey the city, giving you an idea of its structure that permits a grasp of how all these details may hang together? This does, of course, mean sacrificing your desire for even more information about even more details. But any sensible person would choose that option: here, again, *less is more*. In sum, at one end of the spectrum, we have myriad historical details but without any grasp of the whole; at the other end, we have a grasp of the whole but at the expense of a less precise and exact knowledge of the details.

Both extremes must be avoided, so the only sensible course is to find the juste milieu between them. As you will see later in this chapter, this dilemma is typical of all historical writing, which poses a new problem. As far as I know, no philosophy of history ever put the search of such a juste milieu on the agenda. My hunch is that everyone knows the problem of the less is more and of the juste milieu to exist and to be quite prominent in the actual writing of history, whereas at the same time no one took it seriously enough to pay attention to it. When addressing it, the obvious first thing to do is to establish whether the problem, or a close variant of it, has been discussed in the philosophy of science already; and, if so, whether something about the writing of history can be learned from it. And, indeed, as I will show, a positive answer to that question can be given if we have a look at Popper's fallibilism.[14]

To begin with, let's agree that both the sciences and historical writing have their point of departure in what is given to us as observable fact—as the outcome of experiments in the sciences and as archival evidence in

---

14. This may be a surprise because Popper's philosophy of science is not held in high esteem today. Illustrative is the merely marginal role assigned to Popper in John H. Zammito, *A Nice Derangement of Epistemes. Post-Positivism in the Study of Science from Quine to Latour* (Chicago: University of Chicago Press, 2004). For a "rehabilitation," of Popper, see Franklin Rudolf Ankersmit, *Peter Munz's Evolutionist Philosophy of History and the Anthropocene*, forthcoming.

historical writing. No facts, then no science and no historical writing either. If the sciences move from fact to *theory*, one might wonder whether historical writing does so as well. As we all know by now, it does not: HRs are not theories. But there might be interesting analogies. It would be overhasty to reject any comparison between history and the sciences as a useless enterprise because of the differences between HRs and theories. So let's explore this path a little further and see where it leads us.

The journey from fact to theory in the sciences is a long one, and many things change along the way, but somehow the continuity between fact and theory is never broken or abandoned. "*Natura non facit saltus*"—as Leibniz famously put it.[15] And so it is here. Think, for example, of how (logical)-positivists such as Hume, Carnap, or Reichenbach hoped to make the move by induction. The universal law was to be drawn directly from the empirical facts. The doctrine of the theory-ladenness of facts revealed the naivety of these (logical)-positivist hopes—but to do so, it proposed its own version of the idea that there is always a continuity between fact and theory, and vice versa. There are no facts without theory and no theories without facts.

Since then, several types of theories have tried to explain the shift from fact to theory including conventionalism; the philosophy of scientific continuity (Duhem); instrumentalism (Toulmin); the philosophy of continuing comparison (Agassi); and so on. But all of them suppose that both fact and theory formulate statements about reality and that both fact and theory therefore find their ultimate justification in what reality is like. Pragmatist approaches to the philosophy of science, for example, have introduced the idiom of truth as a "warranted assertion," a manner of speaking clearly rooted in the idea that scientific statements predicate certain properties of reality.

In sum, all these philosophies of science share two things. First, they suppose a continuum between fact and theory—with the qualification that each new philosophy of science was developed to add additional nodes

---

15. "Rien ne se fait tout d'un coup, et c'est un de mes grandes maximes et des plus vérifiées que *la nature ne fait jamais des sauts*, ce que j'appelais *la Loi de la Continuité*, lorsque j'en parlais dans les premières Nouvelles de la République des lettres, et l'usage de ce loi est très considérable dans la physique" (italics in original). Gottfried Wilhelm Leibniz, *Nouveaux Essais sur l'Entendement Humain. Chronologie et introduction par Jacques Brunschwig* (Paris: Garnier Flammarion, 1966), 40.

and loops to the continuum such as so-called epistemic values[16] (or even the quasi-political tricks that scientists sometimes indulge in to "win" in scientific debate.)[17] Second, each offers a justification of scientific knowledge with the help of an analysis as detailed and careful as possible of all the steps made on this long continuum between fact and theory and of how each step leads to and necessitates the next one. In this way they are all justificationists. This justificationist thesis—and specifically its notion of this continuum between fact and theory—suggests a movement from elementary data (facts) to the conclusions that can be based upon them (i.e., theories). Traditional empiricism argued from facts to theory in exactly this way. At least from *this* perspective, contemporary justificationism has remained in the orbit of eighteenth- and nineteenth-century empiricism in spite of the wide variety of positions in the justificationist philosophy of science.

Whatever one makes of these approaches to the philosophy of science, in both the Leibnizian system and in historical representation, such a movement from fact to theory is absolutely impossible to defend. There may be continuity between historical fact and how facts are described, but there is *no* continuity between monads and the domain of the PBF nor between historical facts and historical representations. The bridge between fact and theory built by the doctrine of the theory-ladenness of empirical fact has no counterpart in either Leibniz or the domain of historical representation. That bridge may well be a very complicated structure in the case of theory, but in that of historical representation there is no such bridge *at all*. In the case of historical representation, facts belong to the past, when it still was "past reality." However, the HRs live their lives in a completely different metaphysical domain, that of the strong individuals discussed earlier. There is an asymmetry between how facts relate to scientific theories, on the one hand, and how facts relate to historical representations, on the other. Justificationism in the philosophy of science, as just noted, has always owed its plausibility to the claim that there is a continuity (however defined) between fact and theory.

---

16. Herman Paul, *Historians' Virtues. From Antiquity to the Twenty-First Century* (Cambridge: Cambridge University Press, 2022).

17. Bruno Latour, *Science in Action: How to Follow Scientists and Engineers Through Society* (Cambridge, MA: Harvard University Press, 1987).

But whether or not this argument provides a warrant for the truth of scientific propositions, no such support is available in the case of historical representations.

Indeed, historical facts only *indirectly* decide the fate of HR's.[18] It is not the historical facts but *the battle between HRs* that determines which HR will be preferred. Surely, facts have an important role to play, but their role resembles that of the pieces in the moves the chess player makes to gradually maneuver his opponent into an ultimately hopeless position. The pieces are not themselves the moves; they are not the links in an unbreakable chain *justifying* a certain inescapable conclusion. Their presence on the chessboard merely registers the present state in a game of chess. As such they are just as indispensable as signs are for Leibniz's *calculatio caeca*; but as it is with Leibniz, they do not determine the outcome of the game. In the historical text, facts are organized horizontally rather than vertically. Facts are used in historical writing tactically or strategically and always with an eye on the moves of possible opponents, whereas in the sciences the facts that the justificationists have in mind are anticipations of theories, and theories are the transfiguration of facts. Justificationism may make sense for the sciences, but it is an inappropriate model for the writing of history.

When listing the philosophies of science succeeding (logical)-positivism, I deliberately omitted Popper's falsificationism, or fallibilism as its later variant was called.[19] Popper's falsificationism is the only philosophy of science that can do without justificationism. It does not claim that the assessment of scientific theories is dependent on their being justified in one way or another by what reality is like. Of course, Popper's falsificationism was meant to be a philosophy of *science* in the first instance. But because it severs the justificationalist link between fact and theory, it also captures perfectly the absence of any fixed or codifiable algorithmic procedure for moving from fact to historical representation in the writing of history.

How might Popper's falsificationism contribute to our understanding of the growth of historical knowledge? Falsificationism, as the name indicates,

---

18. See chapter 3, section 5.
19. For a fuller discussion, see Ankersmit, *Peter Munz's Evolutionary Philosophy of History*, forthcoming.

emphasizes not *truth* but *falsification*. The closest you can get to truth is having a theory that is *not yet* falsified. The efforts of all scientists will then be directed at falsifying that one too, and at finding a new theory scoring better in the test of falsification. The contrast with justificationism could not be stronger. Justificationism aims above all at elevating beliefs to the desired status of truths, or "warranted true beliefs."

Several conclusions can be inferred from this difference between justificationism and Popper's antijustificationist falsificationism. First, Popper's falsificationism offers an account of the growth of scientific knowledge that never needs to appeal to the idea of what physical reality actually is like. Recall here Cassirer's warning against the most tempting misunderstanding of Leibniz and how it was echoed in Munz's warning against the belief that there should be "a face underneath the masks we press upon the past" (see chapter 2). Similarly, for Popper it suffices to explain the mechanism of falsification hanging high above physical reality without ever getting into touch with it. The only exception is the moment a theory is falsified—and if that happens, one is momentarily empty-handed. In sum, if it is asked which philosopher of science since the early 1900s came closest to Leibniz, the answer is Popper. Both are intensionalists rather than extensionalists—in the epilogue I explain that this opposition underlies most of the argument in this book.

Next, not surprisingly, Popper likes to insist that he can do without an ontology (as in the philosophy of history proposed in this book that the past is robbed of its former metaphysical status). The justificationist is compelled to accept an ontology comprising minimally the world as investigated in the sciences. Hence, its perennial extensionalist bias. But together with the justificationist's continuum between fact and theory, fact and theory themselves have to surrender their privileged status to falsification in Popper's philosophy of science. Neither fact nor theory but falsification, arbitrating between the two, is the decisive factor in the growth of scientific knowledge. Facts only enter on the scene when they succeed in falsifying a theory. Nor are there any true theories in the strict sense of the word in Popper's falsificationism. He offers only theories that have not yet been falsified. To put it all in one sentence, Popper is an antijustificationist because there simply *is* nothing to be justified. Finally, having thus gotten rid of the fact and theory duality and its associated attitudes, the very idea of the continuum between fact and theory can also be rejected.

The only exception is that Popper agrees with the antiempiricist claim that theories determine the description of facts.[20]

Popper's radically antijustificationist approach fits perfectly well with my account of historical representation. In historical representation, fact and representation belong to wholly different worlds. The gap between the two is as deep as that between the metaphysics of the weak individual and that of the strong individual. So the notion of a continuum between fact and theory is untenable if applied to historical representation. The whole issue of justificationism loses all meaning and relevance as far as the writing of history is concerned.

These findings should encourage us to look for more parallels between Popper's philosophy of science and my theory of historical representation. This returns us to Leibniz's perspectivism, as suggested by his so unfortunate metaphor of a city visible from many different perspectives while yet remaining one and the same city—and to the two ideas of less is more and of the juste milieu that were invited by it. These two ideas have, indeed, their counterpart in Popper's philosophy of science.

Recall Popper's notion of "empirical content." According to Popper, a scientific theory should "forbid" as much as possible. The more it forbids, the greater its empirical content will be. Observe the sheer provocation of this claim: intuitively, the *more* a theory tells us about reality, the *better* it is. But, as Popper points out, looking for that kind of theory results in empty truisms, such as "tomorrow it will rain, or it will not rain," i.e., in truths that will always be true of the world regardless of what the world is like. Put differently, they are always true and, paradoxically, precisely because of this their empirical content is nil. Much the same can be said about metaphysical claims such as "man is good" or "man is evil": each of them can be made to agree with empirical evidence about human behavior. Hence, the phrase *less is more* fits both Popper's claim that the more a theory forbids the greater its empirical content and Leibniz's claim that the best point of view from which to see a city is the point of view forbidding an overwhelming number of useless details. On the other hand, both the philosopher of

---

20. Popper fully agrees with the antiempiricist thesis of the theory-ladenness of empirical fact in the sciences. In descriptions of states of affairs, there undoubtedly *is* a continuum between theory, on the one hand, and the description of states of affairs (as expressed in factual statements about these states of affairs), on the other. Justificationism is, however, a thesis about theory *formation* that must not be confused with the issue of the description of states of affairs.

science and the historian hope to explain *more* rather than *less* of that part of the world that is investigated by them. The physicist aims at theories that explain other theories and that, therefore, go deeper than these, whereas the historian aims at HRs having the widest possible scope. Here more is better than less. In this way both the scientist and the historian have to negotiate the juste milieu between the less is more principle, on the one hand, and the principle of more is better than less, on the other.

Before examining further how these Popperian insights can be applied to historical representation, consider this preliminary remark. Both Popper's falsificationism and my account of historical representation sever the continuum between fact and theory, or in our terminology, between fact and historical representation. Furthermore, this caesura has a metaphysical support. In Popper's case, this support is derived from an ontology that comprises no more than what is necessary to falsify a theory. Similarly, in the case of historical representation, HRs refer us to the domain of the PBF and models. HRs fight their wars on a level that is no longer part of historical *reality*.

This does not mean, however, that facts are marginalized in either case. Popper fully agrees with the justificationists believing in the continuum between fact and theory that the sciences are essentially *empirical* sciences. Likewise, the account of historical representation given here does not question that historical writing is impossible without historical facts. But scientific and historical facts only get access to the domains of scientific theory and of historical representation, respectively, after having been invited there for good reasons. Without such an explicit invitation, they can only cause confusion.

Let us see now whether Popper's claim that the more a theory forbids the greater its empirical content applies to historical writing as well. Think of a circle C_1 whose circumference contains all the models and PBF for some part of the past available at time t_1. Think, next, of a somewhat larger circle C_2 doing much the same for the state of historical knowledge at a later time t_2. Now move C_2 over C_1 in such a way that their centers coincide. In that case we can say that historical knowledge has grown between t_1 and t_2, but gradually, and no knowledge was lost in the process. This is probably how the (logical)-positivists thought about the growth of scientific knowledge.

Now let us move the center of the larger circle C_2 away from that of C_1. Initially, the picture will remain fairly close to that just described. But we can move C_2 so far away from C_1 that there is almost no overlap between the two circles. Then we will have the situation that Popper had in mind: the *less* overlap there is between C_1 and C_2, the *more* C_2 can be said to forbid—with the qualification that the term *forbidding* must be associated with that part of C_1 no longer covered by C_2. Hence, what is forbidden is *not* the product of anything external to both C_1 and C_2. I have explicitly stipulated that facts not explicitly invited to play a role in either C_1 or C_2 are not to be taken into consideration. Next, observe that the more you move C_2 and C_1 apart from one another, the more C_2 will forbid (because the surface of C_1 no longer covered by C_2 will become greater). At the same time, C_2's empirical content (i.e., the part of C_2 exceeding C_1) will grow continuously.

Observe, in the first place, that we may discern here a criterion of historical truth: if for Popper the theory "forbidding" most (other things being equal) is the "best" theory, the theory with the greatest "verisimilitude" or the "truest theory," so it is, too, in the writing of history. In both cases Popper's notion of "empirical content" is the objective measuring rod for measuring degrees of truth. The implication is, indeed, that you don't have in historical writing HRs that are "true" or "false," but always *degrees* of truth and falsity. As we might have expected from the fact that historical truth is at all times a matter of HRs being *compared to each other* and not of a *correspondence* of HRs with the past. If you compare A with B the result will always be that A satisfies some standard better than B (or the reverse), whereas correspondence is a matter of yes or no. Saying that A satisfies a standard better than B leaves room for the possibility that HR C, or D satisfies it even better. Correspondence, however, is an all or nothing matter *tertium non datur*; no room for degrees of truth (and falsity) there.

The historian, having lived through this evolution in the writing of history between t_1 and t_2, will have to conclude that it apparently pays to be a revolutionary in historical writing. To put it differently, there is merit in proposing audacious and perhaps even profoundly counterintuitive HRs. Compare the situation when C_1 and C_2 still had the same center; it is true that new historical knowledge was achieved in that situation as well. But it represented the absolute minimum growth of knowledge because C_1 was allowed to remain fully intact and could thus succeed in minimizing C_2's novelty. But the more successful the audacious historian is in defending their new HR, the more empirical content C_2 will secure for itself at the expense of C_1. The process culminates when C_2 has no longer any overlap at all with C_1. Its empirical content will then be at its greatest, and we will have witnessed a complete revolution in the field of historical writing in question.

However, the strivings of historians for a "permanent revolution" will always be tempered by the fact that historical writing must respect the presumption of consistency. If a revolutionary HR is proposed for some part of the past, the question immediately arises of whether it can be reconciled with the state of the art expressed in HRs in closely related fields. The presumption of consistency is nonnegotiable, so this new HR will have to pass this test too. A revolutionary new HR will fail to gain acceptance if too many doubts can be raised about the agreement between the new theory and generally accepted HRs in adjacent areas of historical research.

In sum, the growth of historical knowledge requires finding the juste milieu between intellectual originality and audacity, on the one hand, and the inexorable and nonnegotiable rule of the presumption of consistency, on the other. Perhaps it may even result in a kind of division of tasks among historians in the sense that some historians will temperamentally prefer to propose provocative new insights, and others will believe it to be their task to serve the cause of the growth of historical knowledge by poohpoohing such daring theses. For there to be genuine growth in historical knowledge, both approaches are needed. Everyone needs everyone else; and the quality of historical writing can only benefit from the, admittedly, uncomfortable coexistence of the Ejlert Løvborg's, on the one hand, and the Jørgen Tesman's, on the other. Whereas their coexistence was fatal for Hedda Gabler, historical writing thrives on it.

If it should happen that attempts at reconciliation prove impossible because the available models and PBF do not offer the material needed for bridging the gap between the two, we will find ourselves at an impasse. One can only wait and hope that more HRs on that topic will be written. This may explain why historians continually produce new monographs on the same historical topic, whereas those outside the profession may be tempted to ask themselves what is the use of yet another book on feudal law or on the French Revolution. The more articles, books, and monographs there are, the more opportunities there are to discover if bridges can be built between them, and the more effective the presumption of consistency will prove to be.

An increase in the number of monographs on some historical issue has much the same function as a microscope in biology: it gives the historian access to details of historical reality that would have remained unperceived when only a few HRs were available to illuminate the domain of the PBF with their isolated circles of light. And where would the biologist be without his microscope? Moreover, *"Dieu est dans le détail,"* as the saying goes: a small detail may upset the whole picture. For example, republicanism as understood by Franco Venturi, Quentin Skinner, and John Pocock and many others is still the dominant model for how historians conceive of seventeenth- and eighteenth-century political thought. This consensus would be seriously undermined by even a brief but well-documented HR on the low opinion that both eighteenth-century political philosophers and the political elite of that time had of Dutch, Venitian, and Genoan republics. Had I chosen a different intellectual career, I would very much like to have written that book.

Jouni-Matti Kuukkanen has proposed five criteria for representational success:

> 1) *exemplification*: the descriptive content of a colligatory expression has to exemplify the historical data it subsumes; 2) *coherence*: the material highlighted has to be chosen and constructed so that it forms a maximally coherent set; 3) *comprehensiveness*: the concept that applies to a larger amount of historical material than its rival on the assumed historical phenomena is to be preferred and 4) *scope*: everything being equal, a colligatory concept with a larger scope of application to historical phenomena is preferable to one with a more limited scope, originality: 5) everything being equal, a more innovative and original concept should be preferred to a more customary one.[21]

Three comments are in order here. First, Kuukkanen refers to so-called colligatory concepts (such as the Renaissance, Hellenism, or the Cold War) and, hence, not to *individual* HRs. Nevertheless, these colligatory concepts are historical representations that should, presumably, be regarded as the hard core of the most successful HRs about the period in question. The question of how historians reach consensus about that hard core is best

21. Kuukkanen, *Postnarratavist Philosophy of Historiography*, 123–28.

phrased in terms of the growth of historical knowledge. It can be answered by the account of that growth proposed in the beginning of this section.

Second, Kuukkanen's criterion of exemplification is applicable to colligatory concepts only: for example, the colligatory concept "the Cold War" clearly satisfies the criterion of exemplification because the conflict between the West and Soviet Russia never resulted in a third World War. But I shall leave the issue of colligatory concepts outside of the present discussion because most HRs have no names such as the Baroque or the Cold War. A more detailed discussion, including the issue of the characterization of historical periods by devising a catchy metaphor for doing so, would distract from what is at stake here.[22] Moreover, such metaphors are ordinarily used to refer to sets of HRs having a certain subject-matter in common; hence, these names refer to HRs and not to what they are about. So the issue is not likely to shed much new light on the nature of historical representation.

Third, there is an intimate connection between Kuukkanen's next three criteria. Specifically, "coherence" and "comprehensiveness" can both arguably be subsumed within the "scope" criterion. It is hard to imagine that an HR's scope would not be diminished by a reduction of either its coherence or its comprehensiveness (or both). Hence, the second and third criteria are really alternative specifications of the fourth rather than

---

22. Chiel van den Akker grants exemplification a crucial role in his book: "we should reflect on the distinction between description of the past in the Ideal Chronicle's list and retrospective understandings of the past as they can be found in the historian's narrative. The exemplification theory of history . . . holds that the past as represented in some narrative exemplifies the historical thesis of that narrative. As such the theory explains how the past receives its meaning." Van den Akker, *The Exemplifying Past*, 102.

Van den Akker's exemplification theory reverses how we would normally define the representation and the represented. Usually we see the historical text as the representation and the past as the represented. In Van den Akker's exemplification theory, however, "the given" (i.e., what we normally associate with the represented) is the historical thesis that the past must exemplify (the role that we normally attribute to the representation). A similar reversal of the representation and the represented characterized the discussion of the "projection theory of representation" in chapter 4, section 2.

In the first three chapters, I have consistently distinguished between the past and historical reality. If one were to conflate these two things and call them collectively "the past," my argument would come quite close to the one proposed by Van den Akker. If what I called the *models* accompanying HRs were understood as being situated in the past, they could be said to *exemplify* HRs in Van den Akker's sense. For a review of Van den Akker, *The Exemplifying Past*, and of Paul Roth, *The Philosophical Structure of Historical Explanation*, see Franklin Rudolf Ankersmit, "A Narrativist Revival?," *Journal of the Philosophy of History* 15, no. 2 (2021), 215–40.

a wholly separate and independent instrument for measuring representational success. With regard to the fifth, Kuukkanen effectively shares my position. So, overall, I am in agreement with Kuukkanen's criteria.

There are, however, two reservations. The first one concerns the term *scope*. Obviously, this is a spatial metaphor; I have appealed to it myself in earlier writings. But a metaphor still requires that one explain what the view or theory intimated by the metaphor is and why the metaphor does this so successfully. Any use of metaphors entails risks the danger that their very suggestiveness can obscure important issues. In this case, the metaphor leaves unanswered the question of what the scope is a scope *on* or *of*. Kuukkanen presumably has in mind the past, but this gives rise to the difficult question of how to capture in exclusively literal language what it means to say about a past perhaps many centuries old that it is "falling within some historian's scope." The past is no longer there, no one has ever 'seen' it and it makes no sense to say that my scope on it is larger than yours. This is why I eschewed the notion of "a scope on the past" in our current account of representational success. Only after having translated the spatial metaphor into language usable for speaking about an HR's PBF and models and about the surface covered by them in the domain of the PBF (as was done in chapter 4, section 6) can we avoid the problems raised by this metaphor.

My second reservation concerns Kuukkanen's view of the argumentative dimension of HRs.[23] Nobody will deny that HRs often contain arguments; for example, arguments demonstrating what conclusions can validly be inferred from the evidence the past has left us. Such arguments typically are used in the context of achieving more precision in our knowledge of states of affairs in the past and in the statements describing them. Obviously, here we are still on the level of the facts associated with historical research (Geschichtsforschung) that were distinguished from the level of historical writing (Geschichtsschreibung). But what about arguments on that second level?

Here we should distinguish between (1) the question of whether HRs *themselves* can be regarded as arguments, and (2) arguments *for* and *against* individual HRs and about the merits and shortcomings of HRs when compared with others (i.e., historical debate). In the former case,

---

23. Kuukkanen, *Postnarrativist Philosophy of Historiography*, 157–67.

the question arises whether we should prefer *this* HR or some *other* HR; in the latter, the question arises whether the arguments against *this* HR are more convincing than the arguments in favor of it. These are, obviously, different things. In the former case, we have to deal with *two* HRs, but in the latter with just *one*.

Next, the answer to question (1) depends on how arguments are defined. If they are defined as a set of considerations leading to a "detachable conclusion," HRs are not arguments. Mink has argued convincingly that there are no detachable conclusions in history:

> But despite the fact that the historian may "summarize" conclusions in his final chapter, it seems clear that these are seldom or never detachable conclusions: not merely their validity but their meaning refers backward to the ordering of evidence in the total argument. The significant conclusions, one might say, are ingredients in the argument itself not merely in the sense that they are scattered through the text but in the sense that they are represented by the narrative order itself.[24]

Anyone agreeing with Mink, as I do, has two options. The first one is to decide that narratives or HRs are *not* arguments. The second is to retain the view that narratives or HRs *are* arguments—albeit arguments of a *quite peculiar* type because they lack detachable conclusions as is normally the case with arguments. Both options are possible in principle. But there seems to be no reason to hold the second position. There is no virtue in employing the term *arguments* in a way that is at odds with how the word is commonly understood.

These considerations place Kuukkanen in a dilemma, however. Recall that his *Postnarrativist Philosophy of Historiography* is supposed to be "postnarrativist" precisely because of its emphasis on *argument*. Yet when Kuukkanen investigates how historians use arguments, it is clearly narrative (or historical representation) that he is discussing.[25] Kuukkanen, in other words, is dealing with arguments in Mink's sense. So *either* Kuukkanen is a postnarrativist when he insists that it is only argument that counts, *or*

---

24. Louis O. Mink, *Historical Understanding*, ed. Brian Fay, Eugene O. Golob, and Richard T. Vann (Ithaca, NY: Cornell University Press, 1987), 79.

25. See Kuukkanen, *Postnarrativist Philosophy of Historiography*, 123-30, 155-58.

he believes that the criteria for narrative or representational success he discusses are applicable to historical narratives and representations. If he is the former, however, then the kind of arguments (requiring detachable conclusions) he has in mind are useless for assessing narratives and historical representations (as Mink has argued). But if he holds the latter belief, then it is difficult to see why he sees himself as a "postnarrativist" and not simply as a narrativist *tout court*.

There is also the issue of the role of argument in discussions about HRs and their relative merits and shortcomings when compared with other HRs. As all historians know, these discussions are only rarely disputes about facts. They focus predominantly, if not exclusively, on representation. As I remarked, the historian should always try to find the juste milieu—"the narrow optimum" between intellectual audacity, on the one hand, and the obligation to respect the rule of the presumption of consistency, on the other.

This requirement imposes three parameters to which the contestants in historical debate will and must appeal. Advocates of the audacious new HR will argue: (1) that part(s) of the model(s) entailed by the audacious HR overlap with existing historical knowledge, whereas others do not; (2) that those parts that do not overlap are larger than those that do overlap; and (3) that the new HR comprises a larger part of the domain of the PBF than those HRs supporting existing historical knowledge, while respecting the rule of the presumption of consistency. Their (conservative) opponents will deny one or more of these claims. In this way, discussions between the advocates of the new HR and their opponents can be opened, pursued, and eventually decided.

4. HISTORICAL TEXTS AS SIGNS: MAXIMA AND MINIMA

Just like mathematics and the sciences, historical representation is possible only thanks to the signs it uses. Nevertheless, the signs used by historians differ significantly from those used in the formal and natural sciences. In the first place, their number is far larger because it cannot be restricted to that of the already existing HRs but must instead be identified with the totality of all possible HRs, and their number is literally infinite. Historians awaken the HRs they wish to propose to their fellow historians from their *merely apparent* nonexistence. HRs as signs are logical entities—and these are just as little subject to space and time as are numbers. This quasi-awakening from their eternal slumber proceeds via *individuation*; that is, by means of sentences such as M_1 is s_1, M_1 is s_2, M_1 is s_3 ... M_1 is s_n. In each sentence, M_1 is the subject-term, and everything attributed to it is already part of M_1. In this sense, M_1 precedes the enumeration of its properties and can, therefore, be said to have existed before the process of its individuation.[26] Again, this is a very Leibnizian idea. Monads are eternal and indestructible, and so are HRs, with the qualification that eternal should not be understood in the sense of having existed since the Big Bang but rather standing outside of time and space. Time and space belong to the domain of the PBF. One could characterize HRs as "noumenal" in the Kantian sense.

Not only is the number of historical signs infinite, they also are incredibly large and complex when compared with the simplicity of arithmetical or mathematical signs, such as 2, 6, π, $\sqrt{-1}$, dy/dx, $\int f(x)$, and so on. They may extend to the length of books of some 800 to 1,000 pages. The obvious explanation is, of course, that HRs consist of statements about the past. Moreover, such individual statements sometimes take up an awful lot of room—especially in the eyes of the average philosopher of language used to dealing with the smallest bits of language (and having an innate aversion to longer bits). This is why they immediately feel an irresistible urge to divide these monstrous (heaps of) sentences produced by historians into smaller and more manageable parts and why they will be deeply frustrated if told that they are not allowed to do so because that would result in new and different HRs. It might be objected that this categorical ban on changing even one word of an HR is at odds with the fact that signs are typically arbitrary—as is the case with mathematical signs—whereas those of the historian are claimed to be anything but arbitrary. This objection is simply mistaken for three reasons. First, it is true that mathematical signs are simple. But as soon as a mathematical sign

---

26. One might object that the same is true of objects referred to by means of proper names or unique identifying descriptions. Reference is only possible after the objects referred to have come into being. However, as Leibniz pointed out, objects individuated in this fashion have a purely logical existence and can, therefore, be said to exist from the beginning of time till the end of time. They are timeless. Temporal (and, perhaps, spatial) denominations come in only if one wishes to tell the story of the interaction between HRs; but just as the actors in a play preexist a performance of that play, so it is with HRs.

has been adopted, the categorical ban on changing it obtains there as well. Second, the issue of the complexity of the sign is wholly irrelevant. It is not only in historical writing that we find complicated signs that are the result of careful reflection. Think again of musical scores. It is a naive prejudice that all signs must conform in complexity to those of mathematics (or to traffic signs, for that matter). It need not be surprising, therefore, that in some cases the form given to signs is wholly arbitrary (for example in arithmetic), in others of some interest, and of the greatest interest in still others (as in historical representation). Third, it may be objected that leaving out or adding just one or two sentences to an HR does not alter its meaning. The answer is that this inevitably results in a different sign, and more important, that the appeal to meaning is not permitted because HR are signs and *signs have no meanings*.

HRs are typically immensely long and complex signs. A proper understanding of historical representation must address why this is so. Unfortunately, little help is available. Most philosophers of history have little experience with signs at all, let alone with such huge signs as historical texts. They probably assume that the texts written by historians are too long to be signs at all. But there is no rule that signs must always be simple. However, even signs that look simple can sometimes be extremely complex—think of the barcode on the products for sale in our supermarkets or of digitally scannable Quick Response (QR) codes that since COVID have become part of everyday life. These images can encode enormous amounts of uniquely identifiable information just using some black squares on a white background; what we do not see is the application to the image via software of a complex mathematical algorithm that the thinking done by its programmers has turned into computer code. So complex signs are found in many places in contemporary life, and the fact that historical signs are quite complex is not a matter of much relevance.

I said that historical writing is war. Obviously, historians themselves are perfectly aware of the permanent battle being waged over the models, the PBF, and the meanings of their HRs. Equally obviously, they hope to keep control of the fate of their HRs as much as possible and, in particular, to leave as many lasting traces in historical reality. Hence Thucydides's description of his history of the Peloponnesian Wars between Athens and Sparta was said to be a *ktèma eis aei* (a possession forever). Historians wish to provide their HRs with all the weapons needed for both attack and defense. They will do everything to secure their HR's success in this permanent struggle for survival.[27] So in what way can these signs contribute *as* signs, *as* texts, to an HRs survival?

Think of a historian who has devised a provocative historical thesis, for example, that our contemporary Western democracies are an uneasy fusion of medieval political representation and the absolutism of prerevolutionary Europe.[28] How best can we expound this thesis so it will have the strongest possible impact? A short book will be manhandled by more conservative colleagues and dismissed as just one more weird idea about the origins of modern democracy. But in a very long book, covering all the loose ends, the provocative character of the thesis will be obscured by the countless attacks on how the inevitably numerous loose ends have been dealt with. The result will be no less disappointing: "*Mega biblion, mega kakon.*" So once again the author's best option is to find the juste milieu, or the *right balance* between these two extremes.

This imaginary author's dilemma is, in fact, paradigmatic for the kind of problem historians encounter when deciding how to present their HRs as texts, or better as *signs*, to their readers. These dilemmas occur literally *everywhere* in the practice of historical writing. Recall what was said in the previous section about the juste milieu. The most basic is the need to steer a prudent middle course between newness and audacity and the nonnegotiable demands of the presumption of consistency. Most of the dilemmas historians encounter in the practice of historical writing originate here. There never is a *perfect* answer to the historian's search for the best HR—understood here as the HR *perfectly* satisfying *all* of the variables and desiderata the historian must take into account. Complete satisfaction of one of these variables or desiderata inevitably comes at the expense of the satisfaction of others. Put differently, the realm of

---

27. It is tempting to invoke a war of all against all here, after the Hobbesian state of nature: HRs exist in a state of nature toward one another. Then one HR emerges that acquires (temporary) "sovereignty." Historians "contract" or agree with one another to install it for the time being, until a challenger emerges that can overthrow it by the Hobbesian right of conquest. This also nicely captures the potential "political" quality or implications of historiographical debates. I'd like to thank Luke O'Sullivan for this helpful suggestion.

28. It is an "uneasy fusion" because medieval political representation and the absolutist notion of sovereignty are irreconcilable. There is, therefore, a paradox at the heart of our Western representative democracies. See Frank Ankersmit, "Synecdochical and Metaphorical Political Representation. Then and Now," in *Creating Political Presence: The New Politics of Democratic Representation*, ed. Dario Castiglione and Johannes Pollak (Chicago: University of Chicago Press, 2019), 231–54.

HRs does not admit of perfection, only of the *greatest possible* perfection. Beyond this we cannot go—we must content ourselves with a less than perfect representational universe. We can only hope to achieve the greatest possible perfection.

This is a basic idea; one could even see it as the heart of a whole Weltanschauung. This Weltanschauung originates in Leibniz's thought—specifically, in two of its most conspicuous features. First, because Leibniz attributed perfection to God, one would have expected the perfect Being to be able to create a perfect world. But this is not the case. God disposed of certain means to create the universe, but an unrestrained appeal to one of those means would be detrimental to what could be achieved by one or more of the others—and vice versa. The use of any given means did not always and necessarily mutually reinforce the use of any one of the others. On the contrary, an ill-considered use of one might undo what could be achieved via the others. Thus, although God Himself is indeed perfect, even He cannot create a perfect world—only the most perfect world that is possible (*le meilleur des mondes possibles*). Leibniz thus throws perfection overboard; all God could do is figure out the optimal use of the means available at the moment of the creation. Leibniz himself often illustrated this argument with the example of someone trying to put as many mosaic stones as possible within a certain surface.[29] The metaphor is a happy one insofar as it suggests that even the most perfect way of arranging the mosaic stones will not be perfect in the sense of leaving nothing uncovered by the mosaic stones. Perfection is simply impossible.

The word *optimum* brings us to the second reason for Leibniz's decision to exchange perfection for "the greatest perfection possible." Gilles Deleuze has pointed out that in Euclidian geometry before Leibniz all other geometrical forms were supposed to be reducible to the straight line in order to be understood.[30] The *straight* line was the perfect form underlying all existing forms. But after Leibniz and Newton independently discovered

---

29. Gottfried Wilhelm Leibniz, "Über den letzten Ursprung der Dinge," in *Mit Einleitung und Erläuterungen im Deutschen ausgegeben von Robert Habs*, ed. Kleine Schriften and G. W. Leibniz (Leipzig: Philipp Reclam jun., 1883), 218–19.

30. Gilles Deleuze, *Le Pli: Leibniz et le Baroque* (Paris: Éditions de Minuit 1988), 5, posits "un labyrinthe" between the domain of the soul and that of matter. He claims that Leibniz succeeded in discovering the secrets of this labyrinthe thanks to his notion of "le pli" (the fold), which could not be accommodated in Cartesian geometry. "Si Descartes n'a pas su les résoudre, c'est parce qu'il

the calculus around 1680, the straight line had to surrender its privileged position to the *curved* line. This development in mathematics had its counterpart in the arts. The dominance of the straight line in Renaissance architecture was exchanged for the forms of the baroque and, later on, of the rococo where everything started to move, to swing, and to dance. The Leibnizian Weltanschauung of the greatest *possible* perfection has its ground in this exchange of Euclidian and Cartesian mathematics for that of the calculus. And who would wish to surrender the calculus to return to Euclid and Descartes? Taking mathematics as our guide, we can only acquiesce in the imperfection of perfection and the perfection of imperfection. Apparently, mathematics may teach us some very deep lessons!

This may explain, furthermore, why the conception of the historical text proposed by Hayden White is unhelpful for a proper understanding of what historians are trying to achieve in the practice of their profession. (This is certainly not meant to diminish in any way the value of White's numerous fascinating and often thought-provoking insights.) Recall the tropological grid White had proposed in his *Metahistory*.[31] The grid enabled White to label all historical texts as "metaphorical," "synecdochical," "metonymical," or "ironic." White denied that attaching any of these four labels to a text implied that it would be "better," "more plausible," and so on than texts carrying any of the other labels. This may explain why White's grid—whatever its merits—can be of no help for the historian hoping to write texts that are better or more plausible rather than less so.

However, this is not yet the end of the story. Whether this was White's intention or not, his grid implies a standard for measuring historiographical success. Observe, first, that these four notions—metaphorical, synecdochical, metonymical, and ironic (if responsibly defined)—mutually exclude each other on the level of their meaning. Self-evidently, this need not be true of the texts that they characterize. It may be that some historical texts contain both metaphorical and synecdochical elements, and so on. In fact,

---

a cherché le secret du continu dans des parcours rectilignes, et celui de la liberté dans une rectitude de l'âme, ignorant l'inclinaison de l'âme autant que la courbure de la matière." Deleuze's title originates in Leibniz's observation that was quoted in Dietrich Mahnke, *Leibnizens Synthese von Universalmathematik und Individualmetaphysik* (1925: repr. Stuttgart: Friedrich Frommann, 1964), 135, that "in jeder Seele könnte man die Schönheit des Universums erkennen, wenn man alle Falten ('pli' in French) auseinander legte; aber gerade dass sie in 'Falten' zusammengezogen ist, in jeder Seele in auf eigene Art, das steigert die unendliche Fülle unendlichmal."

31. Hayden White, *Metahistory. The Historical Imagination in the Nineteenth Century* (Baltimore, MD: Johns Hopkins University Press, 1973).

according to White, this ordinarily is the case. So far, so good. Nevertheless, if this is the case, we can only describe such a text as confused because it combines incompatible elements. This provides us with a standard: the worst texts are those where all four tropes go together in an inextricable tangle. They make a mess of White's tropological grid, so to speak. On the other hand, texts that are purely metaphorical, synecdochical, and so on are the best ones. It will be obvious that this standard is Cartesian rather than Leibnizian, in the previous sense. It defines a straight Cartesian line running from complete imperfection, on the one hand, to complete perfection, on the other. It has, therefore, no room for a specific point where a curve that had been moving upward starts its movement downward. So, again, the philosopher of history must conclude that no real help is to be expected from White in his effort to understand historical writing and representation.[32]

The calculus is, among many other things, the mathematics of the local optima and minima of curves. Each nth grade function has n − 1 local optima and minima where the curve in question begins an upward or a downward move. The miracles of the calculus provoked in Leibniz a lifelong fascination with maxima and minima that he does not share, as far as I know, with any of the other great philosophers in the history of Western thought (although he had a predecessor in Cusanus).[33] This stimulated him to see where he could apply the idea of the maxima and minima outside the

---

32. White arguably gave up attempting a philosophical analysis of the practice of historical writing fairly early on in his career—although few of his commentators ever noticed as much, myself included I must confess. So it would, perhaps, be unreasonable to blame him for having no answer to the question of historical rationality. For this issue, see Herman Paul, *Hayden White: The Historical Imagination* (London: Polity Press 2011), 80: "*Metahistory* was perhaps the last occasion on which White invited *professional* historians to change their mode of realism. In the 1980s White came to the sobering insight that a non-ironic realism is more likely to be found outside the historical discipline. Encouraged by the rather enthusiastic reception of his tropology among students of literature, White began to put his hope more in novelists and film directors than in historians. Whereas ... he continued his battle against irony with undiminished zeal." White started his attack on historians and professional historical writing in his first essay on philosophy of history. See Hayden White, "The Burden of History," in *Tropics of Discourse: Essays in Cultural Criticism* (1966; repr. Baltimore, MD: Johns Hopkins University Press, 1978), 27–51.

33. Mahnke, *Leibnizens Synthese*, 163: "Da es nun aber der neuen Unendlichsrechnung doch gelingt, das Transzendente und Infinite mathematisch zu bewältigen, so ergibt sich hieraus die neue philosophische Grundanschauung Leibnizens, dass auch das Transzendente der wissenschaftlichen erforschbaren Erkenntis Wirklichkeit immanent ist. Besonders bedeutsam ist die Erkenntnis der realen Bedeutung des zweiten Differentialquotienten (als der Richtungsänderung der differenzierten Funktion) für Leibniz geworden, ja, Wundt hält sie für 'vielleicht das epochemachendste Ereignis, das er überhaupt in seinem Denken erlebt hat.'"

domain of mathematics. One application was his theological claim previously mentioned, that God had decided to create the best possible world (*le meilleur des mondes possibles*).

But Leibniz's fascination with the calculus also left its mark on his *Monadology*: mathematics is as inalienable a dimension of his thought as metaphysics and logic. The next crucial step in Leibniz's argument was his move from substance to function—a development described in Ernst Cassirer's *Substanzbegriff und Funktionsbegriff* (1910). The idea is that each monad is the series of representations it has of the universe from the day of its creation down to the end of the world. There always is a relation between each stage of its "life" and the representation it *then* has of the universe. In this way, the latter is a *function* of the former.

Here, the mathematical notion of "function" has become part of the concept of the substance or monad. Leibniz speaks of the "lex series," that is, the *law* of the succession of the states in which the monad finds itself.[34] Perhaps it will be objected that we ought to distinguish between the lex series and the actual monadological program that is determined by it. But clearly this objection makes no sense: a mathematical function just *is* itself what it determines to be the case.[35] Hence, Leibniz's introduction of the notion of the lex series is unobjectionable.[36] Next, if this lex series has,

---

34. Mahnke, *Leibnizens Synthese*, 54, defines the law-of-the-series as the "Lebensgesetz eines ganz bestimmten Individuums. Und doch hat auch dies 'individuelles Gesetz' einen ebenso universelle Charakter wie ein mathematischer Funktionszusammenhang, insofern es die Gesamtheit der Lebensvorgänge gleichfalls einheitlich übergreift und in allem Wechsel der momentanen Zuständlichkeiten identisch verharrt." See also Mahnke, *Leibnizens Synthese*, 25: "eben dahin gehört auch Leibnizens gelegentliche Annäherung an Lotzes Lehre, das die 'die Dinge Gesetze sind,' d.h. dass an Stelle der Substanzen mathematische Funktionsgesetze treten müssen, die die Reihe ihrer wechselnden Zustände und Verhältnisse in einen Inbegriff zusammenschliessen."

Modern readers will associate the phrase the law-of-the-series with the laws of nature. Leibniz would not object. But, as Michael Futch, *Leibniz's Metaphysics of Time and Space* (Boston: Springer, 2008), 33, insists, Leibniz's conception of the laws of nature is not identical with ours: "by 'natural' I (and Leibniz) do not mean 'refers to laws of nature' or 'refers to natural causes.' Rather, something like the following is intended: For any thing S having a property P, a reason R will count as a sufficient reason for S having P if and only if it explains S having P by referring to S's nature. Whatever we assert to be true of something must be explainable by that thing's nature and essence."

35. For a similar argument, see J. A. Cover and J. O'Leary-Hawthorne, *Substance and Individuation in Leibniz* (Cambridge: Cambridge University Press, 1999), 220.

36. Leibniz's move from substance to function is vital. Leibniz's metaphysics was inherited from neo-Scholasticism, which was in turn derived from Aristotelian logic. This type of logic is not suited for modern science. Leibniz's notion of the "lex series" was a step toward a relational logic, but a modest one, in the sense that it related only different stages of one and the same monad to each other, while leaving it just as windowless as it was before.

in principle, the form of a mathematical function, it can be differentiated as well. Then the derivative function can show us where to find its local maxima and minima, which will tell us where something of real importance or significance "happens" in a monad's life. In contrast, the relatively straight trajectories of the function will be comparatively uneventful.

Finally, let us ask what this might mean for historical representation. It is true that the Leibnizian system focuses mainly on the relationship between God and His creation. The attempt to translate his system to historical representation is, admittedly, a Godless enterprise because it places the historian in God's position. However, this has occupied my entire argument from the beginning, so I will just have to risk God's (and Leibniz's) wrath and press on to the final stage. Paraphrasing the well-known title and first line of the Dutch poet Willem Kloos's (1859–1938) best-known poem one might say: "the historian is a God in the depth of his thoughts."[37] The historian is lord and master of historical reality, and he can decide the fate of the reputation of emperors, kings, and nations in a way that they could never do themselves in the past.[38]

Moreover, Leibniz himself had applied calculus and his notion of the differential to texts. He did so in a way that brings him quite close to our own preoccupations with the historical text. The two following quotes are instructive. In his "Discourse on Metaphysics" (1684) Leibniz wrote:

> Some general remarks can be made . . . about the ways of providence in the government of affairs . . . he who acts perfectly is like an excellent geometrician who knows how to find the best construction of a problem; or a good architect who makes the most advantageous use of the space and the capital intended for a building, leaving nothing which offends or which lacks the beauty of which it is capable; or a good family head who makes such use of his holdings that there is nothing uncultivated and barren; or a skilled machinist who produces his work by the easiest process that can be chosen;

---

37. Titled "Ik ben een God in 't diepst van mijn gedachten."
38. There is the limiting case in which they are the same person. Think of Churchill speaking to the House of Commons on January 23, 1948: "it will be found much better by all parties to leave the past to history, especially as I propose to write that history myself." But the exception only proves the rule; most government people are not their own historians. This remark is often corrupted into "History will be kind to me for I intend to write it," which Churchill probably did not say; but if taken seriously, this would be a dereliction of historical duty because it preferred self-interest to truth. See https://literature.stackexchange.com/questions/2341/interpretation-of-a-churchill-quote. I'd like to thank Luke O'Sullivan for this comment on Churchill.

or a learned author who includes the greatest number of subjects in the smallest possible volume.[39]

And in a late text (1714) Leibniz wrote:

It follows from the supreme perfection of God that he has chosen the best possible plan in producing the universe, a plan which combines the greatest variety together with the greatest order; with situation, place, and time arranged in the best way possible; with the greatest effect produced by the simplest means; with the most power, the most knowledge, the greatest happiness and goodness in created things which the universe would allow. For as all possible things have a claim to existence in God's understanding in proportion to their perfection, the result of all these claims must be the most perfect actual world which is possible. Without this it would be impossible to give a reason why things have gone as they have rather than otherwise.[40]

Isolating elements from these quotations that are applicable to historical writing and historical representation, Leibniz's criteria for historical rationality can be summarized as follows: the best representation is the one that succeeds in combining a maximum of variety with a maximum of order, a maximum of effect with a minimum of means, a maximum of unity within a maximum of diversity or the greatest number of subjects in the smallest possible volume. When trying to satisfy this principle of historical rationality, historians must steer a careful middle-of-the road course (the juste milieu) between two or more principles that may obstruct each other to a greater or lesser extent.

Historians may try to convince their readers by drowning them with hosts of hard historical facts. Or perhaps they take for granted some substantive

---

39. Leibniz, *Philosophical Papers and Letters*, 305, 306.
40. The text in question is titled "The Principles of Nature and of Grace based on Reason," which Leibniz would elaborate into the *Monadology* to be published later in that same year. See Leibniz, *Philosophical Papers*, 639. Leibniz formulated his principle in his *Discourse on Metaphysics* of 1684: "as for the simplicity of the ways of God, this is shown especially in the means which he uses, whereas the variety, opulence, and abundance appears in regard to the ends and the results." Leibniz, *Philosophical Papers and Letters*, 306.

philosophy of history that dogmatically differentiates the relevant and the irrelevant historical facts. In the former case, the historian's readers will ask themselves in despair what message the historian wanted to convey with his text. In the latter, readers will ask why they should accept such a reckless thesis and demand more reasons to support it. Both solutions are unsatisfactory. So historians will respond by navigating between these two extremes, searching for the right balance (or juste milieu) between both approaches. In this way, the pendulum between thesis and content moves back and forth constantly.

No resulting balance (or equilibrium) will bring perfection, but if all goes as it should, it will realize the greatest possible perfection (or approximations of it). Let us spell out what this means for the notion of historical explanation, which was so hotly disputed in the past that it seemed to be the only problem worthy of the philosopher of history's attention. Strictly speaking, there is *no* such thing as historical explanation—at least not in the same sense as an explanation of, for example, the collision of two trains. In the cause of such exclusively kinetic interactions, a perfect explanation is, in principle, possible. A perfect explanation is possible also when a consequence can logically be derived from a general law and the relevant initial conditions are in agreement with the "covering law model." But explanation, as that notion is commonly understood in the philosophy of history, is a poor and misguiding model for a proper grasp of the practice of historical writing, and we had better drop it from the philosopher of history's vocabulary. This is why historians will revolt as soon as an allegedly perfect explanation of the physical or formal kind is offered to them. They will be quick to point out what this perfect explanation fails to account for.

To put it more forcefully, a historical explanation presenting itself as a candidate for being a perfect explanation has to be rejected straightaway precisely because of its pretension *to be* such a candidate. There are no perfect explanations in historical writing. If this idea of a perfect historical explanation is to have an understandable meaning, it must sui generis be redefined as the search for the best possible representation. Leibniz also has a suggestion for what the historian should focus on in his representations of historical reality. Here we may recall Leibniz's notion of a monad's lex series and apply it to the historical text. The following passage in the *Essai de Théodicée* (the only book Leibniz published during his lifetime apart from the brief manifesto of his *Monadology*) is of interest here:[41]

> For as a lesser evil is a kind of good, even so a lesser good a kind of evil if it stands in the way of a greater good; and there would be something to correct in the actions of God if it were possible to do better. *And as in mathematics, when there is no maximum nor minimum, in short nothing distinguished, everything is done equally, or when that is not possible nothing at all is done*: so it may be said likewise in respect of perfect wisdom, which is no less orderly than mathematics, that if there were not the best (optimum) among all possible worlds, God would not have produced any.[42]

This observation, and the mathematical simile on which it is based, can easily be translated to the domain of the writing of history.

Think of the simplest of simple functions—$f(x) = x^2$—and try to map it on historical writing. The idea behind such mapping can be found in the italicized portion of the passage where Leibniz addresses the issue of where "things happen" or where "nothing happens" (*il ne se fait rien du tout*). Now, examine this function. If x moves from 0 to 1, $f(x)$ moves similarly from 0 to 1. This is only a small change. But if you add 1 to 5—to make 6—the value of $f(x)$ moves from 25 to 36. This is a far larger increase: eleven times greater! And if we focus on the surface defined by the move from 0 to 1 and 5 to 6, we find in the latter case that it is even 123 times as large as in the former (if I figured it out correctly). If we treat surfaces as a measure of the amount of historical events of average importance

---

41. Leibniz changed his mind so often on crucial issues that the attempt to write a book would have inevitably resulted in an endless rewriting of it. Fortunately, he was an exceptionally enthusiastic letter writer, and it is possible to keep track of his perpetual metamorphoses via his correspondence.

42. Gottfried Wilhelm Leibniz, *Essai de Théodicée. Sur la Bonté de Dieu, la liberté de l'Homme et l'Origine du Mal. Chronologie et introduction par J. Brunschwig* (Paris: Garnier Flammarion, 1969), 108: "Car comme un moindre mal est une espèce de bien, de même un moindre bien est une espèce de mal, s'il fait obstacle à un bien plus grand; et il y aurait quelque chose à corriger dans les actions de Dieu, s'il n'y avoit moyen de mieux faire. *Et comme dans les mathématiques, quand il n'y a point de maximum ni de minimum, rien enfin de distingué, tout se fait également; ou quand cela ne se peut, il ne se fait rien du tout*; on peut même dire en matière de possible sagesse, qui n'est pas moins réglée que les mathématiques, que s'il n'y avait pas le possible (*optimum*) parmi tous les mondes possible, Dieu n'en aurait produit aucun" (italics added).

corresponding to the function $f(x) = x^2$, it seems obvious that we will capture more historical events in proportion as we move away from zero into the direction of both $x = +\infty$ and $x = -\infty$.

This looks promising, but it is not how Leibniz looks at it. He would reject it as a Cartesian way of thinking about "where things happen" and urge us to prefer thinking about that notion as the calculus requires us to do. That is to say, Leibniz relates the notion of where things happen to local maxima and minima; hence, to where the amount of historical events of average importance is *least*, and to where we will observe, instead, a *trend break* or tipping point,[43] in the sense that what used to go upward now goes downward, or the other way around. The Leibnizian curve is decisive here, whereas moving away from the curve that provides us with a local maxima or minima will give us stretches of a function's diagram approaching, asymptotically, the Cartesian straight line. Preferring Leibniz's curve to the Cartesian straight line is—*mutatis mutandis*—not at all a bad guide for historical writing with respect to both the writing of HRs and their interpretation. In fact, it is in agreement with the practice of most historical writing.

5. THE RATIONALITY OF HISTORICAL WRITING

This chapter and chapter 4 addressed the issue of historical rationality; that is, the question of what rational criteria decide between competing HRs. One may agree with Kuukkanen that argument has an important role to fulfill here. On the level of historical research (Geschichtsforschung), it is, indeed, together with an accurate research of the available sources, decisive. But its role is questionable on the level of the writing of history. All depends on how the word *argument* is understood. If it is understood as a "detachable conclusion" derived from a set of premises, the word fails to do justice to the type of considerations guiding the historian's disciplinary aim of representing the past. Mink correctly observed that the historical text offers no detachable conclusions. If we decide to hold onto the dictionary meaning of the word *argument*, we will find no arguments on the level of

---

43. One may also think here of Hegel's so-called nodal line of measure relations as discussed in his *Wissenschaft der Logik*; the best example being what he wrote on the shift from mere quantitative to qualitative change (someone loses—quantitatively—his hair over the years and then suddenly we come to see that he has become bald—a qualitative change).

historical representation. If we drop that meaning, we are free to use the word *argument* with regard to the historical text as well. The advantage of this option is that it leaves no room for doubting the rationality of historical writing as a scientific discipline. Its disadvantage is that it invites us to look for that rationality in the wrong place.

At the end of chapter 3, we found that a search for the rationality of historical writing requires us to focus on the models and PBF accompanying each HR. At the end of chapter 4, we saw what kind of disciplinary considerations enable historians to decide about the relative merits of the models and PBF accompanying mutually competing HRs. In this chapter three additional remarks were made about historical rationality. First, it was argued that the historian must always steer a prudent middle course between audacity and the presumption of consistency. Popper's philosophy of science proved to be remarkably helpful in support of that claim. Second, the historical text as such has rarely been discussed in a fruitful way.[44] It is, however, a topic that Leibniz put on the agenda. The calculus—discovered by both Leibniz and Newton—proved to be the appropriate model here. Third, it was argued (1) that no account of historical writing is complete that fails to address the topic of the growth of historical knowledge, and (2) that this growth of historical knowledge is the unintended result of the interaction of different HRs and can, therefore, not be translated backward into specific recommendations to individual historians for how to write history. Although the better individual HRs satisfy the standards of historical rationality, the greater the growth of historical knowledge resulting from their unintended interaction will be—all other things being equal.

In sum, one must agree with all philosophers of history having defended the rationality of historical writing against those who evaded this issue for whatever reason, and even more against those who openly rejoiced in undermining it. At the same time, the defenders of historical writing and its rationality have not always been its ablest and most convincing advocates.

---

44. Needless to say, the historical text was always central in the numerous and profoundly influential writings by Hayden White. However, White never addressed the issue of historical rationality for the simple reason that he did not believe in it. His writings are, therefore, of no interest in the context of this book (which is not meant to deny their interest in *other* contexts).

CONCLUSION
Nontrivial Circularity

I hope I have drawn the main contours of my argument in this book with sufficient clarity to be forgiven for not concluding here with a summary of the most important findings in the preceding chapters. I am well aware that some readers might have welcomed such a summary, above all because most people unacquainted with Leibniz's system find it counterintuitive and difficult to grasp. They have probably felt much the same about this book. It is true that Leibniz's system has its own kind of difficulty. It is not difficult in the way the Kantian system is difficult, which is because of its intricacies (all "its ropes and pulleys" as Ryle once nicely put it), or in the way Hegel's *Phenomenology* is difficult because of its impenetrable prose, or in the way the contemporary philosophy of language is difficult due to its often technical vocabulary. Leibniz's system is difficult because it is a system in which everything seems to be upside down. Let me explain.

Most philosophy departs from the world as we know it and moves upward to abstraction. This is even the case with Platonism, in spite of its claim that "everything transient is just a parable" (*alles Vergängliche ist nur ein Gleichnis*), to quote Goethe's deft summary of the Platonist intuition.[1] But in the Leibnizian system—and unique to it—the immense richness and variety of the phenomena of our own world are reflections of the similarly

---

1. See the final words of Goethe's *Faust Part II*.

immense richness and variety of the monadological universe. Leibniz *starts* with the complex reality of his monadological universe and moves downward to the no less complex world in which we live. No philosopher before or since Leibniz has attempted anything similar.

It is no surprise, therefore, that Leibniz's system is difficult to grasp. Doing so requires something akin to a Gestalt switch. Specifically, what is involved is a change from a Fregean, Russellian, or Strawsonian "descriptive metaphysics" to the descriptive metaphysics of Leibniz as foreshadowed by that of the Scholastics. The switch is encapsulated in the difference between the concepts of the "weak and strong individual." But as soon as one has made the switch, all the problems associated with the contemporary philosophy of language can be seen from a new perspective.[2] The very idea that such a switch is possible at all is thought-provoking: it suggests the existence of an unsuspected philosophical universe parallel to the familiar one presented by the Anglo-Saxon philosophy of language.

Unless one is prepared to temporarily place between parentheses the "descriptive metaphysics" that can be traced back to Frege and Russell (who were the founders of the Anglo-Saxon philosophy of language), it remains impossible to make sense of historical representation. Such has been my argument. In the case of historical writing, realizing the old Platonic goal of carving the world at its joints requires a willingness and an openness to see the world of philosophy in general, and that of the philosophy of history specifically, from a perspective different from the one to which the Anglo-Saxon philosophy of language has accustomed us; namely, from that of Scholastic and Leibnizian "descriptive metaphysics."

Finally, in the hope of making this Gestalt switch understandable and to avoid losing the reader in the sometimes mind-boggling complexity of Leibniz's thought, I left room for a certain amount of repetition in my exposition of the nature of historical representation. The powers of conservatism are never stronger than when a Gestalt switch is involved. Think of the Necker Cube or of the Jastrow/Wittgenstein rabbit/duck drawing: the shift from one Gestalt to the other always involves a micro-revolution in one's perceptions, and the experience of that micro-revolution is invariably unpleasant and involves a moment of vertigo. This may explain why we often feel an irrepressible urge to return to our favored way of seeing the

---

2. See the epilogue for this.

CONCLUSION

Necker Cube and the Wittgenstein drawing. Then the strategy of *frappez, frappez toujours* is the only hope for getting one's message across and keeping the reader aware of it. Repetition may stop the reader from all too easily falling back to their preferred way of seeing things. Moreover, repetition also may be helpful to occasionally remind the reader of the current stage of the argument. I can only apologize if this strategy of repetition irritated some of this book's readers. Rather than testing their patience still further by rehearsing my argument yet again, I conclude with some general remarks.

First, I prefer to describe the current work not as a Leibnizian philosophy of history but rather as a philosophy of history developed with Leibnizian instruments. My aim has been to do justice to the nature of historical representation, not to Leibniz's thought. I am undaunted, therefore, by any and all accusations that I have misunderstood Leibniz. As far as I am concerned, I will be at peace with such misunderstandings if they helped me penetrate deeper into the secrets of historical representation. I would not venture to contradict the Leibniz scholar who says I have sinned against Leibniz's true intentions; even if he is indisputably right, my conscience will remain untroubled.

Second, I made clear from the outset that my goal is to derive a theory of historical representation from just *one* axiom—namely, the axiom that HRs can be defined as the total sum of all true statements about the past state of affairs constituting an HR.[3] In that sense, the argument in this book is structurally similar to Leibniz's thought. Russell was right when stating that all of Leibniz's thought can be derived from a limited number of axioms. The list of abbreviations in the glossary provide a good idea of the axioms in question. Among the five to ten greatest philosophers in the history of Western thought since antiquity, Leibniz has a unique place thanks to the elective affinities of his thought with mathematical argument.

Third, since the Hempel/Dray debate, the philosophy of history has arguably been the philosophical subdiscipline that has seen the least progress. The last real progress in the philosophy of history was made by Louis O. Mink, whose essays date back to the 1970s, almost half a century ago.[4]

---

3. See the introduction.
4. I should make an exception for Chiel van den Akker, *The Exemplifying Past: A Philosophy of History* (Amsterdam: Amsterdam University Press, 2018).

CONCLUSION

Mink's major contribution was to demonstrate that understanding the practice of historical writing required abandoning the paradigm of the proposition as the vehicle of meaning at the sentence level for that of "narrative" (or of historical representation). Mink's arguments, however, were too often ignored. Even those philosophers who explicitly subscribe to Mink's narrativist paradigm often relapse to treating statements as fundamental.[5] This sorry situation has persisted to the present day, which raises the question of why this is so.

Several factors have play a role here, but I restrict myself to what has, in my view, been the most important cause of this lack of progress in the philosophy of history. To begin, in all kinds of inquiry, whether scientific or philosophical, one should clearly distinguish between one's premises, assumptions, or axioms, on the one hand, and the conclusions one hopes to derive from them by means of valid argument, on the other. The necessity of the distinction is indisputable. Recall, for example, what was said in the introduction about geometry. Without the premise that the circle is the set of all points having the same distance to a point P, the geometrician can move no further. As soon as the premise is there, a number of the circle's properties (1) can be inferred from it, e.g., its having a center, a radius, and a diameter; and (2) a set of eight theorems on the circle. The former three still belong to the stage of the premises and only the latter can be said to be theories about the circle. All of them are circular in the sense of having their ultimate ground in the premise(s) of the circle. They are already present in the premise(s).

Next, mathematicians often distinguish between trivial and nontrivial truths. A trivial truth is a truth that is too obvious to be stated. For example, anyone can see that the area of a circle must be πr^2, where r stands for the

---

5. These relapses typically result from the following three factors: (1) the lack of a clear and well-defined conception of a narrative; (2) the doctrine of the theory-ladenness of empirical fact; and (3) the lack of a clear distinction between historical research and historical writing. The relapse begins with (1) the vague intuition that theory and narrative are roughly similar and therefore (2) can be applied to historical writing, which is then taken to prove that (3) is true. The result is the assumption that the only sound model for narrative is the notion of fact, which again means surrendering the paradigm of narrative or of historical representation for that of the statement. But (3) is false because statements have the subject/predicate form, whereas sets of statements don't have that form. Moreover, there is no way to bridge the logical gap between the two. An example is the otherwise most valuable book by Paul Roth, *The Philosophical Structure of Historical Explanation* (Evanston, IL: Northwestern University Press, 2020).

circle's radius and π is a constant standing for the relationship between a square's area and that of a circle. One need only draw a square around the circle with sides being 2r long to see as much. But the truth that the circumference of a circle is 2πr is far from trivial! The circumference C of a circle is the derivative of the circle's area A with respect to its radius r. Hence, C = dA/dr (i.e., 2πr). It requires, therefore, the mathematical sophistication of the calculus to find the length of a circle's circumference. Still, that length can be established on the basis of the definition of the circle. Hence, in this admittedly peculiar sense, the derivation of the length of the circle's circumference can be said to be nontrivially "circular."

Now let's return to the philosophy of history. As this example of the mathematician's dealings with the circle suggests, argument in the philosopher's text must be located in one of two places: either it is an argument about premises, or it is an argument about what can be inferred from these premises. As far as I know, this distinction is never made by philosophers of history, the result being that one can never be sure whether a philosopher of history's argument is meant to give argumentative support to (one of the many possible) proposals of what, according to *this* philosopher, the nature of historical writing *is*, or whether the argument is intended to derive one or more claims about the nature of historical writing from the (tacitly presupposed) proposal adopted by the philosopher. This uncertainty spills over into the latter domain, i.e., that of the claims allegedly inferred from the philosopher's premise(s). This uncertainty entails that one can never be sure whether a philosopher of history's finding is a trivial truth derived from an overly laborious, but never explicitly defined notion of historical writing—which had best be integrated into a definition of historical writing—or a nontrivial truth inferred from a concise and precise definition of what historical writing is.

Moreover, in the first case, the issue is whether the writing of history has been properly and responsibly characterized by the philosopher of history. This is a matter of assessment, of "judgment," in the sense of Kant's third critique rather than a matter of truth or falsity, but it is nonetheless important for all of that. In the second case, we have only argumentative validity. In the first case, we come close to the statement of a matter of fact, i.e., what should be regarded as the decisive facts about the nature of historical writing; whereas in the second case argumentative validity is the only thing at stake.

CONCLUSION

This also has consequences for whether the philosopher's argument yields trivial or nontrivial results. If the argument pertains to how historical writing should be characterized, the characteristic is trivial in the same way definitions are necessarily trivial—although, again, without axioms and definitions there are no conclusions. The conclusions inferred from an axiom or definition of historical writing are nontrivial. Hence, the scope of these nontrivial conclusions is ultimately decisive for the value of a work on the philosophy of history. Failing to keep these two issues—the definition of a subject-matter and the conclusions that can be derived from that definition—sufficiently apart from each other condemns debate in the philosophy of history to a permanent *dialogue des sourds* in which no progress is possible.

This certainly goes a long way to explain why the philosophy of history came to a grinding halt after Mink, with the result that it fell apart into an ever-expanding host of subfields no longer having any common ground. The philosophy of history exploded into myriad private undertakings in which everyone went their own way,[6] and no one was interested in how all of these individual initiatives still hang together. There is no longer a common purpose. As it says in the Book of Judges 21:25: "In those days there was no King in Israel: every man did what was right in his own eyes." That this is the present situation in philosophy is clear from the table of contents in the issues of the leading journals in the field. There surely is something refreshing in this unfettered freedom. However, if philosophers of history hope to contribute to a better understanding of historical writing, a minimum amount of discipline is indispensable. This discipline requires, among other things, the philosopher's willingness to be subject to the demands of rational debate. Specifically, only when conclusions are derived from a well-defined definition can we be told something that we did not yet know and that is worth knowing.

A few suggestions for how to restore the possibility of meaningful debate in the philosophy of history follow from the foregoing. First, issues of how to *define* the writing of history should be carefully kept apart from the issue of what follows from that definition. Second, the definition of

---

6. For a similar diagnosis of the present health (or, rather, lack of it) of the philosophy of history, see Herman Paul, "A Loosely Knit Network: Philosophy of History After White," *Journal of the Philosophy of History* 13 (2019): 3–20.

CONCLUSION

historical writing should preferably be brief, succinct, and have maximum plausibility. For example, had Hayden White followed the strategy I am recommending, he would have begun by defining the writing of history as literature. It would then have been clear straightaway that such a definition is not a very good idea: even a child can distinguish between a work of history and a novel. Third, the issue about what definition of historical writing is most plausible deserves more attention than is paid to it. Think, for example, of the tradition proposing that Verstehen (historical understanding) is the aim of all historical writing.

But this "hermeneuticist tradition," as it is often called, has two variants. In the Anglo-Saxon variant from Collingwood to Davidson (often referred to as the study of "the other mind" problem), the focus is on the beliefs and intentions of (historical) actors. In German hermeneutics, there is a shift to the interpreter. In that variant of the Verstehen tradition, the crucial question is "how can we succeed in understanding a historical actor better than he understood himself?" Needless to say, it is either one or the other: one cannot focus *exclusively* on what supposedly went on in the mind of the historical actor and at the same time *go beyond* this. So one would expect debate in hermeneutics to start by dealing with this dilemma, but lo, there has been no such discussion. Needless to say, this is both strange and worrying. But, alas, this is the result to be expected in a philosophical tradition averse to begin by clearly and ambiguously stating what exactly it *is* that its practitioners decide to investigate. The hermeneuticists I have in mind here are like geometricians investigating the circle without worrying about a definition of what a circle *is*.

This may explain the structure of this book. I began with two definitions of historical writing: (1) historical writing is historical representation, and (2) a historical representation is the totality of statements (either singular or general) that are true of the historical states of affairs that are mentioned in them. As I said in the introduction, (1) is debatable: alternative characteristics of historical writing would be Verstehen, "explanation" (having gathered since Hempel many more varieties than hermeneutics), or "narrative," and one might think of others as well.[7] My argument against all of these alternatives is that they never escape from the level of

---

7. To avoid possible misunderstandings, advocates of the narrativist tradition never agreed with the representationalist thesis defended here, nor is the latter a variant of the former.

historical research and therefore never enter the domain of historical reality as understood in this book's title. Next, (2) is the only axiom informing this book. As such, it is just as plausible as the definition of the circle as the set of all points have a certain distance from a point P. And it is completely unambiguous. In chapter 1 a number of trivial conclusions were inferred from this axiom. I leave it to the reader to decide whether these are still mere *properties* of HRs or should already be seen as nontrivial *theorems* on HRs. Nevertheless, these conclusions follow from the axiom defining historical representation. In this sense, these conclusions are circular, whether trivial or nontrivial.

But the real challenge is how to move beyond these fairly obvious conclusions to those concerning the truly decisive and nontrivial truths about historical representation. I made that move using the Leibnizian system. On several occasions in this book, I discussed the amazing discovery that that system is, in fact, better suited to clarify the nature of historical writing than to serve the purposes for which Leibniz had constructed it. A striking example is the PBF that Leibniz never succeeded to integrate convincingly in his system, which is suggested by his appeal to the metaphor of the rainbow to explain the relation between the domain of the substances or monads, on the one hand, and that of the PBF, on the other.[8] His attempts to deal with the problem resulted in a metaphysical spillover from one of the two domains into the other. But following the suggestions by Danto and Munz that "historical reality only comes into being when the past no longer exists," it proved to be possible to drive a metaphysical wedge between "historical reality" and "the past," thereby preventing any possibility of such "metaphysical leakage." In the first place, this allowed us to bring to the Leibnizian system a greater perfection than it has as it stands. Whatever Leibniz's own intentions may have been with his system, the five chapters show that any inconsistencies or major problems in it disappear *du moment* it is applied to historical writing. In the second place, by avoiding the temptation to suggest any identification of the PBF with "the past" by upholding Leibniz's claim that the PBF depend on monads

---

8. The metaphor suggests a coincidence or common ground of the domain of the monads and that of the PBF that cannot be reconciled with Leibniz's decision to grant existence to his substances or monads only.

CONCLUSION

(or HRs), it proved to be possible to do justice to both Leibniz's requirement that monads (or HRs) only perceive other monads (or HRs), i.e., not the PBF or "the past," and the claim that scientific debate in historical writing is not a debate between HRs themselves but about the PBF accompanying them, so any short-circuit between the PBF and "the past" should and has been avoided.

Surveying it all, it could be argued that the historical PBF and the notion of the sign have been the big winners in this account of historical representation. The past and the notion of the HRs will not be regarded as particularly novel ideas (regardless of how they are defined in this book or elsewhere). But the Leibnizian idea of the PBF—and its transposition to historical representation—surely is such a novelty. Moreover, without Leibniz's conception of the monad and the PBF as its spinoff, I would have had to rely on "the past" to explain historical debate and the growth of historical knowledge—and that would have meant the collapse of my argument. I do, therefore, warmly agree with Chladenius's, Ranke's, Cassirer's, Meinecke's, Koselleck's, and Beiser's assessment that we owe the historicist discovery of the historical world to Leibniz. Then I dealt with the sign. Speaking about HRs is a promising beginning—but not more than that. We also need to be clear about what kind of logical entities they are. The answer—as we have seen—is that HRs are symbols that stand for themselves, i.e., signs. And, next, that sign and meaning should be decoupled: we may give meanings to signs, but *as signs* they have no meaning. Only after having enriched our technical vocabulary with the notion of the sign was a comprehensive analysis of historical representation possible.

Finally, only the future will tell whether this book meets with some sympathy among my esteemed colleagues. I hope they will, in any case, agree that adopting its structure would not be a bad idea. That is to say, the philosopher of history should begin by stating what, in their view, historical writing *is*; next, they should encapsulate this view in a clear, succinct, and unambiguous definition of historical writing and, finally, derive by means of valid argument from that definition conclusions clarifying the nature of historical writing—*as* it had been defined. As long as the philosopher of history does not follow this strategy, the argument may be a master piece of erudition, profundity, and technical refinement, but it will not even reach the level of trivial circularity because we simply can't tell of what these claims are meant to be true.[9] The argument will then be like the public prosecutor's brilliant and eloquent closing speech, moving the hearts and minds of all who are present in the court room—but without there being a crime and a defendant.

---

9. The starting point of the philosopher of history's argument should be what Leibniz referred to as a "primary truth": "first truths are those which predicate something of itself or deny the opposite of its opposite, for example, A is A, or A is not non-A. . . . All other truths are reduced to first truths with the aid of definitions or by the analysis of concepts; in this consists proof a priori, which is independent from experience." See Gottfried Wilhelm Leibniz, *Philosophical Papers and Letters*, 2nd ed., trans. Leroy E. Loemker (Boston: Reidel/Springer, 1976), 267. A valid argument has its point of departure in a truth that is a truth about itself. Leibniz also distinguishes "*nominal definitions*, which contain only marks for discerning one thing from others," from "*real definitions*, through which the possibility of the thing is ascertained." When defining X by means of a primary or a first truth, X must be possible. Leibniz, *Philosophical Papers and Letters*, 293.

EPILOGUE

Intensionalism Versus Extensionalism: The Historical Period (Leibniz) and Its Enemies (Davidson)

Car disant tout homme est animal, je veux dire que tous les hommes sont compris dans tous les animaux, maix j'entends en même temps que l'idée de l'animal est comprise dans l'idée de l'homme. L'animal comprend plus d'individus que l'homme, mais l'homme comprend plus d'idées ou formalités; *l'un a plus d'exemples, l'autre plus de degrés de réalité; l'un plus d'extension, l'autre plus d'intension* (Leibniz) (italics added).[1]

Perhaps I [Davidson] should add that I think our actual scheme and language are best understood as extensional and materialist.[2]

1. WHY AN EPILOGUE TO THIS BOOK?

This book develops a theory on the nature of historical representation, but it does more. Historians typically use ordinary language—anyone who can read the newspapers can also read a work of history— and write their books in a natural language such as English, French, or German. Historical language is not an artificial language such as the language used by physicists or biochemists.[3] This explains why philosophers of language never showed any interest in the writing of history. If historians write their works in a

---

I am deeply indebted to Jaap den Hollander for making me aware of the ramifications of the opposition between extensionalism and intensionalism and for drawing my attention to the essay by Itay Shani. I am also grateful to Chiel van den Akker for an illuminating correspondence I had with him from April to June 2022 regarding Davidson's views. I cannot thank him enough for explaining Davidson's intention to me and for his patience with me. For Van den Akker's own views on Davidson, see Chiel van den Akker, *The Exemplifying Past: A Philosophy of History* (Amsterdam: Amsterdam University Press, 2018), especially chap. 6.

1. Gottfried Wilhelm Leibniz, *Nouveaux Essais sur l'Entendement Humain. Chronologie et Introduction par Jacques Brunschwig* (1765; repr. Paris: Garnier Flammarion, 1966), 432.

2. Donald Davidson, "On the Very Idea of a Conceptual Scheme," in *Inquiries Into Truth and Interpretation* (Oxford: Clarendon Press, 1985), 183–99, especially 188.

3. Although appearances deceive, historical representation has a logical structure setting it apart from other uses of a natural language such as fiction, legal codes, or the instructions for the use of a tool.

natural language and if most (although not all) philosophers of language study natural language, what good reasons would they have to be interested in the writing of history? Surely, as reasonable and open-minded people, philosophers of language respect historical writing as a scientific discipline having its own challenges to meet that justify a thorough philosophical analysis. But philosophers of language assume that, whatever these challenges are, it is not their job to deal with them.

The philosopher of language's attitude to historical writing is understandable but wrong for three reasons. First, there is the problem of the (historical) text mentioned in the preface to this book. Admittedly, this problem is not peculiar to historical writing; it includes novels, newspaper articles, the letters and emails we write to each other, and even the texts that philosophers write themselves. So it is all the more surprising that philosophers of language have been so little interested in the use of language in texts because discussing each other's work is part of their job in dealing with texts on a daily basis. Philosophers of language have investigated the most outlandish aspects of language, but the text: never.[4] Second, at the end of chapter 4, five levels were identified in the historical text. This structural hierarchy has implications for the use of language outside of historical writing too, thanks to the overlap between historical writing and the use of a natural language. So one had better be aware of it.

But more important than the philosopher of language's disregard of these two features of the text (historical or not) is the opposition between the "weak" and the "strong" individual, which is discussed at the beginning of chapter 3. I argued that this opposition both exemplifies and explains the difference between the philosophical DNA of the contemporary philosophy of language and the philosophy of language that is needed to account for historical representation. On the one hand, there is the Fregean, Russellian, and Strawsonian notion of the "weak individual" inspiring the "descriptive metaphysics" of the contemporary philosophy of language; on the other, there is the "descriptive metaphysics" of the Scholastics and of Leibniz accounting for the "strong individual."

This brings us to the key question of how to think of the difference between the weak and the strong individual. Specifically, what is the

---

4. Part of the explanation is that almost all philosophers of language adopt the Cartesian method of dividing complex problems into smaller more manageable ones. Applying that method makes you move from the text to the sentences constituing them. And while making this move the problem of the text has evaporated into thin air.

deeper level in terms of which we can meaningfully articulate this difference? My conjecture is that this deeper level is best identified with the opposition between extensionalism and intensionalism. The extensionalist accepts the world as it is, with all of its objects—i.e., weak individuals—having certain properties: this is where the extensionalist philosopher's quest begins. The fact that these weak individuals can be reduced to the variables of quantification is proof of their weakness. It is the other way around with the intensionalist. The best example of the intensionalist's use of language is in historical representation. But what is a historical representation? As was argued all through this book, in a historical representation each sentence from the second down to the last one is tied to all of the former by means of a meta-sentence having all existing sentences and a new sentence as their object-sentences. The meta-sentence in question has the form "this HR is s," where HR stands for all the sentences this HR contains plus all the meta-sentences tying these together, and s stands for the sentence being added to the existing set. This quasi-endless ongoing process is exclusively *intensionalist* because its logical function is to guarantee the continuous increase of the HR's *intension*.

At this level, there is no room for extensionalism. Extensionalism only manifests itself on the level of the truth or falsity of statements (either singular or general) about past states of affairs. But on the intensional level this has no role to play. In fact, even false statements can (intensionally) be included in an HR as easily as a true one—unless D_{nc} would resist such inclusion because it would result in a contradiction with one (or more) of an HR's statements.

Five conclusions can be inferred from the foregoing: (1) that language can be used for both extensionalist and intensionalist purposes because it is neutral with regard to the extensionalism versus intensionalism opposition; (2) that the existing philosophy of language has a strong extensionalist bias; (3) that it tends to be blind, therefore, to the intensionalist use of language and to those contexts in which a reliance on the intensionalist use of language is conditional for the possibility of human communication and scientific progress; (4) that a fair and unbiased account of our use of language requires the philosopher of language to take the intensionalist use of language no less seriously than its extensionalist counterpart; and above all (5) that all of these issues can be addressed only after having passed through a thorough and painstaking discussion of the extensionalist versus intensionalist opposition. This epilogue is a contribution to that discussion;

it is, therefore, part of this book on historical representation at its more or less logical conclusion.

Briefly, this book would be incomplete without a descent into the deeper underlying level of the issue of extensionalism versus intensionalism.

2. EXTENSIONALIST AND INTENSIONALIST TRUTH

The philosophical term *intension* was used for the first time in the history of philosophy by Leibniz in his *Nouveaux Essais* (published posthumously in 1765).[5] The suggestion evoked by the last sentence of the quote from Leibniz at the beginning of this chapter is that language could be regarded as a kind of switchboard, with a switch that one can move either to the left or to the right. Move the switch to the left and language loses intension but gains in extension; move it to the right and language's extension is diminished in favor of its intension. If we want to know less about more, we move the switch to the (extensionalist) left. If, on the other hand, we want to know more about less—typically about just one and the same thing (and think here of a thing in the widest possible sense)—we must move it to the (intensionalist) right. This inverse relationship between extension and intension has often (especially since Kant) been referred to as the reciprocity principle. The principle can be expressed algebraically as E = c/I, where E stands for extension, I for intension, and c is a constant.

Debates about the reciprocity principle focus on how the intension and extension of a concept C_1 compares to those of a concept C_2.[6] That is to say,

---

5. Leibniz, *Nouveaux Essais sur l'Entendement Humain*. Also see Mary Spencer, "Why the 'S' in 'Intension'?", *Mind* 80, no. 317 (January 1971): 114–15. Spencer adds that Leibniz's notion had its direct predecessor in the notion of "comprehension" used by Leibniz's conversation partner Arnauld.

6. Ellen Walther-Klaus, *Inhalt und Umfang. Untersuchungen zur Geltung und zur Geschichte der Reziprozität von Extension und Intension* (Hildesheim, Germany: Georg Olms, 1987), 2, 3, 6. Whereas the term *extension* stands for the objects "falling under a certain concept C," the distinction between a larger and a more restricted extension seems to be relatively unproblematic. But a similar distinction is less easy to make for a concept's intension because it would require a waterproof procedure to split a concept into its individual components. It seems unlikely that such a procedure exists. Moreover, Bernard Bolzano argued that even if this problem has been solved the reciprocity principle can be falsified. Using an example given by Peirce, the concepts C_1 "man residing in Europe" and C_2 "man residing in Europe, drawing breath north of the equator, seeing the sun rise before those in America" have the same extension, whereas C_2 has a far larger intension. The debate about this issue is ongoing. Walther-Klaus, *Inhalt und Umfang*, 112–20, 124.

EPILOGUE

the claim stating that the greater the intension the more restricted the extension, and vice versa, is not applicable to one concept because the relation between the two is fixed; it is only applicable to sets of individual concepts in which that relationship typically varies from one concept to another. It should be emphasized that choosing between extension and intension is not a matter of a choice between truth and falsity. *Both* options give us truth, albeit of a different kind—or more precisely it gives us truth serving different purposes. One might call the former extensionalist truth and the latter intensionalist truth.

But this even-handed assessment of the two, however just and unobjectionable, requires a qualification to do justice to where the two differ from each other. Recall the switchboard metaphor wherein the extensionalist left side should be associated with reality in all its manifestations, from daily reality, via physical and phenomenological reality, to metaphysical reality. "Reality" here is whatever our true statements are supposed to be true *of*. Extensionalist truth is, predominantly, the kind of truth we have in mind when saying that a statement is true or false.

Intensionalist truth is less easily explained. As is clear from the first epigraph to this chapter, Leibniz credited intension with *plus de degrés de réalité*. This immediately raises questions about what Leibniz had in mind by writing of "degrees of reality" and of how this conception can explain intensionalist truth. Two remarks are of interest in this context. First, in an illuminating essay on how and when the term *intension* came to be included in the philosopher's vocabulary, Mary Spencer quoted the following passage from Sir William Hamilton's *Discussions on Philosophy* (1866):

> This distinction [between extension and intension], as limited to the doctrine of single notions, was signalized by the Port Royal logicians, under the names of *Extension* and *Comprehension*;[7] Leibniz and his followers preferred the more antithetic titles of *Extension* and *Intension*: though Intension be here somewhat deflected from its proper meaning—that of degree. . . . The best expression, I think, for the distinction is *Breadth* and *Depth*.[8]

---

7. The notion of comprehension defended by the logicians of Port Royal comes close to Louis Mink's discussion of that term in "History and Fiction as Modes of Comprehension." See Louis O. Mink, *Historical Understanding*, ed. Brian Eugene Golob and Richard T. Vann (Ithaca, NY: Cornell University Press, 1987), 43–61.

8. Spencer, "Why the 'S' in 'Intension'?," 114.

EPILOGUE

Now recall that in *Nouveaux Essais* Leibniz referred to the fact that the notion of "animal" contains more individuals than the notion "human being," whereas the notion "human being" is said to be "richer in ideas or formalities." Clearly, if Leibniz endowed the latter with "a greater degree of reality," it is because he thought it contained more meanings (or intension) than the notion of "animal." But Leibniz also thought it contained a greater *truth*. To see why, recall Hamilton's observation that Leibniz's use of the term was "somewhat deflected from its proper meaning," by which he had in mind the meaning originally given to intension in Scholasticism.

In Scholasticism, the term *intension* was used to express *degrees of intensity*: "a quality such as 'luminosity' has various degrees; when heightened it is said to be intense, when low it is remiss."[9] Thus, the light of the sun was more intense than that of a candle.[10] Leibniz, the last great Scholastic thinker, took this idea over from Scholasticism when claiming that the light of truth may shine with a greater or a lesser "intensity." This, then, is how we should think of "intensionalist *truth*." In sum, if a notion is said to have a greater intension than some other, this means that it is richer in *meaning*; that it contains "a greater degree of *reality*"; and that it possesses, therefore, a greater degree of *truth*.

Because extensionalism is associated with reality in all the senses given to that term, it is not surprising that it has prevailed over its intensionalist counterpart—even to the extent that intensional phenomena were wholly forgotten about. The Cartesian notion of the *res extensa* and Locke's empiricism contributed to the triumph of extensionalism, and the successes of seventeenth- and eighteenth-century science were regarded as decisive proof that the extensionalist triumph over its intensionalist counterpart was well deserved. It need not surprise anyone, therefore, that no great modern Western philosopher—with the sole exception of Gottfried Wilhelm Leibniz—hesitated for a moment to join the extensionalist chorus.

---

9. Itay Shani, "The Myth of Reductive Extensionalism," *Axiomathes* 17, no. 2 (2007): 155–83, at 180.

10. As the example suggests, this has a theological resonance. See, for example, the depiction of the Annunciation on the middle Panel of the *Mérode Altar* by the Master of Flémalle (perhaps Robert Campin), c. 1425–28, now in the Metropolitan Museum of Art in New York. The light of the candle is extinguished by the infinitely more "intense" light of the divine Truth told to the virgin Mary by the Angel.

EPILOGUE

But in our own time, intensionalism can no longer be so easily overlooked. The most important discoveries of modern physics—relativity, quantum mechanics, and so on—are relentlessly theoretical in the sense of having their origin in exclusively mathematical operations. A striking example is the Higgs boson (or the Brout-Englert-Higgs particle, to give it its full title), which was predicted on purely mathematical grounds by François Englert and Robert Brout in 1964. Its existence was empirically confirmed only in July 2012 with the Large Hadron Collider. Mathematics—which together with the writing of history is the intensionalist discipline *par excellence*—anticipated empirical findings by almost half a century. Furthermore, in sections 5 and 6 of chapter 3, I commented on the reversal between empirical evidence and scientific theory: experimental data about the behavior of extensional entities are no longer the foundation of scientific theory, but instead are the *models* of the scientific theory's abstract calculus. The intensionality of theory has overruled the priority given to empiricist truth in extensionalism. A strictly extensionalist account of modern physics can no longer be upheld. As Shani puts it, "rather than vindicating extensionalism contemporary science undermines the position, and the lesson to be drawn from this surprising fact is that extensionalism need no longer be espoused as a regulative ideal of naturalistic philosophy."[11]

And this is not yet all. Thanks to one of these amazing paradoxes with which history sometimes surprises us, we found that we need an *intensionalist* philosophy of history to explore the secrets of historical writing—and of "historical truth" as found in historical representation. A discovery going back as far as to Chladenius in the middle of the eighteenth century. Whereas at first sight the writing of history seems more deeply rooted in the realities of daily life than any other discipline (and therefore more hospitable to extensionalism than any other), in fact, it made its "intensionalist turn" already at the end of the eighteenth century with the emergence of historicism. In this epilogue, I contrasted this intensionalist philosophy of history with the extensionalist version, which was defended from antiquity through the eighteenth century (here called the "autopsic model" of historical writing that has miraculously survived here and there to the present day next to the historicist tradition.

---

11. Shani, "The Myth of Reductive Extensionalism," 155.

EPILOGUE

Two conclusions follow. First, when raising the issue of intensionalist versus extensionalist truth, Leibniz can no more be left aside than could Kant in a discussion of transcendental idealism. And second, because intensionalist truth is still unfamiliar to most philosophers, it might be worthwhile to sketch some of its main features. For this I draw on an exceptionally helpful essay by Itay Shani, although the Leibnizian intensionalism presented here is more radical than Shani's version.

I argue furthermore that Donald Davidson's extensionalism obviates the recognition of the essentially intensionalist conception of historical periods, a notion at the heart of modern historical writing. In fact, each historical text satisfying the demands of historical writing as expounded in this book can be regarded as proposing the delineation of a *historical period*. It is a historical period because the mechanisms of recursive self-definition expounded endow the historical past represented in the historical text with the unity and cohesion that are the hallmark of the idea of the historical period.[12]

---

12. The purpose of this epilogue is to investigate the extensionalist's and the intensionalist's positions with regard to the notion of the historical period. It is true that in this context the notion of the so-called historical idea would have been a more appropriate candidate than the notion of the historical period. For the early German historicists, the quasi-Platonic notion of the *historische Idee* was suggestive of what is present in the manifold manifestations of some historical phenomenon. Think of the notion of the Zeitgeist, probably the best example of the historische Idee: the Zeitgeist of a period or an epoch subsumes in itself all that is characteristic of that period's culture, politics, social order, the organization of its economic reality, and so on. However, this unity in manifold historical phenomena could also take the form of the *thesis* a historian had developed for how to understand some part or aspect of the past, and then there is no longer a necessary link with the historical period. This is how the notion of historical representations has been understood throughout this book. As Ranke puts it, "das Real-Geistige, welches in ungeahndeter Originalität dir plötzlich vor Augen steht, lässt sich von keinem höheren Prinzip ableiten. Aus dem Besonderen kannst Du wohl bedachtsam und kühn zu dem Allgemeinen aufsteigen; aus der Allgemeinen Theorie gibt es keinen Weg zur Anschauung des Besonderen." Leopold von Ranke, *Politisches Gespräch: Historisch-politische Zeitschrift*, Vol. 2 (Berlin: Duncker und Humblot, 1833–1836), 790. Or think of Humboldt: "Das Geschäft des Geschichtsschreibers in seiner letzten, aber einfachsten Auflösung ist die Darstellung des Strebens einer Idee, Dasein in der Wirklichkeit zu gewinnen." Wilhelm von Humboldt, Über die Aufgabe des Geschichtsschreibers, in *Gesammelte Schriften*, Vol. 4 (1877: repr. Boston: de Gruyter, 2020), 36. For a further discussion of the notions of the "historische Idee and that of the 'Zeitgeist,'" see Allan Megill, "History's Unresolving Tensions: Reality and Implications," *Rethinking History. The Journal of Theory and Practice* 23, no. 3 (September 2019): 279–304, and my forthcoming book, Franklin Rudolf Ankersmit, *Peter Munz's Evolutionist Philosophy of History and the Anthropocene*, chap. 6.

This epilogue ends, however, with a critique of the extensionalism upheld by Davidson in his essay on conceptual schemes. His conceptual schemes come closer to the notion of the historical period than to that of the historical idea, so the former will be at stake in this epilogue.

EPILOGUE

3. WHAT ARE INTENSIONALIST PHENOMENA?

Our primary intuition about intensional phenomena is that they are noetic—that is, they are entities of the mind, the ideas or concepts we need to think or speak about the world. This intuition entails that the world, understood as (physical) reality—hence, the domain of extensional phenomena—logically precedes intensional phenomena, thus adding further ammunition to the conviction that the latter are of merely ephemeral interest compared to extensional phenomena. So the idea is that language may well be intensional but nature is not. Broadly speaking, this yields the extensionalist picture of the world inherited from the seventeenth century: a Cartesian dualism of mind and matter, of *res cogitans* and *res extensa* (albeit allowing for the reversal in the hierarchy between the two effected by Locke's *nihil in intellectu quod non prius fuit in sensu*).

An important qualification, however, is that the extension of "matter" can also include abstract entities such as mathematical figures.[13] As Shani put it, "the extension of 'triangle' [consists] of all triangles and its intension of the triangle's attributes such as figure, three lines, three angles, the equality of these three angles to two right angles, and so on."[14] As the example suggests, one may speak of intrinsic connections between these attributes or patterns of organization that may be investigated and elaborated upon without any reference to the triangle's extension.

Much discussion of intensional phenomena has focused on the distinction between so-called intensional and extensional contexts. Shani writes that "an extensional context is one in which denoting terms whose denotata are co-instantiated (e.g. co-valent sentences, co-extensive predicates, and co-referential singular terms) can be intersubstituted *salva veritate*; an intensional context is one in which substitutivity cannot be guaranteed."[15] Hence, in extensional contexts, if both x and y are true of a, then "a is x" can be replaced by "a is y," *salva veritate*, whereas any such substitution is no longer guaranteed in an intensional context.

---

13. The (Platonic) notion of the triangle is an abstraction of all the triangular forms that may be discerned in the world. These triangular forms in the world are its extension. The transition to the domain of intension is made via theorems, for example, the proposition that the three angles of a triangle add up to 180 degrees or that the surface of a triangle is half the product of its base and its height. Abstraction must be distinguished from geometry.

14. Shani, "The Myth of Reductive Extensionalism," 159.

15. Shani, "The Myth of ReductiveExtensionalism," 159.

For example, if the two sentences S_1 "all human beings have two eyes" and S_2 "all human beings have a lymph system" are both true, S_1 can be exchanged for S_2 *salva veritate* because they are both true of (or coinstantiated in) human beings. But in the case of S_3 "X believes that S_1" and S_4 "X believes that S_2," no such substitution is possible. S_3 may be true of X, but S_4 may not be because X believes S_2 to be false or because the person is simply ignorant of what a lymph system is. If S_4 is false, S_3 cannot be replaced by S_4. Sentences like S_3 and S_4 in which propositional attitudes are reported are said to be intensional because they place sentences such as S_1 and S_2 in an intensional context.

Specifically, sentences like S_3 and S_4 consist of two parts: there is the part stating "X believes that . . ." and the part stating the belief. The crucial fact is that the latter part cannot be described exclusively in extensional terms. It is, after all, about a *belief* and, as previously noted, beliefs belong to the noetic domain of *intensions* containing the ideas, concepts, sentences, and so on. This is the domain we use for expressing our beliefs about (physical) reality. Hence, there is no *extensional* reality proving beyond any conceivable doubt that if X believes S_1 he will also believe S_2.

This is, so to speak, the revenge effect of distinguishing between extension and intension. If you decide to make that distinction, and if truth is understood as extensionalist truth as previously described (in terms of an opposition between truth and falsehood), one should not be surprised that truth and falsity no longer apply to the intensionalist domain. Worse, we can't apply that distinction to truth and falsity. Could truth be anything else but true; could falsity be anything else but false? The only way to escape this conclusion would be to transform the intensional domain to which X's beliefs belong into a kind of pseudo-extensional reality. But then we face the awkward question of the consequences of that maneuver. Have we now eliminated the extension/intension distinction, or have we only raised it to a higher level? The former option, elimination, is not very attractive. Leibniz's distinction in the *Nouveaux Essais* seems reasonable enough. But the second option is a prototypical first step in a *regressus ad infinitum*.

From the perspective of historical writing, it is of considerable interest that the distinction between extensional and intensional contexts has its counterpart in that between first-order and second-order observation. The distinction has been proposed by the German theoretical sociologist Niklas Luhmann (1927–1998) in his systems theory. First-order observation is how you and I observe the world from our perspective; one might call it "the *me* (or *we*) perspective." But when I observe you or one or more others (e.g., you or the family next door) observing the world, second-order observation has come into being. Here one could speak of "the *he* (or *they*) perspective." In the first case, I/we speak about my/our observations; and in the second case, I/we speak about the observation of others (whether it be your observations or those of the family next door).[16]

It could be argued that there is a kind of blind spot between first- and second-order observation. To see this recall that there is a moment of vertigo if you move from one way of seeing the Necker Cube or Wittgenstein's rabbit/duck drawing to the other. Den Hollander offers the following explanation:

> Summing up, we may say that the distinction guiding all our observations remains itself unobservable, as a kind of blind spot. We know, of course, through communication with others, that there is a distinction between the environment and ourselves, but this is irrelevant to the observation theory under discussion. The crucial point is that we cannot observe it. For example, I cannot see what is behind my back right now. Others are only in the position to do this and to exclaim: "Watch out, behind you!" With the asymmetry between my position of observer and the position of others as observers, we arrive at the crucial difference between first and second order observations. Whereas I observe only my own environment, other people observe me in my own environment. They notice that I observe the world from a particular point of view, while I am unable to see this. This means that second order observation introduces an element of perspective and contingency in our way of observing.[17]

---

16. Unfortunately, the meaning Luhmann gives to his central concepts—such as first- and second-order observation—vary with the texts in which he uses them. Nevertheless, the interested reader may be referred to Niklas Luhmann, *Introduction to Systems Theory*, trans. Peter Gilgen (Cambridge: Polity Press, 2012), 212. It must also be emphasized that for Luhmann a first-order observer may become a second-order observer of himself—for example, when he suddenly becomes aware of the unintended consequences of his actions.

17. Jaap den Hollander, "Historicism, Hermeneutics, Second Order Observation: Luhmann Observed by a Historian," in *Social Sciences and Cultural Studies—Issues of Language, Public Opinion, Education and Welfare*, ed. Asuncion Lopez-Varela (Rijeka: Intech Open Access, 2012), 39–59, especially 53. Den Hollander's important conclusion is that the writing of history is the second-order observation discipline *par excellence*.

Historicism came into being at the end of the eighteenth century with the discovery (by Chladenius) that historians are essentially second-order observers.[18] They explain the beliefs and actions of historical actors in terms of the point of view from which *they* saw their world without being aware of it. By doing so, they move from the extensional to the intensional context—hence, from extensionalism to intensionalism.

4. THE ONTOLOGY OF INTENSIONALIST PHENOMENA

Shani now makes the decisive step in his argument when asking whether there exists such a thing as, what he calls, the category of intensional entities: "intensional entities are characterized by the fact that they contravene the extensionality principle, i.e., the principle that equivalence (as in the case of equivalent sets), or co-presence (as in the case of co-present individuals), imply identity. That is, if F and G are two intensional entities such that $F \equiv G$, or that F and G are co-instantiated, it does not follow that $F = G$."[19] To return to the earlier example, the concepts of "having two eyes" and of "having a lymph system" are coextensive but mutually distinct. This also holds for abstract intensional entities such as "4^2" and "16."

Shani insists, however, that not *all* intentional entities are noetic: "neither properties nor relations are such that when co-instantiated they are necessarily identical."[20] This is a surprising statement for several reasons. For one thing, properties such as having two eyes and having a lymph system are not necessarily identical if coinstantiated. But why would this imply that these properties are not noetic? Until this point, Shani has described entities such as ideas, concepts, or sentences as noetic, and he does not make clear why properties (such as the *property* of having two eyes or a lymph system) should be dropped from the list because properties apparently fit well within the picture with which Shani began. On the one hand, there is a (physical) reality, and on the other, the noetic domain of language, thought, ideas, concepts, and so on in terms of which we speak about that reality. For example, when saying things such as "all human beings have a lymph system" or "P has two eyes," surely having a lymph system or having two

---

18. For an elaboration of this claim, see section 5.
19. Shani, "The Myth of Reductive Extensionalism," 162.
20. Shani, "The Myth of Reductive Extensionalism," 63. Shani never returns to relations again, so I only mention them briefly in the remainder of this epilogue.

eyes are properties that we can truly predicate of all human beings or of P. Clearly, properties are noetic entities we appeal to in order to express our knowledge of the world. They live their life in language. This claim also has the support of the extensionalist tradition.

Shani could answer the objection as follows. He could say that we must discriminate between predicates and properties (e.g., in the statement "this flower is red," the *predicate* "is red" attributes the *property* of being red to this flower). Predicates are noetic whereas properties are not; properties are in the world or aspects of what the world is like, and it is properties of things in the world that he has in mind. This is why we can maintain at first sight the somewhat surprising conclusion that properties are intensional but *not* noetic.[21]

Against this background, it will be no surprise that Shani elevates the question of properties into an *ontological* one. He writes that "being instrumental in accounting for the intensional character of concepts, propositions, attitude reports, and so on, properties suggest themselves as the quintessential intensional entities and as the key to a more insightful account of the ontology of intensional phenomena."[22] The suggestion is clearly that properties are ontologically more deeply entrenched than the objects that they are the properties of. Equally clearly, this compels us to exchange our trusted traditional extensionalist ontology for an intensionalist one, which is exactly what Shani recommends that we do. Should we follow his advice? As a corollary, should we reject any extensionalist argument casting doubt on the ontological status of properties?

5. PROPERTIES, ASPECTS, AND THINGS

Shani mentions three strategies that the adherents of the extensionalist thesis use to deny the ontological status of properties. The first one, advocated by Quine, is the claim that there are no clear identity conditions

---

21. C. B. Martin and John Heil, "The Ontological Turn," *Midwest Studies Philosophy* 23 (1999): 34–99, at 44, argue: "Whatever properties are, they cannot be simply whatever answers to predicates. Some predicates designate properties, no doubt, and, in general, predicates hold true of objects in virtue of properties possessed by those objects. But it would be a mistake to imagine that every predicate, even every predicate that figures in a going empirical theory, designates a property."

22. Shani, "The Myth of Reductive Extensionalism," 165.

for properties. Whereas coinstantiation secures the identity of individuals and coextension for sets, no such instruments are available for properties. Shani most shrewdly turns Quine's argument against itself: properties are deeper than individuals or sets of them because it is *they* that allow us to identify them, whereas there is nothing more basic than properties that we can use to identify properties. Properties are logically primitive. It is (sets of) individuals that are secondary in the ontological hierarchy.

A second time-honored extensionalist attack on properties is the claim that properties are universals and hence "too spooky to be taken as primitive constituents of physical reality."[23] Many versions of the attack exist, and it serves no purpose to rehearse them here. Let us say simply that it would be overly hasty to tie the fate of properties to that of universals, let alone to identify them without further discussion. Instead, Shani urges us to regard properties as modes or as tropes. As you may recall, tropes have been introduced into modern philosophical parlance "to denote particular instances of qualities. Thus, two shirts with the same shade of red exemplify two red tropes, two particular instances of redness. Tropes, however are not particular instances of universals."[24] When equating properties and modes or tropes, Shani follows John Heil.[25] Heil prefers the terminology of modes to that of tropes because the adherents of the trope vocabulary tend to see tropes as the building blocks of the universe and objects as nothing but bundles of tropes. However, Shani (and Heil) don't explain what's wrong with the bundle view of tropes (or modes).[26] This is regrettable because

---

23. Shani, "The Myth of Reductive Extensionalism," 169.
24. Shani, "The Myth of Reductive Extensionalism," 169.
25. Equating the two is surprising because both modes and tropes owe their philosophical interest to their pulling together of objects and their properties. Within the mode and trope vocabulary, the property of "being eloquent" differs in (1) "Clinton is eloquent" and (2) "Obama is eloquent" because Clinton's eloquence differs from Obama's eloquence.
26. Martin and Heil, "The Ontological Turn," 45, write that "a common name for properties thus considered is 'tropes.'" I have resisted the term, however, because I differ from other friends of tropes in rejecting the idea that objects are nothing more than bundles of tropes. I won't go into detail here, but bundle theory treats properties appositely as parts of objects. Objects can have parts, but an object's properties are not its parts. They are particular ways the objects is.

Here, Martin and Heil depart from Leibniz's intensionalism. Leibniz would consider "the bundle theory of tropes" a perfectly acceptable way of describing his concept of substances or monads. At the same time, Leibniz would reject as incomprehensible the idea that a substance's or a monad's properties should be regarded as "ways the object [i.e., a substance or monad] is." The account of the intensionalism of historical representation given in this book agrees with Leibniz and not with Martin and Heil.

their rejection of that view implies, according to them, that objects should be something more than mere "bundles" of tropes.

This position raises two questions. First, is this not a concession to the extensionalist seriously compromising the intensionalist's case; and second, what exactly is this "something more"? But both Shani and Heil leave these questions unanswered. A similar problem is occasioned by Shani's claim that exchanging the trope for the mode vocabulary has the alleged advantage of implying that properties are not constitutive parts of things in which they inhere but rather are "constitutive *aspects* of things; in the familiar parlance, they are 'ways things are.'"[27] This raises the problem of what things are *more* than their aspects; they *must* be something more because Shani claims that *they* are *not* "constitutive part of the things in which they inhere."

Both Shani and Heil are silent about this "more," and I regard it as a liability rather than an asset in the intensionalist's argument. It is difficult, if not impossible, to see what purpose is served by holding onto it. Moreover, its omission agrees with my reading of Shani's otherwise useful introduction of the notion of the aspect. Someone's rear or front is an *aspect* of their physical appearance—but also at the same time a *constitutive part* of it. Your rear is

---

More generally, Martin and Heil's habit of speaking without any reluctance of "the redness of tomatoes" or "the sphericity of balls" suggests a logical priority of objects over their properties that is irreconcilable with Leibniz's conception of substances or monads. As far as I can see, there is no difference between the extensionalist conception of objects and their own views, whereas objects are logical entities for the intensionalist. In both the Leibnizian system itself and in the Leibnizian version of intensionalism defended in this book, logic and metaphysics are two sides of the same coin.

John Heil, *From an Ontological Point of View* (Oxford: Oxford University Press, 2003), 128, reveals its residual extensionalist bias: "Tropes have come to be identified with views championed by G. F. Stout, D. C. William, Keith Campbell, and Peter Simons, among others. These authors regard objects as 'bundles' of tropes. Objects, however, are not made up of their properties in the way a clock is made up of its parts: screws, gears, a spring, an escapement, and a case. Parts of objects are objects, not properties. Properties—modes—are particularized ways objects are." A similar argument can be found in John Heil, *The Universe As We Find It* (Oxford: Oxford University Press, 2012), chap. 6.

This makes perfectly clear how Heil thinks of the matter, but not *why*. Heil's argument that parts of objects are objects, not properties, misses its target: modes and tropes are neither objects nor properties. It is their defining characteristic that they must not and cannot be divided into objects such as a clock's screws, gears, and so on, on the one hand, and their properties, on the other. Much the same kind of argument (occasioning the same problem) can be found in Heil, *The Universe As We Find It*, chap. 6.

27. Shani, "The Myth of Reductive Extensionalism," 170.

no less part of your body because it is also being defined and determined by the point of view on your body that presents your rear. Returning to my argument about landscapes at the outset of chapter 4, we might even maintain that objects are nothing but *the totality of their aspects*.[28] The idea of the object is an inherently incomplete notion. It is an anticipation of what will never truly be given to us, the totality of something in all of its *aspects* at once. The assumption that a concrete content can be given to the idea of an object as a "totality" of this kind is also unclear. How, for instance, could you tell that *no* aspect is lacking from that totality? The extensionalist conception of the object lives on even in Shani's account.

Indeed, this brings us to a new issue in our discussion of the opposition of extensionalism and intensionalism. We cannot fail to be struck by the fact that all this talk of objects—not only by Shani but by Heil and Armstrong as well—suggests that an unpurged relic of extensionalism survives in their work. Their (basically extensionalist) argument is that objects having certain properties exist. But in their account, the notions of the aspect and of properties will get in the way of one another if one embraces the intensionalist thesis. As I have argued elsewhere, "aspects are constituent parts of an object and like the object itself they can be said to have properties, *but they are not properties themselves*. Aspects are less than things and more than properties and must be located somewhere between the two."[29]

Aspects are as close to objects as one can get because they are unique bundles of properties and in this sense suggestive of objects. But they will never actually *become* objects because no list of an object's aspects, however long, can ever support the claim that it should be *the total set* and, therefore, constitute an object. Objects understood as the extensionalist presents them, as totalities, turn out to be like limits in mathematics that can be approached asymptotically but can never actually be reached. All we really have, however, are objects in *statu nascendi* or *par manière de dire*.

One last word about objects, aspects, and properties. It might be argued that the extensionalist has greater sympathy for this notion of the aspect

---

28. Although this is not true of their properties. In the case of extensionalist objects, aspects and properties must be distinguished: having a property is true of an object, an aspect is part of it.

29. Franklin Rudolf Ankersmit, *Meaning, Truth and Reference in Historical Representation* (London: Cornell University Press, 2013), 106.

than the intensionalist. After all, the extensionalist has the notion of the object in his vocabulary so he might welcome the notion of the aspect as suggestive of bundles of properties that at least come close to being identifiable with the object itself. But this only suggests, once again, that Shani and Heil still have not wholly abandoned the notion of the object. A reference to HRs can be helpful in showing that this is the case. Remember that an HR is self-referentially defined by all the statements it contains, but there is no explicit mention in the HR that this HR is self-referentially defined by *this* set of statements and no other. That this is the case is, nevertheless, a hard fact. We have established that adding one sentence to, or dropping one of them from, a certain HR inevitably results in a *different* HR. The HR does not possess a separate component that defines its closure. Even more so, it doesn't need one because it is part of the HR's nature that any change made to it results in another HR. Objects, however, need closure, which is achieved by such simple instruments as a logical proper name or an identifying description. The contrast is between the objects of extensionalism, which turn out to be what we have called weak individuals, and those of intensionalism, which are strong individuals that demonstrate their strength by not requiring closure to be and to remain what they are. They leave no one in doubt for a moment about what does belong to them and what does not.

There is another dimension to this difference between aspects and properties. We can attribute properties to intensional entities, but it would be odd to speak of their aspects. If we take HRs—which are arguably the prototypical intensionalist entities, together with Leibniz's substances and monads—it surely makes sense to say that they highlight certain *aspects of the past* they are about. It is true that they do so in an indirect and uncertain way, as we saw in chapter 5 when discussing the debate about the PBF and models of HRs. But it makes no sense to say of HRs *themselves* that these should have aspects as well. This is where intensional entities differ from extensional ones. Being mere sets of statements about past states of affairs, HRs surely have properties (the property of containing sentence s_1, sentence s_2, sentence s_3, and so on), but they have no aspects. Similarly, the distinction between predication and attribution makes sense in an extensionalist but not in an intensionalist context.

I said that we must discern between predicates and properties (e.g., in the statement "this flower is red," the *predicate* "is red" attributes the *property* of being red to this flower). Now, in an extensional context like that of the flower, the functions of predication and the attribution of properties are clearly discernible. Predication (1) is stating that a certain predicate is true of what the subject of a statement refers to; but attribution (2) is stating that a thing has a certain property. Predication remains within the domain of language because it does not move from the statement's subject-term to its object of reference, whereas attribution crosses the demarcation line between the two. Consider the following example: if object A is one meter long and B is two meters long, it can be truly *predicated* of B that it is twice as long as A, but it is not a *property* of B to be twice as long as A. Similarly, whereas being two meters long is a property of B, being twice as long as A can only be predicated of it. Likewise, relations can be predicated of objects (either extensional or intensional), but they cannot be an object's properties.[30]

This extensionalist distinction between properties and true predication will make no sense for the intensionalist because, for the intensionalist, there are only individual entities that are recursively defined by their properties. There is no entity that is logically prior, apart, or above this recursive self-definition.[31] Predication then coincides with attribution. Again, recall the case of historical representation: the meta-sentence "H_1 is s_1" attributes the property of being s_1 to HR_1 and truthfully expresses at the same time that being s_1 is a predicate of H_1. No reference to any entity outside H_1 is implied or suggested; the dualism of object and property characteristic of extensionalism is replaced here by the monism of properties and entities consisting of properties only.

Shani insists that aspects or properties are "inherently *dynamic* in the sense that the possession of an aspect either constituted an activity of a thing or a disposition for active causal influence. Thus, spinning around their centres of gravity is something planets do, while seemingly static aspects, such as shapes, constitute various dispositions for interaction.[32] Indeed, aspects are not mere "ways things are." We see once more how close the intensionalist Shani's manner of speaking comes to the extensionalist's

---

30. Leibniz himself made this point, see chapters 2 and 3.
31. This does not mean there is no room for relations and relational statements within intensionalist language. The last sections of chapter 4 show this inference to be unwarranted. Admittedly, the road from intensional entities to relational statements is a complicated and arduous one.
32. Shani, "The Myth of Reductive Extensionalism," 178.

vocabulary. As Shani goes on to say, aspects can more appropriately be described as "'the ways' things unfold," where each such "way" is a distinct arrow of determination in a field of possible causal chains.

Finally, the ontology of aspects seems to presuppose not only that the things in which they inhere are complex, organized, and dynamic but also that "they manifest intrinsic patterns of organization."[33] Admittedly, these are rather vague and tentative formulations; nevertheless, my proposal to conceive of things or objects as constituted by being recursively defined by their aspects or properties clearly does better justice to the intensionalist cause than Shani's own suggestion of things being logically prior to their aspects or properties. Paraphrasing Luigi Pirandello, one might say that in the intensionalist picture properties are in search of an object, whereas in the extensionalist one—which still lingers in Shani—objects are in search of their properties.

6. THE LIMITATIONS OF EXTENSIONALISM

I used an epigraph from Leibniz's *Nouveaux Essais* to oppose extensionalist and intensionalist truth at the beginning of this epilogue, which aimed to show that both have their own "claim to truth." In certain cases, the extensionalist account will come closest to what we need, and in others the intentionalist view will prevail. We must now address the question of how to map the opposition between extensionalism and intensionalism onto the world in which we live as it is investigated by the sciences. When speaking of "the sciences" 'I have in mind *both* sciences like physics *and* the humanities. One thing can be said straightaway. The world of daily experience inhabited by the well-known "medium-sized dry goods," such as human beings, animal, plants, mountains, rivers, and so on, agrees best with the extensionalist conception of the world. This apparent alliance between extensionalism and common sense grants extensionalism a tremendous advantage over its intensionalist rival. Moreover, as Shani points out, the impressive successes of classical physics from the seventeenth to the beginning of twentieth century also contributed to the triumph of extensionalism over intensionalism. It was as if science had proved that the extensionalist philosopher had been right all along.

---

33. Shani, "The Myth of Reductive Extensionalism," 176.

But little is left today of this existensionalist image of science. Einstein's claim that gravitational fields are the only primary reality and his proposal that we might be able to explain the manifestation of particle-like behavior as an intense localized concentration of field energy was the first crack in the wall. But worse was to come with quantum mechanics. Think of Heisenberg's uncertainty principle; the wave particle duality; the later theory of the entanglement of photons (for which Alain Aspect, John Clauser, and Anton Zeilinger received the 2022 Nobel Prize for Physics); particles being treated as quantizations of field processes; or the radicalization of the latter in string theory. Shani sums up the situation:

> Contemporary physics . . . is diametrically opposed to the extensionalist credo. First, it shows that the particles of old—solid, simple, passive, and indestructible chunks of matter—simply don't exist. Second, it shows that the most elementary systems that do manifest particulate qualities, the fundamental "particles" of subatomic physics, are intrinsically fluctuating entities, which manifest process patterns (e.g. the transmutation of a photon into a virtual electron-positron pair) and are sensitive to process patterns in their environment (e.g., when the probing of a detector brings down the collapse of an electron wave function. . . . What seems to follow from all this is a stark denial of the idea that form can be reduced to an ontology of formless material objects. By the same token, it also undermines the idea that aspects are somehow less elementary than objects.[34]

Shani concludes as follows: "My purpose here, however, is not to urge a complete reversal of the extensionalist bias, i.e. to argue that aspects are more fundamental than objects and, consequently, that intensional entities are more basic than extensional ones. For even without going into such an extreme it seems compulsory to conclude that in the present context of scientific development, reductive extensionalism is no longer defensible and, hence, that it need no longer be fluttered as a regulative ideal for naturalistic philosophy."[35]

---

34. Shani, "The Myth of Reductive Extensionalism," 178–79.
35. Shani, "The Myth of Reductive Extensionalism," 179.

EPILOGUE

The shift observed by Shani has its counterpart in the writing of history—although it is, surprisingly enough, much older there. However, its triumphs were never as undisputed as in the sciences. Until now, the extensionalist and intensionalist models have coexisted, and few historians and philosophers of history have been aware of this struggle in their respective fields. To understand this subterranean conflict at the heart of contemporary historical thought, we should bear in mind that ever since antiquity, all through the Middle Ages, and until deep into the eighteenth century the historian was expected to make readers quasi-contemporaneous with the events of the past. The historical text should read like an eyewitness account.[36] Historians of historical writing often use the noun "autopsy" (i.e., having seen something oneself) as a suggestive metaphor for this conception of the historian's task. Guido Schepens puts it this way:

> In the historiographical conception of many historians of Antiquity, characterized by H. Strassburger as "the art of primary research" ("Kunst der Primarforschung"), the *autopsy* of the historian's own observation of the facts constituted the fundamental point of departure for all writing of history.... The idea of the methodological priority of the *autopsy*, which was passed on from Antiquity to the historiography of the Middle Ages and to Early Modern Europe retained its validity down to the threshold of the nineteenth century.[37]

The historian should avoid as much as possible any suggestion that his text was written at a time later than the historical events described in it. Put

---

36. See Noëll Carroll, "History and Retrospection," in *A Companion to Arthur C. Danto*, ed. Jonathan Gilmore and Lydia Goehr (Hoboken, NJ: Wiley, 2022), 152–62, especially 145–49, where Carroll speaks of the "eyewitness view of history" when explaining Danto's notion of "the Ideal Chronicler." This does not necessarily exclude the appeal to rhetoric; e.g., the speeches Thucydides put in the mouths of the main actors in history had the purpose of placing the reader *in medias res* and allowing them to regard themselves as other participants.

37. Guido Schepens, "L'Autopsie dans la Méthode des Historiens Grecs du Vme Siècle avant J.-C.," *Verhandelingen van de Koninklijke Academie voor Wetenschappen en Schone Kunsten van België, Klasse der Letteren* 42, no. 93 (1980): 199 (author's translation). See also Gianna Pomata and Nancy G. Siraiso, eds., *Historia: Empiricism and Erudition in Early Modern Europe* (Cambridge: Cambridge University Press, 2005); and Arno Seifert, *Cognitio Historica. Die Geschichte als Namengeberin der Frühneuzeitlichen Praxis* (Berlin: Duncker und Humblot, 1976).

differently, the historian should present to readers the past as it was for those who lived in it, and he should do so by giving the impression that he had been present himself when the people whose actions he describes performed them.[38]

Now, the idea is that Collingwood still gave a theoretical justification of this conception of the historian's task with his so-called reenactment theory:

> So the historian of politics or warfare, presented with an account of certain actions done by Julius Caesar, tries to understand these actions, that is, to discover what thoughts in Caesar's mind determined him to do them. This implies envisaging for himself the situation in which Caesar stood, and thinking for himself what Caesar thought about the situation and the possible ways of dealing with it. *The history of thought, and therefore all history, is the re-enactment of past thought in the historian's own mind.*[39]

---

38. Upon its death, the autopsy paradigm left an invaluable legacy for later times. One of the weirdest works of history ever written may give us an idea of that legacy. I have in mind here *Histoire des Ducs de Bourgogne de la Maison de Valois 1364–1477* (1824–1826) by the historian and politician Prosper Baron de Barante (1782–1866). Barrante hoped to realize the aims of the autopsy paradigm by deleting the gap between the historian's sources and his own text. He did so by giving it the character of an ongoing compilation of quotes from the work by fourteenth- and fifteenth-century historians, such as Froissart, Monstrelet, Chastellain, Commynes, and so on, who all wrote "contemporary history," as we now call it. In this sense, Barante's history consisted of material contemporaneous with the events related in it. Stephen Bann framed for Barante the apt metaphor of "the historian as taxidermist": the taxidermist historian wants to show to his readers the past as it was seen by those who lived in it. See Stephen Bann, *The Clothing of Clio. A Study of the Representation of History in Nineteenth-Century Britain and France* (Cambridge: Cambridge University Press, 1984), chap. 1.

Continuing Bann's metaphor, one might say that the quotes Barante used were analogous to the materials used by the taxidermist to create the illusion of a real hawk, fox, or eagle. In this way, Barante hoped to paint the *couleur locale* of fourteenth- and fifteenth-century France. (The term *couleur locale* was taken from painting where it stood for the color a thing has if seen in normal daylight.) Thanks to Barante's *Histoire des Ducs de Bourgogne*, readers would be carried back to the life and times of Jean sans Peur, Philippe le Bon, and Louis XI. But the historical text is not a time machine: it also asks questions that nobody in the past itself could have asked or answered. Nevertheless, we can try to *imagine* what it must have been like to live in a certain part of the past. Who could forbid us to do so? But then the techniques of the historian must be exchanged for those of the novelist. This is how the historical novel (and, a generation later, the realist or naturalist novels of Balzac, Flaubert, and Zola) was born from the death of the autopsy paradigm at the end of the eighteenth century.

39. R. G. Collingwood, *The Idea of History* (New York: Oxford University Press, 1961), 215, emphasis added.

EPILOGUE

For two reasons Collingwood's reenactment theory provides a striking exemplification of the extensionalist bias in historical thought. First, when discussing the transition from classical extensionalist physics to modern intensionalist physics, we saw that the former has its origins in a certain conception of daily reality and the kind of objects we may expect to find there. Clearly, when demanding that historians should identify themselves with the person whose actions they wish to explain, the reenactment theorist also demands (1) an identification of the historian's daily reality with that of the historical agent and (2) the belief that such an identification is feasible at all. For if the daily realities of historians and their subjects differed essentially, if both contained systematically different stimuli for human action, the identification of the historian with their object of study could never succeed.

A second argument follows directly from the foregoing. Recall the argument about intensional contexts expounded previously. It is basically an argument against coinstantiation. If we have the sentences (1) "P believes that p (and p is true)" and (2) "p necessarily entails q," we may not infer from (1) and (2) that (3) "P believes that q." The truth of both (1) and (3) are not coinstantiated in this example of a statement like p being placed in an intensional context. Under extensionalist assumptions, however, where reference to the world is the decisive criterion of truth, coinstantiaton is always guaranteed. The world is as it is, so extensionalism requires coinstantiation in the case of (1) and (3): if the world justifies p, it will also justify q. But intensionalism puts a spoke in the extensionalist's wheels. This may explain Quine's and Davidson's visceral dislike of an intensionalist semantics:

> Already in "Two Dogmas of Empiricism" (1953) Quine declared war on "meanings" and was heading in the direction of a purely referential semantics. His extensionalist program is present in full in his *Word and Object* (1960), where he advocated a "flight from intension" (as one of the chapters of the book is revealingly called), namely, a systematic attempt, to rid our scientific vocabulary of any reference to intensional entities.[40]

---

40. Shani, "The Myth of Reductive Extensionalism," 167.

EPILOGUE

Van den Akker has offered a revealing discussion of Davidson's theory of radical interpretation, trying to explain how it is that we understand the utterances of others. Van den Akker shows that Davidson's theory of interpretation rests on three assumptions: (1) we have to know the truth-conditions of the utterance expressing a speaker's belief; (2) we should assume that the speaker holds their beliefs to be true; and (3) we should be able to relate the belief to other presupposed but unmentioned beliefs.[41]

Davidson included the third condition for the following reason. Suppose we read that the Greeks believed the earth is flat. We may then jump to the conclusion that this belief was false. But that's going too fast. We should ask ourselves what the Greeks had in mind when saying that the earth is flat. Perhaps it merely referred to how the earth's surface presents itself to us in daily experience. This question can only adequately be answered against the background of a number of *truths* shared by the Greeks and us. As long as our Greek interlocutor comes up with more statements *we* regard as false, our perplexity will increase. Only shared truths can help us. Generally speaking, we can only identify a belief as false against the backdrop of many true beliefs.[42] This is what has been called Davidson's "triangulation model": his theory claims there is a continuous interaction between the three points represented by (1) a speaker, (2) a radical interpreter of the speaker's words, and (3) the world.

Clearly, the triangulation model is vintage extensionalism: it relies on a conception of daily reality and its truths characteristic of all extensionalism. Indeed, Davidson is explicit about his embrace of extensionalism: "I think our actual scheme and language are best understood as extensionalist and materialist."[43] He assumes a reality to which the speaker's utterances refer and which guides the interpreter's effort to understand the meaning of the

---

41. Akker, *The Exemplifying Past*, 23, 30.
42. Akker, *The Exemplifying Past*, 31. See also my discussion of *The Exemplifying Past* in Franklin Rudolf Ankersmit, "A Narrativist Revival?," *Journal of the Philosophy of History* 15, no. 2 (2021): 215–40, especially 217–24.
43. See Davidson, "On the Very Idea of a Conceptual Scheme,"188–89, which expresses an extensionalist dislike of the category of meaning at 189: "meanings gave us a way to talk about categories, the organizing structure of language, and so on; but it is possible, as we have seen, to give up meanings and analyticity while retaining the idea of language as embodying a conceptual scheme." The end of the quote seems to suggest that Davidson welcomes conceptual schemes. How this rhymes with his condemnation of them is not easy to see.

speaker's words. We can understand each other because we live in a shared world about which we have an overwhelming number of shared beliefs.[44] Furthermore, as the example of the Greek's belief that the world is flat indicates, Davidson's model of how we understand others is not restricted to our contemporaries. It applies equally well to people living at other times and places. For Davidson there is no basic difference between your neighbor telling you strange things and your discovery of the apparently strange things that people told each other in the Middle Ages.

Van den Akker ends his comparison of Davidson with Collingwood with the conclusion that both travel most of the extensionalist road together—although Collingwood takes a further step when raising the question of *why* an agent (in either the past or the present) held a certain belief or performed a certain action. Davidson had no interest in that question. Van den Akker concludes:

> Davidson assumes that when interpretation has to start from scratch, the interpreter is present and able to assign truth-conditions to the utterances in the specific circumstances the speaker is in, and that, obviously, is not the case when it is unclear what the circumstance was of the past utterances studied by the historian. In that case, re-enacting past thoughts by asking questions is all the historian can do. This being said, our conclusion is that [Collingwoodian] re-enactment of past thoughts and [Davidson's] assigning truth conditions to alien utterances are complementary rather than contradictory activities.[45]

Both Collingwood and Davidson remain within the framework of the autopsy model of historical writing, which owes its apparent plausibility to its extensionalist assumptions. In sum, Van den Akker's argument demonstrates that reenactment and the autopsy model are identical with the conception of historical truth that extensionalists such as Collingwood and Davidson must hold.

As the reader will recall two hundred years before Collingwood the autopsy model had already been completely turned upside down by Johann

---

44. Whereas Quine's scepticism questions even analytical truths, Davidson embraces the truth of most of what we say in daily conversation with the argument that such generosity is required to guarantee understanding (i.e., his so-called charity principle).

45. Akker, *The Exemplifying Past*, 38.

EPILOGUE

Martin Chladenius in his *Allgemeine Geschichtswissenschaft* of 1752. This work can be regarded as marking the birth date of (German) historicism because *it shifted the cognitive center from the historical actor to the historian himself* (as all science requires us to do: no scientist identifies themselves with the object they investigate and is interested exclusively in what can be said about it from their point of view). So it is in historical writing: decisive is not what the past was like for *those who lived in it*, what were their thoughts and beliefs, but what *the historian* can tell readers about the past as investigated by him from *his* point of view:

> The point of view is the internal and external situation of a spectator in so far as there follows from it a certain and quite specific way of seeing, regarding or interpreting the things we see. . . . It is a notion that goes together with what is most important in all of philosophy, though it is still not sufficiently appreciated as such in philosophy, even though "der Herr von Leibniz" has drawn our attention to its role in metaphysics and in psychology.[46]

Chladenius's revolutionary intervention—as inspired by Leibniz!—was succinctly summarized by Reinhart Koselleck:

> Chladenius argued that it was ordinarily believed that a history and its representation should coincide. However, in order to represent part of the past and to a assess it, a methodological separation was necessary: the past itself is one thing, but its representation is separate from it and can take different forms. A history as such can, in its uniqueness, only be thought as being free

---

46. Johann Martin Chladenius, *Allgemeine Geschichtswissenschaft. Mit einer Einleitung von Christoph Friederich und einem Vorwort von Reinhart Koselleck* (1752; repr. Vienna: Hermann Böhlaus Nachf, 1985), 100-1: "Der Sehepunkt ist der innerliche and äusserliche Zustand eines Zuschauers, in so ferne daraus eine gewisse und besondere Art, die vorkommende Dinge anzuschauen und zu betrachten, flüsset. Ein Begriff, der mit den allerwichtigsten in der gantzen Philosophie im Paare gehet, den man aber noch zur Zeit zu Nutzen noch nicht gewohnt ist, ausser dass der Herr von Leibniz hie und da denselben selbst in der Metaphysik und Psychologie gebracht hat" (author's translation).

See also Leopold von Ranke, "Erwiderung auf Heinrich Leo's Angriff," in *Leopold von Ranke's Sämmtliche Werke. Herausgegeben von Alfred Dove*, Vol. 53.54 (Leipzig: Duncker und Humblot, 1890), 664-65: "Ich habe mich hier keinem I. Müller und keinem Alten, sondern der Erscheinung selbst anzunähern gesucht, als welche eben so hervortritt, äusserlich nur Besonderheit, innerlich— und so verstehe ich Leibniz—ein Allgemeines, Bedeutung, Geist." Ranke's habit of speaking about historical individuals such as states or nations as "Gedanken Gottes" (thoughts of God) is definitely Leibnizian.

from contradiction, but each representation of it is broken perspectivally. . . . With this claim that a perspectivist account of history and a biased account of it are not one and the same thing Chladenius created a theoretical matrix that is up till now still unsurpassed. . . . Chladenius's theory of knowledge has been an act of liberation. By expanding *autopsy*—traditionally narrowing and limiting the historian's room of manoeuvre the perspective of the historian himself, historical writing acquired a hitherto completely unknown freedom of movement.[47]

I fully endorse Koselleck's assessment of Chladenius's work as the greatest revolution in the entire history of historical thought until the present time—and therefore feel not the slightest reluctance to quote this wonderful passage again.

Chladenius's liberation of historical thought from the shackles of the autopsy model marked its transition in principle from an extensionalist to an intensionalist conception of historical writing; its transition from a belief in the possibility of "a resurrection of the past" à la Michelet to a real science. Of course, the influence of the extensionalist view has persisted to this day. Nevertheless, it was Chladenius who was the true founder of the Leibnizian philosophy of historical representation advocated in this book. This Leibnizian-Chladenian philosophy is, in its essence, a strictly intensionalist interpretation of historical writing—as Chladenius himself so perceptively noted.

The Leibnizian system itself was already strictly intensionalist, leaving no room at all for reference to an extensionalist reality. This being what he hoped to achieve with this opposition between the domain of the substances or monads and that of the PBF. As we have seen, Leibniz's monads—and my HRs that develop the monadological concept—are constituted by recursive self-definition. This process of self-definition proceeds by meta-sentences stating that this monad, or this HR, is p; where p is a sentence expressing a monad's "perceptions" (to use Leibniz's terminology') or, in the case of an HR, a true statement on some past state of affairs functioning as a property recursively defining an HR. "Recursive definition" means that properties

---

47. Reinhart Koselleck, "Standortbindung und Zeitlichkeit. Ein Beitrag zur historiografischen Erschliessung der geschichtlichen Welt," in *Vergangene Zukunft. Zur Semantik Geschichtlicher Zeiten* (Frankfurt am Main: Suhrkamp, 1979), 176–211, especially 185, 187 (author's translation).

are not an entity's properties prior to their being attributed to that entity. Put differently, whereas sentences like *p* can be said to be extensionalist, the meta-sentence certainly is not: it states that *p* is part of itself. It is about its own meaning—and is, therefore, intensionalist.[48]

7. DAVIDSON ON CONCEPTUAL SCHEMES

In 1974 Donald Davidson published an immensely influential essay in which he rejected—successfully in the eyes of almost all his subsequent commentators—"the very idea of conceptual schemes."[49] But although he made clear how he understood the notion of a conceptual scheme, he remained tantalizingly vague about which disciplines and cultural practices actually relied, in his view, on this notion. This is regrettable, for it has remained unclear which disciplines and cultural practices should be

---

48. It could be argued that (historical) representation necessarily implies self-observation or self-reflection—with the interesting implication that this "self" is automatically no longer the self it was previous to this self-observation or self-reflection. The historical self moves to a meta-level from where, if and when this process is made explicit, it can objectify its previous self: "historical reality only comes into being when the past no longer exists." O'Sullivan adds the following observation that raises this question: "to what extent the historian must explicitly contextualise themselves with regard to their own being in time as a result of doing history. Logically and implicitly one can say that they must; but actually seeing oneself in historical terms as an outcome, may remain latent, depending on the historian. Life is normally lived forwards; seeing it in terms of its own past is in a sense deeply unnatural and counter-intuitive." This is right on target and captures exactly what Hegel had in mind when concluding his famous exposition of "Das Verderben der Griechischen Sittlichkeit" (The Destruction of Greek Morality) as follows: "Die Versöhnung ist deshalb zuerst nur im abstrakten Gedanken: so hat Sokrates sie erfasst. Aber sie musste dann noch im Geiste geschehen." [Dialectical] reconciliation inheres, therefore, at first only in abstract thought; this is how Socrates conceived of it. But then it must still be enacted in the Mind. Georg W. F. Hegel, *Vorlesungen über die Philosophie der Weltgeschichte*, Vol. 2–4 (Hamburg: Felix Meiner, 1967), 647. A new state in the history of the Mind is at first only in the domain of the Objective Mind; it enters that of the Absolute Mind only if it is taken up in *self-awareness*. Self-awareness is the seal *authenticating* the development of the Mind.

49. For the essay's influence, see John H. Zammito, *A Nice Derangement of Epistemes: Post-Positivism in the Study of Science from Quine to Latour* (Chicago: University of Chicago Press, 2004), 72–83. Nevertheless, there have been critics. See, for example, Ian Hacking, "Language, Truth and Reason," in *Rationality and Relativism*, ed. M. Hollis and S. Lukes (Cambridge, MA: MIT Press, 1982), 48–66; Ian Hacking, *Representing and Intervening* (New York: Cambridge University Press, 1983); Nicholas Rescher, "Conceptual Schemes," in *Studies in Epistemology*, ed. Peter A. French, Theodore E. Uehling Jr., and Howard K. Wettstein (Minneapolis: University of Minnesota Press, 1980), 323–45; Isaac Nevo, "In Defence of a Dogma: Davidson, Language, and Conceptual Schemes," *Ratio* 17, no. 3 (August 2004) 312–28; Michael Lynch, "Three Models of Conceptual Schemes," *Inquiry* 40, no. 4 (1997): 407–26; and Xinli Wang, "Conceptual Schemes and Conceptual Relativism," *Pacific Philosophical Quarterly* 90, no. 1 (2009): 140–64.

EPILOGUE

regarded as less reliable or trustworthy because of Davidson's attack on conceptual schemes. All he had to say on this was the following:

> Philosophers of many persuasions are prone to talk of conceptual schemes. Conceptual schemes, we are told, are ways of organizing experience . . . they are points of view from which individuals, cultures, or periods survey the passing scheme. There may be no translation from one scheme to another, in which case the beliefs, desires, hopes and bits of knowledge that characterize one person have no true counterparts for the subscriber to another scheme. Reality itself is relative to a scheme: what counts as real in one system may not be in another.[50]

In the context of this book the obvious question is, of course, whether Davidson also has the writing of history in mind here, and specifically, whether he believes *historical periods* to be defined by specific conceptual schemes or not. It is true that there is no explicit mention of historical periods in the quoted passage. But the remark that there are "points of view from which individuals, cultures, or periods survey the passing scheme" surely includes what historians have in mind by "historical periods." Think of Leopold von Ranke's well-known remark that "each epoch is immediate to God" (jede Epoche ist unmittelbar zu Gott) and of what we, as historians, have learned to associate with it. So *if* historical periods were a subvariant of Davidson's conceptual schemes, he was questioning a concept that is presupposed in all historical writing. What would be left of the practice of historical writing if the historian had to abandon the notion of the historical period and many cognate concepts such as an era, an age, a period (such as Hellenism), the time of Louis XIV, and so on? If Davidson's attack on conceptual schemes was successful, contemporary historical writing would be producing myths. Davidson's essay directly challenges my claim that historical representation is anything but a myth; it is, hence, a matter of great urgency for me to show Davidson's argument to be wrong *if applied to historical writing*.

Finally, I must emphasize that the last two sections of this epilogue discuss Davidson's essay exclusively insofar as it is of relevance for historical writing, and specifically for the notion of the historical period. All other aspects of the essay will be left out.

---

50. Davidson, "On the Very Idea of a Conceptual Scheme," 183.

EPILOGUE

Davidson does not say whether history in particular should fear his reasoning, but he gives a number of suggestive examples: "sometimes an idea, like that of simultaneity as defined in relativity theory is so important that with its addition a whole department of science takes on a new look. Sometimes revisions in the list of sentences held true in a discipline are so central that we may feel that the terms involved have changed their meanings." He adds that "languages that evolved in distant times or places may differ extensively in their resources for dealing with one or another range of phenomena."[51] Both examples suggest a conception of a "historical period" as defined by an adherence to certain beliefs (classical physics, or what is expressed by the acceptance of certain meanings) being followed by a later *period* in which these beliefs or meanings were abandoned for new ones. These two examples are good evidence that the notion of the historical period is, indeed, implicated in Davidson's attack on conceptual schemes. So historians have good reason to feel worried about Davidson's argument—all the more so because there is little love lost between Davidson's extensionalism and the intrinsic intensionalism of historical writing.[52]

Before addressing the question of how the essay relates to historical writing in particular, however, we must obtain more clarity about the notion of the conceptual scheme. What, after all, is a conceptual scheme? By far the most usual—but at the same time unexpected—answer to that question is that, for Davidson, the terms *conceptual scheme* and *natural language* are virtually interchangeable. As Davidson puts it, alas without further elucidation:

> We may accept the doctrine that associates having a language with having a conceptual scheme. The relation may be supposed to be this: where conceptual schemes differ, so do languages. But speakers of different languages may share a conceptual scheme provided there is a way of translating one language in the other. Studying the criteria of translation is therefore a way of focusing on criteria of identity for conceptual schemes.[53]

---

51. Davidson, "On the Very Idea of a Conceptual Scheme," 183–84.
52. Davidson, "On the Very Idea of a Conceptual Scheme," 183–84.
53. Davidson, "On the Very Idea of a Conceptual Scheme," 184. Davidson writes at 185 that "we may identify conceptual schemes with languages, then, or better, allowing for the possibility that more than one language may express the same scheme, sets of intertranslatable languages."

EPILOGUE

Although this ties the notion of the conceptual scheme directly to language, it does not properly define the term *conceptual scheme*. Davidson's essay is known to be an attack on conceptual schemes, so we can also examine some of the authors who, according to Davidson, rely on such schemes. We can derive some further information on what he understood by a conceptual scheme from his criticisms. For example, Davidson discussed Benjamin Whorf (1897–1941) and Thomas Kuhn (1922–1996). Whorf is quoted as follows: "language does in a cruder but also in a broader and more versatile way the same thing that science does. . . . We are thus introduced to a new principle of relativity, which holds that all observers are not led by the same physical evidence to the same picture of the universe, unless their linguistic backgrounds are similar, or can in some way be calibrated."[54] It is to be regretted that Davidson was so much absorbed by his effort to make short shrift of the Sapir/Whorf hypothesis that he shut his eyes to what might be the kernel of truth in it. Let's be clear about just this: the roots of the insight go back to such an intellectual giant as Humboldt, and contrary to common wisdom it is far from dead today.[55] The idea here is that each natural language determines how we will see and experience the world and that it does so "from top to bottom." No part of reality is excluded from how it is interpreted by the language we happen to use. Sapir defined the hypothesis as follows:

> it is quite an illusion to imagine that one adjusts to reality essentially without the use of language and that language is merely an incidental means of solving specific problems of communication or reflection. The fact of the matter is that the 'real world' is to a large extent unconsciously built upon the language habits of the group. No two languages are ever sufficiently similar to be considered as representing the same social reality. The worlds in which different societies live are distinct worlds, not merely the same world with different labels attached. . . . We see and hear and otherwise experience very

---

54. Davidson, "On the Very Idea of a Conceptual Scheme," 190.
55. Thus Humboldt: "da auch auf die Sprache in derselben Nation eine gleichartige Subjectivitaet einwirkt, so liegt in jeder Sprache eine eigenthuemliche Weltansicht. . . . Der Mensch lebt mit den Gegenstaenden hauptsaechlich, ja, da Empfinden und Handeln in ihm von seinen Vorstellungen abhaengen, sogar ausschliesslich so, wie die Sprache sie ihm zufuehrt." See Wilhelm von Humboldt, *Schriften zur Sprachphilosophie, in fünf Bänden*. Vol. 3. *Über die Verschiedenheit des menschlichen Sprachbaues und ihren Einfluss auf die geistige Entwicklung des Menschengeschlechts* (1830-35; repr. Darmstadt: Wissenschaftliche Buchgesellschaft, 1963), 434. (I'd like to thank Arthur van Essen for having made me aware of this passage in Humboldt's writings.)

largely as we do because the language habits of our community predispose certain choices of interpretation.[56]

Over the last few decades the Sapir/Whorf hypothesis has made an unexpected comeback.[57]

In Kuhn's case we must think of the "incommensurability" he had claimed for his paradigms.[58] Davidson writes that "according to Kuhn, scientists operating in different scientific traditions (within different 'paradigms') work in different worlds."[59] We could summarize Whorf's and Kuhn's claims in two different ways. First, we could take them as saying that the translation of one language or paradigm into another is not possible without loss of meaning. Second, we could take them to be asserting that the translation of one language into the other always entails a redistribution of truth values. Davidson is an extensionalist, so he naturally prefers the second reading. Like his teacher Quine he has little love of meaning. This is of importance because it could be argued that Davidson's main claim is that his essay shows this second reading to be wrong. This is helpful for our understanding of what Davidson has in mind by a conceptual scheme, but it does not diminish the fears of historians about their discipline being an obvious victim of Davidson's argument—an unintended victim, perhaps, but that rarely is much of a consolation for the unintended victims in question.

But Davidson's criticisms of Whorf and Kuhn still do not amount to a definition of a conceptual scheme. Whorf's and Kuhn's two claims state what conceptual schemes *do* rather than what they *are*. The role of schemes is, of course, to schematize, but that immediately raises the question what schemes schematize. Davidson pays a lot of attention to this issue.[60] Davidson's notion

---

56. See Edward Sapir, *Culture, Language and Personality. Selected Essays*, ed. David G. Mandelbaum (Los Angeles: University of California Press, 1964), 69.

57. See, for example, Arthur van Essen, "Language Universals, Language Individuality and Linguistic Relativity in the Works of Etsko Kruisinga," in *Studies for Antonie Cohen. Sound Structures*, ed. Marcel van den Broecke, Vincent van Heuven, and Wim Zonneveld (Dordrecht: Foris, 1983), 71–79; John Leavitt, *Linguistic Relativities: Language Diversity and Modern Thought* (Cambridge: Cambridge University Press, 2011); John A. Lucy, *Language Diversity and Thought: A Reformulation of the Linguistic Relativism Hypothesis* (Cambridge: Cambridge University Press, 1992); and John Gumperz and Stephen Levinson, eds., *Rethinking Linguistic Relativity* (Cambridge: Cambridge University Press, 1996).

58. Davidson, "On the Very Idea of a Conceptual Scheme," 190.

59. Davidson, "On the Very Idea of a Conceptual Scheme," 186–87.

60. Davidson, "On the Very Idea of a Conceptual Scheme," 191–94.

EPILOGUE

of the scheme is not, as one might have expected, a scheme organizing the concepts constituting a language in some way or other. For the adjective "conceptual" relates to the *noun* "scheme" and not to the *concepts* that are employed in a language to denote individual extensional and intentional entities. Davidson gives the following clarification of the conceptual scheme, and we might, at last, also be able to treat this as his definition of it:

> Something is a language, and associated with a conceptual scheme, whether we can translate it or not, if it stands in a certain relation (predicting, organizing, facing), or fitting experience (nature, reality, sensory promptings). The problem is to say what the relation is, and to be clearer about the entities related. The images and metaphors fall in to two main groups: conceptual schemes (language) either *organize* something, or they *fit* it (as in "he warps his scientific heritage to fit his ... sensory promptings").[61]

For Davidson the idea of the conceptual scheme thus comprises (1) the scheme itself; (2) its content (that which is conceptualized by the scheme); and (3) a view of how scheme and content are related. The scheme of a conceptual scheme (1) may, in the first place, "organize" things in the world. Think of how I might organize my desk drawer by separating pencils from ballpoints and ballpoints from fountain pens. But I might also sort the drawer according to the "scheme" of the relative length of these objects—or even their relative weight. The other possibility is that the scheme of a conceptual scheme determines the conditions of possible experience. Kant's transcendental idealism is the prime example. Kant has only *one* such conceptual scheme, however, whereas for relativists several schemes of that type may peacefully coexist (as, for example, in Hayden White's tropology).

However, the coexistence of conceptual schemes is a precarious idea. Most often—and on good grounds—it is said that the very idea of a peaceful coexistence of conceptual schemes is at odds with what makes conceptual schemes into what they are. So it is with Davidson, and why in his view conceptual schemes are typically not "intertranslatable." Put differently, this is why according to him (as he likes to express it) there is always

---

61. Davidson, "On the Very Idea of a Conceptual Scheme," 191.

"a redistribution of truth values across different conceptual schemes." This invites (1) the problem of relativism and the worrying conclusion that a truth transcending the war of conceptual schemes is forever unattainable.[62] Next, there is the issue of (2), i.e., content. In fact, that question has already been answered. Content may stand either for sense data, for our experience of the world, or for objects in the world—whether these are concrete or relatively abstract, such as the cultural "objects" that constitute a civilization, society, or historical period, for that matter. Finally, we have (3), the relationship between the scheme and its content. According to Davidson, there are two metaphors for that relationship. The first metaphor is that of "organization," which best suits the relationship between a scheme and a content consisting of *objects* in the world. The second metaphor is one of "fitting." This is the one that we will naturally appeal to if the scheme's content is experiential. Davidson adds that the "fitting metaphor" means, in fact, that the scheme "is true of" its content.

Metaphors often suggest new insights, but these insights have to be shown to be correct, which is the task epistemology has traditionally assigned itself. Epistemology can be defined as the philosophical subdiscipline investigating how language and knowledge relate to the world. Clearly, this is what is at stake in Davidson's two metaphors. So if Davidson's essay is an attack on conceptual schemes, it is likewise an attack on epistemology.[63] According to Davidson, epistemology is nothing but the invention of philosophical machineries, as complicated as they are useless, for tying a

---

62. According to Davidson, the idea of a conceptual scheme only makes sense on the assumption that truth-values vary across different conceptual schemes. Hence, Davidson's argument against conceptual schemes requires him to demonstrate that truth-values remain *un*changed if a sentence in one language is translated into some other language. To show this is precisely what he tries to do with his appeal to Tarski, which is discussed in the next section. According to Davidson, truth-values are not redistributed across different languages and can be translated into each other *salva veritate*. He appeals to Tarski to prove his point.

However, Davidson is also in the habit of calling conceptual schemes "languages," even though he criticizes conceptual schemes unlike languages for effecting a redistribution of truth-values. For example, Davidson, "On the Very Idea of a Conceptual Scheme," 186, writes: "We may identify conceptual schemes with languages, then, or better, allowing for the possibility that more than one language may express the same scheme, sets of intertranslatable languages." Davidson here seems to contradict his own claim that according to the idea of a conceptual scheme languages do *not* permit the redistribution of truth-values.

63. Wang, "Conceptual Schemes and Conceptual Relativism," 146. Davidson's rejection of epistemology inspired Rorty's notorious work: Richard Rorty, *Philosophy and the Mirror of Nature* (Oxford: Basil Blackwell, 1980). The book is a history of epistemological thought since Descartes that tries to demonstrate the futility of all epistemology. Kant is again the main culprit.

scheme to its content. Kant and all variants of Kantianism are the main victims here, of course. Davidson replaces the "verticality" of an epistemology supposedly linking mind and object with a "horizontal" ongoing causal (triangular) interaction between the world, speakers, and their interpreters. Although Davidson does not pay much attention to the details of that interaction, this is probably the closest one can get to a formal definition of the idea of a conceptual scheme in his work.

There is one final issue in need of our attention. Davidson's theory of the conceptual schemes owes quite a lot to Quine. But whereas Quine speaks in this context of an "*un*interpreted reality," Davidson is quite clear about holding onto an "interpreted reality." For him there is no such thing as an uninterpreted reality. For Davidson, Kantian transcendentalism is the prototypical model of the (epistemological) relationship between scheme and content in conceptual schemes. In Kant's critical philosophy, the noumenal order about which nothing can be said plays a key role. Davidson wants to reject this "ungraspable" entity about which *ex hypothesi* nothing can be said because a conceptual scheme's content must satisfy the minimal condition of being describable in language. For him the problem of "the very idea of the conceptual scheme" is meaningful only if the content of a conceptual scheme consists of sentences or descriptions of things in the world (whatever these may be). What has, or can be, described in language must, for that very same reason, be an "interpreted reality." Thus, for Davidson, the reality allegedly organized by a conceptual scheme should be an interpreted reality.[64]

---

64. From the point of view of "philosophical strategy," Davidson's move is of considerable interest. In effect, he elevates Kant's noumenon to the status of what we can truthfully say about the world. Whereas, at first sight, the Kantian noumenon seems to have been deleted irretrievably from the philosopher's vocabulary by Davidson, we might also say that the aura of the pure given—inherited from the noumenon—that *ex hypothesi* may not be questioned is now granted to the most elementary truths we may express about the world. This explains a major difference between Quine and Davidson: whereas Quine is the skeptic *par excellence* requiring us to doubt just *any* individual statement we might make about the world, Davidson urges us to accept them all on the condition that they are in agreement with what plain common sense makes us believe. If seen from this perspective, Quine is the consistent anti-Kantian, whereas Davidson reinstates Kantianism again, although combining this reinstatement with an upgrading of the noumenon to the most universally accepted truths we have of the world. Indeed, the belief that below the true statement S—and the set of true statements s_1 to s_n justifying S—there is some noumenal reality making S true is precisely what Davidson refers to as "the Third Dogma of Empiricism." We have this noumenal reality already in the philosophically innocuous guise of these universally accepted truths about the world.

EPILOGUE

Van den Akker points out that Davidson's rejection of the idea of an uninterpreted reality has important implications:

> Davidson also claims that there is no such thing as "uninterpreted reality, something outside all schemes and science." Perhaps a conceptual relativist would immediately object that his position is precisely that there is no such thing as uninterpreted reality, the data of sensation, or the passing scene. He claims after all that reality is relative to some conceptual scheme and what is real according to one culture's or epoch's scheme is not in another. It is rather easy to see why this objection fails. When the notion of uninterpreted reality is the necessary counterpart of the notion of conceptual scheme, and the conceptual realist rejects the former, he cannot hold on to the latter either, and with that to the idea that reality and truth are relative to it. If we give up on the idea that there is something like uninterpreted reality, the data of sensation, of the passing scheme, we also give up on the idea of conceptual schemes and vice versa.[65]

As Van den Akker makes clear, if you abandon the idea of an uninterpreted reality, you must also abandon relativism. The dualism of scheme and content—presupposing an uninterpreted reality or content, on the one hand, and a scheme interpreting it, on the other—will also have to go.[66] As Van den Akker put it: "the dualism of scheme and empirical content, 'of an organizing system and something waiting to be organized,' as Donald Davidson famously argued, 'cannot be made intelligible and defensible.'"[67]

Davidson's rejection of the very idea of the conceptual scheme is, in the end, somewhat puzzling. Recall that Davidson was an advocate of the "doctrine" (as he called it) associating languages with conceptual schemes.[68]

Needless to say, the weak spot of Davidson's strategy is that there are no universally accepted truths about the world. This is why Davidson's extremism leads us back to Quine's extremism that no statement, however robust it may seem, is exempt from revision. Perhaps Popper's philosophical love of the juste milieu shows us the best way to overcome this conflict of extremisms.

65. Akker, *The Exemplifying Past*, 40.

66. Akker, *The Exemplifying Past*, 42, 43, concludes his discussion of the conceptual scheme with an exposition on Davidson's claim that truth and translatability are indissolubly linked together. The implication is that however much two languages may differ the speakers of these languages can nevertheless, in principle, communicate meaningfully with each other on the condition that they aim to speak the truth. Obviously, this is one more argument against relativism.

67. Akker, *The Exemplifying Past*, 40.

So if conceptual schemes have to go, presumably that sounds the death knell for languages too.[69] The implication seems hard to avoid. Yet Davidson's main argument discusses translation by means of so-called radical interpretation—and without languages, there is no problem of translation. I must confess to being unable to solve the puzzle.[70]

8. DAVIDSON'S RADICAL INTERPRETATION AND THE HISTORICAL PERIOD

So far the argument in Davidson's essay regarding conceptual schemes has not been placed into direct confrontation with historical thought. But I did make clear the implication that sooner or later such a confrontation is

---

68. See note 43.

69. Donald Davidson, "A Nice Derangement of Epitaphs," in *Truth, Language and History* (Oxford: Clarendon Press, 2005) 89–109, written twelve years later, concluded at 107 that "there is no such thing as language, not if a language is anything like what many philosophers and linguists have supposed. There is therefore no such thing to be learned, mastered or born with. We must give up the idea of a clearly defined shared structure which language-users acquire and then apply to cases."

At 104, Davidson argues (1) that what we call "language" can only be found on the most elementary level of communication in terms of words or sentences, and (2) that there are no general rules that could properly be said to define a language for what happens on that level. His argument is as follows: "any general framework, whether conceived as a grammar for English, or a rule for accepting grammars, or a basic grammar plus rules for modifying or extending it—any such general framework, by virtue of the features that make it general, will be *insufficient* for interpreting particular utterances."

The argument does not convince. Indeed, such rules are insufficient; but they are *necessary* at the same time. It is true that there are no secondary rules for how to apply primary general rules to individual cases. Aristotle argued as much with his distinction between theory and "πραξις." That application is a matter of "φρώνησις," of "prudentia," of "practical wisdom." So it is in a juridical context: there is the law as formulated by the legislator, and when applying that law the judge will consult the relevant jurisprudence, but in giving his verdict he adds a new item to already existing jurisprudence. All jurisdiction nevertheless begins with the letter of the law (and not with the legislator's intentions, for that matter). Without laws, there can be no jurisdiction either. Hence, Davidson's claim that our use of language does not rely on general rules is like someone inferring from the absence of a rule for the application of rules that there should be no such thing as a civil or a penal code.

70. Davidson briefly comments on the issue himself when answering some of his critics (e.g., Rorty and Pereda). But I am unable see in which way these comments solve the problem. See Donald Davidson, "Appendix: Replies to Rorty, Stroud, McDowell, and Pereda," in *Truth, Language and History* (Oxford: Clarendon Press, 2005), 315–329, especially 324 and 325. Of course, the problem would disappear if Davidson holds that there are some languages at least that are translatable and share truth-values and others that are untranslatable and that have changing truth-values. But his use of the words *language* and *conceptual scheme* throughout the essay militates against this interpretation.

to be expected. I noted the contrast between Davidson's openly professed extensionalism and the fact that authentically historical thought is intensionalist through and through. The conflict finally comes into the open when Davidson turns to what he calls "radical interpretation." This problem engaged hermeneutic and historicist thought from Schleiermacher, Boeckh, Droysen, and Dilthey down to Gadamer.

Davidson never mentions this venerable tradition, which is more than two and a half centuries old, and the reader may be forgiven when complaining that some remarks about this categorical dismissal would have been welcome—if only because this might have made clearer where he disagreed with it. To mention just one intriguing example, what would an extensionalist like Davidson have made of the requirement of German hermeneuticists from Schleiermacher down to Gadamer that the interpreter should "understand an author better than he understood himself"?[71] Davidson was familiar with the idea, which is clear from the following passages he quotes from Gadamer: "the closer these interpretations adhere to Plato's text the more distant they are from clearing the way toward that text. The more distant they are from the world of Plato's language and thought, on the other hand, the closer I believe they come to performing their task. . . . Every conversation presupposes a common language, or, creates a common language. . . . To reach an understanding with one's partner in a dialogue is . . . a transformation, in which we do not remain what we are."[72] And Davidson most surprisingly comments as follows: "I am in agreement with almost all of this. Where I differ (and this may merely show I have not fully understood Gadamer) is that I would not say that a conversation presupposes a common language, nor that it even requires one."[73]

The reader of Davidson's essay will begin to suspect that Davidson may well have been right when fearing that he may have misunderstood Gadamer. Gadamer's assumption about a shared common language merely states the truism that knowledge of the Greek language is indispensable for a meaningful conversation about the *original Greek version* of Plato's

---

71. For a still helpful and illuminating survey of how German hemeneuticists dealt with the issue, see Otto Friedrich Bollnow, "Was heisst einen Schriftsteller besser verstehen, als er sich selbst verstanden hat?," *Deutsche Vierteljahrschrift* 18, no. 2 (1940): 117–38.

72. See Donald Davidson, "Gadamer and Plato's *Philebus*," in *Truth, Language and History* (Oxford: Clarendon Press, 2005); 271–77, especially 262 and 275.

73. See Davidson, "Gadamer and Plato's *Philebus*," 275.

Philebus. If Gadamer was wrong about this, what's the use of all these translations of Plato's works? We should throw them all away as obstacles to an adequate understanding of Plato's intentions and directly confront the Greek text itself, even if we know no Greek at all.[74]

Anyway, it is as it is. And we have, therefore, no alternative but to address Davidson's notion of radical interpretation and to go along with the idea that he and Quine were the first to discover it and to put it on the philosopher's agenda. Central to Davidson's rejection of conceptual schemes is the idea (mentioned a moment ago already) that there should be no retribution of truth-values across different conceptual schemes. That is to say, a true claim in one scheme will also be true in another—provided it is correctly translated. Hence Davidson's rejection of relativism. Davidson's argument against the conceptual schemes requires him to demonstrate that truth-values should remain *un*changed if a sentence in one language is translated in some other language. This, then, is precisely what he tries to do.

Davidson appeals to Alfred Tarski's now widely accepted theory of truth.[75] At first sight, Tarski's theory seems to be a variant of the correspondence theory. Although this is not entirely wrong, it is much deeper because it posits a *meta-language* expressing the correspondence. That is, we are

---

74. Moreover, as Luke O'Sullivan pointed out to me, Davidson's insistence on interpretation is in tension with his insistence on translation; it is just a fact that not all interpretations are literally translatable without a gloss. In the end, Davidson's argument is vitiated because his distinctions are too crude and not fine-grained enough.

Robert Wardy, *Aristotle in China: Language, Categories and Translation* (Cambridge: Cambridge University Press, 2000) is a great case study here. When discussing a seventeenth-century Jesuit translation of Aristotle's *Categories* into Chinese, Wardy concludes that the Chinese translation was perfectly clear, and even better in some ways than the Latin in being more faithful to the Greek. What seventeenth-century Chinese people would have thought was weird was the whole classical Christian complex of ideas that gave the *Categories* or the *Organon* its importance in Christian theology in the first place. They lacked the background/worldview/conceptual scheme in terms of which the Jesuits had come to think Aristotle so important to Christian theology, and this needed to be explained to them in addition to providing them with a good translation before they could see what the point was—although, when that was done, they could see the point, and converts were made ("conversion" being, I suppose, a very practical proof of "translation"). Although one could say in response and furthermore that in fact Chinese Christianity was not a literal copy of the European tradition but the beginning of something new, just as translating a text into a new language is in a way creating a new work, not simply equivalent to just copying out an old one in a different symbolism. All of these questions are absolutely essential to all interpretation—whether radical or not—but they are simply wiped off the table at one sweep as pointless and irrelevant by Davidson. So in the end, what is Davidson's argument true of apart from what it is true of?—just as one may wonder what to make of the assertion "if I see a tree, I see a tree." True, but so what?

75. Davidson, "On the Very Idea of a Conceptual Scheme," 194–96.

supposed to read a seemingly naive statement such as "s is true" as a meta-sentence about what "s" expresses and which is said to be true according to the naive sentence *as a whole* (i.e., s is true) (1). It will therefore take the following form: "s is true" if "s is true" (2). This is by no means an idle redundancy because, unlike (2), it is only the meta-statement that expresses what is the case if s is true.

According to the basic version of the correspondence theory of truth, we are likely to say "the statement in the German language "Schnee ist weiss" corresponds to the facts (i.e., is true) if, and only if, snow is white" (1). The first part of this sentence (ending with Schnee ist weiss) refers to, or is about, the German sentence "Schnee ist weiss." *This is the crucial fact.* As soon as we start to *refer*, or to say something *about* something else, we have (1) the meta-level of referring or of saying something about something else, and (2) the object-level of what is being referred to or of what is being spoken about.

In this way we can say that sentence (1) *as a whole* is a meta-sentence (in English) stating what condition has to be fulfilled to guarantee that the German sentence "Schnee ist weiss," which is the referent of (1), corresponds to the facts. This is how the basic version of the correspondence theory has it. Indeed, if we replace "Schnee ist weiss" by "snow is white"—the result being "snow is white" if and only if "snow is white" (2)—most people would say that this is the correspondence theory of truth all over again. But then they would be overlooking the fact that (2) is, in fact, a meta-sentence about an object-sentence (although both are, in this case, in the same language). The syntactic form of (2) does not register this, but Tarski argued that (2) is, from a logical point of view, more complicated than (2)'s syntax makes us believe. More generally, let S be the name of some true sentence in a foreign language and s that of a translation of that sentence in English. In that case, we can formulate a meta-sentence about S having the following form: "the statement 'S' is true (or corresponds to the facts), if and only if s" (3). Note that in this meta-sentence reference is exclusively to what S (as the meta-sentence's object-sentence) refers to and not to s because s is equivalent to "snow is white," and there is no hierarchy between meta- and object-language. If we have a closer look at (1), we will observe that S is the translation into some foreign language of s in the speaker's language. and that if s corresponds to the facts (or "is true") the same must be the case with S.

Clearly, with Tarski's help, Davidson has demonstrated the correctness of his claim that truth-values do not vary across different natural languages. But as a corollary, he has also signed the death warrant of "the very idea of conceptual schemes" and of the notion of the historical period. There are no conceptual schemes or historical periods fixing truth-values in agreement with the language that happens to be used in them.

Historians who have followed Davidson's complicated and technical exposition will nevertheless find all of this decidedly weird. They will be profoundly puzzled by Davidson's claim that there should be no redistribution of truth-values across different conceptual schemes; that a true claim in one scheme (or historical period) should also be true in another; and that trying to understand a past period should be a matter of "translation." What is left today of the theological truths of the Middle Ages or those of sixteenth-century science? Historians will conclude that Davidson either has a most peculiar conception of what it means to understand historical periods or that what he is talking about has nothing to do at all with the writing of history and what can meaningfully be associated with it. In the latter case, historians can safely conclude that Davidson's rejection of conceptual schemes is irrelevant to them.[76]

Having arrived at this stage we seem to find ourselves at an impasse in our analysis of whether Davidson's notion of the conceptual schemes applies to the practice of historical writing and, if so, how. Davidson will perhaps be at peace with the impasse; he is likely to suggest that we can only expect an impasse if his theory of conceptual schemes is applied to what practicing historians seem to believe they are doing. This is precisely what he had wanted to make clear. Practicing historians, in their turn, will probably be somewhat baffled by so intransigent and little empathetic an interlocutor as Davidson. But since it is part of their profession to overcome this kind of impasse, they will be the last to acquiesce to it and therefore ask themselves how to get discussion going again.

Now, practicing historians will have noticed that Davidson apparently sets great store by the concept of translation and it may then occur to them

---

76. In my correspondence with Van den Akker, he argued that a peaceful coexistence between Davidson's rejection of the conceptual schemes and an acceptance of the historicist notion of the historical period was perfectly conceivable. I admit the possibility but remain unsure on the issue because Davidson's essay left us in the dark about its targets.

that this idea of translating—clearly so important to Davidson—might provide a clue. For "translation" is also part of the practicing historian's vocabulary—even though he will prefer to use it in figurative sense only. We all know David Hartley's metaphor that "the past is a foreign country," to which the phrase "they do things differently there" is often added.[77] If the past is a foreign country, should not past religious, political, social, or juridical meaning be analogous to a "foreign language" for those of us living in the third decade of the twenty-first century? Hence this would be a language whose meaning historians might try to understand. Finally, why not include in all this the language(s) used by our ancestors as well? In that case, the metaphor of the historian's translation of the past into the present would no longer be a metaphor at all but would have acquired literal meaning.

Surely, speaking of languages in need of translation when talking about historical writing is—no doubt—primarily a metaphor for the relationship between past and present. But as we all know, metaphors are often instrumental for the discovery of the literal, nonmetaphorical truth. So open-minded historians will arguably be prepared to see their discipline—or parts of it—as involving a translation of the past into the present and be content to await what clarification is achieved by this metaphor.

What nonmetaphorical content could we give to this idea of a translation of the past into the present? To begin with, it makes us aware of a momentous fact about historical writing that we have not yet addressed; namely, that historical writing *always* implies the translation of extensional into intensional language. Insofar as historical writing is about the behavior of human beings in the widest sense possible, it necessarily involves sentences stating that either individual human beings or collectives thought, believed, hoped, feared, intended, etc. certain things. Recall what was said in section 2 about sentences like "X believes that s," and it will be clear that all these are sentences in an intensional context. Consequently, historical writing must involve the translation of extensional sentences such as "I believe that s" (1), as uttered by a historical actor X, into intensional sentences such as "X believes that s" (2), as uttered by the historian.

At the same time, this may help us see why historians have two good reasons to have reservations about whether Davidson's way of connecting

---

77. See David Lowenthal, *The Past Is a Foreign Country* (Cambridge: Cambridge University Press, 1985).

translation to truth is applicable to historical writing. In the first place, in section 2 we saw that sentence (1) commits X to the belief that s is true, whereas the historian may believe in the truth of (2) but not in that of s. Historians of witchcraft may comment on the *Malleus Maleficarum* published by Heinrich Institoris and Jacob Sprenger in 1486 (the book codifying the belief in witches) while being convinced that most, if not all, of this book is complete nonsense.

Historians will be aware that the truth or falsity of Institoris and Sprenger's claims about witches is of no relevance for their own book or article, which is focused on how to best *understand* the beliefs that made Instititoris and Sprenger write their book and on why it became so popular at the end of the Middle Ages so that the persecution and burning of witches could become a fashion in Europe only in the late 1400s.[78] And that is something entirely different.

More generally, the truth or falsity of past beliefs and convictions are of little or no relevance for historians in their disciplinary attempt to understand the past. Danto explains this irrelevance of the truths or falsity of beliefs in intensional contexts when pointing out that placing phrases about beliefs in an intensional context interferes with the relationship between language and the world. To clarify, Danto uses the adjectives *opaque* and *transparent* to reflect the fact that language, if used in an intensional context, splits into a meta-level and an object-level, with the inevitable result that the language to be situated on the latter level occludes the view or grasp of the world of the language on the meta-level. The example of an

---

78. See Steije Hofhuis, *Qualitative Darwinism—An Evolutionary History of Witchhunting* (forthcoming). Hofhuis argues that one may discern the mechanisms of Darwinian evolution in the different components of the belief in witches. Some components were soon dropped, and others "went viral." The result was a complex complot theory continuously (re)confirming itself in agreement with the Thomas theorem stating that "if men define a situation as real it is real in its consequences."

If everyone believes that witches exist, the result is a social reality indistinguishable from one in which witches really exist. There was no longer an externalist reality that could stop, or even slow down, this proliferation of the demonology on witches. Social reality had become purely intensionalist. This tends to happen in times of religious, mental, and social uncertainty, as at the end of the Middle Ages, and indeed in our own time with the complot theories of QAnon.

To put it provocatively, QAnon *e tutti quanti* are the (unintended) product of the "everyman his own historian" idea. But this retreat into unconstrained subjectivity only produces narcissistic self-delusion. In times of uncertainty, only a strict subjection to the disciplined procedures of historical writing can prevent such fantasies from causing political and social derailment. Historical writing has sometimes been described as "die letzte Religion der Gebildeten." The challenge is now to make it "die letzte Religion der Ungebildeten" as well.

intensional statement like "P believes that s" is telling here: its truth or falsehood is decided by whether P believes it or not, whereas the truth or falsehood of s has become entirely irrelevant. On the other hand, if I say "I believe that s," nothing stands in the way between my beliefs and reality. Opacity has then been exchanged for transparency. As Danto puts it:

> When I refer to another man's beliefs I am referring to him, whereas he, when expressing his beliefs is not referring to himself but to the world. The beliefs in question are transparent to the believer; he reads the world through them without reading them. But his beliefs are opaque to others: they do not read the world through those beliefs; they, as it were, read the beliefs. My beliefs in this respect are invisible to me until something makes them visible and I can see them from the outside. And this usually happens when the belief itself fails to fit the way the world is, and accident has forced me from my wont objects onto myself. Thus the structure of my beliefs is something like the structure of consciousness itself, as viewed by the great phenomenologists, consciousness being a structure that is not an object for itself in the way the things of the world are objects for it. . . . In other words, I do not, as a consciousness, view myself from without. I am an object for others but not for myself, and when I am an object for myself, I have already gone beyond that; when it is made visible it is no longer me, at least from within.[79]

The only thing that matters is saying true things about these beliefs, however false and ridiculous these beliefs may be. Whereas *truth* is—as

---

79. See Arthur C. Danto, *The Transfiguration of the Commonplace: A Philosophy of Art* (Cambridge, MA: Harvard University Press, 1983) I take the liberty to add a note on Danto's eloquence. It may well be argued that Danto has been the greatest stylist among the ten to fifteen most important American philosophers of the previous century (with Quine and Rorty competing for the second place). As Fontaine wrote: "the last chapter of his book *The Transfiguration of the Commonplace* is devoted to metaphor, expression and style. It is as if his whole exploration of the concept of a work of art culminates with his final reflections on the nature of style." Arturo Fontaine, "Writing with Style," in *A Companion to Arthur C. Danto*, ed. Jonathan Gilmore and Lydia Goehr (Hoboken, NJ: Wiley, 2022); 26–33, at 26. But of more importance and interest than anything anyone can and could say about why style mattered so much to Arthur Danto is the last chapter of this *Companion to Arthur Danto*. It is titled "Letter to Posterity" and written by Danto himself shortly before his death. Anyone who is not deeply moved by this "farewell to his readers" and who is unable to see that this provides us with a glimpse of what was at the depth of the soul of Arthur Danto as a philosopher will never understand what inspired all of his thought. See Arthur Danto, "Letter to Posterity," in *A Companion to Arthur C. Danto*, ed. Jonathan Gilmore and Lydia Goehr (Hoboken, NJ: Wiley, 2022), 397–404.

we have seen—one of the two pillars of Davidson's argument about radical translation and against conceptual schemes.

The other pillar is *translatability*. Here the intensionalism of historical representation throws a spanner into the works once again. Again Danto shows us why. He emphasizes that no changes may be made in how a belief is phrased if placed in an intensional context:

> The explanation of the logical peculiarity of intensional contexts is that the words these sentences make use of do not refer to what they ordinarily refer to in routine nonintensional discourse. They refer, rather, to the form in which the things they ordinarily referred to by those words are represented: they include among their truth conditions reference to a representation. Thus when we say that *m* believes that Frege is a great philosopher, this will not be the same as saying that *m* believes that the author of the *Begriffschrift* is a great philosopher, though Frege he is. This is not simply because he may not know that Frege wrote that thing, for he may know that and in fact he may believe that the author of the *Begriffschrift* is a great philosopher. It is that we are referring neither to Frege nor to the author of the *Begriffschrift*, but to a constituent of the way *m* happens to be representing something.[80]

In sum, the way in which sentences are used in an intensional context are "sacred": one may not interfere with how they are phrased.

Needless to add, this also excludes translation. If one translates it, the sentence becomes false: in the intensional statement "X believes that p_1," the phrase p_1 cannot be exchanged for the translation of p_1 in another language—say p_2—for X believes that p_1 and not that p_2. As long as we are dealing purely with extensional contexts covering simple sentences such "snow is white," "this table is round," or "that tree is an oak," Davidson's argument about translation is unobjectionable. But intensional contexts put an effective stop on translation—as Danto shows—by introducing a component resisting translation. An intensional sentence such as "Louis XIV believed that 'L'État—c'est moi'" is undoubtedly true because Louis XIV declared as much himself when entering the Parlement of Paris in 1655 in high boots and with a riding whip in his hand—and yet the French phrase in an intensional context may not be translated into "I am the

---

80. Danto, *The Transfiguration of the Commonplace*, 181.

State" or "Ich bin der Staat" as Tarski's theory of truth (i.e., the truly indispensable chain in Davidson's argument) wishes to have it.[81] Louis XIV believed (and said) "L'État—c'est moi," and not "I am the State" or "Ich bin der Staat."

But this observation needs further development. It will be objected that an English or German historian writing in his own language on the reign of Louis XIV will not hesitate for a moment to translate Louis XIV's statement "l'État—c'est moi" into his own language. So one might protest that this ban on the translation of phrases in an intensional context is a futile trick devoid of any philosophical force because we all know that the phrases "l'État—c'est moi," "I am the State," or "der Staat, das bin Ich" have exactly the same *meaning*. However, this easy and attractive way out is not open to Davidson because it would compel him to recognize meaning as prior to truth, whereas the priority of truth to meaning is the most basic principle of his entire self-professed extensionalist philosophy of language.[82]

We may conclude that the sentence s_1, "l'État—c'est moi," has a meaning if uttered in an *extensional* context—a meaning it loses if quoted in an *intensional* context, together with the possibility of its being either true or false (as we saw a moment ago). Put differently, the phrase s_1 in sentences like "P believes that s_1" is neither true nor false, nor does it have a meaning. It has, therefore, acquired the logical status of a sign. At the same time, this sign s_1 consists of the words "l'État—c'est moi," which can be translated into other languages, resulting in the signs "I am the State" (s_2), "ich bin der Staat" (s_3), and so on. In agreement with this translation of the

---

81. The source of the anecdote is a passage in Voltaire's *Le Siècle de Louis XIV*, chapter 25. Whether Voltaire's report was accurate was subsequently debated; see Reuben Parsons, *Some Lies and Errors of History* (Notre Dame, IN: Notre Dame Press, 1893), 134–42. But the exact phrase Louis XIV uttered does not matter a great deal because there is no doubt that Louis XIV believed the substance of it. Herbert H. Rowen, *A History of Early Modern Europe 1500–1815* (Indianapolis, IN: Bobbs-Merrill, 1960), 393, remarks that "Louis XIV also compelled the courts of justice to give up their independent habits. In 1665 he deprived the *parlements* of their title of 'sovereign courts,' and permitted them only the name of 'superior courts,' lest he appear to share his sovereignty with them. In a *lit de justice* he commanded the *parlements* to register his laws without debate or vote."

82. Wang, "Conceptual Schemes and Conceptual Relativism," 145, doubts Davidson's principle that truth is prior to meaning: "A central source of trouble in interpreting others in the case of radical interpretation is that there is no way to completely disentangle what an alien means from what he believes. To break into such a vicious circle of radical interpretation, Davidson suggests that we should fix beliefs constant while solving for meaning."

sentence "Louis XIV disait/croyait s_1," it will take the form of "Louis XIV said/believed that s_2," "Ludwig XIV sagte/glaubte that s_3," and so on. But the fact that s_1 has its equivalents in s_2, s_3, and so on by no means justifies the claim that s_2, s_3, and so on are *translations* of s_1. Having no meaning, signs can be *replaced* by others but not *translated* into others. The very idea of a translation of signs is nonsensical.

We appear to have gotten stuck here in our attempt to translate the past into the present. The attempt to do so merely results in a proliferation of (meaningless) signs. The result recalls God's intervention during the building of the Tower of Babel:

> But the Lord came down to see the city and the tower the people were building. The Lord said, "if as one people speaking the same language they have begun to do this, then nothing they plan to do will be impossible for them. Come, let us go down and confuse their language so they will not understand each other." So the Lord scattered them from there over all the earth, and they stopped building the city. That is why it was called Babel—because there the Lord confused the language of the whole world. From there the Lord scattered them over the face of the whole earth.[83]

The crucial question then is: *Who* is it, exactly, who has gotten stuck here? It is not the historian, in any case. To see this, I offer two observations. First, when dealing with sentences in an intensional context such as "P believes that s_1," we should distinguish between the part stating that P has a certain belief and the sign standing for the belief—i.e., s_1. Being a mere sign, s_1 is neither true nor false, nor does it have a meaning, it merely stands for a belief, a belief of P, as is the case with its counterparts s_2, s_3, s_4, and so on. But as a sentence in an intensional context, it is a sentence uttered, or written, by the historian—hence, not by P himself. It is a sentence *about* P's beliefs—i.e., not a sentence *expressing* these beliefs.

Recall, too, that this shift from sentences expressing someone's beliefs to sentences about someone's beliefs took place in the context of the shift from extensional to intensional language, occurring in this translation of the past to the present. Hence the shift from sentences like "I believe that s_1" (1) to sentences like "P believes that s_1" (2) is a shift from a context within which s_1

---

83. Genesis 11:5–9.

stands for "l'État—c'est moi" to a context in which s_1 is a mere sign standing for a belief that still needs to be fixed, and hence, for a belief that in all likelihood will never (and perhaps can never) be fixed for once and for all. A sign is a recognizable form written in ink or with a pencil on a piece of paper quietly awaiting whatever people decide to do with it. This is the change we must expect when moving from the *expression* of a belief to *speaking about* that belief.

Put differently, this sign is the birthplace of *another* sign, namely, the kind of sign that I have called the historical representation (HR). It is the place we need for writing down, for example, the sign we may refer to as HR_x, and as soon as we wrote HR_x we cannot write on that same place some other as well, just as we cannot write 25 after having written on that very same place the sign 52 or 103. One sign may occur on different places, but there cannot be different signs in one and the same place. "*Quod scripsi, scripsi*," as Pilate wisely insisted.

We know, too, that each HR is accompanied by other competing HRs. In this way, the shift from the extensionalist type of sentence (1) to the intensionalist type of sentence (2) must remind us of the Lord's intervention in Babel: after it, no longer one but many languages were spoken. At first sight it may seem that this Babylonian confusion of tongues leaves the historian in a hopeless position with intensionalist language. In Davidson's triangulation model of speaker, world, and radical interpreter, there remains an extensionalist reality—consisting of tables, animals, trees, houses, towers of Babylon, London, or whatever—guiding and supervising their interaction. That guide is sadly absent in intensionalism. However, as discussed in chapters 3 and 4, intensionalist language has an alternative to extensionalist reality in the form of the comparison of intensionalist entities. The domain of the PBF and the models provide the intensionalist with a satisfactory alternative to extensionalist reality. We know from the practice of historical writing how such a comparison of HRs in that domain is conducted, and I developed a Leibnizian theory to explain it.

Second, taking our cue from the shift from an extensionalist expression to the historian's intensionalist speaking about beliefs and about the role of comparison in the latter, success in the mutual comparison of intensional entities (HRs) is all that matters here. That is, in sentences like "P believes that s_1," "s_1" has no meaning but is a symbol standing for an as yet wholly unspecified set of beliefs. It is, hence, a sign because signs are symbols that stand for nothing but themselves. Specification only begins with historical debate. Until then, what s_1 stands for is an empty placeholder. It is like the hook on the wall of a farmhouse or tavern to which one can attach anything (see chapter 4). There is no limitation—and this is not a mere manner of speaking!—with regard to what may be appealed to in the comparison of HRs. Anything from the Big Bang to the death of the universe can, in principle, be invoked here on condition that it may further an HR's success in its struggle with other HRs. To paraphrase Nietzsche: after the death of the God of Autopsy, everything is permitted.

Specifically, the effort at developing a copy of the past as suggested by the autopsic model and Collingwood's reenactment theory may sometimes be seen by historians as a sensible idea. Collingwood sometimes compared the historian to a detective, and as long as the historian is no more than a detective, reenactment may be a helpful guide. Even then, though, the detective's findings may be the ingredients for a "history," but they are not themselves a "history." Nor is the detective expected to tell histories. The judge is interested in facts, not in histories; and a lawsuit cannot be modelled on a detective novel, and vice versa. The lawsuit can only take place after the detective has done his work. But far more decisive is that historians will insist that the past they recount is not the past as it was experienced by those who lived in it. The past itself is not history. Historians will support this counterintuitive claim by appealing to Chladenius's observation that historians are expected to tell their readers what the past looks like from *their*, essentially *later*, perspective; and hence, *not* from the perspective of the historical actor(s) whose beliefs and actions they study.

For example, no historian would take seriously an account of the outbreak of the Franco-German war in 1870 that failed to mention that with their aggressive policy concerning the issue of the Spanish succession Napoleon III and his cabinet fell into the trap Bismarck had so carefully set for them—with the undoubtedly unintended consequence of the fall of the Second Empire. The writing of history is, essentially, the story of the unintended consequences of intentional human action.[84] Collingwood (and the autopsic model) was typically blind to this issue: it goes without saying that you cannot account for *un*intended consequences if you have

---

84. Franklin Rudolf Ankersmit, "The Thorn of History: Unintended Consequences and Speculative Philosophy of History," *History and Theory* 60, no. 2 (June 2021): 187–214, especially 198–204.

deliberately narrowed your view to the historical agent's intentions, as the combined authority of the autopsy model and of extensionalism indeed requires you to do.

In sum, the two pillars of Davidson's argument—truth and translatability—succumb under the weight of the practice of historical writing. By this stage in the argument, you should no longer find this surprising: an extensionalist philosophy of language simply cannot support an essentially intensionalist practice.

9. CONCLUSION

I happily leave it to others to decide whether Davidson's argument holds as its stands. My concern is to obtain more clarity about what aspects of our use(s) of language it applies to and where it has no relevance or is even misleading. From the point of view of the lexicographer, Davidson's argument can be regarded as unexceptional (albeit needlessly belabored). If the statement s_1 in language L_1 is true of a state of affairs A, we can expect a reliable lexicon for the languages L_1 and L_2 to inform us what statement s_2 in language L_2 will also be true of A. Truth and translatability will then be the lexicographer's two main guides. One hardly needs Davidson to recognize as much.

But Davidson was not content with providing the lexicographer with a philosophical foundation. This is clear from his mention of Kuhn, Sapir, and Whorf.[85] He not only addressed the problem of how an interpreter might translate simple sentences in a foreign language such as "snow is white" into his own, and vice versa, but pronounced on claims that the speakers of different languages are also worlds apart.

This was a claim Davidson refused to take seriously. After quoting Strawson's remark that it is possible to imagine worlds different from our own, he wrote that "since there is *at most one world*, their pluralities are, however, metaphorical or merely imagined" (italics added).[86] An extensionalist with a penchant toward materialism may declare "that there is at most one world"; but when historians say they are studying "the world of the Middle Ages" or "the world of Goethe," they are surely not positing something only "metaphorical or merely imagined." The world is not the

---

85. Davidson, "On the Very Idea of a Conceptual Scheme," 190.
86. Davidson, "On the Very Idea of a Conceptual Scheme," 187.

earth; the scene of human affairs is not (just) the third rock from the sun, and the fact that it is so is (generally) irrelevant in any case.

As I have repeatedly demonstrated, the results of such studies are intensional realities. Nor should historians fear the accusation of relativism because of their readiness to use the phrase "the world of . . .", because what such phrases denote are HRs. As you have seen, the relative merits of rival HRs can be the subject of reasonable discussions that underwrite the growth of historical knowledge.

If lexicography was all Davidson had in mind, his essay would have been right on target; and, indeed, it may sometimes seem that he had no more ambitious goals. Just think of his assertion that "instead of living in different worlds, Kuhn's scientists may, like those who need Webster's dictionary, be only words apart."[87] But in the writing of history, our subjects are not *words* but rather *worlds* apart. The Frenchmen living after 1815 spoke much the same French as their fathers and grandfathers did before 1789—and still do. But they lived in different worlds or, more accurately, in different historical *periods*. Whoever replies that this phrase of "living in a different world" is a careless way of speaking only proves that they have no idea what the writing of history is about. It is, however, the kind of reply we might have expected from Davidson because his extensionalist convictions drove him to overreach by pronouncing on a domain in which intensionalism holds all the trump cards.

In sum, when attacking theorists like Sapir, Whorf, or Kuhn,[88] Davidson unwittingly extended a philosophical theory of lexicography to a domain where it no longer applies. We have a word for this, namely, parochialism.

Davidson has not been alone in his blindness regarding the extensionalism versus intensionalism opposition and the question of how much room should be granted to the latter.[89] Indeed, the purpose of this epilogue has

---

87. Davidson, "On the Very Idea of a Conceptual Scheme," 189.

88. This does not exclude having other reservations regarding the arguments of these theorists.

89. Commenting on the barriers between "analytic" and "continental" philosophy, Frederick Beiser observes: "there are other areas of philosophy where the old barriers still exist and continue to have their harmful effect. One of these areas, and one of the worst effected, is the philosophy of history. The purpose of my chapter is to explain why this is so, i.e., why the philosophy of history has languished from the distinction between 'analytic' and 'continental philosophy.'" Frederick C. Beiser, "Hermeneutics and Positivism," in *The Cambridge Companion to Hermeneutics*, ed. Michael N. Forster and Kritsin Gjesdal (Cambridge: Cambridge University Press 2019), 133–158, at 150. One might rephrase Beiser's conclusion by saying that continental philosophy tends to be more open to intensionalism than analytical philosophy.

been to draw the attention of Davidson's coextensionalists to that opposition and to show where it can be expected to come into manifest conflict with its intensionalist counterpart. I am the last to claim that an awareness of this conflict should be decisive for all of philosophy. Nor would I wish to reject reductive extensionalism categorically: it has its (many) uses, but it also has its limitations.[90] The need of constant awareness of these limitations is the background against which this book on Leibniz and historical representation should be read.

And that is also its more comprehensive message.

---

90. Walther-Klaus, *Inhalt und Umfang*, 142: "Eine Interpretation der Extensionalitätsthese dahingehend, dass sich die Logik nur mit Extensionen, nicht auch mit Intensionen zu befassen hätte, lässt zich nicht aufrecht erhalten. . . . Umfang und Inhalt eines Begriffes sind—wie schon die Suppositionslehre zeigt—nur zwei Aspekte der logischen Begebenheiten eines Begriffes."

GLOSSARY

ABBREVIATIONS

D_{cc} Doctrine of the complete concept
D_{ii} Doctrine of the identity of indiscernibles
D_{ph} Doctrine of preestablished harmony
D_{et} Doctrine of the excluded third (or the noncontradiction law)
D_{sr} Doctrine of sufficient reason
D_{wm} Doctrine of the windowlessness of monads
HR   historical representation
PBF well-founded phenomena (phaenomena bene fundata)

TECHNICAL CONCEPTS

1. Extensionalism and intensionalism

Extensionalism relates bits of language to bits of the world; intensionalism relates bits of language to bits of language. Extensionalism and intensionalism are not philosophical theories or doctrines themselves but are research programs in the philosophy of language. In extensionalism both the acceptance of the analytic/synthetic distinction and its rejection make sense, but neither of the two are in the intensionalist program because extensionalist objects are absent in it. In intensionalism the notion the "linguistic thing" or "object" makes sense (for this see entry 6 on "strong individuals"), whereas the extensionalist program has no room for it. Extensionalism is hospitable to epistemology; intensionalism is not.

Think now of a philosophical system (PS) that is completely self-explanatory. Three preliminary remarks are in order. First, we must separate a PS from the philosophical text the philosopher wrote *about* that PS. We ordinarily forget this because the two always go together, as it is with a mussel and its shell. Second, a PS is a *description* of what the world is like according to the philosopher and must, as such, be distinguished from *what* it allegedly describes or refers to (R). When Thales said that the world is water, his assertion referred to the world (R) and not to his PS. Had the latter been his intention, his PS had immediately refuted itself. PSs are not water. Third, a PS is defined here as self-explanatory if (1) questions about any object in or aspect of that PS's R can be explained by an appeal to other things in R; (2) questions about R as a whole are not allowed, but answers appealing to R as a whole are permitted; and (3) both questions and answers themselves are outside R. They are ordinarily part of the PS in question.

It will then be obvious that self-explanatory systems are typically intensionalist, whereas those that are not are typically extensionalist.[1] The former consist exclusively of linguistic things, a fact that simplifies the task of the aspirant builder of an intensionalist self-explanatory system. The best example of such a system is the Leibnizian system: the properties of all of its components (i.e., monads) are massively overdetermined by those of the other monads. The system has, however, a fairly impressive gap in its self-explanatory pretensions because of Leibniz's postulate that each monad corresponds to an object or thing in the domain of the PBF. The gap is closed, however, in the adaptation of the Leibnizian system to historical representation.[2]

---

1. I explicitly add "typically" here because in the epilogue extensionalism and intensionalism may each grow indefinitely at the expense of the other, but neither will completely succeed in wiping out the other. The diagram of the function $f(x) = 1/x$ is a good illustration of what I have in mind here. This may explain why there will always be a certain leakage, however small, from the intensional domain to the extensional domain, and vice versa—and in this book from that of the HRs to that of the PBF. It is also why we can only agree with Quine's rejection of the analytic/synthetic distinction—although we should, at the same time, not go along with his anti-intensionalist exaggerations.

2. See chapter 2, sections 3 and 4.

GLOSSARY

Extensionalist systems also contain bits of the world, and these are typically non-self-explanatory (imagine a stone explaining itself). So each extensionalist PS automatically carries a heavy load of non-self-explanatory things within it. That makes it difficult to construct a completely self-explanatory extensionalist PS. The only example I can think of is our universe, on the condition we add that it was created *ex nihilo*.

2. History and the past

History, unless otherwise defined, stands for "historical," and "historical reality" stands for the totality of all possible HRs. "The past" stands for the totality of all past states of affairs in the past. Although the past no longer exists, true statements about the past are possible insofar as they are based on the evidence—available here and now—confirming their truth.

3. Logic and metaphysics

In extensionalism it is (ordinarily) assumed that there is no obvious and certainly no necessary link between both notions; nothing that is said about either of the two entails inescapable conclusions about the other. They could even do without the other. In intensionalism, however, each logical claim has its counterpart in metaphysics, and vice versa. In intensionalism all logic is metaphysical and all metaphysics is logical.

The doctrine of the excluded third (D_{et}) resists the possibility that something is both part and not part of that reality. It follows that there can be only *one* metaphysical reality. Suppose there are two of them: metaphysical realities M_1 and M_2. To make this true, it must be possible to conceive of things being part of either M_1 or M_2, and, if so, *not* of the other. It may seem that this would justify the claim that M_1 and M_2 are two different metaphysical realities. However, in that case, we may conceive of a metaphysical reality M_3—comprising both M_1 and M_2—about which we may claim, again without contradiction, that there is only *one* metaphysical reality, namely M_3.

It might be objected that simply adding M_1 and M_2 goes a bit too fast: it might be that M_1 and M_2 are incompatible and therefore resist being added together. But this is not a very promising move. I define a metaphysical reality as the totality of all that is *possible* in that reality. That is to say, we should not identify metaphysical with its actual state. For example, we would not say we live in a reality different from the one in which we live had there been no President Obama or an Andromeda galaxy. Hence, it we wish to give any bite to the idea of a metaphysical reality M_2 that is incompatible with M_1, we must also be willing to concede that that reality is *impossible*. Which is, in fact, tantamount to saying that there is no metaphysical reality M_2.

4. Models

The notion of the *model* is indispensable for an adequate understanding of how science proceeds. In mathematics and science, the model is not a model in the sense that we may build a model of a ship, an airplane, or an economic system. It is precisely the reverse. Scientists propose wholly abstract mathematical equations from which the behavior of these objects in reality can be derived.

Hence, the behavior of these concrete objects are *models* of abstract mathematical equations similar to Newton's law of gravity about the gravitational attraction between two bodies. The behavior of falling things such as apples falling from a tree, of the earth's movement around the sun, or of how galaxies circulate around their axis can then all be said to be "models" of Newton's law. If we move from models to these abstract equations, we move *upward* from the domain of the PBF to that of the monadological universe—to put it figuratively.[3] The relation between a mathematical equation or a scientific theory and its models has its counterpart in historical writing in the relation between an HR and the historical PBF corresponding with it.

The notion of the model is of central importance in both mathematics and science, and it is no less so in historical representation.

---

3. It is of interest, in this context, to observe that mathematicians have not yet solved the so-called three-body problem, i.e., the problem of how three bodies being relatively close to each other and having roughly the same mass and velocity circulate around each other on the condition that no other bodies interfere with their movement. Suppose one day some mathematician presents an equation solving the three-body problem. In that case, one may say that Newton's law is a "model" of that equation. But more important, observe that only mathematicians can solve the problem. Experimental data about the behavior of three bodies under these circumstances abound (think of stars accompanied by two very large planets, or of two stars with one large planet), but these are of no use for solving the problem. Only pure mathematics can do so.

5. Signs

The category of symbols comprises two subcategories: (1) the subcategory of symbols standing for something other than themselves (as the "fleur-de-lis" stands for pre-Revolutionary France) and (2) the subcategory of symbols that stand for themselves (as the letter "a" stand for the letter "a" or the cipher "5" for the cipher "5"). In sum, signs are symbols that stand for themselves. Signs may be as simple as the letter *a* or the cipher 5 or as large and complex as a lengthy (historical) text. Any change in a sign, even the smallest one, changes it into a different sign. Signs obey the doctrine of the identity of indiscernibles (D_{ii}): no two different signs can be the same sign.

6. Strong and weak individuals

Strong individuals can only be defined by an enumeration of all of their properties; linguistic things such as HRs are strong individuals. Weak individuals can be defined by proper names or unique identifying descriptions. Examples are what is referred to, or denoted, by phrases such as "Louis XV" or "the human being who was King of France between 1715 and 1774." Strong individuals are typically intensionalist, and weak individuals are typically extensionalist. Strong individuals cannot be reduced to or be developed into weak individuals, and vice versa: both are incommensurable *sensu stricto*.

7. Well-founded phenomena (phaenomena bene fundata)

The notion of the PBF is so deeply interwoven with all of the Leibnizian system that it is impossible to give a short and succinct account of it.

To begin, monads are the stuff of which reality is made; nothing exists outside, below, above, or beyond that reality. Monads (or substances)—and only monads—constitute the monadological universe. The monadological universe is the totality of all monads. Each monad (or substance) perceives all of the monadological universe from its own point view. Monads are defined by the point of view from which they perceive the monadological universe. It follows that all monads perceive all of the others, but the fact that they always do so from their own specific point of view makes each of them different from all of the others.[4]

Next is the (*non-metaphysical!*) domain of the so-called well-founded phenomena (PBF): it is the world as we know it with its human beings (including ourselves), its mountains, rivers and woods, stars, planets, galaxies, and all of the universe investigated by contemporary cosmologists. These are mere phenomena. We all know the phrase "the two sides of the coin." Suppose the coin in question is infinitely thin.[5] We then have a good metaphor for how monadological reality and the domain of the PBF relate to each other. The two domains are infinitely close to each other yet infinitely far apart in the sense that we can never directly argue from one to the other.

But there *are* exceptions to this: each monad has its counterpart in some thing or object in the domain of the PBF, and scientists may investigate the domain of the PBF and offer scientific explanation for how certain well-defined sets of PBF hang together and why this is so. Valid explanations present us with a vague reflection of some indefinite state of affairs in the monadological universe, but more than that cannot be said.

Why did Leibniz arrange his system in such a strange and profoundly counterintuitive way? Why did he not simply identify reality with the domain of the PBF and state that we have scientific research to penetrate deeper into that reality? This question is, in fact, *the ultimate* still meaningful question one may ask about the Leibnizian system; answering it presents us with that system's very raison d'être.

The answer is as follows. Each monad perceives all of the others. If we take all of the monads and all of their perceptions of each other together, we have attained a complete grasp of the monadological universe. From that perspective, it is wholly self-explanatory (as explained previously): we could not appeal to anything *outside* it to explain anything *in* it. To put it in contemporary terminology, from that perspective the monadological

---

4. Admittedly, some monads perceive the monadological universe more clearly than others. One may discern a hierarchy here: on top are human beings, next come animals, then plants, and finally inanimate objects. They all have their own place in what Leibniz calls "the great chain of being." But from a metaphysical point of view, none of them can claim to be superior to any of the others: they are all part of metaphysical reality, which is an either/or affair, leaving no room for superiority or inferiority.

5. But it is never actually zero because neither extensionalism nor intensionalism can reduce the other to zero. See chapter 2, sections 3 and 4.

universe is "a theory of everything." This raises the subsequent question: Why does Leibniz need this notion of a theory of everything so badly that he brazenly sacrifices all intuitions of common sense when demanding that we embrace his seemingly weird construction of a monadological universe—and metaphysically distinct from it, the domain of the PBF?

Earlier I explained the relationship between an abstract mathematical equation and its many potential models. This is how Leibniz conceives of the relationship between the monadological universe and the domain of the PBF: everything that is valid in the former is valid in the latter as well. This offers him the indispensable *metaphysical* support of the rationalist claim that everything can be explained. Because the metaphysical reality of the monadological universe is completely explanatory, that reality contains nothing that could not be explained by an appeal to something else in it. The domain of the PBF (the world in which we live) must be regarded as a model of the monadological reality (or as a subset, and a subset of a subset, and so on of it), and that domain must *also* be completely self-explanatory. The relationship between a theory, equation, or whatever and its models guarantees as much. Leibniz leaves no room whatsoever for irrationality, and *this* is precisely what his construction of the monadological universe and the domain of the PBF was meant to achieve. This is why we can know a priori that there is a sufficient reason for all that happens in our world, as is stated by the doctrine of sufficient reason (D_{sr}), and why Leibniz absolutely needs this seemingly so fantastic construction. Leibniz needed the postulate of monadological reality "to make the (phenomenal) world safe for rational scientific inquiry."

I add a final remark to this. We know now why Leibniz opted for his monadological universe; so far, so good. But it may be that one could conceive other types of universes that would fit the bill. Perhaps yes, perhaps no. But whatever is the right answer to that question, we can only agree that Leibniz's option perfectly satisfied his requirement of a completely self-explanatory universe.

Of no less interest is the fact that it fits remarkably well in the world in which we live—hence, what Leibniz refers to as the domain of the PBF. Our most basic intuition about it is that it consists of individual things that all obey universal laws to be discovered by the scientist. I suppose few philosophers would wish to quarrel with that intuition. Now this conception of the domain of the PBF has its antecedents in the monadological universe because one can derive both individuals and universals from it. Leibniz himself said that each monad corresponds a thing in the domain of the PBF. And we have seen that each monad perceives all of the others. Using monad M_1, we can formulate the universal statement "of each x it is true that if x is a monad x, perceives M_1." In sum, when deciding what kind of universe would best serve his purposes, Leibniz also ensured—wittingly or unwittingly—that it would agree with the most elementary makeup of the domain of the PBF.

One more conclusion can be inferred from this. Think again of the domain of the PBF as a model (or models) of the monadological universe. It follows that the PBF will privilege either individual or universals. The former gives us individual things (and the HRs developed in historical writing) and the latter the sciences. This may explain the structural similarities between the scientific revolution of the seventeenth century and the revolution in historical writing of a century later,[6] and why the writing of history must be regarded as the *pater patriae* of the kingdom of the humanities.

Let's now turn to historical writing, because the role of the PBF in historical representation has not been dealt with yet. I must begin here with a preliminary remark, however. As is emphasized in the conclusion to this book, it is not about the place of history and historical writing *within* the framework of the Leibnizian system, much in the way one may ask for the place and function of some specific side chapel within the whole of some medieval cathedral. Instead, this book aims to show how that system may help us understand history and historical writing. It may be that the Leibnizian system is also helpful outside of historical writing[7]— but that issue is not on the agenda in this book.

---

6. The seventeenth-century revolution of science is often associated with Newton's *Principia Mathematica*, but Newton was no philosopher. There can be no doubt that the Leibnizian system provides us with the best philosophical support of the scientific revolution.

7. The relevant aspects of Leibniz's thought have lost nothing of their freshness and their capacity to provoke new avenues of thought in our own time. For contemporary philosophers finding their inspiration in Leibniz, see Richard Halpern, *Leibniz: A Philosopher in Motion* (New York: Columbia University Press, 2003); Jürgen Jost, *Leibniz und die moderne Naturwissenschaften* (Berlin: Springer, 2019); Ralf Krömer and Yannick Chin-Drian eds., *New Essays on Leibniz's Reception in Science 1800–2000* (Basel: Springer, 2012); Jürgen Laurenz, *Leibniz: Prophet of New Era Science* (Newcastle upon Tyne: Cambridge Scholars, 2013); and Lloyd Strickland and Julia Weckend, eds., *Leibniz's Legacy and Impact* (London: Routledge, 2020).

GLOSSARY

What may Leibniz tell us about history and historical representation, and specifically how does the notion of the well-founded phenomena (PBF) fit within the picture? To answer that question, we must start with mapping the Leibnizian system as accurately as possible on the practice of historical writing. The first and most important claim made in this book is to strictly distinguish between the past and historical reality. The past is reality only for as long as it exists. When historians start to write about it, it no longer exists—the phrase "past reality" is a *contradictio in terminis*—and at that very moment historical reality is born. *The death of the past is the birth of historical reality*. Historical reality takes the form of the totality of all possible HRs.[8] Each HR represents that historical reality from its own point of view. Hence, HRs are not representations of *the past* but of *each other*, i.e., of historical reality.

As is suggested by the foregoing, historical knowledge (and its growth) should be associated with the outcome of historical debate rather than with individual HRs (although, admittedly, neither of the two can do without the other).

What can be said about what guides historical discussion? In the first place, we must think here of historical facts, i.e., statements about past states of affairs. It is assumed in this book that HRs typically consist of a huge number of individual true statements about past states of affairs. So in this way the category of the past makes its reentry in the present account of historical representation. But their role remains modest for two reasons. First, they are about a world that no longer exists, and therefore they have a curiously spectral character when compared to what goes on in historical reality. Next, their role is only secondary because

---

8. Needless to say, only an infinitesimally small subset of that totality is known to us and actually activated in the practice of historical writing. It should be pointed out, however, that we should not worry about the fact that the number of HRs actually presented by historians from past, present, and future is negligible when compared to the totality of all possible HRs. Historians discuss only the most important of them, and most HRs constituting historical reality are too bad to be taken seriously if only for a moment. But without the bad the good cannot emerge, so even bad HRs serve their purpose. They will always be present, although invariably at the background, and in the majority of cases they will simply be ignored. They constitute the soft walls guaranteeing fruitful historical discussion and the growth of historical knowledge. This why we must be happy with them even though no historian will ever take any notice of them. They are, in a way, similar to a picture frame: they are not part of the painting but contribute to our understanding of what is shown in the painting.

historians appeal to them to argue the superiority of their own HR when compared to those that had been proposed by others. Historical facts are like the soldiers in a battle: without them no battle can be won. No facts, then no historical representations either. At the same time, it is the general's strategy as expressed in a *HR as a whole* that determines which general will lose or win the battle.

Now, at long last we encounter the (historical) PBF. Recall what was said about the notion of the model as it is used in mathematics and science. On the one hand, we have mathematical equations or scientific theories, and on the other, we have models or groups of historical PBF that can be explained by them. Return to historical representation with this in mind. We will then discover, much to our dismay, that we have until now no counterpart for these models or groups of phenomena. What we have are (1) historical reality consisting of all possible HRs and (2) the past that once was reality but transferred that quality to historical reality when HRs came to be written. But we have, as yet, nothing we could for good reasons regard as the historian's analogue to the scientists PBF.

Needless to say, we will now all feel an irresistible temptation to identify the PBF with the *past*. But that is a very bad idea for two reasons. The PBF are instruments the historian appeals to (among others) to represent and to understand the past, much in the way the scientist appeals to equations to explain the behavior of certain things in the world. But if these explanations are successful, no sensible person would conclude from this that the equations used are somehow present in *explained reality* itself. The explanatory order must be carefully kept apart from the order of the explananda. Nor can we seek our refuge in the claim that each HR is accompanied by its own past reality. Not only was the latter notion unmasked as a *contradiction in terminis*, but it would also confront us with a multiplication of historical realities. If there were such a thing as a historical reality, there can at most be *one* of them. Recall that the category of "reality" was already granted to historical reality (and the HR's constituting them), and the category of reality is a most jealous God who suffers no rivals. The phrase "many realities" is either a figurative use of language to which no one will object or nonsense. In sum, no trap is both so attractive and as fatally wrong as to equate the historical PBF with the past.

But what alternative do we have? That causes a problem that can't be overestimated: it is as if we were to delete the category of the world or of reality in non-Leibnizian accounts of our understanding of the world in which we live. At this stage the account of historical representation so carefully constructed on the preceding pages seems to collapse and to be beyond repair.

But when the need is greatest, salvation is at hand, and so it is here. Leibniz presents us with a system in which everything seems to be topsy-turvy: no one ever actually *saw* his monadological reality, and the daily reality we know so well is reduced by him to the status of the well-founded phenomena. Well-founded, it is true, because they have their *foundation* in monadological reality, but mere phenomena nevertheless. When allowing ourselves to be inspired by Leibniz for an adequate grasp of historical representation, consistency requires us to follow the strategy he adopted under similar circumstances. We must *postulate* a domain of (historical) PBF in which each HR corresponds to some set of historical PBF, just as each monad corresponds to a thing or object in the domain of the PBF.

It might be objected that this can never be more than a postulate. Has anyone ever seen or heard these historical PBF, let alone touched them with their fingers? Obviously, no. **We will not even find them in the text of works of history, though reference will be made to them in these texts. They are in the no man's-land *between* these texts rather than *in* them. This is the domain where historical knowledge (one of the least understood notions in philosophy of history) originates and develops.**

However, it was no different with Leibniz's monads. Even Leibniz himself never actually saw a monad (as he would be the first to admit). Nevertheless, we gave him the benefit of the doubt there. However, these historical PBF can even do without the benefit of the doubt because they constitute the place or space of reason (to use a well-known phrase), where the battle between the HRs is actually fought. Even if we cannot pinpoint a place in the spatiotemporal order where the PBF allegedly reside, it makes its presence immediately felt as soon as a different HR on some historical topic conflicts with another and when historical debate begins.

HRs themselves could be compared to generals guiding the attack on the enemy without actually fighting themselves; the real fighting is done by the soldiers or the HR's PBF; and that fight will decide which general, or HR, will lose or win the day. Both armies come from wholly different countries, with different pasts and different political aims. And this is precisely what made them meet on the battleground. Without differences there are no battles. So it remains at the level of the army generals or the HRs. But on the battlefield the soldiers and the HR's PBF do share, whether they like it or not, in the form of the battlefield a domain where they momentarily achieve Kuhnian "commensurability." The raison d'être of the battlefield is that the two armies can fight their existential conflict there and come to an objective irrefutable conclusion about which of them is best. The outcome of the battle will determine the course of political debate and the growth of knowledge in the case of the HRs and their PBF. (Before being accused of defending nationalist historical writing, I emphasize that the previous sentences were a mere metaphor.)

In sum, the fact that there are such things as historical discussion and the growth of historical knowledge testify to the presence of this so deceptively spectral level of the historical PBF. Admittedly, there is no concrete and tangible evidence of the domain of the historical PBF such as a table or a tree; but if we abandon the notion on that ground, 90 percent of what happens in historical writing and in historical discussion that guarantees the growth of historical knowledge will become wholly incomprehensible.

For more details about the PBF and about how the battle of the HRs is fought, see chapter 2, section 3; chapter 3, sections 5 and 6; and chapter 4, section 6.

BIBLIOGRAPHY

Akker, Chiel van den. *The Exemplifying Past: A Philosophy of History*. Amsterdam: Amsterdam University Press, 2018.
Ankersmit, Franklin Rudolf. "A Dialogue with Jouni-Matti Kuukkanen." *Journal of the Philosophy of History* 11, no. 1 (2017): 38–59.
——. *Meaning, Truth and Reference in Historical Representation*. London: Cornell University Press, 2013.
——. *Narrative Logic. A Semantic Analysis of the Historian's Language*. Boston: Martinus Nijhoff, 1983.
——. "A Narrativist Revival?" *Journal of the Philosophy of History* 15, no. 2 (2021): 215–40.
——. *Peter Munz's Evolutionist Philosophy of History and the Anthropocene* (forthcoming).
——. "Peter Munz and Historical Thought." *Journal of the Philosophy of History* 15, no. 3 (2021): 378–95.
——. "Representation, Truth and Historical Reality." In *A Companion to Arthur C. Danto*, ed. Jonathan Gilmore and Lydia Goehr, 132–42. Hoboken, NJ: Wiley, 2022.
——. "Representationalist Logic." In *Other Logics. Alternatives to Formal Logic in the History of Thought and Contemporary Philosophy*, ed. Admir Skodo, 103–23. Leiden: Brill, 2014.
——. "The Thorn of History: Unintended Consequences and Speculative Philosophy of History." *History and Theory* 60, no. 2 (June 2021): 187–214.
——. "Synecdochical and Metaphorical Political Representation. Then and Now." In *Creating Political Presence: The New Politics of Democratic Representation*, ed. Dario Castiglione and Johannes Pollak, 231–54. Chicago: University of Chicago Press, 2019.
Aurell, Jaume. "What Is a Classic in History?" *Journal of the Philosophy of History* 16, no. 1 (2022): 54–92.
Austin, J. L. *Sense and Sensibilia: Reconstructed from the Manuscript Notes by G. J. Warnock*. London: Oxford University Press, 1964.

BIBLIOGRAPHY

Bach, Johann Sebastian. *Cantata 110: "Wacht auf, wacht auf, ihr Adern und ihr Glieder."*
Bann, Stephen. *The Clothing of Clio: A Study of the Representation of History in Nineteenth-Century Britain and France*. Cambridge: Cambridge University Press, 1984.
Baumgartner, Hans Michael. *Kontinuität und Geschichte: zur Kritik und Metakritik der historischen Vernunft*. Frankfurt am Main: Suhrkamp, 1972.
Beiser, Frederick C. *The German Historicist Tradition*. Oxford: Oxford University Press, 2011.
———. "Hermeneutics and Positivism." In *The Cambridge Companion to Hermeneutics*, ed. Michael N. Forster and Kritsin Gjesdal, 133–58. Cambridge: Cambridge University Press, 2019.
Bollnow, Otto Friedrich. "Was heissst, einen Schriftsteller besser verstehen, als er sich selber verstanden hat?" *Deutsche Vierteljahreschrift* 18, no. 2 (1940): 117–38.
Burke, Edmund. *A Philosophical Enquiry Into the Origins of Our Ideas of the Sublime and the Beautiful*. Oxford: Oxford University Press, 1992.
Carroll, Noëll. "History and Retrospection." In *A Companion to Arthur C. Danto*, ed. Jonathan Gilmore and Lydia Goehr, 152–62. Hoboken, NJ: Wiley, 2022.
Cassirer, Ernst. "Einleitung." In *Hauptschriften zur Grundlegung der Philosophie*, Vol. 2, ed. G. W. Leibniz. Hamburg: Felix Mainer, 1966.
———. *Hauptschriften zur Grundlegung der Philosophie*, Vol. 2, ed. G. W. Leibniz. Hamburg: Felix Mainer, 1966.
———. *Leibniz's System in seinen Wissenschaftlichen Grundlagen. Text und Anmerkungen bearbeitet von Marcel Simon*. Hamburg: Felix Meiner, 1998.
———. *The Philosophy of the Enlightenmen*. Princeton, NJ: Princeton University Press, 1951.
———. *Substanzbegriff und Funktionsbegriff. Untersuchungen über die Grundfragen der Erkenntniskritik*. Darmstadt: Wissenschaftliche Buchgesellschaft, 1994.
Chladenius, Johann Martin. *Allgemeine Geschichtswissenchaft. Mit einer Einleitung von Christoph Friederich und einem Vorwort von Reinhart Koselleck*. Vienna: Hermann Böhlaus Nachf, 1985. First published in 1752.
Cohen, I. Bernard. *The Newtonian Revolution: With Illustrations of the Transformations of Scientific Ideas*. Cambridge: Cambridge University Press, 1980.
Collingwood, R. G. *The Idea of History*. New York: Oxford University Press, 1961.
Couturat, Louis. *La Logique de Leibniz d'après des Documents Inédits*. Hildesheim: Olms, 1961.
Cover, J. A., and J. O'Leary-Hawthorne. *Substance and Individuation in Leibniz*. Cambridge: Cambridge University Press, 1999.
Danto, Arthur C. *After the End of Art: Contemporary Art and the Pale of History*. Princeton, NJ: Princeton University Press, 1997.
———. "Letter to Posterity." In *A Companion to Arthur C. Danto*, ed. Jonathan Gilmore and Lydia Goehr, 397–404. Hoboken, NJ: Wiley, 2022.
———. *Narration and Knowledge: With a New Introduction by Lydia Goehr and a New Conclusion by Frank Ankersmit*. New York: Columbia University Press, 2007.
———. *The Transfiguration of the Commonplace: A Philosophy of Art* Cambridge, MA: Harvard University Press, 1983.
Davidson, Donald. "Appendix: Replies to Rorty, Stroud, McDowell, and Pereda." In *Truth, Language and History*, 315–29. Oxford: Clarendon Press, 2005.

BIBLIOGRAPHY

———. "Gadamer and Plato's *Philebus*." In *Truth, Language and History*, 271–77. Oxford: Clarendon Press, 2005.
———. "A Nice Derangement of Epitaphs." In *Truth, Language and History*, 89–109. Oxford: Clarendon Press, 2005.
———. "On the Very Idea of a Conceptual Scheme." In *Inquiries Into Truth and Interpretation*. Oxford: Clarendon Press, 1985.
Deleuze, Gilles. *Le Pli: Leibniz et le Baroque*. Paris: Minuit, 1988.
Dillmann, Eduard. *Eine neue Darstellung der Leibnizischen Monadenlehre auf Grund der Quellen*. Leipzig: Hanse, 1891.
Dupuy, Jean-Pierre. *The Mechanization of the Mind: On the Origins of Cognitive Science*, trans. M. B. DeBevoise. Princeton, NJ: Princeton University Press, 2000.
Edamura, Shohei. "How to Connect Physics with Metaphysics: Leibniz on the Conservation Law, Force, and Substance." *Revista Portuguese de Filosofia* 74, no. 2–3 (2018): 787–810.
———. "Well-Founded Phenomenon and the Reality of Bodies in the Later Philosophy of Leibniz." https://www.seiryo-u.ac.jp/u/research/gakkai/ronbunlib/j_ronsyu_pdf/no43/08_edamura.pdf. Last accessed November 30, 2023.
Essen, Arthur van. "Language Universals, Language Individuality and Linguistic Relativity in the Works of Etsko Kruisinga." In *Studies for Antonie Cohen. Sound Structures*, ed. Marcel van de Broecke, Vincent van Heuven, and Wim Zonneveld, 71–79. Dordrecht: Foris, 1983.
Ferguson, Adam. *An Essay on the History of Civil Society*, ed. Fania Oz-Salzberger. Cambridge: Cambridge University Press, 1995.
Fontaine, Arturo. "Writing with Style." In *A Companion to Arthur C. Danto*, ed. Jonathan Gilmore and Lydia Goehr, 26–33. Hoboken, NJ: Wiley, 2022.
Frege, Gottlob. "Letter to Husserl 24.5.1891: Extract." In *The Frege Reader*, ed. M. Beany, 149–51. Oxford: Oxford University Press, 1997.
———. "On Concept and Object." In *The Frege Reader*, ed. M. Beany, 181–94. Oxford: Oxford University Press, 1997.
———. "On Sinn and Bedeutung." In *The Frege Reader*, ed. M. Beany, 151–72. Oxford: Oxford University Press, 1997.
———. "Über Sinn und Bedeutung." *Zeitschrift für Philosophie und philosophische Kritik* 100 (1892): 25–50.
Futch, Michael. *Leibniz's Metaphysics of Time and Space*. Boston: Springer, 2008.
Garber, Daniel. *Leibniz, Body, Substance, Monad*. Oxford: Oxford University Press, 2009.
Gartenberg, Zachary Micah. "Brandom's Leibniz." *Pacific Philosophical Quarterly* 102, no. 1 (March 2021): 73–102.
Gerhardt, Carl Immanuel. *Die Philosophische Schriften von Gottfried Wilhelm Leibniz*, vol. 3. Ed. C. I. Gerhardt. New York: Georg Olms, 1978.
Goldstein, Leon. *Historical Knowing*. Austin: University of Texas Press, 1976.
———. *The What and the Why of History: Philosophical Essays*. Boston: Brill, 1996.
Gombrich, Ernst. "Meditations on a Hobby Horse." In *Aesthetics Today*, ed. Morris Philips, 172–87. New York: New American Library, 1980.
Gracia, Jorge J. E. *Individuality: An Essay on the Foundation of Metaphysics*. Albany: State University of New York Press, 1988.
———. *Introduction to the Problem of Individuation in the Early Middle Ages*. Washington, DC: The Catholic University of America Press, 1984.

Gumperz, John, and Stephen Levinson, eds. *Rethinking Linguistic Relativity*. Cambridge: Cambridge University Press, 1996.
Hacking, Ian. "Language, Truth and Reason." In *Rationality and Relativism*, ed. M. Hollis and S. Lukes, 48–66. Cambridge, MA: MIT Press, 1982.
———. *Representing and Intervening*. New York: Cambridge University Press, 1983.
Halpern, Richard. *Leibniz: A Philosopher in Motion*. New York: Columbia University Press, 2023.
Hansmann, Wilfried. *Schloss Augustusburg in Brühl*. Worms: Wernersche Verlagsanstalt, 2002.
Hegel, Georg W. F. *Vorlesungen über die Philosophie der Weltgeschichte*. Vol. 2–4. Hamburg: Felix Meiner, 1967.
Heil, John. *From an Ontological Point of View*. Oxford: Oxford University Press, 2003.
———. *The Universe as We Find It*. Oxford: Oxford University Press, 2012.
Herbertz, Richard. *Die Lehre vom Unbewussten im System des Leibniz*. New York: Georg Olms, 1980.
Hertog, Thomas. *On the Origin of Time: Stephen Hawking's Final Theory*. London: Penguin Random House, 2023.
Hofhuis, Steije. *Qualitative Darwinism—An Evolutionary History of Witchhunting* (forthcoming).
Hollis, Martin, and Steven Lukes, eds. *Rationality and Relativism*. Cambridge, MA: MIT Press, 1982.
Hollander, Jaap den. "Contemporary History and the Art of Self-Distancing." *History and Theory: Studies in the Philosophy of History* 50, no. 4 (December 2011): 51–68.
———. "Historicism, Hermeneutics, Second Order Observation: Luhmann Observed by a Historian." In *Social Sciences and Cultural Studies—Issues of Language, Public Opinion, Education and Welfare*, ed. Asuncion Lopez-Varela, 39–59. Rijeka: Intech Open Access, 2012.
———. "The Meaning of Evolution and the Evolution of Meaning." *Journal of the Philosophy of History* 8, no. 2 (2014): 243–65.
Howard, Michael. "Lords of Destruction." *Times Literary Supplement*, November 13, 1981, 1323.
Humboldt, Wilhelm von. *Schriften zur Sprachphilosophie, in fünf Bänden*. Vol. 3. *Über die Verschiedenheit des menschlichen Sprachbaues und ihren Einfluss auf die geistige Entwicklung des Menschengeschlechts*. Darmstadt: Wissenschaftlich Buchgesellschaft, 1963. First published 1830–35.
———. "Über die Aufgabe des Geschichtsschreibers." In *Gesammelte Schriften*. Vol. 4. Boston: de Gruyter, 2020. First published in 1877.
Jong, Henk de. "*Kennst du das Land? Italië-reizigers, Rome-ervaringen en Duits historisch besef in de Negentiende Eeuw*." PhD diss., Amsterdam University, 2020.
Jost, Jürgen. *Leibniz und die moderne Naturwissenschaften*. Berlin: Springer, 2019.
Kenny, Anthony. *Frege: An Introduction to the Founder of Modern Analytic Philosophy*. Oxford, Oxford University Press, 1995.
King, Peter. "The Problem of Individuation in the Middle Ages." *Theoria* 66 (2000): 159–84.
Köhler, Paul. *Der Begriff der Repräsentation bei Leibniz. Ein Beitrag zur Entstehungeschichte seines Systems*. Bern: Francke, 1913.

BIBLIOGRAPHY

Koselleck, Reinhart. "Standortbindung und Zeitlichkeit. Ein Beitrag zur historiografischen Erschliessung der geschichtlichen Welt." In *Vergangene Zukunft. Zur Semantik Geschichtlicher Zeiten*, 176–211. Frankfurt am Main: Suhrkamp, 1979.

Krämer, Sybille. "Kalküle als Repräsentation. Zur Genese des operativen Symbolismus in der Neuzeit." In *Räume des Wissens: Repräsentation, Codierung, Spur*, ed. H. J. Rheinberger, M. Hagner, and B. Wahring-Schmidt (Hrsgb.), 111–23. Berlin: Akademie, 1997.

Krins, Hubert. *Barock in Süddeutschland. Mit Fotografen von Joachim Feist*. Stuttgart: Konrad Theiss, 2001.

Krömer, Ralph, and Yannick Chin-Drian. eds. *New Essays on Leibniz's Reception in Science 1800–2000*. Basel: Springer, 2012.

Kuukkanen, Jouni-Matti. "Moving Deeper Into Rational Pragmatism: A Reply to My Reviewers." *Journal of the Philosophy of History* 11 (2017): 59–83.

———. *Postnarrativist Philosophy of Historiography*. Basingstoke: Palgrave MacMillan, 2015.

Latour, Bruno. *Science in Action: How to Follow Scientists and Engineers Through Society*. Cambridge, MA: Harvard University Press, 1987.

Laurenz, Jürgen. *Leibniz: Prophet of New Era Science*. Newcastle upon Tyne, UK: Cambridge Scholars, 2013.

Leavitt, John. *Linguistic Relativities: Language Diversity and Modern Thought*. Cambridge: Cambridge University Press, 2011.

Leibniz, Gottfried Wilhelm. *Die Hauptwerke*. Stuttgart: Alfred Kröner, 1967.

———. *Essai de Théodicée. Sur la Bonté de Dieu, la liberté de l'Homme et l'Origine du Mal. Chronologie et introduction par J. Brunschwig*. Paris: Garnier Flammarion, 1969.

———. "Meditations on Knowledge, Truth and Ideas." In *Philosophical Papers and Letters*, 2nd ed., trans. Leroy E. Loemker, 291–95. Boston: Reidel/Springer, 1976.

———. "Methodus Nova de Maximis et Minimis." *Acta Eruditorum* (October 1684): 467–73.

———. "Monadology." In *Philosophical Papers and Letters*, 2nd ed., trans. Leroy E. Loemker, 643–45. Boston: Reidel/Springer, 1976.

———. *Nouveaux Essais sur l'Entendement Humain. Chronologie et introduction par Jacques Brunschwig*. Paris: Garnier Flammarion, 1966. First published in 1765.

———. "Nova Methodus pro Maximis et Minimis." *Acta Eruditorum* (October 1684): 467–73.

———. *Philosophical Papers and Letters*, 2nd ed., trans. Leroy E. Loemker. Boston: Reidel/Springer, 1976.

———. "The Principles of Nature and of Grace Based on Reason." In *Philosophical Papers and Letters*, 2nd ed., trans. Leroy E. Loemker, 635–42. Boston: Reidel/Springer, 1976.

———. "Über den letzten Ursprung der Dinge." In *Mit Einleitung und Erläuterungen im Deutschen ausgegeben von Robert Habs*, ed. Kleine Schriften and G. W. Leibniz, 218–19. Leipzig: Philipp Reclam jun., 1883.

Lowenthal, David. *The Past Is a Foreign Country*. Cambridge: Cambridge University Press, 1985.

Lucy, John A. *Language Diversity and Thought: A Reformulation of the Linguistic Relativism Hypothesis*. Cambridge: Cambridge University Press, 1992.

Luhmann, Niklas. *Introduction to Systems Theory*, trans. Peter Gilgen. Cambridge: Polity Press, 2012.

Lynch, Michael. "Three Models of Conceptual Schemes." *Inquiry* 40, no. 4 (1997): 407–26.
Mahnke, Dietrich. *Leibnizens Synthese von Universalmathematik und Individualmetaphysik*. Stuttgart: Friedrich Frommann, 1964. First published in 1925.
Mann, Thomas. *Doktor Faustus. Das Leben des deutschen Tonsetzers Adrian Leverkühn, erzählt von einem Freunde*. Frankfurt am Main: Fischer Taschenbuch, 1990. First published in 1947.
Mates, Benson. *The Philosophy of Leibniz: Metaphysics and Language*. New York: Oxford University Press, 1986.
Martin, C. B., and John Heil. "The Ontological Turn." *Midwest Studies in Philosophy* 23 (1999): 34–60.
Maurin, Anna Sophia. "Tropes." *Stanford Encyclopedia of Philosophy*, March 16, 2023, https://plato.stanford.edu/entries/tropes/.
McCullough, L. B. *Leibniz on Individuals and Individuation: The Persistence of Premodern Ideas in Modern Philosophy*. Dordrecht: Kluwer. 1996.
Megill, Allan. "History's Unresolving Tensions: Reality and Implications." *Rethinking History. The Journal of Theory and Practice* 23, no. 3 (September 2019): 279–304.
Meinecke, Friedrich. *Die Entstehung des Historismus. Herausgegeben und eingeleitet von Carl Hinrichs*. Munich: R. Oldenbourg, 1965. First published in 1936.
Mink, Louis O. *Historical Understanding*, ed. Brian Fay, Eugene O. Golob, and Richard T. Vann. Ithaca, NY: Cornell University Press, 1987.
Munz, Peter. *Philosophical Darwinism: On the Origin of Knowledge by Means of Natural Selection*. New York: Routledge 1993.
———. *The Shapes of Time: A New Look at the Philosophy of History*. Middletown, CT: Wesleyan University Press, 1977.
Nevo, Isaac. "In Defence of a Dogma: Davidson, Language, and Conceptual Schemes." *Ratio* 17, no. 3 (August 2004): 312–28.
O'Sullivan, Luke. "Heinrich Gomperz and 'Vienna Contextualism.' Historical Epistemology and Logical Empiricism." *Contributions to the History of Concepts* 17, no. 2 (winter 2022): 70–94.
———. "Worlds of Experience: History." In *The Cambridge Companion to Oakeshott*, ed. Efraim Podoksik, 42–64. Cambridge: Cambridge University Press, 2012.
Paetzold, Heinz. *Ernst Cassirer. Zur Einführung*. Hamburg: Junius, 1993.
Parsons, Reuben. *Some Lies and Errors of History*. Notre Dame, IN: Notre Dame Press, 1893.
Paul, Herman. *Hayden White: The Historical Imagination*. London: Polity Press, 2011.
———. *Historians' Virtues: From Antiquity to the Twenty-First Century*. Cambridge: Cambridge University Press, 2022.
———. "A Loosely Knit Network: Philosophy of History After White." *Journal of the Philosophy of History* 13 (2019): 3–20.
Pereyra, G. Rodriguez. "Leibniz's Argument for the Identity of Indiscernibles in Primary Truths." In *Individuals, Minds and Bodies: Themes from Leibniz*, ed. M. Carrara, S. M. Nunziante, and G. Tomasi, 49–61. Munich: Franz Steiner, 2004.
Pomata, Gianna, and Nancy G. Siraiso, eds. *Historia: Empiricism and Erudition in Early Modern Europe*. Cambridge: Cambridge University Press, 2005.
Poser, Hans. *Gottfried Wilhelm Leibniz. Zur Einführung*. Hamburg: Junius, 2005.
Puryear, Stephen M. *Perception and Representation in Leibniz*. Pittsburgh, PA: University of Pittsburgh Press, 2006.

BIBLIOGRAPHY

Ranke, Leopold von. "Erwiderung auf Heinrich Leo's Angriff." In *Leopold von Ranke's Sämmtliche Werke. Herausgegeben von Alfred Dove*. Vol. 53.54. Leipzig: Duncker und Humblot, 1890.
———. *Politisches Gespräch: Historisch-politische Zeitschrift*, Vol. 2. Berlin: Duncker und Humblot, 1833–1836.
Rescher, Nicholas. "Conceptual Schemes." In *Studies in Epistemology*, ed. Peter A. French, Theodore E. Uehling Jr., and Howard K. Wettstein, 323–45. Minneapolis: University of Minnesota Press, 1980.
———. *The Philosophy of Leibniz*. Englewood Cliffs, NJ: Prentice-Hall, 1967.
Rorty, Richard. *Philosophy and the Mirror of Nature*. Oxford: Basil Blackwell, 1980.
Roth, Paul A. *The Philosophical Structure of Historical Explanation*. Evanston, IL: Northwestern University Press, 2020.
Rowen, Herbert H. *A History of Early Modern Europe 1500–1815*. Indianapolis, IN: Bobbs-Merrill, 1960.
Russell, Bertrand, and Alfred North Whitehead. *A Critical Exposition of the Philosophy of Leibniz*. London: Allen and Unwin, 1967.
———. "On Denoting." *Mind* 14 (1905): 479–93.
———. *Principia Mathematica*. Cambridge: Cambridge University Press, 1962.
Rutherford, Donald. *Leibniz and the Rational Order of Nature*. Cambridge: Cambridge University Press, 1995.
———. "Metaphysics: The Late Period." In *The Cambridge Companion to Leibniz*, ed. Nicholas Jolley, 124–75. Cambridge: Cambridge University Press, 1995.
———. "Phenomenalism and the Reality of Body in Leibniz's Later Philosophy." *Studia Leibniziana* 22, no. 1 (1990): 11–28.
Sapir, Edward. *Culture, Language and Personality: Selected Essays*, ed. David G. Mandelbaum. Los Angeles: University of California Press, 1964.
———. *Language: An Introduction to the Study of Speech*. Cambridge: Cambridge University Press, 2014.
Savile, Anthony. "The Rainbow as a Guide to Leibniz's Understanding of Material Things." In *Individuals, Minds and Bodies: Themes from Leibniz*, ed. M. Carrara, A. M. Nunziante, and G. Tomasi, 193–203. Munich: Franz Steiner, 2004.
Schepens, Guido. "L'Autopsie dans la Méthode des Historiens Grecs du Vme Siècle avant J.-C." *Verhandelingen van de Koninklijke Academie voor Wetenschappen en Schone Kunsten van België, Klasse der Letteren* 42, no. 93 (1980).
Schiffman, Zachary Sayre. *The Birth of the Past*. Baltimore, MD: Johns Hopkins University Press, 2011.
Seifert, Arno. *Cognitio Historica. Die Geschichte als Namensgeberin der Frühneuzeitlichen Praxis*. Berlin: Duncker und Humblot, 1976.
Shani, Itay. "The Myth of Reductive Extensionalism." *Axiomathes* 17, no. 2 (2007): 155–83.
Simon, Zoltán Boldiszár. *History in Times of Unprecedented Change: A Theory for the 21st Century*. New York: Bloomsbury Academic, 2019.
Simon, Zoltán Boldiszár, and Marek Tamm. *History and Theory* 60, no. 1 (March 2021): 3–23.
Spencer, Mary. "Why the 'S' in 'Intension'?" *Mind* 80, no. 317 (January 1971): 114–15.
Stipriaan, René van. *De Zwijger. Het leven van Willem van Oranje*. Amsterdam: Querrido, 2021.

Strawson, Peter F. *Individuals: An Essay in Descriptive Metaphysics.* London: Methuen, 1964. First published in 1959.

——. "Singular Terms and Predicates." In *Philosophical Logic,* 69–89. Oxford: Oxford University Press, 1973.

Strickland, Lloyd, and Julia Weckend, eds. *Leibniz's Legacy and Impact.* London: Routledge, 2020.

Vogl, Joseph. *Der Souveränitätseffekt.* Berlin: Diaphanes, 2015.

Walther-Klaus, Ellen. *Inhalt und Umfang. Untersuchungen zur Geltung und zur Geschichte der Reziprozität von Extension und Intension.* Hildesheim, Germany: Georg Olms, 1987.

Wang, Xinli. "Conceptual Schemes and Conceptual Relativism." *Pacific Philosophical Quarterly* 90, no. 1 (2009): 140–64.

Wardy, Robert. *Aristotle in China: Language, Categories and Translation.* Cambridge: Cambridge University Press, 2000.

White, Hayden. "The Burden of History." In *Tropics of Discourse: Essays in Cultural Criticism,* 27–51. Baltimore, MD: Johns Hopkins University Press 1978. First published in 1966.

——. *Metahistory: The Historical Imagination in the Nineteenth Century.* Baltimore, MD: Johns Hopkins University Press, 1973.

Williams, Donald C. "On the Elements of Being: II." *Review of Metaphysics* 7, no. 2 (1953): 171–92.

Wittgenstein, Ludwig. *Philosophical Investigations.* Oxford: Oxford University Press, 1974.

——. *Tractatus Logico-Philosophicus,* trans. C. K. Ogden. New York: Dover, 1999.

Zammito, John H. *A Nice Derangement of Epistemes: Post-Positivism in the Study of Science from Quine to Latour.* Chicago: University of Chicago Press, 2004.

TOPICAL INDEX

If an entry has many sub-entries the first letter of the most prominent word in the sub-entry will be enlarged and in bold in order to facilitate the reader's access to the entries in question. The sub-entries are enumerated in alphabetical order.

Aggregates of monads, 54
van den Akker, C., 198n22, 217n4, 225, 248, 260, 265n76; **c**omparing Davidson and Collingwood, 249; on **D**avidson's theory of radical interpretation, 248; defending the logical distinction between historical **r**esearch and historical writing, 181–183; on Davidson's rejection of Quine's belief in an **u**ninterpreted reality, 266
Algorithms, as distinguishing mathematics from historical writing, 122, 203; in historical representation, 191; and Leibniz's *calculatio caeca*, 121–125; and signs, 137
Archilochos, xi
Arguments in HRs, 199, 201, 213; Kuukkanen on, 178, 179, 199–201, 213, 214
Aristotle/Aristotelian: in China, 263n74; as marshalled against Davidson, 261; and D_{cc}, 45; and Leibniz, 208; (metaphysical) reality, 157; and mathematical concepts, 157, 158
Art as opposed to historical writing, 51, 55
Association, 20n6, 95, 96, 128; and consciousness, 20n6, 52, 87, 96n4, 146n30, 268
Aquinas, T., 23
Aurell, J., on what is a classic in history?, 166n58
Austin, J. L., 45n39
Autopsy, defined 5, 8, 9; Chladenius's rejection of, 5, 8, 9, 101, 254–256; and Kosselleck, 5; and Lessing, 5
Axiom(s), 97, 98, 217–222; underlying this book's argument, 16–23; their relation to D_{et} and D_{ii}, 1–18

Bach, J.S. 129, 130
Bann, S., on Prosper de Barante, 262n71
Baumgartner, H. M., on narrativism as a transcendentalist category, 102n59

TOPICAL INDEX

Beiser, F. C.: on Chladenius, 3–5; on Chladenius as "the GermanVico," 3; on Chladenius's perspectivalism, 3–5, 100; on historicism, 1
van Berkel, K., on I. Bernard Cohen, 104n62
Berlin, I. xi
Bernheim, E., on Chladenius, 3n4
Biden, J., 172
Biology and representation, 28n11
Black, M., on D_{ii}, 19n3
Bollnow, O. F., 262n71
Bolzano, B., on the reciprocity of extensionalism and intensionalism, 229n6
Brandom, R.: on Leibniz, 111n3; criticized by Gartenberg, 111n3
Burke, E., on the substitution theory of representation, 112n6. See also representation

Calculus (the), 128, 140n33, 138; Leibniz's use of for establishing maxima and minima, 206–214
Cantor, G., on the infinite in mathematics, 55
Carroll, N., 245n36
Cassirer, E., 2; on the metaphysical reality of the monadological universe, 32, 33, 117; on "substance" vs "function," 141n38, 208; on there being nothing below, behind or beyond Leibniz's metaphysics, 32, 33, 117
Circularity (trivial and non-trivial), 16, 215, 224
Chladenius, H. M.: as **a**nticipating the PBF, 103, 104; vs the **a**utopsy model, 5–9, 101, 254–256, vs **C**ollingwood and Davidson, 250, 251; as "the **G**erman Vico," 3; as having **i**nitiated the historical revolution 100–104; **K**oselleck on, 5, 6; as inspired by Leibniz, 5, 6; on the **m**etamorphosis of history into narrative, 102; on **n**arrativism, 10, 101; and **p**erspectivalism, 3–, 100; as exchanging "**v**erticality" for "horizontality," 101

Clarke, C., 176
Clarke, S., 140n33
Clausius, R., on entropy 185n10
Clemens Augustus, Prince-Archbishop of Cologne, 134
Cohen, I. B., on the Newtonian revolution of science, 104–108
Collingwood, R. G.: and autopsy, 246, 273; and Davidson, 221, 249; and extensionalism, 249; his blindness to the unintended consequences of human action, 273
Consciousness, 20n6. See also association
Continuity between fact and theory in the sciences 189ff. See also thesis of theory-ladenness of fact and justificationism
Couturat, on the identity of the representation and the represented, 114n11
Comparison: of HRs with the past is impossible, 94; as criterion for deciding about HRs, 50, 58, 90; of intensionalist entities, 272, 273, 286
Consistency: of the past with itself, 2, 3; of the representationalist universe, 42, 95, 161; seen by Leibniz as the sign of truth, 161. See also presumption of consistency.
Cover, J. A., and J.O'Leary-Hawthorne: 77n20, 84n34, 171, 208n35; on individuals, 76n18; on individuals and D_{ii}, 44n34; on relational statements 152–155; their supervenience theory of relational statements, 154, 155, 171
Crisis of historicism, as a storm in a neo-Kantian cup of tea, 2, 3
Cusanus, as having anticipated the calculus, 207
Marquis de Custine, A., on the hopelessness of the Russian people, 175n65

Danto, A. C.: on the birth of history from the death of the past, 7, 8, 116, 117; and Davidson, 268, 269; on the Ideal Chronicle, 137; on

TOPICAL INDEX

intensional contexts, 267–269; his perspectivalism, 7,8, 245n36; on narrative sentences 59n67, 179, 180
Davidson, D., 252–276; on "conceptual schemes," 252ff.; and German hermeneutics (Gadamer) 262, 263; and intensional contexts, 266ff.; his visceral dislike (shared by Quine) of intensionalist semantics, 247, 248; vs Kant 258, 259; his "parochialism," 275; vs Quine on uninterpreted reality 259; and Tarski's semantic theory of truth 263–265; on radical translation, 257, 262ff.; his radical translation as contradicted by historical practice, 267ff.; his extensionalist "triangulation model," 248; on the retribution of truth values across conceptual schemes, 258
Deleuze, G., on Leibniz vs Descartes, 206, 206n30
Descartes, R., and analytical geometry, 97
Descriptive metaphysics: defined by Strawson, 64–67, 147, 148, 216; Aristotle's and Strawson's coincide, 158
Determinism, in Leibniz, 31n19, 44n37
Dialogue des sourds between German and Anglo-Saxon hermeneutics, 221
Dillmann, E.: on representation in Leibniz, 25; on there being nothing behind or beyond Leibniz's metaphysics, 33
Duns Scotus, on "haecceitas," 77
Doctrine of Complete Concept (D_{cc}), 88, 106; allegedly counter-intuive essentialist implications of, 44n37; and D_{ii}, 55; as principle of individuation, 79; leaves no room for universals, 63
Doctrine of Identity of Indiscernibles (D_{ii}): and D_{cc}; 55, 73, 113, 114, 281; defined 18; Leibniz's account of, 18; derived by Leibniz from D_{sr}, 19; Russell's criticism of, 18
Doctrine of the Excluded Third (D_{et}), 30, 31, 41, 42; defined, 18; and the presumption of consistency obtaining in the domain of the PBF, 160ff.

Doctrine of Preestablished Harmony (D_{ph}), 35; defined 28–31; and relational statements, 149
Doctrine of Sufficient Reason (D_{sr}), 19, 148, 283; defined, 18; and metaphysics, 159
Doctrine of the Windowlessness of Monads (D_{wm}): defined 27; 28, 35, 37, 38n29, 42, 128n2, 242, 147

Edamura, S., on PBF, 38n29
van Essen, A., 256n57
Evans, Richard, 176
Evidence (historical), 31, 39, 94, 188, 231
Extensionalism, 13, 14, 227–252; its approach to individuality, 81; Davidson's, 225, 254, 262, 275, 276; definition of, 14, 227–229; complementarity with intensionalism, 81, 228, 276n90; metaphysics of, 88; extensionalist and intensionalist truth, 228–231; and the world/language dichotomy; 84

Facts: as based on historical evidence, 31, 39, 94, 188, 231; used as arguments by and in HRs, 30; used in debate on historical reality, not on the past, 39
Ferguson, A., on unintended consequences, 7
Ferguson, N., 176
Fischer, F., 176
Frege, G.: on comprehensive knowledge, 68, 89, 89; comprehensive knowledge and historical writing, 70; comprehensive knowledge and the individual, 75, 81, 85; comprehensive knowledge and universals, 68, 69; notion of the "Dritte Reich," 21n9; on individuation, 66; on proper names, 68
Futch, H., in Leibniz's concept of the laws of nature, 208n34

Garber, D., on phenomenalism and antiphenomenalism, 161, 162
German rococo, 135

TOPICAL INDEX

Geschichtsforschung (historical research) vs Geschichtsschreibung (historical writing), 31, 58–61, 174, 179n3, 183, 199; distinction resists thesis of theory-ladenness of facts, 58, 59
God: and D_{ph}, 30; in Leibniz's cosmology, 29; in Leibniz's thought, 18, 19 150; the historian as, 209; nothing short of an omniscient can help Leibniz out of the problems occasioned by relational statements, 150
Goethe, J., 62n1, 215; and comparativism 51n56); and "individuum est ineffabile," 70
Goldstein, L. J., on constructivism, 11
Gombrich, E., on representation, 112
Goodman, N.: individuals and identity, 64n2), on representation, 112n4
Gracia, J. J. E., on individuals, 75n15, 76n19
Growth of historical knowledge, 162, 166, 177, 184, 185; not to be related with the "classics" of historical writing, 166n58; to be situated between rather than in HRs, 177; as stimulated by the search for the juste milieu between intellectual daring or originality and the presumption of consistency, 196, 136; as the unintended result of the interaction of individual HRs, 185

Hamilton, W., on the notion of intensionalism, 229, 230
Hawking, S., and the information paradox of black holes, 123n18
Hart, H. L. A., 2
Hegel, G. W. F., 252n8
Heil, J., 237n21, 238
Heimsoeth, H., 34
Herbertz, R., on the identity of representation and the represented in Leibniz, 114n10
Herder, J. G., 1

Hertog, T., on the information paradox of black holes, 123n18)
Hilbert, D., and the formalization of mathematics, 97
Historical Enlightenment, political necessity of for our time, since it is no longer capable of distinguishing truth from patent lies, 175
Historical explanation, there is no such thing as, 211
Historical language, 22, 61, 85, 170, 226; complexity of, 170; six levels in, 171; as different from ordinary language 225n3
Historical rationality, 12; Leibniz's criteria for 210–214; prevails over norms and values, 58; not undermined by the notion of the growth of historical knowledge, 186
Historical reality: Chladenius and, 103; Danto on, 8, 116, 117; emergence of after the death of the past, 8, 9; the historian as a quasi-God in, 209; Kuukkanen, on, 178, 179; Munz on, 9, 10, 24, 47. 48, 103; to be distinguished from the past, 39, 136; and representation, 117; self-consistency of, 43, 95, 158–160; (past) is what true statements about past states of affairs are true of, 229; and strong individuals, 88; what is, 8–10, 38–42, 22, 279
Historical representation (a)*: xi, xii, 10; and the growth of historical knowledge, dialectical relationship between, 185; incompatible with justificationism, 190; seen in the light of Leibniz's monadology, 43–54; difference between Leibniz's monadology and the account of historical representation given in the present book, 39ff.; where the notion of the **PBF** agrees with our intuitions about, 46n41

---

* Historical representation can refer to either of two things: a) the procedure of representing historical reality or b) individual representations of historical reality (abbreviated as HRs). The distinction is similar to Spinoza's distinction between 'natura naturans' (nature doing what nature does) and 'natura naturata' (nature already created). The entry on 'historical representation' covers 1); the entry on HRs covers (2).

TOPICAL INDEX

Historical representations (b), (HRs), **a**ctualized or non-actualized, 52, 53; the **b**attle of, 10, 12; are **c**hecked against each other and not against the past, 94; are **c**ompetitive, 50; **c**onsistency of all with each other, 42, 43, 49, 156; **d**ebates about competing are fought out with the *PBF* belonging to them, 43, 93–99, 160–170, 176, 186, 210, 213; **d**efined, 17, 18; are **e**ternal, 21, 50, 131, 202; the notion of is **i**ndispensable from a logical point of view for the philosopher of history, 183; **i**ndividual are recursively defined by 1) the statements contained by them and 2) the meta-sentences guaranteeing them to be thus defined, 19, 63, 182, 251; are **i**ndivisible, 54, 55; **i**nternal vs external definitions of individual, 22; semantic **l**evels in, 170; are **l**inguistic things or objects, 45; as the historical counterpart of a **m**athematical calculus in the sciences, 99; the contours of the **m**eanings gain in precision with their number (*one* HR is *no* HR, *two* HRs is the beginning of history as a science), 137; and **n**arrativism, 24, 25; and **n**ominalism, 22; and **n**ovels, 22; and **PBF**, 93–100, 131, 132; and the **p**resumption of consistency, 160, 161, 167, 196, 201; **p**roperties of are 1) consist of singular or general/ universal **s**tatements about past states of affairs contained by them and 2) the metasentences guaranteeing them to be thus defined, 17–22, 44, 45; **r**epresent themselves and all other, 46, 47; as compared to **s**cientific theories, 189; are **s**igns from a logical point of view, 11, 67, 68; are strong individuals, 73. *See also* identity and signs

Historical period: and conceptual schemes, 265–275; (implicitly) questioned by Davidson, 253, 254, 258; intensionalism of the notion of, 231, 232; and the Rankean "historische Idee," 232n12

Historical text, the two functions of, 124

Historical writing: focusing on selection rather than meaning, 133; is war, 94, 131, 132, 203; as a science, 55; scientific, 166; as opposed to art, 55, 56, 165, 166

Historicism, 25, 26, 62; and the asymmetry between past and present, 183; Chladenius as the "Newton" of the revolution of, 3–6; as the exchange of a generalizing for an individualizing approach (Meinecke), 62; "we are all historicists today" (F. C. Beiser), 2; involves a metaphysical and a logical claim, 63; revolutionized historical writing, 1–3, 99–104

History, and the past, 279; as the science of the *ex post facto*, 6; two conclusions implied by seeing as the science of the *ex post facto*, 6, 7; why the teaching of is a *conditio sine qua non* for having a politically enlightened electorate, 165, 171–175

den Hollander, J. C., on contemporary history, 92n43; 99n53, 123n17, 235

von Humboldt, W., 232n12, 255

Identity: of HRs is defined by the set of all of their sentences and metasentences, 54; of representation and represented, 114–116, 146; substantial and numerical, 18. *See also* Doctrine of Identity of Indiscernibles (D_{ii})

Identity, theory of, 114–116. *See also* theories of representation

Inconsistencies, in Leibniz, 13. *See also* PBF

Individual(s), 64–82; five Scholastic principles for what makes an, 76n19; Gracia on, 66n4, 67n15, 76n19; King, on the Scholastic notion of, 78n24); Leibniz's notion of, 33, 34; Strawson on, 64, 71, 72, 67: to be distinguished from the unique, 72, 73

Individuation: Cover and O'Leary-Hawthorne on, 44n34, 84n34; HRs awakened from their eternal

Individuation (*continued*)
slumber by, 202; is internalist, 21, 177; McCullough on, 23nn11–12; principle of, 20–32; reference and, 20–23; in Scholasticism, 75–79

Infinity: Cantor on, in mathematics 55; Leibniz on, and the process of individuation of monads, 44n34; length of HRs is never, 45; but the number of HRs is in principle, 53, 89; search for the best possible HR should not take the notion of as its guide, 213

Intensionalism, 12, 14; <u>a</u>ffinities of with mathematics, modern physics, and historical writing, 232–236; and extensionalism, <u>c</u>omplementarity of, 81, 108, 228, 243, 276n90; <u>D</u>avidson vs, 54; <u>d</u>efined, 227, 228, 277–280; and <u>e</u>xtensionalist truth, 228–231; and <u>F</u>rege, 21; and **HRs**, 227, 241–245, 251–257, 272–276; and <u>i</u>ntensional contexts, 59, 233–236, 247, 267–271; and <u>i</u>ntensionalist phenomena, 233–237; incompatible with <u>j</u>ustificationism, 190; Leibniz first to use word in modern sense, 229;—and <u>m</u>eta-sentences of HRs, 108; of <u>R</u>anke's "historische Ideen," 232n12; <u>r</u>ealism and, 21; Return of intensionalism in modern physics, 231ff; that defended in this book more radical than that proposed by <u>S</u>hani, 232; and <u>s</u>trong individuals, 81, 241; as used in <u>s</u>cholasticism, 230; and <u>t</u>alk about objects, 240ff.; and <u>w</u>orld/language dichotomy, 84ff.

Jacquelot, xii, 27

Juste milieu: historian must aim for (between abundance of detail and irresponsible sweeping statements), 188, 193; historian must aim for (between originality and the presumption of consistency), 196, 201; as invited by the "less is more" principle, 194; in Leibniz, 210, 211; per Mahnke, Scholasticism is the (between Leibniz's predicational logic and Russell's set theory), 71n12; as soon as more options are available to him, the search for ought under *all* circumstances be the historian's primary rule of life, 188, 204; in science, 108

Justificationism, 190; cannot be upheld for historical representation 190, 191; defined, 190; in philosophy of science, 190, 191; rejected by Popper, 191–193

Kant, I. 2; and the crisis of historicism, 2, 3; and Davidson, 257; compared to Leibniz, 35, 38; on the reciprocity between extensionalism and intensionalism, 228

Kenny, A., on Frege, 66

King, P., on Scholastic notion of the individual, 78n24

Köhler, P., on Leibniz's theory of representation; 25, 33, 49n50

Koselleck, R.: on autopsy, 5; on Chladenius, 4, 6; on Chladenius's perspectivism, 10, 250; and the crisis of historicism, 3; and his *Geschichtliche Grundbegriffe*, 3

Krämer, S., on sign and algorithms, 122, 123n17

Kuhn, T., 176, 255

Kuukkanen, J. M.: on argument in historical writing, 199–201, 213; criticizing notion of HRs as signs 125n20; on deciding between rival historical narratives, 177; proposing five criteria for representational succes, 197, 199; reservations about the theory of historical narrative as proposed by, 199–201

Landauer, R., on information theory and signs, 123n18

Language: difference between the historian's and ordinary, 164; language/world dichotomy, 82–86,

157–159; six levels in the historian's, 170; of professional historians 164
Latour, B., 164n57
Leibniz, G.W.: (a) general comments, (b) specific comments.
(a) General comments: Leibniz's system can be derived from a few axioms only (see Russell); his *calculatio caeca*; 119; succeeded in giving a philosophical meaning to the calculus, 12, 206–209, 213; his thought leaves little or no room for epistemology, 38; is the greatest individualist of all times (Heimsoeth), 34; introduced the notion of intension in modern philosophical vocabulary, 225; logic and metaphysics in, 10, 64; was the father of mathematical and symbolic logic, 122; anticipated the notion of the abstract model, 98, 99n54, 103–108; and reality, 10; why the Leibnizian system is difficult to grasp, 215, 216; his system greatly gains in plausibility if applied to historical representation, 13, 41, 222; his monadological universe as fully enclosed in itself (Cassirer, Dillman, Köhler), 32, 33; was one of the ten greatest philosophers in the history of Western thought, xi, xii
(b) Specific comments: Leibniz on (anti-) phenomenalism; 36, 37, 161, 162; replies to Pierre Bayle's criticisms, 49n50; and the application of the calculus to texts, 209, 210; on why consistency is the sign of truth, 161; on "the great chain of being," 86; Chladenius on, 4; on cosmology, 29; on Duns Scotus's "haecceitas," 7; on why being an individual means being indivisible, 76, 79; and individuality, 78n26; remains closest to Abelard, Ockham, Buridan and Suarez *re* individuality, 78n26; on knowledge, 52n58; on the lex series, 208; why the light of truth shines from within, 50; on maxima and minima, 140n3,

207, 212, 213; on "le meilleur des mondes possibles," 205; and the monadological universe, 10; on "natura non facit saltus," 189n15; and nominalism 43; and perspectivism, 4, 111, 193; problems occasioned by his view of relational statements 140–143; on relational statements, 138–121; on representation, ii, 25, 35, 114–117; developed the notion of the sign required in the *calculatio caeca* of all mathematics, 118, 119; and Suarez, 28n12, 33, 44n44, 75, 79; and the shift from an Aristotelian "Substanzbegriff" to a modern (Russellian)" Funktionsbegriff" (Cassirer), 208; on trendbreaks or tipping points in history, 213; and tropes, 34n24, 78n25, 207, 238, 239; on the world/language dichotomy, 82–86, 157–159. *See also* the calculus; D_{cc}; D_{ii}; D_{et}; D_{ph}; D_{sr}; D_{wm}; individuals; intensionalism; mathematics; metaphysics; PBF; monads/monadology; representation; signs
Luhmann, N, 234, 235

Mahnke, D. 12n16, 114n11;—on what the discovery of the calculus meant for Leibniz as a philosopher, 207n33; on Leibniz's perspectivism, 49n50; aimed at a synthesis of mathematics and the science(s) of the individual, 133, 123n16; on Leibniz's predicational logic vs Russell's set theory, 71; on Leibniz and representation, 25
Mann, T., 127, 130n24
Martin, J. B., 237n21, 238
Mates, B., 77
Mathematics: and historical representation, analogies between, 125; and the calculus, 99, 138, 208, 213, 214; and historical representation, common ground of, 12, 13, 137–140; why Descartes's is of the Renaissance and Leibniz's is of the baroque and the rococo, 124; the formalization

Mathematics (*continued*)
of, as anticipated by Descartes in his analytical geometry, 97; **f**ormalization of by Hilbert; 97, 98; and **h**istorical representation, similarities and differences, 12, 13, 124, 125; **HRs** are the historian's counterpart of the abstract calculus in 99; where **h**istorical writing diverges, 124; and signs, **K**rämer on, 123, 124; **L**eibniz on models of abstract theorems in, 99n52; and signs, **L**eibniz on, 119–123; **M**ahnke on Leibniz's mediation between and the science(s) of the individual, 109n1; **N**ewton's use of, 106, 107; and the **m**odel, 12; decides against **p**erfection and in favor of the imperfection of perfection and/or the perfection of imperfection, 206ff

Maurin, A.S., on tropes 78n25

McCullough, D.: on Leibniz's account of individuality and individation, 64n2, 76nn17–18; individuals have nothing in common with each other, 79; on relational statements, 141

Meaning: how to conceive of **a**nalytical? answer: can only be fixed by decision, 127; is **a**ssociative, 127; of words used in the present **b**ook is of two kinds: 1) as defined in dictionaries and 2) as technical innovations whose meaning is defined in this book in such a way that no room for ambiguity is left, 14, 19; **F**rege on , 67n8, 68, 70, 73; **F**rege on comprehensive, 69; of the concept of the **i**ndividual, 77, 74; the ties attaching to **HRs** can be of two kinds: **r**eferential and causal, 128ff.; **L**eibniz on, 26, 40, 118, 119; **m**athematics categorically excludes all, 119–124; problem of **r**elational statements about HRs sidestepped by rephrasing them as non-relational statements about PBF, 169; in historical **r**epresentation meaningful discussion is possible only thanks to **m**eaningless signs 128; attached to historical **r**epresentations not communicable (unless fixed by decision), 128; of a **s**entence is unaltered if used in different HRs, 59, 60; signs have no, 119–126, 128; may be attached to **s**igns having no meaning themselves, 126

Megill, A., 232n21

Meinecke, F., 1, 62; definition of historicism by, 62

Metaphysics/metaphysical: **a**greement of Leibniz's and his logic 30, 30n15); **e**xception to the rule that speculation is always idle, 158; **e**xtensionalist, 84–86, 121; **f**usion of the—of the world and that of language into one, 86, 87; of **h**istorical representation, 5, 70; are necessarily **i**ncompatible with each other, 89; **i**ntensionalist, 84, 121; issue of in Leibniz as complicated by **l**anguage, 157, 158; **L**eibniz on, 159n52; and **l**ogic, 109, 208, 239, 279, 280; **M**ahnke on, in Leibniz, 110, 114n11; **m**onadological, 34, 64, 114, 162, 126n56; and **r**elational statements, 149, 152, 153n45; and the **s**cientist/historian, 156; 160; **S**trawson on descriptive, 64 67, 216, 226; of **s**trong and weak individuals, 90, 94, 134, 193n26); of the **w**orld in which we live and/or the monadological, 60, 61, 64. *See also* monadological universe; reality; representationalist universe

St. Mill, J., 97, 133

Mink, L. O., 54n63, 132n26, 229n7

Mommsen, T., 24

Mommsen, W., 176

Models: defined , 98, 99, 100; since neither models nor PBF are part of historical reality, consistency of the domain of the PBF and/or—models can never be more than a *desideratum*, 107, 108; in practice models and PBF are often interchangeable, what can be said about the former also

TOPICAL INDEX

holds for the latter, and vice versa 99,104, 108, 128–133; notion of revolutionized both science and history, 160; undermine monopoly of extensionalism, 108, 109

Monadological universe: and Leibniz's metaphor of the city, 40, 187; and D_{ph}, 149; conflicts with common sense, 35; created by God, 28; hierarchy in, 86; contains only individuals, 64; some monads see more of other and others less so, 43; and **PBF**, 35–37, 91, 95–142, 216, 280; as perceived by monads, 6, 44; as seen from different monadological points of view, 52, 111; has no universal properties, 63; as represented by monads, 47; is totality of all monads, no less and no more, 10, 28, 32, 43, 117, 243

Monads/monadology, xii, 10, 28; difference between Leibniz's and the account of historical representation given in the present book, 39ff.; and historical representation, 11, 43–54; "hylomorphism" of Leibniz's, 36n28); inconsistencies in Leibniz's theory of and PBF, 13; are indivisible, 54, 76, 90; and the **PBF**, 35–40; some perceive more of the monadological universe than others, 6; have (subconscious) perceptions, 63; perceptions of the monadological universe agrees with that of all the others, 29, 30n15; as model for the HRs, 16; and the monadological universe, 35, 37; are points of view on the monadological universe, 6, 10; are all that can be truly predicated of them, 44; and the rainbow metaphor, 37, 38n29; as (historical) representations 11, 17, 52; no room for universals in, 34; monadological universe contains only, 27, 32, 33; and Scholasticism, 20n7

Munz, P.: on historical reality, 24, 24n1, 117; Leibnizianism of, 47, 48, 103; HRs represent themselves and all of the others, 47, 48, 192

Music, its score 129, 130

Myth: most powerful myth about historical writing (owing its remarkable success to its creeping so surreptitiously in the mind of both historians and philosophers of history) is that the historian has at his disposal not only 1) the facts about the past (which is *correct*) but 2) "the past" as well (which *is* the myth), 46n41; "the Myth of the Given" (Sellars), 74

Narrativism, 23; what is wrong with, 24–26; why the notion of representation captures the nature of historical writing better than, 25.

Neumann, B., 134

Newton, I., 1, 12; and the scientific revolution, 104–108; I. B. Cohen distinguishes between the "scenario" and the "style" of in his scientific writings, 105–107

Novelties: the three main proposed in the present book are 1) the appeal to the PBF in order to explain the nature of historical debate and 2) the notion of the sign and 3) that the historicist philosophy of history as proposed by Chladenius, Ranke, Humboldt, Burckhardt, Cassirer, Meinecke, Koselleck and Beiser is basically correct, *passim*

Oakeshott, M., 137n30

Objects: are weak individuals in the hope of becoming at the end of times strong individuals. The hope is necessarily idle. This is why they are, in fact, objects in *statu nascendi* or *par manière de dire*, 115ff, 240

Objectivity, guaranteed by subjectivity, 6

O'Sullivan, L., 137n 30), 204n27, 209n38, 252n48, 263n74

TOPICAL INDEX

Paetzold, H., 110n1

PBF, 281–288; are a HR's "**b**oots on the ground," 99; and **C**hladenius, 104, 108; and the metaphor of the **c**ity, 40, 187; are all **c**ommensurable with each other, 177; **c**onsistency of domain of a desideratum, 160, 161; mobilized for historical **d**ebate, 168–170; problem of is not **e**pistemological, 38; and **HRs**, 128–138; greatest common denominator of is what "historical **k**nowledge" basically comes down to, 163; and **K**uukkanen, 199–201; and **m**odels, 99–104, 108, 128–133; why the—are a **p**ain in the ass for Leibniz and a windfall for the philosopher of history, 40–42, 87; and (anti-)**p**henomenalism, 36, 37; **P**opper's maximalization of empirical content and, 194–197; **p**resumption of consistency and , 161, 166, 167, 196, 201; **r**ainbow as Leibniz's model for dealing with the problem of—, 37, 103, 170n63, 222; where the notion of—agrees with our intuitions about historical **r**epresentation, 46n41; as **s**cene where battle between HRs is fought, 94–99, 124; domain of—not **s**elf-consistent, 43; **s**elf-consistency of domain of—is not in need of any metaphysical support, 43, 160; Leibniz's permanent **s**truggle with, 37, 91, 223, 223; are as the **w**orld appears to us, 35, 36

Peirce, C. S. M.: theory of the sign, 113n8; and extensionalism 228n6

Pereyra, R., on Leibniz and D$_{ii}$, 19n4

Perceptions: do they create a relationship between the perception and the perceived?, 143–150

Perspective/perspectivism/perspectivalism: and Chladenius, 3–5, 40, 10, 101, 251; and Danto, 7; vs Puryear's projection view of Leibnizian representation 111; and relativism, 4, 49. *See also* point of view

Philosophy/philosophers of history: never grew into **m**aturity due to the instinctive abnegation of formalism of its practitioners, 52, 97, 117; never were aware that they should care about what **m**ethodology they should adopt, let alone that they ever adopted one—apart, then, from that of "vogue la galère," 16, 218–220, 223, 224; in the last two decades, **e**xploded like a large house on which a bomb had been dropped: bricks, doors and furniture flew all over the place, while an incoherent multitude of tiny little cabins arose wherever the debris hit the ground, 220; **P**aul's soothing description of "post-explosion" as "a loosely knit network," 220n6; did too little to close the gap between themselves and professional **h**istorians, 164n57; produced since Chladenius little more than what are, at best, **t**rivial and/or half truths, 218, 219

Philosophy/philosophers of language: why it is not interested in philosophy of history, 25; 226; the extensionalist bias of, 227, 274, 276. *See also* Davidson and Quine

Pictorial representation and the identity of the representation and the represented, 114, 115

Plato, 215

Point of view: Chladenius on, 3–7, 11, 101–103; God's, 143; **h**istorians about, 56–58, 187, 188, 193; and **h**istorical representation, 21; in **h**istory, 38, 39; **HRs** subsuming other HRs in their, 50, 52, 54; and intensional contexts, 235, 236; Leibniz on, 10, 28; the **p**ast only becomes the past from a later one, 116, 250; and **s**cope, 48; and the **u**nintended consequences of intentional human action (Ferguson), 7, 8. *See also* perspective

Popper, Karl: on empirical content, 193; and the juste milieu 194; replaces his falsificationism for fallibilism, 191, 192; is an intensionalist rather than an extensionalist 192; his present undeserved unpopularity, 188n14; minimizes the role of ontology 192; translated into the vocabulary of representationalism, 194, 195; according to whom scientific debate is not settled by correspondence but by comparison, 195

Poser, H., 27n8

Predicates/predication: co-extensional, 233; D_{cc} and, 44n35, 45; and D_{ii}, 55; Gracia, on, 76n19; individuals cannot be to each other, 147; Leibniz's individuals consist of all that can truly be of them, 4, 44, 84; Leibniz on, 224n9; Mahnke on, 71n12; and properties, 237, 237n21, 242; relational statements and, 19; relational statements resist the subject/predicate form, 153–155; Russell on, 19n3; sentences having the subject/predicate form, 59; Strawson on, 71n13). *See also* tropes

Preestablished harmony, Leibniz on, 28. *See also* D_{ph}

Presumption of consistency: adopted by all professional historians, 166; enhances the empirical content of historical writing, 214; and the growth of historical knowledge, 161, 167; guarantees the juste milieu between overhasty audacity and blind conservatism, 196, 201, 204; and the PBF, 17, postulate of, 160; solves the problem of relational statements in historical debate, 167

Projection theory of representation, Puryear on, 111. *See also* theories of representation

Properties: defining the nature of the individual, 76; cannot be dissociated from what they are true of, 78, 79; Frege on, 68, 69; each HR recursively defined by all the statements that are its properties and the meta-sentences tying them to itself, 20, 20n8; in case of HRs of a finite length they can be individuated/identified by a subset of all of their, 21; individuality vs uniqueness and, 72, 73; indivisibility as the defining one of individuality, 76; for Leibniz a thing is the totality of all properties that can be truly predicated of it, 17, 44, 45, 52, 89; Leibniz's universe has no universal, 63, 64; meta-sentences of an HR's tie that HR's properties to that HR, 20; and proper names or uniquely identifying descriptions of HRs, 21; and reference, 89; if two things share all of their, they are one and the same thing (D_{ii}), 18, 19; Russell's transformation of into universals in his "canonical notation," 70, 71, 72; Strawson on, 65, 66; universals and, 63; and the world/language distinction, 85, 86

Puryear, S. M.: Leibniz as an advocate of the projection theory of representation, 111; Puryear's account rejected, 112

Putin, W., 165, 171, 175n65

Quine, W. V. O., "canonical notation" of, 71; claim that there are no identity conditions for properties, 207; dislike of an intensionalist semantics, 247; "on what there is," 75n16; and the triumph of the universal over the individual, 112; on (un-)interpreted reality, 259. *See also* Russell

von Ranke, L., 1, 232n12, 250n46, 253; anticipating the role of the PBF in historical writing, 99n35

Rationality, historical: and the growth of historical knowledge, 186; triumph of over norms and values, 58; of historical writing, 13, 43, 54; Leibniz's criteria for historical, 210–213; of science, Leibniz's belief in, 11, 282ff.

TOPICAL INDEX

Realism: and Frege's notion of the "Dritte Reich," 21n9; White's dislike of, 207; in the Scholastic sense of the term must be rejected for HRs, 2, 78, 83; and the (historical) novel 246; and Davidson, 260

Reality: metaphysical–in the Aristotelian sense, 157; metaphysical–and (in-)consistency, 158, 159; (past) is what statements about the the past are true of, 229. *See also* historical reality; monadological reality.

Reciprocity in relations, 144–150. *See also* relational statements

Relational statements: according to **C**over and O'Leary-Hawthorne all commentators on Leibniz from Russell to Mates failed to solve the problem of Leibniz with-by forgetting "that there aren't relational ways things are," 152; **C**over and O'Leary-Hawthorne's account of, 152–155; **C**over and O'Leary-Hawthorne's 'Supervenience theory' allegedly overcoming the problem of in Leibniz, 154; why **C**over and O'Leary Hawthorne's Supervenience theory is of no help of in the effort to legitimate on HRs, 155; **d**efined, 130; **e**xternalist approach to, 150–155; **i**nternalist approach to, 138–150; Leibniz on, 140, 141; **L**eibniz's debate with Clarke on, 140, 140n33; why **L**eibniz's nominalism invited him to seriously underestimate the problem of,140; explaining what **m**ean is a conditio sine qua non for each theory of historical representation deserving to be taken seriously, 151; and the **PBF**, 155–176; **r**eciprocity is silent about them—it states mere correspondence as expressed in D_{wm} and thus presupposes acceptance of Leibnizian metaphysics, 149; **r**eciprocity can, therefore, not solve the problem of, since the statements expressing it are no *at all*, 148; could **r**eciprocity shield Leibniz against the challenge of?, 144–148? (answer: no!); real **s**ize of the problem of, 142; no **r**oom for in Leibniz's thought and, hence, neither in historical representation, unless safely shut up in true statements about past states of affairs (*there* they can do no harm), 19, 44n36, 59n68, 150; **R**ussell on Leibniz's struggle with relational statements, 19, 140n35, 151, 152; **s**tatements/theories in the sciences (often) have the form of, 98, 183, 189–201, 286; nor does **t**ransitivity solve the problem of, 148; **S**cholasticism offers (self-evidently) no way out of the problem of, 147. *See also* Cassirer on the concept of "function" vs that of "**s**ubstance"

Representation, and biology, 281n11

Resemblance theory of representation, 112, 113. *See also* theories of representation

Ritter, G., 176

Röhl, J., 176

Roth, R., 180, 181, 246n38

Rule of the idleness of all metaphysical speculation: debate about world/language dichotomy is exception to, 157; results of the present book (if considered to be of some interest) is such an exception, too

Russell, B.: and "canonical notation," 70, 71, 74, 80, 151, 152; enabling us to refute Max Black's argument on D*ii*, 190n3; on D_{ii}, 18; extensionalism and set theory, 84n36; attempt to bypass Leibniz's appeal to God for D_{ii} is obviated by the problem of relational statements; 19; claim that all of the Leibnizian system can be inferred from a limited number of axioms, 13, 18n2; and metaphysics, 84; on relationship between monadological universe and PBF, 30n15); argument that *Leibniz* had better do with just one monad, like Spinoza instead

of with an infinity of them, 30n15, 147n41; on Leibniz's struggle with relational statements, 19, 140n35, 151, 152; and the *u*nique, 72
Rutherford, D.: on Leibniz and phenomenalism, 36n28; on why Leibniz's thought is incompatible with the rejection of the so-called myth of the given and the thesis of the theoryladenness of fact, 77

Sapir, E., 256
de Saussure, F., 128, 131
Savile, A., 37n29
Schiffman, Z. S., on the reality of the past, 9n12
Scientific revolution (Newtonian), 1, 104–108
Scholasticism/Scholastics: Leibniz and, 28n12, 75n36, 208n46; as more successful dealing with problem of the individual (and closely related topics) than philosophy of language, 75; Hamilton on, 230; Scholastic notion *unitas est entitas*, 75n16
Seiffert, A., 245n37
Sellars, W., 6, 179
Self-consistency: of historical reality, 42, 158; in science, 156; and the PBF 159, 160
Shani, I., and aspects, 240; and coinstantation, 234–236; on extensionalism *in* intensionalism, 233; on intensional contexts, 233, 234; intensionalism advocated in this book more radical than, 232; on objects, 240; on ontological status of intensional objects, 237, 243; and tropes, 238–240
Shannon, C., on information theory, 123n18
Signs: **c**alculation in mathematics is possible only thanks to there being ones that stand only for themselves, 119; signs and Leibniz's *c*alculatio caeca, 121, 122; and **D**avidson, 271, 271; **d**efined (the sub-class of symbols that stands for themselves), 119; **d**ichotomy of and objects in Frege, 66–70; problems with the **d**ichotomy of sign and object in Frege: is the Renaissance a sign or an object?, 68; **d**ichotomy of sign and object loses its point and purpose in historical writing, 70; **h**istorical text is, 118; **HRs** are, 118; "**i**nformation (as conveyed by signs) is physical" (Landauer), 123n18; **L**eibniz and, 118; are the *identity* of the representation and the represented, 116; are no less **i**ndispensable for historian than for scientist, 124, 138, 201, 202; have neither **m**eaning nor reference, 120, 203, 204; precisely since they have no **m**eaning themselves, one is free to associate *any* meaning with them, 125; **m**eanings associated with them can be tied to them either referentially or causally, 129; no sign without their *p*hysical manifestation (Krämer), 122, 123; and **r**epresentation, 113–129, 135–138; neither in **s**cience nor in historical representation can one be changed on the pain of giving us a *different* one (cf. D$_{ii}$ and D$_{cc}$), 125; can be both **s**imple and as complex as a historical text, 124; and **t**raffic-signs, 135; and **HRs,** 113–129, 135–138; have been one of the two **w**inners of this book (the other being the PBF), 233
Siraiso, N., 245n37
Simon, Boldiszar Z., on contemporary history (i.e. the Anthropocene), 92n32
Spencer, M., on intensionalism, 228n5, 29
Spinoza, B., 30n15
Strawson, P. F., 64–67, 72, 75; on "descriptive" and "revisionary metaphysics," 65, 157, 158; and weak individuals, 80, 226
Strong individuals, 73–75, 79, 80, 53; explained 281
(True) statements about past states of affairs, the main function of–is to function as *a*rguments in a HR

(True) statements about past states of affairs (*continued*)
and in the debate over HRs, 10, 39; HRs can be defined as the totality of all-contained by them, 54, 217, 285; amount to large part of what a HR consists of, 17; are never incompatible with each other, 31; and PBF, 95, 170; historical research (Geschichtsforschung) and historical writing (Geschichtsschreibung) and, 60; (historical) reality is what they are true of, 229

Suarez, F.,—and D_{cc}, 44n34; as Leibniz's source of inspiration, 28n12, 33, 75, 78n26, 79

Substitution theory of representation, 12, 113. See also theories of representation

Substance (synonym of monad). See monads/monadology

Tamm, M., and contemporary history (i.e. the Anthropocene), 92n43

Tarski, A., and his semantic theory of truth, 14, 23n13, 263–265

Texts: as promising candidates for being included in Leibniz's "great chain of being," 87

Thesis of the theory-ladenness of empirical fact: was the rejection of the neoposivist dogma of having direct and unmediated knowledge of what is given in experience and as it is expressed in so-called "Protokollsätze" (the dogma also known as "the Myth of the Given"), becomes, in its turn, a stultifying dogma if applied to the Leibnizian monadological and the representationalist universe, 58 60, 133, 134; clashes with the fact that monads/HRs have nothing in common, 79; clashes with the dichotomy of historical research and historical writing, 31, 57–60, 180–184

Theories of representation: identity theory of, 114–116; projection theory of, 110–112; resemblance theory of, 112; substitution theory of, 112, 113. See also signs

Trend-break or turning points in history, Leibniz on, 167–170, 212, 213

Troeltsch, E., 2

Tropes (literary), as used by H. White, 207

Tropes (or modes), 238, 239; defined, 34n24; Maurin on, 78n25; as standing for an object having a (certain set of) properties, 34n24; first defined by D. C. Williams, 78n25

Trump, D. J., 165, 171–174

Truths/true: **a**nalytical, 44; **c**omparison, non correspondence is the safest road to, 195; **c**onditions, 182, 248, 249; **c**onsistency is for Leibniz the sign of,161; **d**egrees of, as proposed by Popper, 195; being capable to distinguish between **d**e re and **d**e dicto is a condition of a democracy's political health, 171; the fatal inability of the major part of the American electorate to apply the distinction between **d**e re and **d**e dicto protects Trump's demagogery like an impenetrable armor; 171; **d**egrees of, in historical representation, 195; **e**xtensionalist, 229; **i**ntensionalist, 229–234; for **L**eibniz all statements about the monadological universe are analytically, 44; **L**eibniz on true knowledge, 52n58, 224n9; two **l**evels of in historical writing, 60; the (historical) **l**ight of shines from within, 50, 53; about the past is necessarily **e**x post facto, 7; **l**ogical-positivism and the truth of Protokollsätze, 180; and **m**eaning of relational statements in Leibniz and representationalism, 151; in history, **M**unz on, 9, 47, 48; (**n**on-)trivial truth, 218, 219, 222; and **p**olitics, 172–175; triumphs over and **n**orms and values, 58; for **P**opper the scientist should aim at falsification and maximalization of empirical content rather than, 193;

TOPICAL INDEX

Popper on, and verisimilitude, 195; relationship representation and, xii; and strong (weak) individuals 75; theological, 2; translate/translating/translation/translatability/ and, 254–274; truth-values of sentences, 130; as "warrantable assertion," 189, 192

Unintended consequences (of intentional human action), 7; Collingwood's blindness to, 273; Ferguson on, 7; growth of historical knowledge is the result of the—of the interaction between individual HRs, 184–186, 214, 217, 273; of the fatal inability of the American judiciary system to adequately deal with the lawsuits against D. J. Trump, 173
Unity in diversity, as inspired by Leibniz's mathematics, 75
Unity of Science, 12, 108

Viète, F., sixteenth-century inventor of letter algebra, 121
Vinculum substantiale, 20n7

Vogl, J., establishing an elective affiniy between liberal economy and the Leibnizian system, 50n55

Walther-Klein, E., on the reciprocity of extension and intension, 228n6, 276n90
Wang, X.: on Davidson and conceptual schemes, 258n63; vs Davidson's claim that truth is prior to meaning, 270n82
Weak individuals. *See* strong individuals
White, H., 206, 207, 220, 221, 257
Wiggins, D., on individuals and identity, 64n2
William I of Orange, stadholder of the Netherlands, defending freedom of opinion and religion, 167
Williams, D. C., on tropes, 34n24
Windelband, W., on uniqueness, 74
Wundt W., on Leibniz's obsession with the philosophical implications of the calculus, 207n33

Zammito, J. H., 252n49

Printed in the USA
CPSIA information can be obtained
at www.ICGtesting.com
LVHW091915041124
795688LV00034B/952